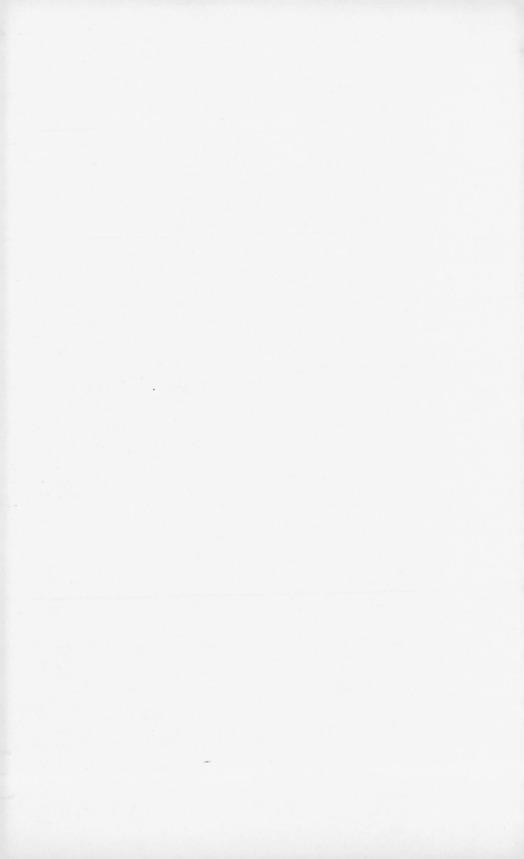

THE CLASSICS
OF **WESTERN
SPIRITUALITY**

THE CLASSICS OF WESTERN SPIRITUALITY
A Library of the Great Spiritual Masters

President and Publisher
Lawrence Boadt, C.S.P.

EDITORIAL BOARD

Abraham Miguel Cardozo

SELECTED WRITINGS

TRANSLATED AND INTRODUCED BY
DAVID J. HALPERIN

PREFACE BY
ELLIOT R. WOLFSON

PAULIST PRESS
NEW YORK • MAHWAH, NJ

Cover artist: Rose Halperin, M.D., was trained in medicine at Harvard Medical School and in internal medicine, nephrology and psychiatry at Duke University Hospitals. From 1978 through 2001, she has tended the sick in various settings—most recently, a private practice of psychiatry and psychotherapy—and has delivered thoughtful, responsible, compassionate care of body and soul to those under her care. She is currently an artist and devotes her energies to conveying emotional states in oil paintings. The painting on the cover is her vision of Abraham Miguel Cardozo, after her interpretation of a Titian self-portrait, no known portrait of Cardozo having survived.

Book design by Theresa M. Sparacio

Cover design by A. Michael Velthaus

Library of Congress Cataloging-in-Publication Data

Cardozo, Abraham Miguel, d. 1706.
   [Selections. English. 2001]
     Abraham Miguel Cardozo : selected writings / translated and introduced by David J. Halperin.
     p. cm. — (The classics of Western spirituality)
   Includes bibliographical references and index.
   ISBN 0-8091-4023-3 (paper); ISBN 0-8091-0532-2 (cloth)
   1. Judaism. 2. Shabbethai Tzevi, 1626-1676. 3. Messiah—Judaism. 4. God (Judaism) 5. Cabala. 6. Sabbathaians. 7. Cardozo, Abraham Miguel, d. 1706. I. Title: Selected writings. II. Halperin, David J. III. Title. IV. Series.

BM550 .C32213 2001
296.8′2—dc21

                                             00-140085

Published by Paulist Press
997 Macarthur Boulevard
Mahwah, New Jersey 07430

www.paulistpress.com

Printed and bound in the United States of America

Contents

CONTENTS

Translator of This Volume

DAVID J. HALPERIN was trained in Semitic languages at Cornell University, in Near Eastern studies at the University of California at Berkeley, and in rabbinics at the Hebrew University of Jerusalem. He received his Ph.D. from Berkeley in 1977. From 1976 through 2000, he taught the history of Judaism in the Department of Religious Studies at the University of North Carolina, Chapel Hill, where he was repeatedly recognized for excellence in undergraduate teaching.

He has published numerous scholarly articles and three books: *The Merkabah in Rabbinic Literature* (1980), *The Faces of the Chariot: Early Jewish Responses to Ezekiel's Vision* (1988), and *Seeking Ezekiel: Text and Psychology* (1993). Most recently he has written a novel, *Mirage*, which weaves Jewish and biblical themes together with themes of the modern supernatural. He is currently working on a second novel, about Abraham Miguel Cardozo.

He lives in Durham, North Carolina, with his wife Dr. Rose Halperin, the artist whose painting is on the cover of this volume.

Author of the Preface

ELLIOT R. WOLFSON is the Abraham Lieberman Professor of Hebrew and Judaic Studies and director of the program in religious studies at New York University. He is the author of many publications in the history of Jewish mysticism, including *Through a Speculum That Shines: Vision and Imagination in Medieval Jewish Mysticism* (Princeton University Press, 1994), which won the American Academy of Religion's Award for Excellence in the Study of Religion in the Category of Historical Studies, 1995, and the National Jewish Book Award for Excellence in Scholarship, 1995. In addition, he is the author of *Along the Path: Studies in Kabbalistic Hermeneutics, Myth, and Symbolism* and *Circle in the Square: Studies in the Use of Gender in Kabbalistic Symbolism*, both published in 1995 (State University of New York Press). His most recent book, *Abraham Abulafia—Kabbalist and Prophet: Hermeneutics, Theosophy, and Theurgy*, was published in 2000 (Cherub Press). He is currently working on two monographs, *Language, Eros, and Being: Kabbalistic Hermeneutics and the Poetic Imagination* and *Venturing Beyond: Law, Ethics, and Asceticism in Kabbalistic Piety*.

Preface

Perhaps one of the most significant contributions of postmodernist hermeneutics to the study of religion is the recognition that truthfulness of religious experience is not to be discovered in the indivisibility that ostensibly renders one tradition coherent but in the crevices that open up spaces in between different traditions. The binding of oneself to a particular faith community serves the dual role of delimiting options and expanding horizons. The metaphor of the fence is especially helpful in demarcating the seemingly contradictory tasks of letting in and keeping out. That is, just as a fence keeps the undesirable out but also affords access to the alluring, so joining a particular group to the exclusion of another sets up a boundary that both divides and unifies. As the rabbis of old used to say, it is incumbent to make a hedge to surround the law. Surely, the "original" intent of this dictum was to advocate for strict adherence to ritualistic exclusivity in the effort to set rigid borders separating Jews and Gentiles. In good rabbinic fashion, however, we may subversively preserve the ancient wisdom by (re)interpreting the hedge as a mechanism that not only excludes by inclusion but also includes by exclusion. When viewed from this perspective, we can speak meaningfully of letting in by keeping out and keeping in by letting out.

Well before the contemporary tendency to transgress boundaries, select individuals, whether by force of historical circumstance or psychological disposition, have demonstrated the ability to dwell in intercultural spaces that destabilize an inside/outside dichotomy. In the history of Judaism in the modern period, Abraham Miguel

Cardozo (1627–1706) is exemplary of a person who was centered from the margins. Cardozo was born into a Marrano family in Spain and thus was accustomed to living in a state of dissimilitude, externally professing allegiance to Christianity and internally preserving attachment to Judaism. His physical departure from Spain in 1648 (together with his older brother Fernando who later became Isaac) represented a spiritual odyssey that brought him back to his Jewish heritage. He eventually changed his name from Miguel to Abraham to mark the return to the faith of his ancestors. In spite of this return to Judaism and the disavowal of Christianity, Cardozo's writings attest that throughout his life he remained faithful to the double vision of a Marrano, looking from inside out and outside in.

The duplicitous identity, which is essential to the Marrano experience, provides the key to understanding Cardozo's complex relationship to Sabbatai Sevi, who was proclaimed messiah by Nathan of Gaza in 1665. A distinctive feature of this messianic phenomenon, as many scholars have noted, centered on the blatant acts of breaking traditional rituals and customs, culminating in the ultimate act of betrayal, the conversion of Sabbatai Sevi to Islam on September 16, 1666. These intermittent acts of antinomianism and the fateful apostasy were transformed by faithful followers of Sabbatai Sevi into a theology of paradox, largely expressed through presuppositions of Lurianic kabbalah. That is, the abrogation of Jewish law and the adoption of the Muslim faith, which Nathan and other Sabbatians referred to as *ma'asim zarim*, "strange acts," afforded the alleged messiah the opportunity to descend to the realm of the demonic shells *(qelippot)* in order to perform the ultimate rectification *(tiqqun)*. In several texts of Nathan of Gaza, the theology of paradox, or what Scholem tellingly called "redemption through sin," is expressed in terms of the statement in *Tiqqunei Zohar*, "he is good on the inside but his garment is evil" *(tav milegav u-levusha' dileih bish)*, which is associated exegetically with the scriptural description of the messianic king, "yet humble, riding on an ass" (Zech 9:9). The verse from Zechariah relates the paradox to the image of riding upon the ass. In light of the symbolic association of Ishmael and the ass, this is an entirely apt image to signify the sense of being subservient to the faith of Islam, a subservience that actually bespeaks the mastery of the messiah over the demonic realm to which he has succumbed in order to redeem the fallen sparks of his soul-root. From the outside, then, it seems as if the messiah were lacking good deeds and proper piety. In truth, however, the apparent poverty is a mark of genuine spiritual wealth, for it is the sublime excellence of the messiah's soul that allows him to descend into the depths of impurity in order to separate the holy and profane.

For his part, Cardozo related this characteristic of Sabbatai Sevi's messianic pretensions to the existential situation of the Marrano. Thus, in a letter that he wrote to his brother, sometime before April 1668, Cardozo proclaimed that the messiah "will don the garments of a Marrano, and on account of that the Jews will not recognize him. In short, in the future he will be a Marrano like me." In this text, Cardozo is not asserting that he is the messiah, but only that the redeemer will "don the garments of a Marrano," for necessarily there will be a discrepancy between who is he on the inside and how he appears on the outside.

An even more striking expression of the spiritual tug of war that Cardozo experienced between his Marrano past and his Sabbatian belief is found in *Derush Qodesh Yisra'el la-YHWH*, written between 1682 and 1686. Cardozo identifies the two messianic figures in Jewish tradition, the messiah son of David and the messiah son of Ephraim, respectively with Sabbatai Sevi and himself. He notes that the two saviors move in spiritual paths with antithetical trajectories: The Davidic messiah descends from holiness to impurity, whereas the Ephraimite messiah ascends from impurity to holiness. The allusion here is obviously to the fact that Sabbatai Sevi converted from Judaism to Islam, whereas Cardozo returned from Christianity to Judaism. Moreover, since the messiah son of Ephraim was born amongst the "uncircumcised," it is his special task to combat the Christological belief in the trinity and the doctrine of incarnation, which affirm the divinity of Jesus. Indeed, his very name, Michael, reflects his unique messianic function, for he must constantly ask the rhetorical question, *mi ka'el*, who is like God?, so that people will understand that there is none comparable

to the divine including the messiah himself. This is clearly a reference to Sabbatians who affirmed an incarnational theology
whereby the messiah was explicitly identified as the embodiment of
the divine. As Cardozo informs the reader, to combat this error it
was necessary for the messiah son of Ephraim to delve into the
heretical theology and idolatrous practices of Christianity.

Cardozo utilized Christological motifs to formulate the messianic belief nurtured by kabbalistic symbolism even if his ultimate
objective was to distinguish between the two realms. The charge
that Christianity served as a major influence on Cardozo's messianic teaching was leveled against him by Jacob Sasportas.
Interestingly, in one of his letters to his brother, which is extant in
Spanish, Cardozo accepts the idea that there are similarities
between Christian belief and true messianism, which can be
explained by the fact that Christians received their traditions from
the sages of Israel. It is thus not merely rhetorical when Cardozo
employs the word *sod*, "secret," in his depiction of the Christian
doctrine of the trinity in a passage from *Derush Zeh 'Eli wa-
'Anveihu* (composed between 1683–84). The presumption that the
Christological doctrine is derived, albeit in a distorted manner,
from Jewish esotericism underlies Cardozo's remark in the same
context that kabbalists could answer his queries about trinitarian
theology that even Christian thinkers could not solve.

The complex interrelatedness of Christianity and esoteric
Judaism is also attested in the homology that Cardozo establishes
between veneration of Mary in Christian liturgical practice and
worship of *Shekhinah* in kabbalistic practice. To be sure, Cardozo's
view that Mary is reminiscent of the kabbalistic symbol of
Shekhinah is a reversal of the psychological process that he
undoubtedly underwent, that is, his conception of *Shekhinah*
reflects his prior knowledge and experience of Mary from within a
Christian milieu. Still, it is instructive that he noted this analogy. I
surmise that his repeated emphasis that Jews do not worship
Shekhinah is isolation from the holy One, blessed be he, must be
seen in a polemical context. Cardozo presents in encapsulated form
a history of monotheism from the perspective of the gender of the

divine. Jews pray to the holy One who is androgynous, comprising the *Shekhinah* in himself just as (according to the creation narrative in the second chapter of Genesis) woman was thought to be contained in Adam; Christians worship the male Jesus and the female Mary; and Muslims exclusively worship the male deity. Christian praxis, therefore, is closer in spirit to the kabbalistic orientation than that of Islam, for the kabbalist also acknowledges masculine and feminine aspects of the divine to whom worship is directed. There is, however, a major difference between Christian and kabbalistic liturgical practices insofar as the latter unites the genders separated by the former.

Finally, let me note that in another treatise, *Derush Boqer 'Avraham*, composed between 1670 and 1672, Cardozo remarked that Christian faith comes from "wicked Jews" who believed in Jesus and who tried to anchor their belief in the wisdom of kabbalah. The link that Cardozo draws between the promotion of Christian dogma and the need on the part of some Jews to spread kabbalistic teachings is most telling. Apparently, Cardozo is responding to Jews who would have buttressed the premise of Christian kabbalists that the Christological teachings were based on ancient secrets, the *prisca theologia* of Jewish tradition. Notwithstanding his protestations, Cardozo himself at times gives credence to this orientation and supplies the scholar with some of the most interesting articulations of living in the breach between the two religious cultures.

We are indebted to David J. Halperin for providing a biography of this most extraordinary figure in Jewish history that combines painstaking textual specificity and breathtaking methodological sophistication. In the first part of this work, Halperin deftly brings the reader into the Cardozo's universe. It is to the author's credit that he broadens the canvas by discussing various aspects of Cardozo's personality, to wit, his background as a Marrano; his study of kabbalah; his mission as bearer of the messianic message; his training as a theologian; his experience with the occult science of magic; and his social condition as a wanderer. In painting this intellectual portrait, Halperin combines a very fine historical sense with analytic acuity. In the second part, Halperin has made available in English translation for the first time portions of Cardozo's extensive writings. Halperin's translations are philologically sound and literarily superb. In addition, his learned notes will undoubtedly open many doors for scholars in future generations. Halperin has succeeded in producing a learned volume that is nevertheless accessible to a wider audience. His study should prove to be of great interest to anyone who seeks to understand the place of liminality in the formation of religious experience.

Elliot R. Wolfson
New York University

Acknowledgments

This book had its beginning in the summer of 1989. The previous academic year I had been on sabbatical, studying Kabbalah in preparation for a project of translating Sabbatian literature. The following summer I flew to Israel to immerse myself for eight weeks in Sabbatian texts. It was then that I first encountered Abraham Miguel Cardozo.

For this experience, I owe to many a great debt of thanks. I was supported during my sabbatical by a leave from the Department of Religious Studies at the University of North Carolina, Chapel Hill, and by a Pogue Research Leave from the university. The National Endowment for the Humanities awarded me a Travel to Collections Grant for my trip to Israel, and the American Philosophical Society helped support my stay in Israel with a research grant. Professor Yehuda Liebes, one of the foremost Israeli scholars of Sabbatianism and Kabbalah, took time to guide me through the often bewildering universe of Sabbatian thought. His wife, Ms. Etti Liebes, librarian of the Gershom G. Scholem Collection of materials on Jewish mysticism in the Hebrew University Library, Jerusalem, helped me orient myself to the resources under her care.

The UNC Institute for the Arts and Humanities, under the directorship of Professor Ruel W. Tyson, gave me a warm and lively setting of scholarly collegiality in which to pursue my Kabbalistic studies in 1988–89. During the years that followed, as I worked on my Sabbatian translations, I turned again and again to the institute for intellectual fellowship and for financial support.

Again and again, the institute proved more than generous. I was honored with a faculty fellowship for the summer of 1990, with a Lyman Cotton Faculty Fellowship for the fall semester of 1992— supplemented by a generous grant from the Memorial Foundation for Jewish Culture—and with a Chapman Family Faculty Fellowship for the spring semester of 1997. I fondly remember the Tuesday afternoons around the institute's lunch-and-seminar table that spring, exchanging ideas with colleagues in all disciplines of the humanities, during a semester's leave devoted entirely to the life and thought of Abraham Cardozo. The institute's generosity made that semester, and hence this book, possible.

My former student, Ms. Elizabeth L. Mosley, kindly read an early draft of my translation of the *Epistle to the Judges of Izmir* (chapter 9 of this volume) and provided me with valuable comments. Professor Tom Tweed of the UNC Department of Religious Studies, and Professor David Winston of the Graduate Theological Union in Berkeley did the same for *This Is My God and I Will Praise Him* (chapter 10). The wonderful students in my honors course for the spring of 1998 ("Shylock, Spinoza and Sabbatai Zevi: Judaism in the Early Modern World") read drafts of most of the translations offered in this volume and offered me their collective advice on the editing of Cardozo's so-called autobiographical letter (chapter 12). It is my pleasant duty to thank each of them one by one: Jennifer Alzos, Karen Bandel, Priscilla Chappell, Gail Goers, Tyrell Haberkorn, Kelley Harris, Matthew Kirby, Tyler Ladner, Sarah Manekin, Katherine Massey, Amy Nelson, Amy Smith, Justin Tolley, and Marion Traub-Werner.

To the erudition of my colleague, Professor Lance Lazar, of the UNC Department of Religious Studies, I owe the suggestion that made it possible to identify the woman whom Cardozo saw on the moon one summer night in 1683 (chapter 6). Professor Lazar also provided me with sources on Cadmus and suggested a comparison of Cardozo with Ignatius of Loyola. Professor Lucia Binotti, of the UNC Department of Romance Languages, worked with me in my efforts, eventually fruitless I am afraid, to identify the "Christian Carabusa" with which Cardozo came into conflict (chapter 6). My former student, Mr. Jonathan I. Tepper, generously shared with me his knowledge of Spanish and Judeo-Spanish and translated for me from the Spanish the decree of the Leghorn Jewish community excommunicating Cardozo (chapter 3).

Nearly three-quarters of the Cardozan material included in this book—*This Is My God* (chapter 10), *Israel, Holiness to the Lord* (chapter 11), the "autobiographical letter" (chapter 12)—was originally published in Hebrew by the Ben-Zvi Institute for the Study of Jewish Communities in the East (Jerusalem), in its massive volume on Sabbatianism: *Sefunot* 3–4 (1960). I am deeply grateful to the Ben-Zvi Institute, and to its academic secretary, Mr. Michael Glatzer, for allowing me to publish translations of this material. I am grateful to the Bialik Institute (Jerusalem) and to Ms. Ilana Toucatly for permission to publish my translation of the text, originally published by the Bialik Institute, of the *Epistle to the Judges of Izmir* (chapter 9); to the Library of the Jewish Theological Seminary of America (New York) and to Dr. Mayer E. Rabinowitz for permission to publish a translation of extracts from their ms 1677 (chapter 8); and to the Russian State Library (Moscow) and to Ms. Ekaterina Nikonorova for permission to publish a translation of the poem in Cardozo's honor that appears on the title page of their ms Ginzburg 660 (chapter 13). Ms. Odelia Levanovsky of the Library of the Jewish Theological Seminary kindly located for me the library's microfilm copy of ms Ginzburg 660, and arranged to make for me a copy from the microfilm.

Ms. Joanne Seiff, my research assistant, helped me immensely in the final stages of preparing the manuscript. She was a fine and sensitive editor who repeatedly flagged awkwardnesses and unclarities in my writing and often suggested ways to improve them. She was a resourceful and skilled researcher, to whose tireless detective work I owe many of my details of Cardozo's times. For her help in tracking down sources on the 1672 revolution in Tripoli, I am particularly grateful. (I am grateful, too, to Mr. Robert Clements of the London Public Record Office, who prepared for me a copy of Nathaniel Bradley's unpublished manuscript account of the revolution.)

I thank Professor Elliot R. Wolfson, one of this country's foremost scholars of Kabbalah, for having contributed the preface for this volume. I thank Ms. Katherine Gaul, graduate student in the

ABRAHAM MIGUEL CARDOZO

UNC Department of Geography, for preparing the map of Cardozo's world that appears on page xxxii; and, for putting me in touch with Ms. Gaul, I thank the chair of the Geography Department, Professor Leo Zonn. The sefirotic diagram (page 27) was prepared by Ms. Lynn Else, of Paulist Press, on the basis of a diagram originally used for an earlier volume in the Classics of Western Spirituality series: Daniel Matt's magnificent *Zohar: The Book of Enlightenment* (Mahwah, N.J.: Paulist Press, 1983), which sets a standard for all translators of Kabbalistic texts. Working with the people at Paulist Press has been a pleasure from beginning to end: Professor Bernard McGinn, editor of the Classics of Western Spirituality series; Ms. Joan Laflamme, copy editor, Ms. Kathleen Walsh, editor in charge of the project, whose diligent labor and unceasing good humor saw my manuscript through its complex process of transformation into a Paulist Press book, and the indexer, Ms. Dolores Grande.

I thank Ms. Keedrah Sidberry for her help in the selection of the cover art. I thank Mr. Jacob Cooley, Ms. Jane Fish, Dr. Walter Guild, and Ms. Dorothy Loring for their input and encouragement of the artist. I thank Mr. Seth Tice-Lewis for his photograph of the artist's painting.

Above all, I thank the artist herself, Dr. Rose Halperin. She has been my wife for more than eighteen years, my closest friend for more than twenty. For ten years she and I together have gotten to know Abraham Miguel Cardozo, warts and all—not always wise, not always lovable, not always very spiritual—but always deeply human, calling out to us through our common humanity. It was Rose the psychiatrist who helped me understand Cardozo's soul. It was Rose who pointed out for me the way to tell his story. It was Rose the artist who saw in a self-portrait of Titian's the material for a portrait, created from her intuitive understanding, of this lonely and weary Messiah of whom no other portrait exists. It is to Rose, my beloved life's companion, that I dedicate this volume.

Durham, North Carolina
February 15, 2001

Note to the Reader

Abraham Cardozo (1627–1706) is known today, to the extent that he is known at all, as a Sabbatian enthusiast, that is, a follower and defender of the false messiah Sabbatai Zevi. This is a pity. Cardozo was a Sabbatian believer, of course, but he was a great deal more. He was one of the most vivid, complex, and original personalities to emerge within Judaism during the seventeenth century. He was an early modern Jew who was, above all, an individual. Like his contemporary Spinoza, he suffered horribly for his individuality; yet, unlike Spinoza, he remained faithful until his death to what he believed to be true Judaism. He deserves to be known for himself.

Cardozo is often a hard person for the modern reader to get to know. This is not because he was an inept writer. Quite the contrary. He wrote his books and treatises in a Hebrew style that his contemporary critics might despise as "vulgar,"[1] but which is better described as simple and direct, vivid and powerful. It is the style of a man who has something to say that he passionately believes in and wants to say it as clearly and forcefully as possible.

The problem is that Cardozo lived not only in a different world from ours but in a different universe. His was not the universe of Newton and Descartes, but the magical universe of Kabbalistic mysticism, which has mostly vanished today. It requires substantial effort from most of us, nowadays, to think ourselves into the universe as Cardozo and his like-minded contemporaries imagined it. Cardozo, moreover, had made himself at home in a rich and complex tradition of Jewish scholastic thought, and he normally assumed that his readers were at least moderately familiar with this tradition. It is no wonder that reading him can sometimes present difficulties.

I have tried to ease the reader's way as much as possible. To begin with, I have provided, as part one of the volume, a general orientation to Cardozo. Much of this orientation is biographical. Cardozo's life's work and his sense of his life's mission are bound up closely with the events of his life. Yet only one biography of Cardozo has ever been written: in 1707, the year after his death, by a man who (for reasons presently to be explored) detested him. Abraham Cardozo's older brother, Isaac, is the subject of a marvelous biography by Yosef H. Yerushalmi.[2] For Abraham, however, there is nowhere the reader can go for a biographical account other than Gershom Scholem's article "Cardozo, Abraham" in the *Encyclopaedia Judaica*. I have tried to fill this gap.

Much of part one, however, is devoted less to Cardozo himself than to the landscape of his mental universe, particularly the Kabbalah and the Jewish Messianic tradition. This is essential. If the reader does not know, at least very roughly, what is meant by the Zohar or the Shechinah, or the ten *sefirot* or the "Five Persons," or the centrally important Kabbalistic concept of the "Mending"— or if he or she is not aware that the Jewish tradition out of which Cardozo emerged found room not just for one Messiah but for *two*—that reader is bound to miss out on a great deal of what Cardozo is saying. My aim in part one has been to provide all the background that is necessary without encumbering the reader with superfluous detail.

I have prepared individual introductions for each of the four major texts translated in this volume (chapters 9–12). To several of the translations, I have added an introductory section called "Background Texts." The reason is this: In the course of the text that follows, Cardozo will build upon and presuppose familiarity with some passage or passages from the Bible or the rabbinic or Kabbalistic literature. If the reader has not read these passages, or has not looked at them recently, he or she will be at some disadvantage. The reading of Cardozo will go much more easily if the reader comes to it fresh from the sources that Cardozo has utilized. (In the case of the biblical passages, it has often been necessary for me to translate them, not as a modern scholar would understand them, but as *Cardozo himself understood them*. Such, for example, is the case with Isaiah's famous prophecy of the Suffering Servant, in chapter 9.)

In annotating Cardozo's writings, I have kept in mind that these annotations will appear at the end of the book rather than at the bottom of the page. The reader should not have to keep turning back and forth to the notes in order to understand what Cardozo is trying to say. I have therefore inserted some notes into the text itself (indented, in brackets) in order to provide the reader with the guidance that is needed, as it were, in mid-course. I have reserved the notes for other purposes: citing Cardozo's sources; discussing textual, philological, biographical, and historical problems; and providing information that is indeed important for those seriously interested in the text, but that is not essential for a first understanding.

Often, when Cardozo touches upon some subject, I provide a note referring the reader to some place in the volume where that subject is discussed. (Normally, the reference will be to part one, and the reader is directed to the pertinent chapter and subchapter.) There will be times, however, when the reader will come upon a name or a term, have no recollection of what it is, and find no note giving directions to where that information may be found. The reader is best advised, then, to turn to the index, where I have marked **in bold type** the page where a term is defined or an individual described.

There are a few specific points that need to be noted:

Dates. Cardozo, like most Jewish writers of his time, normally dates events by the Jewish calendar. Years are counted from the supposed date of the creation of the world; they are lunar rather than solar; and they begin in the autumn (with the festival of Rosh Hashanah, the Jewish New Year). One can roughly translate the Creation-Era year into the Christian-Era year by subtracting 3760. Thus, Cardozo's 5426 corresponds more or less to the year 1666, but the reader must be aware that 5426 begins in the autumn of 1665 and ends in the autumn of 1666. Needless to say, I do not lay the burden of doing this arithmetic upon the reader; I provide, in brackets, the Gregorian equivalents for Cardozo's dates.

The Jewish month begins and ends at new moon and is therefore either twenty-nine or thirty days long. Since the resulting year is only 354 days long, after a few years the lunar Jewish calendar will begin to lag behind the solar calendar. When this happens, a thirteenth month is inserted (in late winter) in order to catch up. The consequence is that the day-and-month date of the Jewish year never corresponds two years in a row to the same day-and-month date of the Gregorian year (for example, Heshvan 15, 5457 = November 10, 1696; but Heshvan 15, 5458 = October 30, 1697).[3] Still, one can make a rough equivalence of Jewish months and Gregorian months: Tishri (the first month of the Jewish year) corresponds to September-October, Heshvan to October-November, and so forth. (See Table I, at the end of this "Note to the Reader," for a complete list.)

Place-names. Cardozo sometimes speaks of Constantinople and Adrianople, calling these ancient cities by their classical names. At other times, he uses their modern names: Istanbul and Edirne. In my translations I have not tried to impose consistency upon Cardozo but use whichever name he has preferred in any given passage. Cardozo invariably speaks of Izmir (not Smyrna), and I follow him on this. He normally writes the name of the city of Leghorn, Italy, as *ligorna*, and I accordingly call it Leghorn, not Livorno.

Source-citations. To understand the method Cardozo uses for citing passages from the Zohar, it is necessary first to understand that Jewish liturgical usage divides the Pentateuch into fifty-four "portions" *(parashiyyot)*, each of which is to be read in synagogue one week of the year. In this manner the entire Torah is read aloud, from the beginning of Genesis to the end of Deuteronomy, over the course of the Jewish year. Each Torah portion is named after the first significant Hebrew word that occurs at the beginning of that portion. Thus, Genesis 1:1—6:8 is "the Torah portion *Bereshit*," Genesis 6:9—11:32 is "the Torah portion *Noah*," and so forth. (See Table II for a complete list.)

NOTE TO THE READER

The Zohar is structured as a commentary on the Pentateuch. Cardozo therefore cites it by referring to "the Zohar on the Torah portion *Bereshit*," "the Zohar on the Torah portion *Noah*," and so forth. (He sometimes uses the same method for other texts whose structure follows the Pentateuch, the Torah commentary of Nachmanides, for example. But he most commonly uses it for the Zohar.) Sometimes, when he wants to pinpoint his source more precisely, he also gives the page number of the three-volume Mantua edition of the Zohar, which was the standard edition in Cardozo's time, as it is today. He does *not* give the number of the volume, since he regards this as self-evident from the name of the Torah portion.

Cardozo's other source-citations will present few problems for the reader. Citing biblical passages, Cardozo occasionally gives the number of the chapter, never of the verse. He cites Talmudic passages only by the name of the tractate. I supply, in brackets or notes, all the information Cardozo has left out. (I cite the Babylonian Talmud, as is customary, by the tractate and folio page of the standard edition; and I use the abbreviations "BT" and "PT" for the Babylonian and Palestinian Talmuds.)

Unless indicated otherwise, all quotations from the Bible and other Jewish religious texts are my own translations.

Other. When he quotes his sources, Cardozo naturally does not always quote them in their entirety. He often omits those words or sentences that are not essential for his point. Sometimes he marks his omissions with the Hebrew equivalent of an ellipsis, sometimes not. Where he omits words from a quotation *without* indicating the omission, I mark this in the translation with a bracketed ellipsis ([...]).

Cardozo has divided his treatise *This Is My God and I Will Praise Him* (*Zeh eli ve-anvehu*, translated in chapter 10) into chapters, and it is often convenient for me to cite this text by chapter number. This opens the possibility of confusion between chapter numbers of *This Is My God* and chapter numbers referring to the chapters *of this volume*. To avoid any such confusion, I use Roman numerals for the chapters of *This Is My God* (chapters I, II, III, etc.)

and Arabic numerals (chapters 1, 2, 3, etc.) for the chapters of this volume.

I provide information on the source or sources of each Hebrew text I am translating, in the first note of the translation, which the reader will find attached to the translation's title.

TABLE I
The Jewish Calendar

Tishri	September-October
Heshvan	October-November
Kislev	November-December
Tevet	December-January
Shevat	January-February
Adar	February-March
Nisan	March-April
Iyyar	April-May
Sivan	May-June
Tammuz	June-July
Av	July-August
Elul	August-September

(A thirteenth month, Second Adar, is often inserted after Adar)

TABLE II
Weekly Torah Portions

GENESIS:

Bereshit	1:1–6:8
Noah	6:9–11:32
Lekh Lekha	12:1–17:27
Vayyera'	18:1–22:24
Hayyei Sarah	23:1–25:18
Toledot	25:19–28:9
Vayyeze	28:10–32:3
Vayyishlah	32:4–36:43
Vayyeshev	37:1–40:23
Miqqez	41:1–44:17
Vayyiggash	44:18–47:27
Vayyehi	47:28–50:26

EXODUS:

Shemot	1:1–6:1
Va'era	6:2–9:35
Bo	10:1–13:16
Beshallah	13:17–17:16
Yitro	18:1–20:26
Mishpatim	21:1–24:18
Terumah	25:1–27:19
Tezavveh	27:20–30:10
Ki Tissa	30:11–34:35
Vayyaqhel	35:1–38:20
Pequdei	38:21–40:38

LEVITICUS:

Vayyiqra	1:1–5:26
Zav	6:1–8:36
Shemini	9:1–11:47

CHRONOLOGY OF THE LIFE
OF ABRAHAM CARDOZO

1627—Miguel Cardozo born to a Marrano family in Medina de Rio Seco, Spain

1648—Cardozo leaves Spain with his older brother, Fernando; they settle in Venice, convert to Judaism; Fernando Cardozo takes the name Isaac, while Miguel becomes Abraham

Early 1650s (?)—Cardozo in Egypt, studying Kabbalah

1659—Cardozo in Leghorn

1663—Cardozo in Tripoli, physician to Osman Pasha and Rejeb Bey

1665—Nathan of Gaza proclaims Sabbatai Zevi the Messiah

September 16, 1666—Sabbatai Zevi converts to Islam

1668—Cardozo writes an early version of his defense of Sabbatai Zevi's Messiahship

1669—Cardozo writes the *Epistle to the Judges of Izmir*

1670–72—Cardozo writes *Abraham's Morn*

1672–73—Osman Pasha and Rejeb Bey killed in a revolution; Cardozo leaves for Tunis

1674—Cardozo excommunicated, expelled from Tunis; tries to settle in Leghorn

1675—Cardozo forced out of Leghorn, settles in Izmir

September 17, 1676—Sabbatai Zevi dies

1678—Cardozo's family decimated by plague

1680—Cardozo expelled from Izmir, moves to Constantinople

Summer-autumn 1681—Cardozo prophesies Redemption for the following Passover; he is excommunicated, his life threatened; he withdraws to Rodosto

December 1681–January 1682—Sabbatai Zevi's widow, Esther, proposes marriage to Cardozo; he returns to Constantinople

Spring 1682—predicted Redemption fails to materialize; Cardozo leaves Constantinople for the Dardanelles

1682–86—Cardozo lives by the Dardanelles (Gallipoli, Canakkale); writes *Israel, Holiness to the Lord*

1683—the great apostasy at Salonica (mass conversion of the Sabbatians to Islam)

1685 or 1686—Cardozo writes *This Is My God and I Will Praise Him*

1686—Cardozo tries to settle in Adrianople (Edirne); expelled, he returns to Constantinople

1687—plague again strikes Cardozo's family

1696—Cardozo leaves Constantinople for Rodosto; he is prevented from returning to Izmir

1696–97—Cardozo settles in Adrianople, is expelled (in autumn 1697) at the instigation of Samuel Primo; back to Rodosto

1701—Cardozo in Candia (Iraklion), Crete; drifts back and forth between the islands of Crete and Chios; eventually goes to Alexandria

1701 (or shortly afterward)—Cardozo writes his "autobiographical letter"

Ca. 1703—Cardozo tries unsuccessfully to move to Palestine, perhaps in anticipation of Sabbatai Zevi's return; is not permitted to enter; goes back to Egypt

1706—Cardozo stabbed to death by his nephew

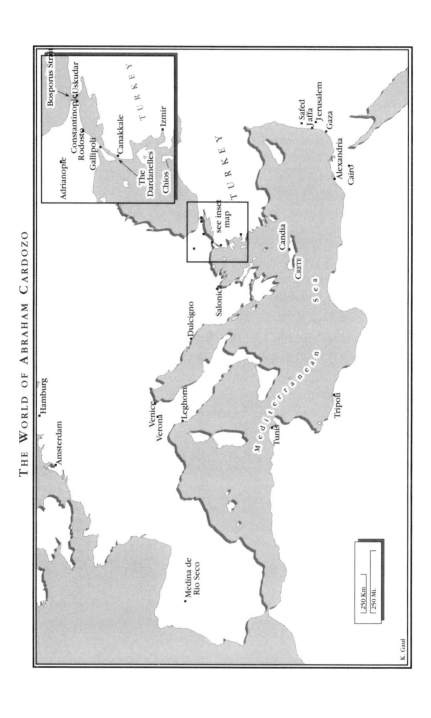

THE WORLD OF ABRAHAM CARDOZO

Bosporus Strait

Constantinople Uskudar
Adrianople
Rodosto
Gallipoli
Canakkale

TURKEY

Izmir

The
Dardanelles
Chios

TURKEY

see inset
map

Hamburg
Amsterdam

Venice
Verona
Leghorn

Dulcigno

Salonica

Candia

CRETE

Mediterranean Sea

Tunis

Tripoli

Safed
Jaffa
Jerusalem
Gaza

Alexandria
Cairo

Medina de
Rio Seco

250 Km
250 Mi.

K. Gaul

Part One

THE MAN AND HIS UNIVERSE

At a certain Village in *La Mancha*, which I shall not name, there liv'd not long ago one of those old-fashion'd Gentlemen...nigh fifty Years of Age, of a hale and strong Complexion, lean-body'd, and thin-fac'd....Some say his Sirname was *Quixada*, or *Quesada* (for Authors differ in this Particular)....

You must know then, that when our Gentleman had nothing to do (which was almost all the Year round) he pass'd his Time in reading Books of Knight-Errantry...so wholly...that a-Nights he would pore on 'till 'twas Day, and a-Days he would read on 'till 'twas Night; and thus by sleeping little, and reading much, the Moisture of his Brain was exhausted to that Degree, that at last he lost the Use of his Reason. A world of disorderly Notions, pick'd out of his Books, crouded into his Imagination; and now his Head was full of nothing but Inchantments, Quarrels, Battles, Challenges, Wounds, Complaints, Amours, Torments, and abundance of Stuff and Impossibilities; insomuch, that all the Fables and fantastical Tales which he read, seem'd to him now as true as the most authentick Histories.

—Cervantes, *Don Quixote*

Miguel de Cervantes died in 1616. Some eleven years later, in 1627, another Miguel was born, in the town of Medina de Rio Seco in Cervantes's Spanish homeland, to the family Cardozo. The family had at one time been Jewish. Now they were professing Christians, and—although no record of the event survives—Miguel Cardozo was certainly baptized into the Catholic Church.[1]

No portrait or physical description of Miguel Cardozo survives. We do not know to what extent he resembled Miguel de Cervantes's most famous creation. His one and only biographer, who detested and despised him, described him as a bon vivant with

3

a taste for ad hoc religious rituals that tended to involve plenty of good food and wine, a man given to "fondling a woman with one hand and a pastry with the other."[2] A "lean-body'd, thin-fac'd" Don Quixote would, perhaps, not quite fit this description. Yet Miguel Cardozo went hungry often enough during the long struggles with loneliness and rejection that marked the extraordinary crusade on behalf of his God, to which he dedicated his life.

In his spirit, at any rate, Cardozo was like Quixote; more grandiosely ambitious, even, than the original. He sallied forth into the world to redeem it, with weapons and armor made of brilliant illusion. He failed dismally, and he died a strange, desperate, and horrifying death, shattered by what he could not allow himself to understand.

In his failure, Cardozo was incandescent. His notions, false as most of them certainly were, have about them a radiance that can bedazzle but also illuminate and guide. He fascinated many of his contemporaries. He has the power to fascinate us today. He also has the power to teach us about ourselves, our souls, our faith.

Who was this man?

Chapter 1
Cardozo the Marrano

1.

> I am the man they call, at times, *mem-bet-aleph*, which are the [Hebrew] initials of *Michael ben Abraham*. At other times I am called *aleph-mem-koph: Abraham Michael Cardozo*. I am of the Marranos of Spain.[1]

In this often mysterious passage—we shall return to consider some of its darker elements—Cardozo defines his origins as being *min ha-anusim asher bi-sefarad*, literally, "of the forced [converts] who are in Spain." To Cardozo's seventeenth-century contemporaries, this reference would have needed no further clarification. There can have been few people anywhere in the Jewish world who did not know the agony and the tragedy of the Spanish and Portuguese Jews.

Down to the end of the fourteenth century, these had been among the proudest, freest, most prosperous Jews of the world. But, starting with the anti-Jewish riots of 1391, things had turned sour. Persecution, harassment, and humiliation grew worse through the fifteenth century. In 1492 the Spanish Jews were finally given the choice between conversion and exile. Five years later the Jews of Portugal—along with the Spanish exiles who had settled there—were forced into Christianity.

Even before the expulsion of 1492, hundreds of thousands of Iberian Jews had become Christians. With their new religion they took on Spanish or Portuguese names. Once baptized, they left behind them all the legal oppressions that went with the profession of Judaism. Many of them entered the government, the church, the learned professions. Some came to be among the richest and most powerful people in Spain.

What they did not leave behind them was the hatred and suspicion of their "Old Christian" neighbors. Jews were bad enough when they were openly Jewish. Now that they had become "New Christians," could mix with Spanish Christians on equal terms, and seemed to be rising with weird and baffling ease to wealth and influence—who knew what insidious evils they might bring upon Spain? They were all the more sinister in that at least some of them seemed not really to have become Christian at all. Some of them— or maybe all of them, people thought—were still as Jewish as ever, behind their facade of Christianity. They still kept Jewish festivals, lit candles on the Sabbath, avoided eating pork. Baptism had not managed to wash away the essential Jewish evil of their nature. True, they had entered Christian society. But they had done so only to destroy it more effectively, from the inside.

Cervantes can say, in Sancho Panza's praise, that he "was something of a Gentleman by Descent, or at least the Offspring of the old Christians"—as opposed to the "New Christian" *conversos*. Sancho can boast of himself that "I firmly believe whatever our Holy *Roman* Catholick Church believes, and I hate the *Jews* mortally."[2] By Sancho's time, the latter part of the sixteenth century, there were no openly professing Jews left in Spain for him to hate. But there were the "New Christians"—*Marranos*, "pigs," as they had often come to be called—who had inherited a burden of loathing and terror worse than anything their Jewish ancestors had carried.

Beginning in the 1480s this loathing and terror found institutional embodiment in an organization that had as its most essential goal the project of hunting out any trace of "Judaizing" among the New Christians—and then destroying it, with hideous torture, with burning at the stake. This was the Spanish Inquisition.

2.

> When I was six years old, my parents made known to me
> that I was a Jew. When I was twelve…I took to reading
> the [Old Testament] Scriptures in Latin, despite the
> tremendous danger that this entails everywhere in Spain.[3]

We cannot generalize from the Cardozo family to all, or most,
of the Marranos. Very possibly by the seventeenth century most of
the *conversos'* descendants were true Christian believers, whose
"Judaism" consisted at most of a few residual customs whose meaning no one remembered. (The Inquisition, which inherited the
property of any "Judaizers" they could execute, had every motive
for wanting to exaggerate these customs into a full-fledged crypto-
Judaism.) Yet the ancient religion was often stubborn, and might
often reappear in unexpected ways.[4]

Take the case of Uriel Da Costa (1583/4–1640), whom we
may usefully compare with the much younger Cardozo:

> I was born in Portugal [Da Costa tells us] in a city of the same
> name but commonly called Oporto. My parents were of the
> nobility, originally descended from those Jews who were forced
> to embrace Christianity in that kingdom. My father was a true
> Christian and a man of unquestioned honor and integrity. I
> had a good education at home, servants always at my com-
> mand.…According to the custom of the country, I was edu-
> cated in Roman Catholicism. When I was but a youth the
> dread of eternal damnation made me anxious to observe all its
> doctrines punctiliously.…

Yet Da Costa, like young Miguel Cardozo, turned to the study
of the Old Testament and convinced himself thereby "to become a
convert to the Law of Moses."

> Having made this decision and finding it unsafe to profess this
> religion in Portugal, I began to think of changing my resi-
> dence and leaving my native home.…When I had concluded
> all the necessary arrangements, my mother, brothers and

myself boarded a ship, not without danger for it is illegal for those who are descended from Jews to depart without a special permit from the King....At the end of our voyage we arrived at Amsterdam [in 1615] where we found the Jews professing their religion with great freedom, as the Law directs them. We immediately fulfilled the precept concerning circumcision.

This was a reasonably common story in the seventeenth century,[5] and one that sounds as though it ought to have had a happy ending. In Da Costa's case, unfortunately, it did not. As a young man, he had become skeptical of Christianity. He came soon to be skeptical of the Judaism of the rabbis (which seemed to him a "Pharisaic" invention, alien to the Old Testament), and eventually of the Old Testament itself. All religions, he decided, were human inventions. God was revealed only through nature and through the natural laws that He had laid down.

The Jewish communities of the "Marrano Diaspora" (to use Cecil Roth's term) did not care for Da Costa's biblical fundamentalism, nor did they care for his subsequent Deism. He was excommunicated in Venice in 1618, in Amsterdam in 1623 and again in 1632 (or 1633). He was reconciled with the Amsterdam community in 1639, after being forced to endure a humiliating public ceremony of repentance. In 1640 he shot himself to death.[6]

3.

While I was in Spain, among the Christians, they used to demand that one avoid saying *alabado sea Dios* [praised be God] when stepping into another's house, to avert all suspicion of being a Jew. Rather, we were supposed to say *Ave Maria: Salvation is with you, Maria.*[7]

If we are to believe Miguel Cardozo, he was burdened at an extraordinarily young age with the dreadful and potentially lethal secret of his Jewishness. From age six he lived knowing that he was not who he seemed to be: "My parents made known to me that I was a Jew."

Trapped in the land of the Inquisition, in the shadow of the stake and the torture chamber, the child felt himself driven to seek out who he really was: "I would wander about the countryside, meditating, seeking God." "Difficult problems," he tells us, presented themselves to his mind. Cardozo's main "problem," however, was not the "dread of eternal damnation" that tormented the young Da Costa. It was something far more abstract, which we can hardly imagine being even intelligible to a twelve-year-old, much less coming to obsess him. Yet it was the germ of the fixed idea that was to dominate his entire life.

In the books of philosophy he had apparently taken to reading, young Miguel had learned about the "First Cause." This was God, as the medieval philosophers had perceived Him, or, we might perhaps better say, "had perceived *It*."[8] The First Cause was a being utterly abstract, utterly transcendent, utterly pure of any such human characteristic as gender. It has no shape, Cardozo learned. No language of substance or motion can apply to It. And—this was the point that particularly impressed itself upon the boy—It has no name whatever. Could *this* be the God of the Bible?

> I posed to my father the following question: You affirm, do you not, that the First Cause has no name?…Well, then: how do you make sense of the fact that the Torah, the Prophets, and the Holy Writings all call the First Cause by the name YAHVEH…? He Himself told Moses that He has a name….[9]

And the elder Cardozo tried to explain.

We do not know the name of Cardozo's father. About his mother we know nothing whatsoever. Two sisters, with the Spanish names Rica and Luna, appear briefly in his stories about his later years in the cities of Ottoman Turkey.[10] He had an older brother, too.

Fernando Cardozo was born in 1603 or 1604. When his brother Miguel was born, he was already a man of 23 or 24; a physician, with university training in philosophy and a doctorate in medicine from the University of Valladolid. He was also becoming a minor Spanish literary figure. When the playwright Lope de Vega—who disliked and despised Jews—died in 1635, one of those asked to contribute to a volume in his memory was Fernando Cardozo.[11]

Fernando lived in Madrid at least from 1630 onward. At some point, it would seem, his young brother came there to live with him. The bookish child from Medina de Rio Seco hit puberty, and for a few years he had other things on his mind. Years later, Fernando could remind him, to his embarrassment, "of the old days when they were back in Spain, when this would-be prophet was sowing his wild oats, and spent his nights fiddling and strumming in the streets of Madrid with companions as dissipated as himself."[12]

Miguel Cardozo, like his brother, grew up to be a physician. Again like his brother, he was educated in the wisdom of the Gentiles, though we have no idea where he studied, and only a fairly vague idea of what he studied. Later in life he would claim that he had spent two years, during his Christian youth, studying "their theology."[13] He would explain to his readers how the "Messiah son of Ephraim"—a Messianic figure with whom he had come to identify himself—was

> destined to be born among the uncircumcised. Unwillingly, therefore, will he worship their idols. He will learn their sciences, including that science of Divinity that they call *teologia*. As a result, there will not be a single one, of all the distorted doctrines to which the uncircumcised give credence, with which I am not conversant.[14]

Cardozo exaggerates. His writings do not suggest any profound or exhaustive knowledge of the details of Catholic doctrine, and they contain some statements that point to a certain lack of attention to his theological studies. Take, for example, his explanation of why Christians call the devil by the name Lucifer. Satan, he says, was once named *Luz Bel* (Lovely Light). But, with his fall, his name was changed to *Luz Feo* (Ugly Light), which in Cardozo's Spanish was pronounced *Luz Fer*.[15]

CARDOZO THE MARRANO

I cannot say whether this remarkable etymology was Cardozo's own invention. Someone trained in Latin and in Christian theology—as Cardozo claims he was—should surely have known that *Lucifer* is not Spanish at all, but the Latin word meaning Light-bearer. We might at first be tempted to suppose that Cardozo's nighttime activities, in the streets of Madrid, left him too tired for much theological education. But there is also another explanation.

Cardozo's later writings are marked by a ferocious, and absolutely understandable, antipathy to Christianity. "A monstrous heresy," he calls it, "the like of which has never been found in any nation."[16] What does he think of Christian doctrine? "Lies, every word....The Christian religion is false, down to every last detail."[17] Jesus? Cardozo could see him only as Satan's man, a devilish parody of a Messiah, whose essence is *nada*, "a *Nothing*, the very denial of true Being."[18]

This hatred was only one side of a profound ambivalence. We shall see how thoroughly Cardozo's thought was saturated with the influences of the religion in which he was educated, and which he so loathed. Is it any wonder, though, that the teen-age Miguel Cardozo might have found it hard to concentrate his mind on the fine points of Catholic theology? That even so serious and religious-minded a boy might have preferred to go wild in the streets? The Christian religion, with its torture chambers and public burnings, had alienated him and his entire family from what they knew to be their essential being. Jesus's purpose on earth, Cardozo believed, was to "see to it that his people would forget the divinity of our Blessed God."[19] He could see, day after day, Jesus's church doing the same thing.

Even as he plodded his way through his Latin theology books, Miguel Cardozo must have seen himself as a prisoner in the heart of Satan's empire.

Miguel made his escape, with his older brother, Fernando, in 1648. We know none of the details. We do not even know how many members of the Cardozo family went with them. Neither

Fernando nor Miguel mentions their parents in any subsequent context, and it seems a fair assumption that by 1648 they were both dead.

A generation earlier the Da Costas had escaped Portugal for Amsterdam, which was the freest place for a Jew in the seventeenth-century world. The Cardozos went instead to Venice. Like the Da Costas, like thousands of others, they made formal conversion to Judaism. They took new, Hebrew names: Isaac for Fernando, Abraham for Miguel. Their choice is a little strange. After all, as the older brother—he was forty-four by this time, Miguel only twenty-one—we would expect Fernando to have named himself after the senior patriarch.[20] My wife, Rose Halperin, has offered me what I think must be the explanation for their choice.

Each of the Cardozos gravitated toward the biblical figure with which he identified himself. Fernando/Isaac was the dutiful son. As physician—first in Venice, later in Verona—he became a pillar of the Jewish community and of the traditional faith. When Sabbatai Zevi appeared in 1665, claiming to be Messiah, Isaac frowned his disapproval. He would later win fame and honor throughout the Jewish world with his masterful defense of the merits of traditional Judaism: *Las Excelencias y Calumnias de los Hebreos* (Amsterdam, 1679). No wonder he identified himself with the faithful, obedient Isaac of the Book of Genesis, who walked trustingly with his father even to the altar where he was to be sacrificed.

How different was Father Abraham! The Bible, to be sure, tells us next to nothing about the patriarch's younger days. But Jewish legends, from ancient times through the Middle Ages, made up for the Bible's silence. These legends, and the Judeo-Spanish popular songs based on them, told of a young Abraham who was an explorer, a pioneer, a bold smasher of idols, without any excessive respect for his society or its traditions, a fearless and independent-minded intellectual adventurer.[21]

Abraham's quest—say the legends—began at a very early age. His mother had given birth to him in a cave and left him there. She came back twenty days later to find him grown, already a young man, studying the skies, reasoning his way toward knowledge of the true God.[22] Once he had found his truth, the most savage persecution could not stop him from proclaiming it to one and all. His reward was God's favor and friendship and the command: "Get thee out of thy country, and from thy kindred, and from thy father's house, unto the land that I will show thee" (Gen 12:1).

Miguel Cardozo, the precocious child grown to manhood, recognized Abraham as the companion of his spirit. He took on the patriarch's name. In large measure he took on the patriarch's life as well. He had already "gotten himself out" of his ancestral country. He would dedicate his life, as had Abraham, to discovering and proclaiming the true God, and, in the service of that quest, would "get himself out" of place after place, time after time, in the years to come.

Few of his departures would be voluntary. Before he died Cardozo would undergo a string of excommunications, expulsions, and public humiliations that would make Uriel Da Costa's trials seem trivial by comparison. Unlike Da Costa, Cardozo did not kill himself. He struggled onward until his death, led by a God in whom only he believed, toward a fantastic land of Redemption that only he could see.

4.

I learned Scripture, Mishnah, and Gemara. My teachers were the flawless scholars Rabbis Abraham Vallensi, Samuel Aboab, and Moses Zacuto....[I studied] the Bible commentators, the Geonim, and the midrashim.[23]

Samuel Aboab and Moses Zacuto were two of the leading rabbinic scholars of Venice. Under their tutelage—if we are to take his word for it—Abraham Cardozo threw himself into the task of mastering the intricacies of his religious tradition. The cornerstone of this tradition was of course Scripture: the "Old Testament," or, as Jews called it, the Torah, Prophets, and Writings.[24] But—as former Marranos like Da Costa were often appalled to learn—seventeenth-century Judaism was heir also to a complex and ramified system of religious literature, thought, and practice that had grown far beyond its biblical roots.[25]

To begin with, there were the vast literatures created by the ancient rabbis of the first through sixth centuries C.E. These were the men who, after the destruction of the Second Temple in 70 C.E., reshaped Judaism from a sacrificial, priest-led religion into a scholastic faith, the central values of which were prayer and (above all) study. They studied the Bible, deeply and imaginatively. Out of their involvement with the Bible, they created texts called *midrashim*. (The singular is *midrash*; -*im* is the Hebrew masculine plural.) These are not so much commentaries on the Bible, in the modern sense of the word *commentary*, as creative efforts to search out the inner meanings of the Scriptures—often by plucking out passages from different parts of the Bible and setting them side by side to interpret one another.

These midrashic interpretations are often dazzlingly brilliant and insightful. Yet they are normally arbitrary and fanciful as well. For later Jews, such as Cardozo, their authority rested less on the plausibility of their biblical exegesis—which was often not evident—than on the authority ascribed to "our ancient sages, of blessed memory," who were their authors.

Interpreting the Scriptures was an important goal for these ancient rabbis. Still more important was the project of defining and transmitting the authoritative religious law, or *halakhah*, as it is called in Hebrew. This law, the rabbis believed, had been revealed to Moses at Mount Sinai: both in written form (the Pentateuch) and in the form of an *Oral Torah* handed down through generations of rabbis. Early in the third century C.E., the rabbis had codified their Oral Torah in a book called the *Mishnah*. They developed it further in two enormous commentaries on the Mishnah, composed in Palestine (in the fifth century) and in Babylonia (sixth century). Each of these commentaries was called *Gemara*. Each, taken together with the core text of the Mishnah, was called *Talmud*.

The Babylonian Gemara, and thus the Babylonian Talmud, was by far the more important of the two in the eyes of later generations. When Cardozo says, "I learned Scripture, Mishnah, and Gemara," it is the Babylonian Gemara that he intends.

14

Like Da Costa, Cardozo had a few shocks waiting for him: "I subsequently began my study of Gemara. I found there…statements that left me appalled. That God prays, for example, that He wears phylacteries, that He studies the Torah and performs the commandments."[26]

These are a few examples of the strange Talmudic and midrashic passages that Jews called *aggadot shel dofi,* "tainted texts." (An *aggadah* is a rabbinic passage containing some nonlegal teaching, often about God and His ways; *-ot* is the Hebrew feminine plural.) What these "tainted texts" had to say about God was often so bizarre—how does God pray? and to whom does He pray?—that Jews often preferred to forget they existed. They might try to explain them away. They might even use them as evidence that the entire rabbinic tradition was false and degenerate.

Not so Cardozo. Like another intellectual conquistador centuries later, Sigmund Freud, Cardozo sensed intuitively that it was precisely the jumbled, the bizarre, the disreputable and seemingly senseless, that would serve as royal road into the secrets of divinity. The "tainted texts," he was to write many years afterward,

> teach no sound lesson, not of law nor of morality nor even of courtesy; they offer no good counsel, convey no wisdom in the usual sense of the word.…Did not the sages know this?…[Yet they] wrote these passages quite deliberately. For, with their aid, the pure-hearted investigator may discover, at the end of the exile-time, the Mystery of God's Divinity.[27]

In the Venetian years Cardozo was still at the beginning of his quest. He studied, as he tells us, Mishnah and Gemara and midrash. He studied the writings of the Geonim: the legal authorities who presided over the Iraqi rabbinic academies of the early Middle Ages, of whom the greatest, Saadiah Gaon (882–942), was a formidable philosopher as well as master of *halakhah.* He studied the Bible, not only with the ancient midrashim, but with the commentaries of medieval scholars: the great Rashi (1040–1105), whose Bible and Talmud commentaries were the foundations of an ordinary Jewish education, and the Kabbalists Nachmanides (1194–1270) and Bahya ben Asher (d. 1340). We may presume that it was in Venice that he made his acquaintance with the masterworks of the greatest Jewish rationalist of the Middle Ages, Moses Maimonides (1135–1204): the halakhic *Code of Jewish Law* and the philosophical *Guide to the Perplexed*.

He had his contacts with more up-to-date currents of thought as well. The "aristocrats of the Venetian Senate," whom he had perhaps come to know through his budding medical practice, felt comfortable enough with Cardozo to share their religious opinions with him. He learned that the rulers of Christian Venice were not precisely Christians. On the contrary, they "ridicule Jesus and everyone who believes in him."

> These men maintain the simplicity of the First Cause, and insist upon the premises that the First Cause admits of no alteration, nor does It speak to any living creature [and therefore certainly could not have revealed a sacred Scripture]. They hold, as an article of faith, that humanity's "Torah" consists of the dictates of reason, and of that sense of justice and truth with which the Creator (whom they suppose to be the First Cause) has endowed the human intellect....Many of them say that the real reason for our [that is, the Jews'] having spent more than sixteen hundred years in exile—humiliated, degraded, accursed—is that we have claimed falsely that our Torah derives from the First Cause.[28]

Cardozo tried to answer back. But dozens of biblical passages that speak of God having human limbs or human feelings—not to mention those awful "tainted texts" of the Talmud—stood in his way. He was eventually forced to concede, to himself if not to his debate partners, that "the Torah and all its contents are infinitely remote from the First Cause." Bible and Talmud, he came to realize, are filled with utterances that, "if God were the First Cause... would be blasphemous heresies which not even a Gentile would dare to speak."[29]

But is it thinkable that God and the First Cause are two distinct beings? Does it even make coherent sense to say such a thing? (If so, what will become of Jewish monotheism?) No wonder Uriel

Da Costa, like the Venetian senators, abandoned revealed religion and became a Deist. Cardozo found another path.

"God is true, and the Torah is true," he would write many years later. "Whoever knows the Torah's real Author will understand the Torah's truth. And whoever recognizes and concedes the truth of the Torah will be in a position to discover the true God."[30]

Chapter 2
Cardozo the Kabbalist

1.

At that time, a certain monk in the city of Venice preached a sermon in which he challenged all the scholars of the yeshiva to tell him the true nature of the God of Israel....And there was no one, among all the rabbis of Venice, who could answer him.[1]

The monk's challenge did not concern the First Cause. It raised the problem of a different entity: She whom the rabbinic and Kabbalistic traditions called the Shechinah.

The word *Shechinah* has a long and checkered history.[2] It derives from the Hebrew root *sh-kh-n*, meaning "to dwell," as in Exodus 25:8, "they shall make Me a sanctuary and I will dwell" [*ve-shakhanti*] among them." For the rabbis of Talmud and midrash, therefore, *Shechinah* designated that aspect of God that "dwells among us," that is present to us and hears our prayers. God is infinite, fills heaven and earth. Cosmic distances, unimaginable in their vastness, separate us from His Throne of Glory. Yet He is with us, so long as we choose to be with Him, and that aspect of Him that is "with us" is what the ancient rabbis called the Shechinah. "Whenever ten people"—or five or three or two or even one—"sit and busy themselves with Torah, Shechinah dwells among them" (Mishnah, *Pirkei Avot* 3:6).[3]

Now, the Kabbalistic mystical tradition, which emerged out of rabbinic Judaism in the twelfth and thirteenth centuries (in southern France and northern Spain), worked a remarkable transformation upon this rabbinic term. The Shechinah became a female element within God. The Kabbalists conceived God not only as a gendered being but as an androgyne: male and female in one.

The Bible itself testified to this. God had created Adam ("humanity") "in His image; in the image of God He created him; male and female He created them...and He called their name Adam in the day they were created" (Gen 1:27, 5:2). The Scripture seems to teach that Adam is not just the man but the man and woman together, and that this androgynous human being—split into two sexes only at a later stage—was created in the image of an androgynous Deity.[4]

The ancient rabbis do not seem to have intended anything of the sort when they spoke of the Shechinah.[5] Nor, when they spoke of God as "the Blessed Holy One" *(ha-qadosh barukh hu)*,[6] did they mean to suggest that this was the distinctively *male* aspect of God, as opposed to the Shechinah. All of this was Kabbalistic innovation. But, when the Kabbalists read the Talmud or the ancient midrashim, they could not but suppose that their revered ancestors had used the terms *Blessed Holy One* and *Shechinah* in the same way they themselves did. And so it came to pass that the Jewish Goddess—perhaps a very ancient goddess, at that[7]—reasserted Herself in the midst of the noisily masculine Jewish God.

We must not exaggerate. Medieval Kabbalah was not striving toward gender equality within the Godhead. The Kabbalists' ideal, rather, was the absorption of the female Shechinah into the male.[8] When God is whole and complete, His female aspect loses its distinctive identity and becomes an inseparable part of His maleness. (Humanity was created in God's image, and it is only when Eve is cut away from Adam that she exists as a woman. When the two fuse, sexually, he can fantasize that she becomes part of him again.) Yet it remains true that the Kabbalists do recognize a female aspect of God, which they call by the ancient term *Shechinah*. No less than Eve from Adam, She has been separated from the Blessed Holy One, who is Her mate. This alienation of God from God is at the root of the world's pain.

How did this alienation come to be? Through human sin, beginning with Adam's, extending through the sins of the Jewish people. This is why Isaiah says: "Where is your Mother's bill of divorce, by which I sent Her away?…For your sins was your Mother sent away" (50:1). The Kabbalists understood the speaker to be the Blessed Holy One, and "your Mother" to be His beloved Shechinah. The separated lovers call out to one another in the Song of Songs. The male voice that speaks in these passionate poems—according to the Kabbalists—is that of the Blessed Holy One, while the female is the Shechinah.

How are they to be joined together and the universal wound thus healed? Through meticulous performance of the rituals of Judaism, which were instituted for precisely this purpose. Every ritual act a Jew carries out, the Kabbalists taught, should be prefaced by a statement of intent: *to unify the Blessed Holy One and His Shechinah*, and this formula, which goes back at least to the sixteenth century, has left its marks upon the Jewish liturgy to this day.[9]

Note well: the Blessed Holy One *and* His Shechinah. Is it one God, or two? This was the challenge that the monk whose sermon so impressed the young Cardozo threw down before the rabbis of Venice. Say that the Shechinah is a divinity, as the Kabbalists believed She was, and you can hardly escape the charge that Judaism has two gods. But you are no better off if you take the alternative path, laid out by medieval philosophers like Saadiah and Maimonides, of saying that the Shechinah is a being subordinate to God (like an angel), which He Himself has created. For then you must admit that the Jews worship a created being, and to worship a created being is idolatry.

The monk was no ignoramus, as far as matters Hebraic were concerned. "He opened all these books and read aloud from them, to us and to the Christians.…He went on to sharpen the dilemma, with arguments based on the teachings of our ancient sages. And there was no one, among all the rabbis of Venice, who could answer him."[10]

2.

My head swirled. I found myself once again caught in a web of doubts. To escape them, to find for myself some kind of spiritual equilibrium, I set out for Egypt....I wanted medicine to heal this wound of mine.[11]

Cardozo's "medicine" was Kabbalah. He spent five years in Egypt, he tells us, studying with some of the leading Kabbalists of his time: men like Samuel Vital, and Hayyim Kohen of Aleppo.

Considerable doubt attaches to Cardozo's narrative at this point. It seems very likely that Cardozo did indeed spend time in Egypt, presumably in the early 1650s.[12] But did he really study with Vital, Kohen, and the others he claims as teachers?[13] If so, why does his earliest work of systematic theology (the treatise *Abraham's Morn*) start off with what seems like a defensive admission that he was self-taught in Kabbalistic matters? He there claims his teachers in Kabbalah to have been no other than...Elijah and Moses! After all, he explains, he has learned his Kabbalah from the classics of the Kabbalistic literature, and what difference does it make whether you learn orally from a teacher or from books?[14]

Perhaps we can resolve this tension in a way that gives Cardozo the benefit of the doubt. Yes, he did go to Egypt in his twenties to find among the great Kabbalists "medicine to heal this wound of mine." But, no, he found no such medicine. "To put the matter in a nutshell," he says explicitly of his Egyptian teachers, "nothing they could tell me gave me any relief whatever."[15] False Kabbalah one could learn from the likes of Samuel Vital and Hayyim Kohen. For true Kabbalah, one had to go to the sources: to the classic texts, to Elijah and Moses.

The Kabbalist's path back to the mystical secrets of Elijah and Moses led through an ancient rabbi named Simeon ben Yohai.

In 1558–60, a three-volume work called the Zohar was printed and circulated throughout the Jewish world.[16] The book was structured as a commentary on the Pentateuch. It consisted largely of a string of rambling, free-associative, weirdly evocative discourses, which took verses from all over the Jewish Bible and wove them into shimmering webs of mystical fantasy about the secret inner life of God.

Where had the book come from? No one quite knew. What *was* known was that it had first surfaced in Spain, around the end of the thirteenth century, and that it claimed to be something far more ancient. The speakers of its discourses—which were mostly in the Aramaic language—were rabbis who had lived in Palestine in the second century C.E. Foremost among them was Simeon ben Yohai, a somewhat mysterious figure famed for his holy and ascetic life.

The Zohar thus gave every appearance of being a mystical counterpart to the Talmud. Rabbinic Judaism, we recall, believed that Moses had received from God not only a written law, but an Oral Torah as well, and that the tradition of this Oral Torah was preserved by the rabbis of the Mishnah and the Talmud. Now, it seemed, there was a mystical Oral Torah, too. Moses's elementary, straightforward teachings about the nature of God, which could be understood by scholar and simpleton alike, had been laid out in the Bible for all to read. The esoteric teachings had been handed down by tradition—the word *Kabbalah* literally means "tradition"—to be recorded in the second century, in secrecy, by Rabbi Simeon ben Yohai and his colleagues, and to be rediscovered, by a remarkable act of divine grace, in thirteenth-century Spain.

Not quite everyone believed this, even in the sixteenth and seventeenth centuries. A few skeptics, like the famous Venetian rabbi Leone Modena—who died in 1648, the year the Cardozo brothers arrived in his town—noticed incongruities in the Zohar that suggested the book was not quite what it claimed to be. But Modena and the rest normally kept their doubts to themselves. The Zohar, and Kabbalah with it, had become wildly popular in the six-teenth century. Well into the eighteenth century, Kabbalah would remain *the* theology of Judaism, understood by few, no doubt, yet revered by almost all. One did not want to come out too publicly with criticism of its Holy Zohar.

We know today that the Zohar was written at the end of the thirteenth century by a Spanish Kabbalist named Moses de Leon. It is no Talmud, no midrash, but an extraordinary theosophical novel, invented more or less from scratch. De Leon used all his formidable literary and imaginative talents to give haunting poetic expression to the doctrines of medieval Kabbalah.[17]

Cardozo himself certainly had no inkling of this. For him, the Zohar was a text as ancient as the Mishnah, more ancient than Gemara or midrash. The esoteric teaching of Moses and the prophets pulsated within it. For him, it was a source inspired and authoritative, which could be used by a seeker of truth—like himself—to test the things he had learned from his teachers of Kabbalah.

3.

> I judge…that in all our Diaspora there are hardly three or four people who truly know the Kabbalah; albeit many do study it.[18]

Kabbalah was hard to understand in Cardozo's time. It is hard to understand today. We have already become acquainted with one element of it: the androgynous character of the Kabbalistic God, with the Blessed Holy One as the male aspect of Deity and the Shechinah as the female aspect. But there is a great deal more that must be understood if Cardozo himself is to become intelligible, and much of it does not make for easy reading.

Perhaps it will be best to follow in Cardozo's own footsteps. In his treatise *This Is My God*, written some thirty years after his stay in Egypt, Cardozo sets forth what he intends to be a basic orientation to the Kabbalah.[19] He begins his sketch from the loftiest and most abstract aspect of the Kabbalistic Divinity:

> The Kabbalistic tradition…asserts that, from the First Cause (which the Kabbalists call *Ein Sof*, "the Infinite"), there emerges a single pure spiritual entity: a holy Intelligence, simple in its nature.…The Kabbalists call this First Emanation *Keter*, "Crown."…
>
> From the First Cause and *Keter*, a second Intelligence is emanated. This is…*Hokhmah*, "Wisdom."…Through the

power of *Keter* and the will of the First Cause, *Binah* ("Understanding") is produced from *Hokhmah*. This is...a third Intelligence....

From *Binah* comes *Hesed* ("Grace")...from *Hesed* comes *Gevurah* ("Power")...from *Gevurah* comes *Tif'eret* ("Splendor") ...from *Tif'eret* comes *Nezah* ("Eternity")...from *Nezah* comes *Hod* ("Glory")...from *Hod* comes *Yesod* ("Foundation")...and from *Yesod*, by the power that flows forth from the superior entities, comes *Malkhut* ("Kingship")....

Ein Sof ("the Infinite") and the ten *sefirot* (Cardozo's "Intelligences") constitute the backbone of the Kabbalistic doctrine of God. But what does it mean? What, exactly, are the *sefirot*?[20] Cardozo will tell us, first, what they are *not*.

These *sefirot* are not created beings. A *creation* is necessarily delimited and distinguished from the essence of its creator, like a stone that is carved out from a mountain....But the *sefirot*, say the Kabbalists, are *emanated* from the First Cause, much as light and heat are emanated from the sun.

The word *emanation* indicates a reality that has emerged from the inner being of that entity that has caused its existence...like the light that emerges from the sun and yet remains unified with its source; such that the power of the Emanator perpetually inheres within the Emanated.

This all sounds very abstract. Reading it, we are bound to visualize the *sefirot* as something like ten shining spheres of light, emitted from the greater sphere that is their source and yet somehow remaining one with it. (Cardozo's solar analogy is a good way to get a handle on this paradox.) This image is not altogether misleading. Some Kabbalistic diagrams, in fact, represent the *sefirot* as a series of concentric circles.

Yet the Kabbalistic imagination does not leave the *sefirot* at this abstract level. It gives them shape, color, personality, sex. For each individual *sefirah*[21] it finds dozens of vividly tangible images drawn from the Bible or from Jewish liturgy or ritual. The *sefirot*, taken together, become something like the body of God, within which the endless and unknowable *Ein Sof* manifests Itself inside our corporeal reality. Taken individually, they become something like a pantheon of deities—some male, some female—a Many within which the One manifests Itself inside our multiplex reality.

We shall talk, presently, about the *sefirot* as limbs that function together in the divine Body. We shall talk about them also as distinct entities that beget one another, nourish one another, at times struggle against one another, that copulate and separate and yearn for one another. Yet, for the Kabbalists, *sefirot* and *Ein Sof* are all aspects of the One God. To quote Cardozo, they are

> more closely unified with one another, and the entire collective with each individual member, than the human intelligence and will are with the human soul....The First Cause [that is, the *Ein Sof*] incorporates Itself within them, as though It were their soul....It is forbidden even to think about the First Cause, other than through the *sefirot*; impossible to give It worship or blessing, other than through them.

Judaism, in other words—Jewish ritual, Jewish prayer, the Jewish Bible—is all about the ten *sefirot*. It is through the *sefirot* that Divinity can give of Itself to human beings. It is through them, too, that humans can have impact on Divinity.

Some Kabbalistic diagrams, as I have said, represent the *sefirot* as a series of concentric circles. But the more familiar diagrams prefer to arrange them as a series of triads, one above the other. The ten, together, thus constitute a stylized representation of the human body.

The human body? Or the Body of God? The latter, but it turns out to be much the same thing, given that the androgynous Adam-and-Eve was created in God's image. This biblical doctrine, the Kabbalists say, does not mean that God has arms and legs and genitalia in any literal sense. Rather, our own arms and legs and genitalia serve as representations, within this tangible universe, of super-tangible realities to which they correspond. These super-tangible realities are what the Kabbalists call the *sefirot*.

Consider the following very crude and approximate illustration: We are silhouettes of God, projected onto a screen by His light. The silhouette, unlike its source, is black and two-dimensional. If silhouettes could think and talk, they would no doubt imagine that their source must be black and two-dimensional like themselves. Living in their silhouette world, they could not conceive any reality that transcends two-dimensionality and monochrome blackness. We cannot conceive—any more than the thinking silhouette could—the reality of the sefirotic Body in whose image we were created. We can only gain some inkling of that Body through a series of images, drawn from our own bodies and from the material universe, which is itself a shadow of the divine Body. The investigation of that Body, and of its workings within this shadow universe of ours, is what the Kabbalah is essentially about.

The Body's head is constituted by the supreme triad of *sefirot: Keter, Hokhmah, Binah*. The apex of this triangle is *Keter*. This is the "Crown," a *sefirah* so lofty that at times it seems hardly distinguishable from the Infinite out of which it emerged. It is an intellectual power, as are the two *sefirot* beneath it. (We might gather this from their names: *Hokhmah* and *Binah*, "Wisdom" and "Understanding.") But they are not quite at *Keter*'s level of abstraction, and their function in the sefirotic system is to begin the transformation of Divine Thought into tangible action. Unlike *Keter*, they are sexually distinctive. *Hokhmah* is male, *Binah* female.

The next six *sefirot*, together, are the trunk of the divine Body. Within this group, the central member is the male *sefirah Tif'eret* ("Splendor"). The five *sefirot* that surround Him are His satellites. *Tif'eret* is the trunk, in the narrowest sense of the word; *Hesed* and *Gevurah*, which are located above Him in the sefirotic scheme, are His right and left arms, respectively. *Hesed* is "Grace," while *Gevurah* is "Power," which the Kabbalists understand as strict and unbending Justice.[22] Both of these function as potentialities of *Tif'eret*, who synthesizes them within Himself in the form of Mercy.

The Kabbalists regularly refer to the *sefirah Tif'eret* by the title *ha-qadosh barukh hu*, "the Blessed Holy One." In the rabbinic literature this title means simply "God." It is easy to jump from this to the

26

The Ten Sefirot

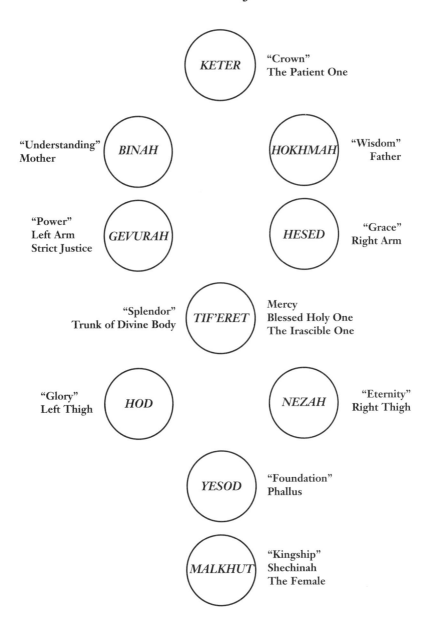

KETER — "Crown" / The Patient One

"Understanding" / Mother — **BINAH**

HOKHMAH — "Wisdom" / Father

"Power" / Left Arm / Strict Justice — **GEVURAH**

HESED — "Grace" / Right Arm

"Splendor" / Trunk of Divine Body — **TIF'ERET** — Mercy / Blessed Holy One / The Irascible One

"Glory" / Left Thigh — **HOD**

NEZAH — "Eternity" / Right Thigh

YESOD — "Foundation" / Phallus

MALKHUT — "Kingship" / Shechinah / The Female

conclusion that the Kabbalists believed the masculine God of the Bible and the Talmud to be none other than the *sefirah Tif'eret*. Many Kabbalists in Cardozo's time in fact drew this conclusion; Cardozo devotes considerable energy to explaining why it is wrong. In trying to get a handle on Kabbalah, however, it is not a bad way to start.

Think of God, as we imagine Him from the Hebrew Bible, as being *Tif'eret*, or better, the group of six *sefirot* of which *Tif'eret* is the nucleus. He may act according to Grace *(Hesed)* or according to strict Justice *(Gevurah)*; we will then speak of Him as operating through His right arm or His left. Or He may act through His own proper blend of the two: Mercy.

He is male. This is why, as we move down the trunk—past the colorless *sefirot* of *Nezah* and *Hod*, which correspond to His two thighs—we find Him with a distinctively male organ. This is the *sefirah Yesod*, "Foundation," which plays the crucial role of uniting Him with His female counterpart, and transmitting the vital fluids of Divinity from Him to Her.

And where is She on the sefirotic diagram? She stands alone, beneath the rest: a tenth *sefirah*, the one called *Malkhut* (a.k.a. the Shechinah). She is the lowest *sefirah*. She is therefore the crucial mediator between the sefirotic world—which the Kabbalists call *'Olam ha-Azilut*, "the World of Emanation"—and the universes that lie beneath it and depend on it.

A life-giving essence, which the Kabbalists call *shefa'* ("effluence"), streams down from the highest *sefirot* to the lowest. Like human semen, which begins (according to medieval medicine) in the brain and descends into the genitalia, it flows down through the sefirotic channels from *Keter* to *Yesod*. *Yesod* ejaculates it into *Malkhut*. *Malkhut* transmits it to the lower realms, such as our own.

When this effluence flows in plenty, all is well. But sometimes, usually due to human sinfulness, the stream dries up. The lower *sefirot*—or, perhaps, all the *sefirot*—then wither. We, who depend on them for our existence, ourselves wither and can barely subsist.

We shall talk later about how this sad situation comes about, and how it can be mended. For the moment, let us note only that the Zohar is filled with vivid images of how the precious effluence is transmitted from *sefirah* to *sefirah*, from the male to the female. It is one of the Zohar's favorite subjects.

The very first passage of the Zohar, for example, represents *Malkhut* as a thirteen-petalled rose. She is sometimes white, sometimes red, depending on whether She is under the influence of Grace *(Hesed)* or of strict Justice *(Gevurah)*. The "covenant"—this being Kabbalistic code for the phallic *Yesod*[23]—"enters into the rose and emits seed into her." This precious ejaculate is the "effluence," here represented by the image of a divine Light, concealed and contained within *Yesod*.

The gender imbalance here is very palpable. The Divine Male is a full body, or at least a full torso. The Divine Female, within the sefirotic system, is truncated and incomplete. As represented in the Zohar's "thirteen-petalled rose," She is hardly more than a receptive genital. It is true that *Malkhut* (the Shechinah-*sefirah*) possesses a full system of ten *sefirot*—including a *Malkhut* of her own—simply by virtue of being Herself a *sefirah*. (This is one of the features that makes Kabbalah so endlessly complicated. Each and every *sefirah* has ten *sefirot* of its own, each of which in turn has ten of *its* own; and so on, ad infinitum.) Yet it also remains true that the Divine Female, as *Malkhut*, is only a single "point" within a system of ten such "points."

Cardozo was troubled by this asymmetry between the male and female aspects of Divinity. This was the reason, he claims, that he became disillusioned with his teachers in Egypt. They were not able to provide any really satisfying resolution to the problem of the Shechinah. Restricting Her as they did to the single *sefirah Malkhut*, they could not form any adequate conception of Her true grandeur.[24] Cardozo was to take this project on, as part of his own life's task.

4.

Cardozo claims, among his teachers of Kabbalah, Rabbi Hayyim Kohen and Rabbi Samuel Vital. These were names to conjure with in Kabbalistic circles in the middle of the seventeenth century. Samuel Vital was the son of Hayyim Vital. Hayyim Kohen was the disciple of Hayyim Vital. And Hayyim Vital was the disciple—the greatest disciple, many thought—of Isaac Luria of Safed, the greatest Kabbalist of all time.

Hayyim Vital had died in 1620, at seventy-eight. His master, Isaac Luria, had died in 1572, at thirty-eight. In the last years of his brief life, Luria had devised a new system of Kabbalah, which, in Cardozo's time, had begun to sweep the Jewish world. The new system was still very imperfectly known in the 1650s, when Cardozo supposedly began his studies in Egypt. Luria himself had committed almost nothing of it to paper. The most authoritative account of what he had taught, which Hayyim Vital had written down in a massive tome shortly after the Master's death, was kept under tight wraps—first by Vital himself, then by his son Samuel. Almost no one was permitted to look at it.[25]

This did not prevent the news from spreading, in the decades before Cardozo was born, that there was abroad in the world a new kind of Kabbalah, one which bore to the older Kabbalah something of the relation of Einstein's physics to Newton's. Only a few years before Luria, the Kabbalist Moses Cordovero (1522–70) had given an encyclopedic formulation to the old traditional Kabbalah, which had been based on a fairly straightforward reading of the Zohar. Now something new had emerged, which made Cordovero's work seem simplistic and outdated.[26] Yet, until well into the seventeenth century, few people knew very clearly just what it was that Luria had taught.[27] It was not until 1649 that Samuel Vital set himself to preparing a new edition of his father's opus, for which he apparently intended a reasonably wide circulation. By this time other versions of the Lurianic-Gospel-According-to-Hayyim-Vital had begun to spread.[28]

Did Cardozo sit at Samuel Vital's feet in the flesh or only in the spirit? We cannot be sure. But it is clear that his youthful Kabbalistic studies, wherever he pursued them, took place in the dawning and still somewhat uncertain light of the Lurianic Kabbalah. We will not understand Cardozo, therefore, without at least a glance at Luria.

Luria, like most Kabbalists, did not think of himself as an innovator. He saw himself as laying out explicitly what was present, though latent, in the Zohar. In very great measure he was right about this. What appear to be his most startling novelties normally have their roots in some Zoharic text—usually one that is obscure and difficult.

We have already seen, in connection with the medieval Kabbalah, that the *sefirot* often tend to take on individual personalities, so that they come to appear less as aspects of a single God than as deities in some mythological pantheon. The Lurianic system takes this tendency to its extreme. Out of the ten *sefirot*, it fashions a hierarchy of five divine figures, which Luria and his followers— Cardozo included—call *parzufim*.

What exactly is a *parzuf*? The Hebrew word[29] literally means "face" or "countenance." Scholem's favored translation for the word, in its Lurianic context, is "configuration."[30] This is a reasonable translation, and if I were discussing Lurianic Kabbalah as a subject for itself and not as a preparation for reading Cardozo, I would certainly use it. But Cardozo tells us quite clearly how he wants to translate *parzufim*. Given that the focus of our interest is Cardozo's perceptions, we have little choice but to follow him.

The Hebrew word *parzufim*, Cardozo says, has as its French (!) equivalent the word *personas*.[31] This is, of course, the Spanish word for the Persons of the Christian Trinity. In his summary of Christian doctrine, moreover, Cardozo uses Hebrew *parzufim* for the Father, Son, and Holy Spirit.[32] There is little doubt that he has read Lurianic Kabbalah through the lenses of Christian theology and envisioned the Five Persons of the Lurianic "World of Emanation" along the lines of the Three Persons of his Catholic upbringing.

Who are the Five Persons? At the bottom of their hierarchy— most relevant to the life of this universe and therefore of the greatest interest to the Kabbalists—stand *Ze'ir ve-Nuqbeh*, "the Irascible One and His Female."[33] The first member of this pair, *Ze'ir* (or *Ze'ir Anpin*), turns out to be none other than the cluster of six *sefirot* we have met earlier: *Tif'eret*, with His five satellites, a.k.a. the Blessed

31

Holy One. *Ze'ir's* "Female" is of course the Shechinah, the *sefirah Malkhut.*

Thus, "the Blessed Holy One and His Shechinah," *Tif'eret* and *Malkhut,* and "the Irascible One and His Female" are three different ways of designating the same pair. These are a Divine Male-and-Female, sometimes mating and sometimes separating, upon whose intermittent sexual harmony the well-being of the cosmos depends.

Above the Irascible One and His Female are the three highest *sefirot, Keter, Hokhmah,* and *Binah.* Lurianic Kabbalah turns each of these three into a distinct "Person." *Hokhmah* becomes *Abba* ("Father") and *Binah* becomes *Imma* ("Mother"), the divine "Parents," that is, of the Irascible One and His Female. The highest *sefirah* of all, *Keter,* is transformed into *Arikh Anpin,* "the Patient One": an androgynous being of nearly inconceivable loftiness whose remote benevolence nurtures the entire system and tempers the wrathful inclinations of the more "irascible" junior Divinity.[34]

Within God, then, there is a "Father" and a "Mother." Their two "children," the Irascible One and His Female, are one another's lovers. (That is why, say the Kabbalists, the divine Lover addresses His Beloved in the Song of Songs as "my sister, my bride.")[35] It makes sense, in this context, to speak of the Irascible One as a divine "Son," and the Zohar in fact does.[36] So do Vital's writings.

Yet it is Cardozo who takes a very special relish in referring to his God by such terms as "Holy Son" *(bera qaddisha)* or "Delightful Son" *(ha-ben ha-nehmad).*[37] He may protest all he likes that he is merely following the Zohar's usage. We will not forget—any more than Cardozo's enemies would let him forget—that he was brought up in an alien religion, dedicated to the worship of the divine Son. In this respect, as in others, Cardozo's childhood faith surely left its imprint on his adult mind.

Between the Five Persons and the incomprehensible *Ein Sof* ("the Infinite") stands an entity whom Luria and his disciples call *Adam Qadmon,* "Primordial Adam" (or "the Primordial Human"). *Adam Qadmon* enfolds the Persons, encompasses them, transcends them, and constitutes the primordial ground from which the Persons emerged.

In his account of Kabbalistic doctrine, Cardozo sets forth the relationship of "Primordial Adam" to the *Ein Sof* (which he calls the "First Cause") and to the Persons:

> Luria taught that one simple, infinite entity, designated "Primordial Adam"…is produced from the First Cause, and that from this entity the ten *sefirot* were produced….It was then that there occurred the "Shattering"…[which] is the "Death of the Kings."
>
> The First Cause's effluence within Primordial Adam afterwards became greater than it had been previously. Ten more *sefirot*…were thus generated. Through them, Primordial Adam mended *[tiqqen]* the vessels and the essences of the prior *sefirot*. From all this was constructed the World of Emanation, with its Five Persons.[38]

In these baffling words Cardozo alludes to the fundamental myth of the Lurianic Kabbalah and to one of its most pivotal conceptions: that of *tiqqun*, the process of "mending." Unless we know what *tiqqun* means, we cannot hope to understand Cardozo or the fantastic crusade to which he dedicated his life. We must therefore linger a little on the "Shattering" as well as on the "Mending."

5.

The Zohar had spoken, enigmatically, of the "Death of the Primordial Kings." By this, the Zohar's author had intended the destruction of a sefirotic system that preceded the current one, a primitive system that was unstable and therefore could not endure.[39]

These original *sefirot*, Luria explained, were vessels emanated from "Primordial Adam," in a time before the category of time had even come into existence. Light, also emanated from Primordial Adam, had been poured into these vessels. But the vessels could not contain the light. They shattered—hence the Lurianic designation of this event as the "Shattering"—and the light fell into the abyss of darkness below.

Primordial Adam mended the broken *sefirot*, and it was from this act of "mending" *(tiqqun)* that the current Five Persons of the World of Emanation were constructed. Yet the "Mending" remained incomplete. Much of the divine light that had fallen at the time of the "Shattering" remained below, imprisoned in darkness. Its fragmented "sparks" were trapped helplessly among the demonic "shells" *(qelippot)*, which fattened themselves off the captive light.[40]

The World of Emanation, moreover, as "mended" by Primordial Adam, had its own instabilities. Each of the Five Persons, in order to be a completed entity, must have a full complement of ten *sefirot*. What, then, shall the Irascible One's Female do? She has only one *sefirah*—one single "point," as Luria's disciples put it—namely, the *sefirah Malkhut*. (This is the old problem, which we have noted above, of the gender imbalance within the sefirotic world.) Can the Irascible One make satisfying love with a Female so truncated, so unequal to Himself?

A solution was at hand. The Irascible One endowed His Beloved with nine extra *sefirot*, drawn from His own. She thus became a completed Female, corresponding to Him as completed Male. All that was necessary for them to mate was for Her to turn wet with "female waters," welcoming Him.

The production of these "female waters" was Adam's task—not Primordial Adam, this time, but rather the human Adam of the Book of Genesis, who had been created in the divine image, for the purpose of "mending" whatever remained flawed and disfigured within that image. "If Adam had not sinned," Hayyim Vital writes wistfully, "he would have stirred up the female waters on that first Sabbath [of Creation], which would have enabled the Irascible One and His Female to make love, face to face."[41]

But Adam did sin, and the nine extra *sefirot*, which the Female had received from Her Lover, left the Divine Female and plunged into the realms of the Demonic. Again they were "mended" and raised, in large part through the virtuous deeds of the pious ancestors of Israel. But the Jews sinned, as Adam had, and with the same result. With the final destruction of the Temple in 70 C.E., the

Female's *sefirot* again descended among the Shells and became incarnated within the Demonic.[42]

"For your sins was your Mother"—the Shechinah, that is— "sent away" (Isa 50:1, as interpreted by Cardozo).[43] Sent away into exile; sent away to become the soul within a demonic body; sent away, far away, from the embraces of Her true Lover. Correspondingly, the Jewish people was sent away—into "bitter and savage exile"[44] among persecuting Gentiles and their twisted faiths. By Luria's time, and by Cardozo's, that exile had dragged on more than fifteen hundred years. With the expulsion from Spain in 1492, it had taken on a dimension of bitterness and savagery that seemed to go beyond anything the Jewish people had previously experienced.

The Kabbalists had diagnosed the problem. The root of the historic Jewish pain was not essentially the Jews' having offended God—as one might imagine from a simplistic reading of the Bible—but from God's own self-alienation. The remedy followed from the diagnosis. To heal our own pain and alienation, we must first heal God's. This was what the Kabbalistic *tiqqun* was all about.

To "mend" a Deity might seem a formidable task. Fortunately— said the Kabbalists—God has provided us with a set of procedures designed precisely for that purpose. This is the *halakhah*: Judaism's numerous and complex ritual demands as revealed in the Written and the Oral Torah.[45]

"Behold, I am prepared and at the ready, to perform the commandment of…[such-and-such] for the purpose of uniting the Blessed Holy One and His Shechinah…in the name of all Israel."[46] That is the way one does it. It is not enough just to say the prescribed prayers and to carry out the prescribed ritual acts, although such mechanical obedience does have a certain positive effect. One must pray and perform with the proper mental attitude—the proper "intention" *(kavvanah),* to use the Kabbalistic term. One must know the essential fact that one is in the process of "mending" the Deity. Ideally, one should also know (in terms of the *sefirot* involved) just how the "mending" is supposed to take place.

For the most part, Kabbalistic ritual consisted of performing normative Jewish rites with the proper internal *kavvanah*. A

Kabbalist's worship did not look, from the outside, different from that of any other Jew. But, beginning in the sixteenth century, the Kabbalists—particularly Luria's followers—began to introduce special rites of their own. They often called these rites *tiqqunim*, "Mending-rites."

We shall encounter Cardozo, in his later years, as a tireless and creative inventor of *tiqqunim*, some of which create a distinctly bizarre impression. In doing so, he stood within a tradition of Kabbalistic *tiqqunim* that was over a century old. Take, for example, the "Midnight Mending-rite" *(tiqqun hazot)*—a particularly dramatic and affecting ritual developed among the Kabbalists of sixteenth-century Safed, which by Cardozo's time had spread through the Jewish world.

To perform the ritual, one was to "rise and dress at midnight…go to the door and stand near the doorpost, remove his shoes and veil his head. Weeping, he should then take ashes from the hearth and lay them on his forehead…bow his head and rub his eyes in the dust on the ground, just as the *Shekhinah* herself…lies in the dust."[47] Then comes the recitation of biblical texts—psalms, and passages from Isaiah and Lamentations—all spoken of course with the proper *kavvanah*. Through these recitations the Shechinah is raised from Her degradation, restored to Her full dimensions, and prepared for lovemaking with the Divine Male.[48]

She will fall again, of course, and will need to be raised again tomorrow night. Yet the "Mending-rituals," performed over and over, have a cumulative effect. The number of the "sparks" that fell into the demonic realms, though large, is not infinite. The Shechinah gathers them during Her dark exile in the abyss. (That, Vital says at one point, is why She is there.)[49] When She is raised, the sparks She has gathered are liberated.

The process is long and painful. But it is not endless. God will be healed. Israel, like the Divine Female, will be redeemed from exile, will be restored to its ancient glory, returned to its proper home. When *tiqqun* is in its final stage, the Messiah will appear, to see the process through to completion.

Chapter 3
Cardozo the
Messiah-Bearer

1.

> In the year 5409 [1648–49] I was studying Torah in
> Venice....I had a dream that the Messiah had appeared,
> and that the people of Venice did not believe in him. But
> God gave me strength, and I seated him on my shoulders
> and proclaimed through the market-places, *"This is the
> true Messiah!"*[1]

Young Miguel Cardozo had surely heard from his Catholic
teachers the story of St. Christopher. This terrifying giant of
old had wandered the world, always seeking "the greatest prince
that was in the world, and him would he serve and obey." He put
himself first in the service of human kings, then of the devil, and
finally of Jesus Christ, who appeared to him as a child.

Christopher carried the child on his shoulders across a river. But
the child turned out to be "heavy as lead, and...more and more waxed
heavy, insomuch that Christopher had great anguish and was afeared
to be drowned....'Christopher [said the child], marvel thee nothing;
for thou hast not only borne all the world upon thee, but thou hast
borne Him that created and made all the world, upon thy shoulders.'"[2]

Several features of the Christopher legend, as it took shape in the later Middle Ages, are strangely suggestive of the Jewish legends of Abraham.[3] It hardly seems farfetched that the two figures became in some measure conflated, perhaps unconsciously, in Cardozo's mind. Once Cardozo came to identify himself with Abraham, the pioneer God-seeker, he went on to identify himself with Christopher, the "Christ-bearer." All that remained was to find a Messiah for him to carry.

2.

By Cardozo's time the Jewish Messianic tradition was well over two thousand years old. Already in the eighth century B.C.E. the prophet Isaiah had predicted the coming of an ideal king whom future generations would call by the title Messiah. This king would be descended from David. The spirit of the Lord would rest upon him. He would be wise, knowledgeable, God-fearing. He would slay the wicked with the breath of his lips, but would judge the poor and the meek in righteousness. In his days peace would reign. "They shall not hurt or destroy in all My holy mountain; for the earth will be filled with the knowledge of the Lord, as the waters cover the sea" (Isa 11:1–9).

Once the concept of the Messiah had taken root in Judaism, other biblical passages came to be understood in a Messianic context. Christianity carried this process still further. The Book of Isaiah had spoken of a mysterious "Suffering Servant" of the Lord, who was "crushed on account of our iniquities...and through his wound we found healing...and the Lord inflicted upon him the sin of us all" (52:13—53:12). Surely, the Christians thought, this was a reference to their own Messiah, who had suffered atrociously in order to take away the sin of the world.

The rabbinic tradition, perhaps in reaction to Christianity, normally avoided talking about Isaiah's Suffering Servant. The rabbis did, at times, make remarks that suggested the Servant was the Messiah. Cardozo, who had his own reasons for being interested in the Suffering Servant, was later to pounce upon these remarks and to declare, falsely, that they represented the rabbinic doctrine in its entirety. But the rabbis also propounded an alternative interpretation, which kept the Servant and the Messiah safely distinct. According to this interpretation, the Servant was a collective representation of the Jewish people, who certainly do suffer and whose suffering is for the benefit of the Gentile nations.[4] In the hands of medieval Jewish commentators this "collective" interpretation of Isaiah 53 became all but canonical.[5] The Servant of the Lord is Israel, not any Messiah who had come or would come.

The Messiah of medieval Judaism often became a mundane, prosaic figure, shorn of anything that might seem superhuman or miraculous. The Christians had it all wrong. Far from being a Son of God, who worked miracles and returned from death to redeem human sin, the Messiah was nothing but an unusually God-fearing and God-favored king.

"You must not imagine," Maimonides warned his twelfth-century readers, "that King Messiah is under any obligation…to do things outside the regular course of nature, resurrect the dead, or anything of that sort." No: his mission is only to

> restore the kingdom of David to its ancient dominion, build the Temple, and gather Israel's exiles.…If a king should arise from the house of David, who studies the Torah, applies himself to the commandments as did David his ancestor…compels the Jewish people to obey and to maintain [the Torah], and fights the Lord's battles—he is to be presumed the Messiah.

Once the Temple is actually rebuilt, once the Jews are back in their ancient Holy Land, there is no more doubt about it. The Messiah has come. All that remains for him to do, says Maimonides, is to fulfill biblical prophecy and "mend the entire world, such that all serve God together."

The Kabbalists allowed their imaginations a little more freedom on the subject of the Messiah. Nachmanides explained (in 1263) that the Messiah's mission was to go to the pope, as Moses had once gone to Pharaoh, and demand that he "let my people go"![6] (Midrashic texts, as Nachmanides was certainly aware, had taught that Moses, the First Redeemer, would serve as prototype for the Final Redeemer.)[7] A few decades later the Zohar laid out in bewildering detail the convulsions of nature—a pillar of fire between heaven and earth, new and fantastic stars, and so on and so forth—that would precede the Messiah's advent (II, 7b–9a).

Yet it was the teaching of Maimonides, the "great eagle," that dominated seventeenth-century Jewish thinking about the Messiah. When the English traveler Thomas Coryate wandered about the Ghetto of Venice (in 1608), asking the Jews he met what they thought of the Messiah, he was dismayed to find that their expectations, though grandiose, were—like Maimonides's—very much of this world. The Messiah was to be "a peerelesse Monarch" who would conquer for them Judea and the countries around it and who would "make the King of Guiana, and al other Princes what-soeuer...his tributary vassals."[8]

3.

Now comes a particularly strange feature of the story, which, if we are to understand Cardozo, we must thoroughly grasp. The son of David *(Messiah ben David)* is not the only Messiah with whom we must reckon. Jews expected also a *Messiah ben Ephraim*, who was to be, in the words of a seventeenth-century English observer, "a Preacher of the *Law*, poor, and despised," servant and forerunner of Messiah ben David. It was the second of the two Messiahs, the "son of David," who "was to be great and rich, to restore the *Jewes* to *Jerusalem*, to sit upon the Throne of *David*."[9]

This "Messiah, son of Ephraim" first appears in a strange pas-sage in the Babylonian Talmud (Sukkah 52a). "'The land shall mourn, each family by itself; the family of the house of David by itself, and their wives by themselves' [Zech 12:12]:...mourning for...Messiah ben Joseph, who was killed." ("Joseph" and "Ephraim" are interchangeable terms, in this context.)[10] Messiah ben David, moreover, somehow sees that Messiah ben Joseph has been killed, which prompts him to make a special request to God, for life.

The Talmud goes on to apply a cryptic verse from the Book of Zechariah (12:10) to this Messiah ben Joseph. "They shall look upon him whom they have pierced, and they shall mourn for him, as one mourns for an only child." Interestingly, this was the same verse that Christians had understood as a prophecy of the crucified Jesus.

The Talmud tells us nothing more. We are left in the dark about who "pierced" Messiah ben Joseph, why he had to die, and how he relates to the far better-known Messiah ben David. But Hebrew apocalyptic writings, from the beginning of the Middle Ages, fill in these details. Messiah ben Joseph, they tell us, will be the first of the two Messiahs to appear. He will gather the Jewish people to Jerusalem and restore the Temple worship. But the all-mighty and sinister King Armillus, "son of Satan and of stone," will make war against him and kill him. His broken (or "pierced") corpse will be cast out before the gates of Jerusalem. Only later will Messiah ben David appear, to complete the Redemption.[11]

From the Talmud, and from the early medieval apocalypses, we would gather that Messiah ben Joseph's doom is wholly inevitable. Zechariah prophesied it—"they shall look upon him whom they have pierced"—and that is that. Yet an extremely influential Kabbalistic text of the early fourteenth century, entitled *The Faithful Shepherd*,[12] suggests that there may be an escape for him after all. Moses, the Faithful Shepherd of the book's title, is there told that he has "suffered many afflictions…in order that Messiah ben Joseph not be slain…and in order that he and his offspring not be profaned amid the idolaters."

In ancient times, the passage continues, King Jeroboam of Israel had brazenly defied the Lord with his worship of idols (1 Kgs 12:25–33). Jeroboam was a descendant of the patriarch Joseph. Messiah ben Joseph was therefore "doomed to be profaned through idol-worship, he and his offspring." But Moses, who turns out to have been the Suffering Servant of Isaiah 53, took the profanation upon himself.[13]

41

Cardozo, as we learn from his later writings, thought long and hard about this mysterious text from *The Faithful Shepherd* and what it implied for his own life. Not long before his death, he was to explain how, in retribution for the sins of the Jewish people, "Messiah ben Ephraim was doomed to worship idols, and to be pierced in the war of Gog and Magog."[14] (Gog and Magog are the barbarous Gentile hordes who are to menace the Jewish people during the last days, as prophesied in Ezekiel 38–39.) He preferred to gloss over *The Faithful Shepherd*'s assurance that Moses had spared Messiah ben Ephraim this burden by voluntarily carrying it himself.

Cardozo knew from experience that Messiah ben Ephraim was indeed doomed to worship idols: the images, that is, that stood in Catholic churches. He had tasted this bitter punishment in his own youth. By the time he reached middle age, he had begun to have some glimmering of the truth that was to dominate his sense of his life's task: that he *himself was Messiah ben Ephraim* and that this Messiah's fate, and Cardozo's own, were one and the same.

(We recall how Cardozo introduces himself: "I am the man they call, at times, *mem-bet-aleph*, which are the initials of *Michael ben Abraham*" [above, p. 5]. We realize now that the Hebrew letters *mem-bet-aleph* can stand not only for *Michael ben Abraham*, but also for *Messiah ben Ephraim*.)

Of the "piercing" of Cardozo, in his role of Messiah ben Ephraim, we shall presently have more to say.

4.

From time to time, through the centuries, visionaries appeared among the Jewish people and proclaimed themselves Messiah or enacted what they believed to be the Messianic destiny. In the thirteenth century, for example, there was the Spanish mystic Abraham Abulafia, in the sixteenth, the Portuguese Marrano—reconverted, like Cardozo, to Judaism—Solomon Molcho.[15] Other Jewish dreamers, less confident or less self-deluded, meanwhile hunted through their holy books for clues to the date when the Messiah would come. Thus the Zohar, basing itself upon a numerical calculation from a biblical passage, predicted that the Redemption of Israel and the resurrection of the dead would come to pass in the year 5408.[16] (This is the Jewish year, counted from the creation of the world, that begins in the autumn of 1647 and ends in the autumn of 1648.)

The long-awaited year came and went. There was no Redemption; there was no resurrection. Instead, there was slaughter and horror. The Ukrainian leader Bogdan Chmielnicki rebelled in 1648 against Polish rule. His rebels had a particular hatred for the Jews, whom they murdered with unspeakable cruelty wherever and whenever they got power over them. By the end of 1648 tens of thousands of Polish and Ukrainian Jews had been butchered, and Jews everywhere had come to feel the bitterness of their "Messianic" year.[17]

Yet a Messiah, of sorts, did appear that year. He declared himself Messiah, it would seem, in June 1648, in his native city of Izmir (Smyrna) on the western coast of Turkey. He was a young man, just under twenty-two years old, perhaps a year older than Cardozo. His name was Sabbatai Zevi.

Hardly anyone paid attention.[18] Sabbatai Zevi had a considerable local reputation as an eccentric: the kind of young fellow who would recite biblical verses about flying up to the skies and then demand to know whether you had seen him levitate, and, when you said truthfully that you really *hadn't*, would rail at you for being insufficiently enlightened.[19] You could not take such a person seriously.

For the time being, very few did.

5.

After the year 5423 [1662–63] had begun...I saw in a dream the following words written out: "The Redeemer will come in the year 5425" [1664–65]....And so it happened.[20]

43

By 1665, when Sabbatai Zevi suddenly turned into an international celebrity, Cardozo had said goodbye to Christian Europe. He was living in Tripoli, in Muslim North Africa, personal physician to Tripoli's ruler, Osman Pasha, or possibly to the commander of its army, Rejeb Bey.

We know very little about his later years in Italy, after he returned from his time in Egypt. We know that in 1659 he was living in the port city of Leghorn (Livorno), which had a substantial Jewish population. We know practically nothing of his life in Leghorn, except that he does not seem to have enjoyed it very much.[21]

By 1663, Cardozo was in Tripoli.[22] His biographer, the tirelessly carping Elijah Kohen, speaks of his move to North Africa as "a sudden windfall." The duke of Tuscany, says Kohen, had brought Cardozo to Tripoli to treat Osman Pasha, "and he gave this devil-goat [Cardozo] his recommendation, as did some of the Turks....And so he found himself in an easy and pleasant berth indeed; and settled in there; and sired sons and daughters."[23]

Cardozo was married by now, and married again—and, perhaps, yet again and again. By the mid-1660s he had at least two wives in his household.[24] By 1674, when he tried (unsuccessfully) to resettle in Italy, he had four.[25] There was no reason, from the standpoint of the Jewish religion, why he should not have had four wives. Neither Bible nor Talmud, neither the Geonim nor the great Maimonides had forbidden a Jewish man from marrying as many women as he could support. Some time around the year 1000, it was true, the German Talmudist Gershom of Mainz had issued a ban against polygamy. But it was only the Ashkenazim—the Jews of medieval Germany and France, later resettled in Eastern Europe—who treated the ban as though it had any authority. The Sephardic Jews of Spain and Portugal (like Cardozo), and the Jews of Muslim countries (among whom Cardozo now lived), cared little about what Gershom of Mainz might have approved or disapproved.

Still, Jews in the seventeenth century were not normally polygamous. It is at least a curious coincidence that, after ten years of hobnobbing with the Muslim grandees of North Africa, Cardozo

44

found himself with precisely the number of wives allowed to a man by Islamic law. The religion of his North African surroundings, we might guess, had found its way into Cardozo's bedroom.

Beyond its possible impact on his marital habits, Islam does not seem to have much influenced Cardozo's thinking. His writings show a superficial but fundamentally accurate grasp of Islamic theology, which he regarded as so similar to that of contemporary Judaism that it was hardly worth distinguishing between them. He remained cheerfully misinformed about the Prophet Muhammad, his life, and his teachings.[26] After the early 1660s Cardozo lived nearly all his life in Muslim lands—first North Africa, later Turkey. Yet Islam made little or no appeal to his imagination. Unlike Christianity, it did not get under his skin.

Writing in 1669, to the religious judges of Izmir, Cardozo depicts his North African life as an idyll of prosperity and ease. He has slaves and servant-girls. He has horses to ride—a remarkable privilege for a Jew in a Muslim country.[27] His medical duties consist of paying, at his own convenience, occasional calls on Rejeb Bey. He has plenty of free time for the study of Torah.[28]

Yet the texture of Cardozo's everyday life, as conveyed in the vivid anecdotes of that same *Epistle to the Judges of Izmir*, has a distinctly grubby feel to it. His polygynous home does not exactly breathe the languid and perfumed sensuality of the stereotypic Oriental seraglio. On the contrary, one gets an impression of a teeming, overcrowded household crammed with children and in-laws and relatives of in-laws, where everybody is more or less continually sick with one ailment or another. Cardozo himself, the physician, seems hardly ever to have been in good health.

All his life Cardozo was a compulsive raconteur. In his *Epistle*, he treats the judges of Izmir to one story after another of the marvelous portents granted him of Sabbatai Zevi's advent. The climactic sign was the appearance in the heavens of a "star, big as the full moon," of which Cardozo had repeated premonitions during the early months of 1666. This was not, of course, the first time in history that an unusual star had been welcomed as herald of the Messiah. We naturally think of the star of Bethlehem. In the Zohar, too, the Messiah's coming was to be preceded by the appearance of new, extraordinary stars.

Yet there are remarkable parallels to Cardozo's star from times closer to Cardozo's own. In 1572 a supernova flared up in the constellation Cassiopeia. The brilliant new star, visible even in the daytime, was observed closely by the budding astronomer Tycho Brahe. Religious leaders hailed it as "the second star of Bethlehem and a portent of the Second Coming of Christ."[29] Another supernova appeared in 1604. Johannes Kepler, who wrote a book about it, thought it portended the downfall of the Turkish Empire.[30] The mysterious Rosicrucian manifestos, which stirred up "frenzied interest" and "wild excitement" among educated Europeans in the years 1614–20, declared that the new star was an omen of a great and imminent dawning. The world would be renewed, the church reformed, and "a great influx of truth, light, and grandeur...poured forth on mankind." The manifestos promised, in another context, that "before the rising of the Sun there should break forth Aurora, or some clearness or divine light, in the sky."[31]

Cardozo's divine light finally broke forth in the eastern sky, half an hour past sunrise on May 15, 1666. "It was the size of the moon; people saw it shining with a clear, brilliant light." Cardozo names several of the witnesses, who watched it for something like half an hour before it began to fade.[32] He himself, however, did not see it. He had contracted an eye disease of some sort and, as often, was sick in bed.

6.

By May 1666 you did not need stars to tell you that Redemption was near. Everyone knew it, had known it for months. A year or so earlier, in the spring of 1665, Sabbatai Zevi had gone to Gaza to consult with Nathan Ashkenazi, a brilliant young Kabbalist with some reputation as a seer. Nathan had declared him to be the Messiah.

Sabbatai had already made this announcement several times on his own behalf, without any perceptible impact. But in 1665 something new and extraordinary happened. "Your savior is come," proclaimed Nathan of Gaza, "Sabbatai Zevi his name," and this prophetic message spread like wildfire through the Jewish world.

Now people believed. Jews everywhere put their faith in the new Messiah. The rich believed; the poor believed. The educated and the uneducated alike hailed Sabbatai Zevi as Redeemer. There were skeptics, to be sure, like the learned Hamburg rabbi Jacob Sasportas, who a few years later was to put together an invaluable collection of documents on the Messianic furor. (He called his book *Zevi's Fading Flower*, an erudite pun on Isaiah 28:1.) But by May 1666 these skeptics found themselves isolated and increasingly frightened.

In Germany "many sold their houses and lands and all their possessions, for any day they hoped to be redeemed."[33] In Yemen "they sold their goods at low prices and made preparations" to go meet their Messiah in Jerusalem.[34] On February 19, 1666, a slightly nervous Samuel Pepys confided to his diary that the London Jews were offering ten-to-one odds that "a certain person now at Smirna" would be "within these two years owned by all the princes of the East…as the King of the world, in the same manner we do the King of England, and that this man is the true Messiah."[35]

This was a fairly modest statement of what, in 1666, was expected of Sabbatai Zevi. A Messianic manifesto, issued the previous September by Nathan of Gaza and circulated throughout the Jewish world, offered a far more dramatic vision of the future.[36] The most important arena of the imminent "Mending" would be the invisible world of the *sefirot* and the Lurianic "Persons." This could be taken for granted. Nathan and Sabbatai Zevi were Kabbalists, as was Cardozo, and saw the Messianic denouement in Kabbalistic terms. The Shechinah, as divine "Bride," would be set face to face with Her Husband for lovemaking. The two would become wholly fused with one another, never again to separate. The Shechinah's "sparks" would all be raised from among the demonic forces. The supreme and benevolent "Person" of the "Holy Ancient One" would reveal itself within the Irascible One, presumably, to replace the divine harshness with a permanent benevolence.

All of this was to be accomplished, or at least aided, by Kabbalistic *tiqqunim* performed by the Messiah and the Messianic faithful. For these faithful—indeed, for the entire Jewish people—the supreme commandment of Judaism was now to have absolute and unquestioning faith in Sabbatai Zevi. The Messiah has the authority, Nathan wrote ominously in his manifesto, "to condemn to dreadful torment even the most pious saint alive, if he were to entertain any doubts about him."

The effects of this "Mending" of the World of Emanation would soon become manifest upon earth. "A year and some months from now," Nathan wrote—that is, by early 1667 at the latest—"Sabbatai Zevi will take power from the Turkish sultan....All the kings will become his tributaries; the sultan alone will be his personal slave." The Messiah would then cross the mythical river Sambatyon, beyond which dwell the Lost Tribes of Israel. There he would be joined with his true and proper bride: the daughter of no less a personage than Moses the lawgiver, who had come back to life (and presumably fathered children) some fifteen years earlier.

In the Messiah's absence, the sultan would rebel. Great tribulation would follow. The Messianic signs prophesied in the Zohar would take place. And Sabbatai Zevi would return—his mouth blazing fire, his mount a monstrous and terrifying lion, his bridle a seven-headed snake—to rule the world. The Jewish Diaspora would be regathered to the Holy Land. The Temple would descend from heaven, fully built. The dead would return to life.

One did not have to be poor or ignorant to believe all this. Nor did one have to be oppressed or downtrodden, as some theories of Messianic movements might lead us to expect. Jews in the 1660s were not, by and large, oppressed.[37] Nor were the Sabbatian faithful particularly downtrodden, either objectively or in their own perceptions.

Cardozo is a case in point. He asks rhetorically, in his *Epistle*, what possible motive he might have for his Messianic belief, beyond sober consideration of the evidence in its favor: "Certainly not my being in exile, for I experience no exile."[38] For him, "exile" is plainly not a matter of locality but of mode of life, and Cardozo's mode of life in Tripoli is entirely satisfactory.

This is why Cardozo neither wants nor expects that the Messiah will bring the Jews back to the Holy Land. On this score he parts company not only with Nathan of Gaza, but with fifteen hundred years of Jewish Messianic dreaming. His own image of the Messianic era is a strangely prescient foreshadowing of the Jewish political emancipation of the eighteenth and nineteenth centuries: "When the Redeemer comes, the Jews will still be living among the Gentiles even after their salvation is accomplished. But they will not be dead men, as they had been previously. Through their redemption they will experience happiness, enjoy dignity and honor."[39]

Happiness. Dignity. Honor. All of these terms might well be used to describe the seventeenth-century Jewish experience in the great, rich, tolerant city of Amsterdam. Not only were the Jews there entirely free to profess and practice their Judaism; they were, by the 1660s, prosperous, proud, and comfortably acculturated. They themselves, or their friends or their parents, might have once sat for a portrait or sketch by Rembrandt, who valued the Jews' friendship as well as their patronage.[40] Surely, like Cardozo, they "experienced no exile" in their Dutch Jerusalem.[41]

Yet nowhere did Sabbatai Zevi find wilder enthusiasts than in Jewish Amsterdam. "Our world," one Amsterdam rabbi wrote proudly at the beginning of 1666, "has been turned topsy-turvy. People have forsworn the dicing houses and the lotteries....Day and night do they contemplate God's Torah; undertaking, mean-while, a perfect penance," in anticipation of the coming Redemption. The man to whom the rabbi was writing—Jacob Sasportas, in Hamburg—was still an unrepentant skeptic. But if only he could see the marvelous transformation of Amsterdam Jewry! "You yourself...would be compelled to admit it is the Lord's doing."[42]

Sasportas was not overly impressed by the newly discovered religiosity of the Amsterdam Jews. What did impress him was the news, which reached him in February 1666, that the rabbinic court of Sabbatai Zevi's hometown of Izmir had abolished the Fast of the Tenth of Tevet (which had fallen on December 18, 1665). It had declared it, instead, "a day of feasting and celebration."[43]

This was important. The Fast of the Tenth of Tevet was one of the four fasts listed in Zechariah 8:19, which Jews understood as having been instituted in order to commemorate and lament the sad events connected with the destruction of the Temple.[44] But in Messianic times, the Lord had promised, all four would become occasions of "joy and gladness...for the house of Judah." The decree of the Izmir court, therefore, was tantamount to an official declaration that the Messiah had come.

The news troubled Sasportas. For the first and only time he wavered in his skepticism. The court had issued its ruling, and Sasportas had it on the Talmud's authority that one need entertain no suspicion that a duly constituted religious court might go astray. Anxiety began to gnaw at him. What if Sabbatai Zevi should turn out to be the Messiah after all, and all the plum jobs in the Messianic administration go to other people? "I cannot convey the pleasure I feel," Sasportas wrote with his usual heavy sarcasm, "as I watch these adolescents, these worthless brats, installed in civic office and credited with wisdom and piety superior to my own....And they may indeed become the Messiah's ministers and his deputies, while I am set to cleaning the manure out of his stables."[45]

7.

As the spring of 1666 warmed into summer, Sasportas found that he had more to worry about than lost patronage. Sabbatai Zevi and his followers had begun to show an alarming fondness for sacralized violence directed against the isolated minority—Sasportas now firmly among them—who could not bring themselves to believe.

Sabbatai had long had a penchant for performing what his contemporaries called "strange acts." (Cardozo would speak more strongly of them: "foul deeds.")[46] These might be peculiar but harmless stunts, like arranging a wedding ceremony between himself and a Torah scroll. They might be minor violations of the Torah or of the normative proprieties of Judaism, like eating forbidden foods or pronouncing aloud the sacred four-letter Name of God. After Nathan of Gaza had proclaimed him to be the Messiah, however, Sabbatai's "strange acts" had turned downright thuggish. In December 1665, for example, he smashed his way into a synagogue during Sabbath prayers, then proceeded to harangue and terrorize the worshipers, forcing them to pronounce the sacred Name.[47]

All this was common knowledge. Yet Sabbatai Zevi's enthusiasts remained strangely unperturbed by it, just as they were unperturbed by Nathan of Gaza's inability to produce any convincing evidence that he was really the prophet he claimed to be. This indifference, in the early months of 1666, was all but impenetrable. Try to penetrate it, try to call attention to the bizarre and unMessiah-like acts of the Messiah, and one might find oneself excommunicated[48]—or worse.

Late in the spring of 1666, news reached Sabbatai Zevi that the believers in Venice had brutally beaten a man who had dared speak blasphemy against the Messiah. That was all right, of course, but the day that they had carried out their beating happened to be the Sabbath. Had they violated the Sabbath, or had they not?

Sabbatai was by then living in comfortable imprisonment in the fortress of Gallipoli,[49] by order of the Turkish authorities, who were aware of his Messianic claims and were not quite sure what to do with him. One of the rising stars in his entourage there was an ambitious and talented young man named Samuel Primo, who had become the Messiah's personal secretary. It was Primo who composed the response to the action of the Venetian zealots that presently went out on Sabbatai Zevi's authority.

Primo's letter shows how far Sabbatai had grown, in the believers' imaginations, beyond the modest human dimensions of Maimonides's Messiah. He is "King of the World…your king and savior, who redeems your souls and your bodies on heaven and on earth, who brings your dead back to life, who saves you from the

51

oppression of the Gentiles and the punishments of Hell." He is the Almighty.[50] He is, moreover—as his name Sabbatai would suggest—the Sabbath incarnate. Defending him against "rebellious" detractors, therefore, is the same thing as keeping the Sabbath.[51] To beat up an unbeliever, therefore, is an appropriate Sabbath-day activity for the faithful.

How Primo must have itched to be Grand Inquisitor, seated at the right hand of the newly crowned King of the World![52] But it was not to be. By September 1666, Sultan Mehmed IV had had enough of the Messianic melodrama that had been playing for months in Gallipoli, in what was supposed to be a prison. He summoned Sabbatai Zevi before him in Adrianople and (on September 16) presented him with the choice between Islam and death.

Sabbatai made his choice. "He began grovelling on the ground before the sultan, begging that he might be allowed to take refuge in the sultan's religion. He threw his [Jewish] cap onto the ground, and spat on it. He insulted the Jewish faith and profaned God's name, in full public view." He thereupon received from the sultan a turban (a mark of his having become a Muslim), the Muslim name Mehmed Effendi, and an honorary position, complete with salary, as "royal doorkeeper" in the Turkish court.

The account quoted above was penned in November 1666 by an "unbelieving" rabbi, one of Sasportas's intimate correspondents.[53] It is easily possible that Sabbatai behaved before the sultan with more dignity than this rabbi was willing to allow. Yet the essential fact could not be denied, despite the believers' earnest efforts (over the next several months) to deny it. Their Messiah had abandoned them in the cruelest and most devastating way imaginable.

They did not abandon him. At least, very many of them did not. Ways were found to rationalize Sabbatai's apostasy, to represent it as an essential but temporary setback in the unfolding of the Redemption. The most popular of these rationalizations drew upon the Lurianic doctrine of the fallen sparks. These fragments of holiness, we recall, had fallen into the demonic realms at the time of the "Shattering" and remained imprisoned there. Over and over again the Shechinah descends into the abyss to gather and redeem them. Now She has the Messiah to help Her. Like Her, he has courageously plunged into the fecal sewer of Gentile-dom—specifically, Islam—in order to rescue the sparks that lie buried in the filth.[54] Soon he will emerge from this "harrowing of hell" to shine in his Messianic glory.

The years passed. Sabbatai Zevi died on September 17, 1676, leaving his faithful with yet another painful wound to be nursed and brooded over and picked at. Nathan of Gaza died in 1680.

Meanwhile, time worked its cleansing magic upon Samuel Primo. By the 1690s his youthful career as secretary to the Messiah had been forgotten. Only a few knew that he still believed in Sabbatai Zevi, believed, in fact, that Sabbatai Zevi was now God, the former God having withdrawn Himself from the universe leaving Sabbatai as Deity in His place. To the rest of the world Primo seemed impeccably orthodox: grave, learned, pious, respected by all. By the 1690s, he was rabbi in Adrianople (Edirne), empowered to judge, to legislate, to order floggings and excommunications.[55] He could turn his inquisitorial talents, then, toward the congenial task of hounding, humiliating, and destroying Abraham Cardozo.

8.

In 1666 Cardozo's conflict with Primo was still far in the future. It is doubtful if the Messiah's secretary had ever heard of Cardozo during the heyday of the Messianic movement, or that he would have stooped to pay him much attention if he had heard of him. If Cardozo was doing anything at this time on Sabbatai Zevi's behalf—apart, of course, from prophesying the appearance of new stars—we do not know what it was. It was not until 1668, when the movement was in eclipse, that Cardozo stepped forward as one of its literary champions.

How major a figure he became within the movement we cannot be sure. Seen from the outside, he might look important enough. Sasportas, for one, took him seriously enough to devote substantial space in his anti-Sabbatian book *Zevi's Fading Flower* to refuting and ridiculing him.[56] He even went so far as to couple Cardozo with Nathan, as a pair of fake prophets vouching for one another.[57] Yet Cardozo never belonged to the movement's inner circle: the privileged ones who continued even after the apostasy to pay court to Sabbatai Zevi and were part of the correspondence network that included Nathan and Samuel Primo. The Sabbatians might speak of Cardozo as a man to be respected but a bit odd nonetheless. He follows a path of his own, they might say. His ways are not quite ours.[58] Nathan seems hardly to have noticed his existence,[59] which will no doubt help explain why Cardozo's own feelings about Nathan grew more and more sour with the passing years.[60]

Cardozo did indeed meet with Sabbatai Zevi and receive from him the warmest and most heartening compliments.[61] This was only years afterward, however, well after Sabbatai was dead. Cardozo had by then developed a notable talent for bringing ghosts back from the other world and hearing from them whatever it was he wanted to hear. In this sad world of ours Cardozo never laid eyes on his Messiah, and, for all that he wrote about Sabbatai Zevi and to Sabbatai Zevi, he never received from Sabbatai Zevi a word of acknowledgment.

"I have come to know," Cardozo wrote in 1669 to the judges of Izmir, "that the true Messiah is Sabbatai Zevi, for whom I am obliged to sacrifice my life."[62] And we are obliged to ask, Why? What was there about Sabbatai Zevi that could evoke so powerful a conviction?

In a sense Cardozo has answered this question in the *Epistle to the Judges of Izmir*. He gives us page after page of elegant, tightly reasoned scholastic argumentation, from Bible and Talmud and midrash, that Sabbatai Zevi precisely fits the profile of the Messiah anticipated by the prophets and the rabbis and even by Maimonides. *This* is why I believe, he tells us: because all the evidence points to Sabbatai as the man we have awaited so long.

Can we be satisfied with this answer? Cardozo lived all his life in a scholastic world, where authoritative texts were the measures of truth. That world was crumbling, even as Cardozo wrote, under the blows of thinkers like Descartes and Spinoza and Newton. Most of us today will not find its premises compelling. If we want to understand why Cardozo believed in Sabbatai Zevi, we will find a satisfying answer—if at all—not in the books Cardozo studied but in the yearnings of his soul. Fortunately, Cardozo has revealed enough of his soul in his writings to make such an inquiry possible.

He gives us a vital clue in one of his letters, which is in effect an early draft (spring 1668) of the arguments he was later to place before the judges of Izmir.[63] Two years earlier, he says in the letter—that is, in the spring of 1666, when the Sabbatian excitement was at its height—he had had a presentiment "that King Messiah would don the garb of a forced convert [or "Marrano"]; that on account of that garb the Jews would not recognize him; that he would become, in short, a Marrano like me."[64]

"A Marrano like me." Cardozo was to edit this remark out of his later, more polished presentation of his case. But surely it reveals the essential truth of his Messianic faith. Cardozo believed in Sabbatai Zevi, because he saw in Sabbatai Zevi *a mirror of the most painful and shameful, yet most essential, aspects of his own experience*. He saw this intuitively, perhaps, even before September 1666, when only the Messiah's "strange acts" might serve as portents of what would be the strangest act of all, his apostasy. When the news of the apostasy reached Cardozo, his faith in Sabbatai Zevi turned to fixed and immoveable "knowledge." The conviction rooted itself in him, not *in spite* of Sabbatai's conversion to Islam, but *because* of it.[65]

Cardozo had known that there was something Messianic about his own destiny long before he had ever heard of Sabbatai Zevi.[66] We see this in his "St. Christopher" dream from his early days in Venice. Here he and the Messiah are fused into one body. His legs carry the Messiah through the marketplaces of Venice. His voice issues the Messianic proclamation.

By 1669, as we shall see from the *Epistle to the Judges of Izmir* (below, chapter 9), Cardozo had begun to believe that he himself was Messiah ben Joseph, over against Sabbatai Zevi's Messiah ben David. We cannot be sure how, at this stage, he conceived his role as co-Messiah. Presumably he still saw Messiah ben Joseph in the traditional category of martyred forerunner, humble "Christ-bearer" to the Messiah who really counted. (Is this what he had in mind when he told the judges of Izmir: "I am obliged to sacrifice my life" for Sabbatai Zevi?)

Yet Cardozo knew, from his reading of the Kabbalistic *Faithful Shepherd*, that it had been part of his Messianic fate to have been "profaned" amid the "idolatrous temples" of the uncircumcised Christians. Once Sabbatai Zevi had converted to Islam, the mirror-like symmetry between the two Messiahs must have seemed to him irresistibly compelling. One Messiah had been a Christian; the other was now a Muslim. The one had been born in Gentile-dom and had left it for Judaism; that other had been born in Judaism and left it for Gentile-dom. Even in 1669 Cardozo must have begun to conceive himself and Sabbatai Zevi as complementary partners, each the other's alter ego: two Messiahs who really were one.

Cardozo had not yet come to believe, as he later would, that he himself was the better, stronger, more effective Messiah of the pair. He did not yet understand, as he later would, what a weak and confused human being Sabbatai Zevi really had been. He would not have dreamed, in 1669, of representing Sabbatai Zevi as the female Messiah, with himself as the male. That was to come later—after Sabbatai Zevi had disappointed him.

The disappointment was not the apostasy. Cardozo took that in stride. Nor was it Sabbatai's failure to crush the Gentile nations, bring the Jews back to the Holy Land, make himself ruler of all the kings of the earth. Cardozo did not care very deeply about any of this. Cardozo's disappointment was that Sabbatai either could not or would not do one thing that had never been a part of the traditional Messianic job description, which nevertheless came to be, for Cardozo, the very heart of the Messiah's task.

The Messiah, Cardozo expected, would "come to recognize through his own inquiry who the God of Israel truly is" and would communicate this knowledge to all. He would "open the eyes of the blind and the ears of the deaf"—who had not previously grasped just who the Being is whom we worship. He would reveal, not only to the Jews but even to the Gentiles, "the mystery of the God who has concealed Himself."[67] Through this revelation he would bring salvation to the Jewish people and to the entire world.

This expectation seems very strange in the traditional Jewish context. It perhaps marks Cardozo as a man with roots in seventeenth-century Europe. Early in the century educated Europeans had gone wild over the mysterious Rosicrucian manifestos, which had promised that new breakthroughs in human knowledge would usher in a divinely transformed world.[68] Perhaps some of this excitement had seeped into Cardozo's Spanish environment.

Yet it is also possible to see Cardozo's near-obsession with recovering the concealed and (he thought) long-forgotten identity of his God as a reflection of his Marrano experience. The core of being a Marrano is that one's *true and essential identity is concealed.* This was the case with Cardozo during his most impressionable years. It was the case with Cardozo's father, to whom the little boy turned, as we have seen, to learn the real truth about God. It was the case, Cardozo came to believe, with God Himself. God's essential identity is concealed, and we suffer from that concealment. Once the mystery is revealed, once the true identity is disclosed, the suffering ends.

Cardozo turned to his Messiah, as he had once turned to his father, to reveal the saving and healing truth. His father, with his ineffectual responses to the boy's questioning, had been a disappointment. Now the Messiah disappointed him too. Cardozo waited and waited for Sabbatai Zevi's public disclosure of the "mystery of Divinity." It never came.

Meanwhile, Cardozo had launched his own inquiries into who the God of Israel truly is. For twenty-two years, he tells us—from about 1648 to 1670, it would seem—he struggled with "the Mystery of this Faith," through "innumerable psychic torments, born of doubts and misunderstandings."[69] Eventually he found the knowledge he was looking for.

Bafflingly, Messiah ben David would not or could not reveal that knowledge. Messiah ben Joseph, then, must do the job. Cardozo was ready to set forth on the redemptive crusade that would dominate and define the rest of his life.

9.

In the meantime, Cardozo's idyllic days in Tripoli were drawing to an end.

In November 1672 a soldiers' mutiny broke out against Osman Pasha. Very soon, the notables of Tripoli—including the leading Muslim clerics, the mufti and the *cadi*—had joined the revolt. The swelling mob went to Rejeb Bey and demanded he be their leader. He refused. Their former love for him—wrote the English consul Bradley in the report he dispatched to his superiors in London—turned to hatred. They besieged Rejeb Bey's house. He first resisted, then surrendered; he was strangled, his head cut off, his body (says Bradley) "thrown into the Street to the Dogges."[70] Cardozo would not see his old patron again for nearly ten years, not until the end of March 1682, when Rejeb Bey's ghost would rise out of hell at Cardozo's summons and sit at table with Cardozo and his disciples and talk with them.[71]

The rebels besieged Osman Pasha in his palace. Resistance was hopeless. Early on the morning of November 28, Osman died. In a strange and disquieting passage, written some thirty years after the event, Cardozo seems to claim that Osman Pasha was murdered, that, moreover, he himself had helped plan the murder.[72] Other accounts do not support Cardozo on this point, though it cannot be ruled out that Cardozo knew more about Osman's last hours than the other sources did. The Pasha was sick all night, Bradley wrote, and died before daybreak. "Some report that he took Poison, but by the Doctors report and those that were with him that night it was known he died with greif...."[73]

Was Cardozo this "Doctor"? We shall never know.

Osman Pasha had been a tyrant, hated for his greed. Tripoli was relieved to be rid of him. The aftermath of the revolution was, by and large, orderly and tranquil. Yet revolutions tend to devour those who carry them out, and this one was no exception. Cardozo, as one of the conspirators—allegedly—was in danger. The mufti, who himself supported the revolution, intervened to save him.

"Any follower of Muhammad," he proclaimed, "who lays a hand on the Jew doctor, is no follower of Muhammad!"[74] But life in Tripoli cannot have been secure. Early in 1673 Cardozo left for Tunis.[75]

He found that his reputation as a propagandist for the apostate Messiah had gone before him. The Jews of Tunis were not sure what to do with him. They wrote to Venice for advice. The Venetian rabbis wrote back: he must be excommunicated. The excommunication failed, but, before long, a bribe for the city's rulers accomplished what the excommunication could not. Cardozo was expelled from Tunis.[76]

He tried to go back to Italy. Under other circumstances he would perhaps have gone to Verona, where his brother Isaac was now a successful physician and a pillar of the community. But the Cardozo brothers were no longer on speaking terms. They had quarrelled bitterly in 1668 over Abraham's Sabbatian activities. There had been a nasty exchange of letters. In his last letter Abraham warned Isaac that he would burn any reply that he might receive from him. If he did receive any reply, we know nothing of it. The break was final.[77]

He went back to Leghorn. Leghorn would not have him. The Jews there tried—with only partial success—to keep him and his family confined in the *lazaretto*, the place where suspected plague-carriers were kept under quarantine. As soon as they could, they shipped him off to Turkey.[78] A year and some months afterward, they gave him a sort of belated godspeed. This was a decree of excommunication, directed not only against Cardozo himself, but also against any "individual of our holy Community, of any rank, gender, or condition whatsoever," who might "write to or communicate with the aforesaid Doctor Cardozo...directly or indirectly."[79]

"I experience no exile," Cardozo had written confidently in 1669 from his cozy berth in Tripoli. Six years later he had begun again to taste that experience. He would taste it again and again, till the day of his death.

Chapter 4
Cardozo
the Theologian

1.

The Mystery of this Faith...I myself did not attain...till I had struggled with it for twenty-two years. Innumerable psychic torments, born of doubts and misunderstandings, did I suffer. Time after time was I exposed to temptation.

For no sensible person could possibly accept this Faith on anyone's say-so; unless that instructor were to work signs and wonders...as Moses did for our ancestors, when he revealed to them the God of their patriarchs. For they, too, had forgotten Him; so long had their exile dragged on....[1]

Some time in 1673, or perhaps late 1672, Abraham Cardozo wrote a long letter to his Messiah. He attached to the letter a treatise he had recently composed, which he had called by the high-flown title *Drush Boqer de-Avraham (Abraham's Morn).*[2] The title was taken from the Zohar (e.g., I, 203a-b). In the Zoharic context, "Abraham" was the biblical patriarch, who, in Kabbalistic code, is a symbol for the *sefirah* of Grace *(Hesed).* But Cardozo was also an

"Abraham," and his "morn" was the dawning light of Grace that this latter-day Abraham was about to shed on the long-hidden mysteries of true religion.[3]

Cardozo dispatched the letter and the treatise by courier to Adrianople, where he naturally supposed that Sabbatai Zevi was residing with the rest of the sultan's court, and waited for a reply.

Abraham's Morn began with a bold statement of intent: "I propose to set forth the Faith of our ancestors, our prophets, and our sages, which for the past thousand years has been forgotten by us, due to the long duration of our exile."

The sages of the Mishnah had known the Faith, Cardozo tells his reader. So, by and large, had the Talmudic sages who came after them. Many of the Geonim, early in the Middle Ages, had preserved its memory. Perhaps a few traces of it survived, here and there, in the dark centuries that had followed. For the most part, however, the Faith had become lost, buried in oblivion, till it should be rediscovered through God's grace at the time of the Redemption. Even Cordovero and Luria, for all their insights and valuable contributions to the science of Kabbalah, had not truly understood its Mystery. The reason was that they lived a hundred years earlier, "in a time when the Final End was still remote. But now, God has enlightened our intelligence, and the Mystery of this Faith has begun to be revealed."[4]

It is at first sight paradoxical that Cardozo should have expected that his Messiah would need enlightenment from him on the subject of the Mystery of the Faith. We have seen that it was the Messiah himself who was supposed to reveal the Mystery to the world. Yet we have also seen that Sabbatai Zevi had done nothing of the kind, and Cardozo was left to wonder why.

It turned out that the Messiah's failure on this score had been predicted, along with so much else, by the prophet Isaiah. "Who is blind, other than My servant?" God had demanded, through Isaiah's mouth (42:18). It was patently clear, from the context, that "My servant" was the Messiah—that very same Messiah whom God had chosen "as a light to the Gentiles, to open the eyes of the blind, to bring...the dwellers in darkness out from their prison" (42:6–7). Yet the Messiah himself is blind, at the beginning! The Messiah, Cardozo wrote, has at first no clear knowledge of the Faith. Only as the Redemption progresses is he enlightened. He, in turn, opens the blind eyes of the Jewish people. Only then can the Jews carry out their divinely appointed task of being God's witnesses (Isa 43:12)—for how can anyone witness to a truth that he himself does not know?—and enlightenment extend to the Gentiles.[5] Only then, when He is witnessed to by the Jewish people, can God truly become God.[6]

In other words, the salvation of humanity and of God alike must begin with the Messiah, who is Sabbatai Zevi. Only, Sabbatai Zevi does not yet know how to be Messiah. Cardozo will explain it to him.

There were a few things that Cardozo himself, at this point, did not yet know. He did not know, for example, that Sabbatai Zevi was no longer in Adrianople, no longer part of the sultan's court. By the beginning of 1673, the sultan had at last grown tired of the once-amusing "Mehmed Effendi." The man would not leave off trying to be Turkish courtier and Jewish Messiah all at the same time! True, he had managed to persuade a number of the Jewish scholars, who continued to pay court to him, to do as he had done and "don the turban." But mass conversions to Islam, which might have justified continued support for him, did not seem to be forthcoming. Besides, how true and sincere could one's Islamic faith be, if one had adopted it out of devotion to the *Jewish* Messiah? Would not the convert remain a Jew afterward, under his or her Muslim robes?

So, in January 1673, Sabbatai Zevi was banished to Albania, to the place (Dulcigno; modern Ulcinj) that the Turks called Ulgun and that Sabbatai's ever-loyal followers called by the biblical name Alkum.[7]

Unaware of this—unaware that his letter and the treatise *Abraham's Morn* would have to be forwarded to the hinterlands of the Turkish Empire, to a man who might or might not ever pay them attention[8]—Cardozo poured his heart into his first serious work of theology, laying out the secrets of Divinity to enlighten the blind eyes of his Messiah.[9]

2.

Abraham's Morn was the first book in which Cardozo set forth the secret of Divinity. It was far from the last. By the end of his life he had written (by his own accounting) "sixty treatises or books to communicate God's Divinity and that of His Name."[10] Scholem has put together a list of fifty-seven such treatises, all of which circulated only in manuscript.[11]

Cardozo did not have anywhere near as much to say as this stunning literary productivity might suggest. Once he had discovered the "Mystery of Divinity," some time around 1670, he did not revise it in any essential way. In treatise after treatise he pounded across the same basic set of ideas, bolstered by the same basic set of proofs, modifying them only to suit the level of Kabbalistic expertise he expected of his readers. To be sure, there was some development. Cardozo seems to have gradually refined, as the decades passed, his idea of the precise hierarchy of super-sefirotic beings out of which the being we call God has His origin. Each treatise normally contains one or two striking ideas, one or two striking images or arguments, that do not occur in the others. By and large, though, once you have read one work of Cardozan theology you have read them all, and as you work your way through the next treatise, you can practically predict what he is going to say.

For this volume I have translated Cardozo's treatise *This Is My God and I Will Praise Him* (written in 1685 or 1686), which is the most lucid and systematic of his theological writings. In the account of his theology I give here, I will take *Abraham's Morn* as my starting point. Yet I will not hesitate to include ideas, images, and arguments drawn from his later works, for the risk of thereby distorting his early thought is small.

By the time Cardozo wrote *Abraham's Morn*, his twenty-two years of "torments...doubts and misunderstandings" were behind him. The truth was in his grasp. He hardly needed to modify it. All he needed to do was convince others of what he already knew: that he had indeed discovered the long-forgotten Faith of their ancestors, their prophets, and their sages. He would thereby redeem them and all the world.

3.

The world, says Cardozo, is currently home to four basic systems of religion. There is absolute, pure, prophetic monotheism, which is represented equally by Judaism and by Islam. There is philosophical Deism. There is Christian Trinitarianism. There is pagan polytheism.[12] *All four are false religions.*

Jewish-Islamic monotheism, Cardozo leaves no doubt, is just as false as the rest. In some respects, indeed, it is inferior to paganism and perhaps also to Deism. (Not, however, to Christianity; Cardozo never wavers in his insistence that Christianity is the worst and most foolish religion that could ever be conceived.) Muslims and Jews—with the partial exception of the Kabbalists—fall into the error of insisting that there is no God except the being that the philosophers call the First Cause: a Being absolutely pure and simple, absolutely *other* than ourselves, absolutely transcendent and bodiless and genderless. "There is no God but Allah," say the Muslims, by which they mean, no God but the First Cause.

Yet the essential content of the message that Moses brought to the children of Israel, when he came to redeem them from Pharaoh, was that there *is* a God other than the First Cause. He is the God whom the Bible calls by the sacred four-letter Name *YHVH (Yahveh)*, whom the ancient rabbis called the Blessed Holy One.

This God, to be sure, is hardly the "Supreme Being." That honor belongs to the First Cause and to the First Cause alone. The God whom Moses preached is, in a real sense, an inferior Deity. Moses's God is entirely dependent upon the First Cause for His existence. He is in some measure dependent also upon human beings to bring down upon Him that effluence from the First Cause that He needs continually in order to function. Yet this God is nonetheless a being august and powerful beyond our ability to conceive. He, and none other, is Creator of the universe and all that it contains. He, and none other, continues daily to guide and sustain His creation. He, and none other, is the proper object of human worship.

This is the nucleus of Cardozo's theology: that God and the First Cause are distinct entities, that God is the lesser of the two beings, *and yet* that it is God—and not the First Cause—who must be worshiped.

To convey this paradox, Cardozo propounds the parable of a fruit tree. The tree is rooted in the earth. It draws its sustenance from soil and water and air and sun. What it absorbs, it converts into foliage and blossoms and, most important, into edible fruits. The tree is derivative and dependent: it could not thrive without the soil, water, and so forth. Yet only a very great fool would, on that account, despise the tree and refuse to eat its fruit, choosing instead to get his nourishment from soil and water and air.

God is like that tree. He is rooted in, and draws nourishment from, entities superior to Himself.[13] (This "nourishment" is the divine effluence, or *shefa'*, that the Kabbalists are always talking about.) But we need God to transform that effluence into a form that is "edible," so to speak, to us lower creatures. If not for God, we could no more make use of the effluence than a hungry person can make a meal off dirt and water.

This is why it is essential to worship God. A Hebrew wordplay helps Cardozo make his point. The same verb, *la-'avod,* can mean "to cultivate" a tree or "to worship" a deity. To worship God is essentially to cultivate Him—to draw *shefa'* down upon him from the higher entities through the magic of ritual language—as though He were a tree on which we depend for our livelihood. "One cultivates the tree, providing it with good soil and plentiful water...in order to improve the tree, that is God...from which we get the fruit."[14]

Worshiping the highest of the entities above God, namely the First Cause—as Jews have been doing for the past thousand years in blind imitation of the Muslims[15]—is about as sensible and effective as eating dirt.

Once the dazzlingly simple truth had dawned on Cardozo, that the God of biblical and Talmudic Judaism is a distinct being from the First Cause,[16] he found proofs for it everywhere. Dozens of biblical stories, hitherto puzzling, now became fully intelligible. Why, for example, did Pharaoh—who certainly knew and revered the First Cause—declare himself to know nothing about the God of Moses (Exod 5:2–3)? Why did neither Moses, nor Aaron, nor the elders of Israel, ever tell Pharaoh that the Being who had sent them was the First Cause?[17] The reason must be that Moses's message had nothing to do with the First Cause, but with a subordinate Deity whose existence, unlike that of the First Cause, is difficult or impossible to prove by rational argument.

The anthropomorphic expressions used of God in the Bible, which had struck the young Cardozo as so weirdly inappropriate for the philosophers' God, now made sense. The Bible wasn't talking about *that* God at all! ("The Torah and all its contents," Cardozo says, "are infinitely remote from the First Cause, about which the Torah does not contain the smallest hint.")[18] The biblical God appears human-like, because in some sense He *is* human-like. The human species, male and female, is in His image, and wise King Solomon filled an entire book with the love songs that His maleness and His femaleness sing to one another.[19]

The "tainted texts" of the Talmud, too, made perfect sense. How unjust it is, Cardozo proclaims, to call them "tainted texts" (*aggadot shel dofi*)! They should be called, rather, *aggadot shel yofi*, "beauteous texts"[20] because they provide us with the precious hints from which "the pure-hearted investigator may discover, at the end of the exile-time, the Mystery of God's Divinity."[21] The Talmud says, for example, that God prays. On the face of it, the statement seems absurd. If God is the Supreme Being, to whom might He pray? Yet the truth is that God is *not* the Supreme Being. There is one higher than He, dwelling within Him, and it is to that Being that His prayers are directed.

Finally, the traditional Jewish liturgy—formulated in remote antiquity before the Jews had forgotten the Mystery of God's Divinity—now becomes wholly intelligible for the first time. Again and again, the liturgy says, "Blessed art Thou, O Lord...," using a passive form of the Hebrew verb. The prayer leader opens the order of worship by declaring, "Bless ye the Lord, who is blessed!" and the congregation responds, "Blessed be the Lord who is blessed for all eternity!"[22] The passive form of the liturgical language testifies to Cardozo's truth. God is not the one who *blesses*, but the one who *is blessed*. There is some being superior to Him, whose blessing He requires, and the whole aim of Jewish worship is to draw that blessing down upon Him, as one would water a fruit tree, so that the world may be nourished from the divine fruit.

4.

Cardozo had a great deal to say about the nature of his God, beyond the negative proposition that He is not identical with the First Cause. It is difficult to go into any detail about Cardozo's doctrine of God without getting lost in a forest of Kabbalistic technicalities. We shall therefore touch rather lightly upon this aspect of Cardozo's thought. Yet there are a few points that can and must be made.

Let us begin by remarking that Cardozo did not see his "Mystery of Divinity" as repudiating or breaking with the Lurianic Kabbalah. True, Isaac Luria had not penetrated to the heart of the Mystery. (The time had not been ripe: when Luria had died in 1572, the Messianic redemption was still a hundred years in the future.) Yet Luria was nevertheless a giant, on whose shoulders Cardozo must sit. If Luria's investigations had not paved the way, no one, Cardozo included, could have discovered the identity of the God of Israel.[23] Cardozo thus describes his God in Lurianic language, in terms of the "Five Persons."

(The reader without Kabbalistic background, who wishes nonetheless to understand Cardozo's doctrine, might do well to turn back to the account of Lurianic Kabbalah given in chapter 2.4 and review who the "Five Persons" are and how they function together.)

God, says Cardozo, has a body and a soul. The "body" may be equated with the World of Emanation as a whole, comprising all five of the "Persons," but, more commonly, Cardozo localizes it in the "Person" of the Irascible One. The "soul" comes from an elusive and rarified realm above and beyond the *sefirot*, which Cardozo often designates "the World of *Ein Sof*" ("the Infinite"). This soul is not the First Cause, but rather an entity emanated from It and therefore inferior to It, far superior, nonetheless, to the "Persons" of the World of Emanation.[24]

We must not take this talk of God's "body" too literally, as though it were something you or I might be able to touch or hold. For Cardozo, both "body" and "soul" are relative rather than absolute terms. A substance can be ethereal and abstract to a degree beyond human imagining and yet be a "body," provided it serves as a vehicle for some other substance that is even more ethereal and abstract than itself. Once we have made this disclaimer, however, we can go on to say that Cardozo thinks of God as an embodied or an "incarnated" being. His body derives from one (lower) level of divine reality, His soul from another.

As often, Cardozo treats the story of Adam, who was created in God's image, as an index to the processes taking place within God Himself. God breathed into Adam's nostrils the "spirit of life" (Gen 2:7), which Cardozo understands as a rational soul.[25] Through that act Adam was transformed into a being akin to God. A parallel infusion takes place in the World of Emanation. The Irascible One is the "Man" of the World of Emanation. He and the human Adam mirror one another. Just as a superior entity breathed His soul into Adam's nostrils, transforming Adam in the process, so a mysterious entity from a realm superior to the World of Emanation infused the Irascible One with a soul superior to the Irascible One Himself. This superior entity (says Cardozo) "loved the Irascible One...raised Him up...fused with Him through His Great Name,"[26] with the result that "the Irascible One...has been transformed into a Deity."[27]

So Cardozo worships an incarnated God, much as during his Spanish youth he worshiped an incarnated Son of God.

68

We have already seen that the Kabbalists might on occasion speak of the Irascible One as the "Son," namely, of the "Persons" called Father and Mother. But Cardozo turns this occasional usage into a fixed practice. His God is the "Holy Son" *(bera qaddisha)*, the "Delightful Son" *(ha-ben ha-nehmad)*, who gets His sefirotic "body" from Father and Mother, His super-sefirotic soul from the loftier entity who has breathed it into him.

How Cardozo detested Christianity! How impossible he found it to tear out the roots that Christianity had planted in his mind!

There is a very practical, and very lamentable, consequence of the fact that God is a being made up of soul and body. This is that God's soul can leave His body, just as Adam's did, just as yours or mine can. When that happens, He does not die. Cardozo is not quite the first "death of God" theologian, although at times he does come close. But God, though not susceptible to death in an absolute sense, does become inert and comatose.

When God is in this state of soullessness, prayers go unanswered. How could they even be heard? Without God's soul, His body does not function. Without His body, His soul's perceptions do not reach beyond the ethereal realms of the "Infinite." Without His bodily organs—namely, the *sefirot*—we have no way to address Him. The *sefirot* themselves can do nothing to help us, since they are only the organs of a soulless body.

> When God [Cardozo means here the "soul" that infuses God] ascends on high, and departs from the Irascible One, the latter is left in a state of smallness. People then cry out, but get no answer, because it is through the Irascible One that God is able to hear prayer....And the Shechinah has descended to the lower realms, and She remains tiny and profaned....[28]

No wonder all the agonized cries of all the Inquisition's Marrano victims evoked no response from on high! God could not hear them. His soul had left Him. To use the imagery of *Abraham's Morn:* the fruit tree is parched and withered for lack of water. We

69

have not "irrigated" the God who is our precious "fruit tree" because we have labored under the delusion that He is the First Cause, all-sufficient, who needs no "watering."

Our task now is to turn the water channels toward Him. We must pray and read the Scriptures with the proper "intentions" *(kavvanot)*. We must perform the proper "Mending-rites" *(tiqqunim)*. Do this—and our saving God will return to life. He will be, in a manner of speaking, newly born.

5.

"A Child is born unto us, a Son is given to us," the prophet Isaiah had proclaimed (9:5). Cardozo had no doubt been taught, as a boy, that this was a prophecy of Christ's birth. Only now could the prophecy be given its true interpretation. Only now, with Cardozo's discovery of the Mystery of Divinity, could it begin to come true.

> In our times...the Mystery of God's faith and the unity of His Shechinah has become revealed. We therefore consider it as though the Deity had been born unto us and given to us, and He is truly the Holy and Delightful Son....
>
> The Irascible One...is called a Child when He is at His lowest stage....The goal of our intentions *[kavvanot]* now is to make Him big.
>
> Next we must concentrate our Intentions on the following goal: that, when the light and the effluence and the blessing flow down upon Him and thus cause His *sefirot* and His qualities to become enlarged, the Shechinah shall also become enlarged. She is to become a complete Person, fit to couple with Her Husband and fully to unite with Him.[29]

Before this could happen, *kavvanot* and *tiqqunim* were necessary. Cardozo undertook to provide them.

Chapter 5
Cardozo the Magus

1.

I was at Edirne [Adrianople] when the news arrived that
Sabbatai Zevi had died at Alkum. I went to...the honorable Rabbi Jacob Ashkenazi, and I said to him: "Sabbatai
Zevi is dead. What says Your Worship to that?" And he
replied, "If Sabbatai Zevi is dead, you had best find yourself another God...."[1]

Sabbatai Zevi died in 1676, at age fifty. He left behind him a
young widow, named Esther, and at least two young children
from a previous marriage. His brother, Elijah Zevi, traveled to
Albania, where Sabbatai's family had gone into exile with him, and,
in 1677, escorted the widow and the children back to Adrianople.[2]

Esther Zevi was the daughter of Joseph Filosoff, a rabbi in
Salonica with some reputation as a scholar.[3] Sabbatai had asked her
hand in marriage the year before he died. Filosoff had accepted the
proposal, thereby getting himself fired from his rabbinical post.[4]
He seems to have insisted, as condition for the marriage, that his
Esther would be treated as a Jewish girl, even in the Albanian
"palace" of her modern-day Muslim Ahasuerus.[5] Filosoff and his
family were not yet ready, as they were eight years later, to become
Muslims themselves.

It is a pity we do not know more about this Esther. (The Sabbatian chronicler Baruch of Arezzo does not even bother to tell us her name.)[6] She emerges dimly from our sources as a smart, ambitious, and resourceful lady with a talent for making Messiahs the men in her life, or where this failed, making the men in her life into Messiahs.

The first of her "Messiahs," after Sabbatai Zevi was gone, was her stepson Ishmael, who was eight years old when his father died. Some of the Sabbatian believers put the wildest hopes in this son of the Messiah. They expected him, indeed, to grow into a Messianic luminary who would outshine even his father. But Ishmael Zevi disappointed his elders by dying (in 1679, most probably). They avenged themselves upon him by forgetting he ever had existed.[7]

By the end of 1681 Esther Zevi had turned her gaze toward the town of Rodosto (modern Tekirdag), on the shore of the Sea of Marmara, where Abraham Cardozo, excommunicated by the Constantinople rabbis and in some fear for his life,[8] was in temporary exile.

2.

Cardozo had by then acquired considerable notoriety. For the past six years he had been living in Turkey. First he was in Izmir, where he had settled in the summer of 1675 after being driven out of Leghorn. Four or five years later the rabbis and community leaders of Izmir managed to arrange his expulsion, and he sailed onward, in high hopes of imminent Redemption, to Constantinople.[9]

He left behind him a tightly organized and intensely loyal circle of disciples, numbering at least two dozen,[10] with whom he would stay in touch by correspondence for the next twenty years. The group was led by two men, both of whom seem to have been in their thirties. One was Daniel Bonafoux, the visionary prophet of Cardozo's circle. (Cardozo fondly refers to him, in the language of Daniel 10:11, as "beloved Daniel.")[11] The other was a young preacher—later to develop, after Cardozo's death, into a very famous author, whose lurid hellfire-and-brimstone tracts were read by Jews all over the world.[12] By an odd coincidence, he had the same name—Elijah Kohen—as the furious Cardozo-hater who would eventually write Cardozo's biography.

Cardozo left much of his family behind him in Izmir—in the graveyard. It had all happened in the summer of 1678, in the space of two ghastly weeks. Plague had struck the city. Three of Cardozo's children, including two teen-age girls, died in a single day. Others followed. A wet-nurse accidentally suffocated his infant child. Another infant, newborn, bled to death when its navel was cut. By the end of the first week of July, thirteen of his children and one of his wives were dead.

All this was God's punishment, Cardozo was sure, because, in the face of the ridicule of the people of Izmir, he had wavered in his dedication to the task of publicizing the Mystery of Divinity: "I had had enough suffering....I would no longer reveal the Mystery of Divinity to anyone."[13]

God, the Irascible One, had made His point. Cardozo went back to revealing the Mystery to anyone who would listen. He revealed it to his disciples in Izmir till he was expelled in 1679 or 1680. Then he revealed it to the new disciples he gathered around him in Constantinople.

3.

As luck would have it, Cardozo found in Constantinople a disciple named Samuel Galimidi, who happened to have a rich father.

Solomon, the elder Galimidi, had believed in Sabbatai Zevi from the very beginning. In the spring of 1666, when the Messianic hope was bright and all the world seemed to believe, he and forty other wealthy householders of Constantinople had signed a solemn pledge to use all their resources to bring obstinate skeptics "here in chains and destroy them utterly, as our good rabbis have directed."[14] All that was past now. The Messiah was dead, the faith forsaken. The rabbis and community leaders of Constantinople were far more willing to turn their resources to "utterly destroying" the believers.

Yet Solomon Galimidi's heart remained faithful. He still believed in Sabbatai Zevi. He believed now in Abraham Cardozo, who had begun openly to proclaim himself Messiah ben Joseph, Sabbatai Zevi's partner in the redemptive task.[15] When his son Samuel became Cardozo's pupil—outstandingly apt, outstandingly zealous—Galimidi opened his home and his wallet to the new Messiah.

Elijah Kohen—the biographer, not the disciple—has a great deal to say about Cardozo's relationship with the Galimidis. Nearly all of it is unpleasant. Not for an instant will Kohen waver from his fixed idea that Cardozo was a mercenary charlatan whose only real goal in life was to take the credulous father and son for all they were worth. This is obviously a hate-filled caricature. Yet it certainly contains an element of truth. For a man of letters or of science in the seventeenth century, a wealthy patron was a resource to be cultivated. The advance of learning, and the attendant benefits to humankind, might require experiment, and the materials for experiment did not always come cheap. For a Kabbalistic investigator like Cardozo, eager as any seventeenth-century scientist to make new discoveries and bring their benefits to the world, the laboratory experiment had its equivalent in the *tiqqun.*

God is flawed, disfigured, internally disharmonious, the male and female aspects of Divinity alienated from one another. Cardozo had learned that from the Kabbalists who came before him. He had also learned that human ritual activity—if performed with the right "intentions" *(kavvanot)*, which necessarily required a detailed awareness of the internal processes within Divinity—could "mend" these flaws and disconnections and that all the world would benefit.

Cardozo was hardly the first to develop special "Mending-rites" for that purpose. A hundred years earlier the Safed Kabbalists had invented their "Midnight Mending-rite" to raise the Shechinah from Her degradation and exile.[16] But Cardozo understood Divinity, and what went on within It, in a way that none of his predecessors had. This had the very practical consequence that Cardozo could devise *tiqqunim* that would be effective beyond the dreams of a Cordovero or a Luria. With the support of an enlightened patron like Galimidi, he and his students could bring these *tiqqunim* into reality.

Prior to Cardozo's arrival in Constantinople, we hear little about his "Mending-rites."[17] Then it all changes. The *tiqqun* becomes the pivotal activity for him and his students. His science has moved, as it were, from the lecture hall to the laboratory.

Kohen makes merry over what he perceives as the lunatic grotesqueness of Cardozo's *tiqqunim*. They do often sound more than a little eccentric, as they are filtered through Kohen's prejudiced pen. Cardozo has left a few prescriptions for his own "Mending-rites," however, and the impression these give is far more dignified and powerful.

One of these texts, which bears the title *Israel—Holiness to the Lord*, is partly translated in this volume (chapter 11). It is unusual among Cardozo's *tiqqunim* in that ritual acts—perhaps we should say, magical acts—play some perceptible role in it. (The disciples are to take different sets of five stones, symbolizing the "Five Persons" or their demonic counterparts. They place them in a stream, take them out of the stream, throw them in one direction or another, and so on and so forth.) Even here, however, the essential "act" of the *tiqqun* is not the manipulation of physical objects but the recitation of carefully selected passages from the Bible.

In this respect, Cardozo's *tiqqunim* sound very much like the old traditional *tiqqunim*, such as the "Midnight Mending-rite." As in the older *tiqqunim*, what matters is not the recitation itself but the disciples' intentions during the recitation. They must concentrate on the hidden meaning of the biblical text, which is the precise mechanism by which the sacred words act to "mend" the rifts within Divinity. This will perhaps explain why Kohen's accounts of Cardozo's *tiqqunim* tend to be so vague. He does not describe the ritual of the *tiqqun*, because in fact there is not much ritual beyond the Bible readings.

The *tiqqun*, according to Kohen, normally involves a ritualized meal. Again according to Kohen, the meal normally involves a considerable quantity of good food and wine, the bill footed by rich Master Solomon. But Kohen also quotes Cardozo's menu for one such *tiqqun*, and it does not sound exactly like a Roman banquet: "Beef. Two ounces of dates. Twenty of nuts. Twenty of olives. Grapes. Pomegranates. Apples. Two wines: one red, one white."[18]

Many of Kohen's *tiqqun* stories are set in late 1681 or early 1682. These were the wild, exciting days when Cardozo and his followers were expecting Redemption to arrive on the coming Passover and were anxious to prepare by "mending" the Divinity as thoroughly as possible. At some point in the fall of 1681, for example, Yom Tov Mevorakh—who was the "prophet" of the Constantinople circle, much as Daniel Bonafoux was in Izmir—had a revelation. The group must perform a *tiqqun* at the grave of the former Turkish sultan Ibrahim, the father of Mehmed IV. Ibrahim would then appear in a dream to his son, the current sultan, and reveal to him that the Messiah has divine authority to redeem all living creatures.

So off they went, and, "after great and heedless expenditure of cash" (Kohen), performed the *tiqqun*. Mevorakh then had another fit of prophetic inspiration: "Thus saith the Lord: On the approaching twelfth of Tevet [December 23, 1681], Sultan Mehmed will go mad; for his father, Sultan Ibrahim, will drive him mad. He will go completely insane, and it will be good, good, good."[19]

4.

The appearance in this *tiqqun* of Sultan Ibrahim's ghost leads us to one of the strangest aspects of Cardozo's activity as expert manipulator of the supernatural. In 1669 Cardozo had assured the judges of Izmir, with a solemn oath, that he had never, in all his life, "exercised power over any angel or spirit of a deceased saint, or over any spirit whatsoever, to compel that entity to reveal itself to me or to answer any question of mine on any subject at all."[20] If this was true in 1669—there is a peculiar loophole in the terms of Cardozo's oath,[21] which suggests that it may not have been altogether sincere—it was no longer true a decade later. By then, Cardozo reveled in his mastery of the world of spirits and his ability to put those spirits to work for him and his disciples.

In Izmir, and later in Constantinople, Cardozo was to boast, many years afterward: "I was granted the power to distribute spirit-guides at my pleasure, to assign whomever I wanted as spirit-guide to whomever I wanted." (We shall return, presently, to the question of what Cardozo means by a "spirit-guide.") He had the power, as well, "to send at my discretion anyone I pleased to the saints' graves to talk with their spirits. I might dispatch one of my students or many of them; the spirits would promptly emerge from their graves in perceptible shapes, and give lucid replies to whatever questions I had sent them to ask."[22]

Cardozo's disciples did not need to perform any of the special preparatory rites that were customary when one went to consult the holy dead. Their success was guaranteed beforehand by special merit of their teacher's achievement. Cardozo had struggled his way toward knowledge of God and had communicated His divinity to the Jewish people. Had it not been for his *Abraham's Morn*, even the holy souls in heaven would not have known who God truly is: "That is why He, who is God of the spirits of all flesh, has ordained that all spirits must reveal themselves at my slightest command, or to anyone I may choose to send."[23]

The spirits might reveal themselves even unbidden. Near the beginning of 1682, for example, a formidable crowd of biblical prophets and ancient and modern Kabbalists—not to mention Sabbatai Zevi himself—showed up to hear Cardozo's lectures on *Abraham's Morn*. (Their purpose, he later discovered, was to pick up some of his pedagogical techniques, so that they could effectively instruct departed souls in the Mystery of Divinity.)[24] But Cardozo might summon the revered dead as well. So he did in the early spring of 1682 in a series of brilliantly successful seances in Solomon Galimidi's house. Hayyim Benveniste, a halakhic scholar of Izmir who had died in 1673, appeared at Cardozo's bidding. So did Sabbatai Zevi. Before the seance was over, Maimonides was there too.[25]

We learn about these seances, it is true, from a letter written by Cardozo some twenty years later. He looked wistfully back on the beginning of the 1680s as a lost golden time when he was undisputed master of the Invisible World, when Redemption seemed on the doorstep and the traumatic events of 1682–83 had not yet happened, when Solomon Galimidi still liked and admired him. Yet we can certainly trust the general accuracy of Cardozo's account, not least because it is easy to see, reading between the lines, where the "spirits" really come from. Cardozo's imagination has produced them. The disciples, desperate to please the master and impress one another, gradually convince themselves that they see the shadowy forms as well.

One latecomer is asked what he sees. His answer at first is: nothing. Only after a fair amount of prodding does the man start to see spirits and to produce details (which, curiously, are quoted mostly in Spanish) of what they look like. Later on, Cardozo demands that Maimonides's ghost state its verdict on a thorny halakhic issue and assigns Yom Tov Mevorakh to "declare you whatever it is that Maimonides says." And poor Yom Tov, who obviously has no idea at all what answer Cardozo is looking for, comes up with a brilliantly meaningless piece of equivocation.

5.

The blessed spirits at Cardozo's command might be summoned, as we have just seen, for an occasional appearance among Cardozo's followers. Alternatively, they might be attached as regular companions to one or another of his favored disciples. When the ghost functions in this latter capacity, Cardozo speaks of him as a *maggid*, a "revelatory entity,"[26] or, as I have chosen to translate the term, a "spirit-guide."

Cardozo did not invent the idea of the *maggid*. It had been well known to the Kabbalists of sixteenth-century Safed. The great halakhic master Joseph Caro, who lived in Safed from about 1536 onward, was visited time and time again by a *maggid*. It spoke through his mouth, with his vocal cords, as a *maggid* often will, yet it addressed him in the second person and revealed to him Kabbalistic mysteries that he believed himself never to have known.

Caro's *maggid* identified itself as the Mishnah personified. Other Safed authorities—Moses Cordovero and Hayyim Vital, both of whom discussed the *maggidim* as a theoretical issue—supposed they were angels, perhaps created on the spot by the pious actions of the individuals whose bodies they were later to enter.[27]

For Cardozo, the *maggidim* are for the most part deceased saints.[28] The saint in question may be very recently departed. Nathan of Gaza, who died in 1680, was one of the spirit-guides whom Cardozo allotted to his disciples. So was Abraham Yakhini, a Constantinople preacher who became a devoted follower of Sabbatai Zevi (and an admirer of Cardozo) before his death near the end of 1681.[29] But the biblical prophet Samuel was also among the spirit-guides at Cardozo's command. So was Isaac Luria,[30] whom Cardozo several times appointed spirit-guide for one or another of his disciples and then dismissed from that post.

Of all Cardozo's many and varied spirit-friends and contacts, the most baffling and enigmatic is the spirit-guide whom Cardozo calls Roshi. This figure crops up again and again in Cardozo's writings from the 1680s onward. Yet his precise nature remains elusive.

There is perhaps a foreshadowing of Roshi in a strange story that Cardozo had related many years earlier, in 1668,[31] describing the portents he had experienced (in Tripoli) of the coming of Sabbatai Zevi. He was sitting at table one day, he tells us, trying to make sense of three visions that had come to him the preceding night. As he sat lost in thought, his three-year-old daughter Rachel walked into the room—

> and she told me, in the most lucid and astonishing manner,[32] what it was I had been thinking about and how the visions were to be interpreted. And when I said to her, "Who told you all this?" she laughed and said, "Do you not see, Papa, the man above your head?[33] Look! look! he's talking to me!" Then she ran out of the room, and afterward remembered nothing of what she had said.

Roshi literally means "my head," and his subsequent appearance in Cardozo's life is surely related to the mysterious man whom little Rachel saw above Cardozo's head, revealing the deepest secrets of Cardozo's thought.

In the stories about Roshi's appearances from the 1680s and the 1690s, he often functions as Cardozo's *maggid*. He may appear to Cardozo and tell him (or fail to tell him) what is going on in heaven.[34] Cardozo may also attach him to other people, with whom, however, Cardozo is closely connected or identified. In *Israel—Holiness to the Lord*, the Izmir disciple Elijah Kohen functions as Cardozo's stand-in for the performance of the "Mending-rite." His *maggid*, on that occasion, is to be Roshi. The same text explains Roshi as a name for Cardozo himself, in his capacity as Messiah ben Joseph.[35]

When Roshi appears to Cardozo's son Ephraim at the head[36] of the "many" *maggidim* who attend him, he appears to Ephraim in Cardozo's own likeness.[37] Roshi, then, is at some level Cardozo himself. He is not the fleshly Cardozo, however, but rather some split-off, idealized, celestial aspect of him. Perhaps he is that Cardozo who is Messiah ben Joseph, as opposed to the Cardozo who (as we will see) is prepared to deny under oath that he is any such thing. Or perhaps he is yet a different aspect of Cardozo's personality, about which Cardozo normally does not tell us very much.

This is suggested by a curious story, set in 1696–97, of how Cardozo made a final heroic attempt to get a clear answer from the heavenly entities as to whether Sabbatai Zevi was really Messiah or not.[38] The answer turned out to be yes, but that is not the part of the story that concerns us here. What does concern us is an episode in which the supreme angel Metatron descends to talk to Cardozo and then departs. As he goes, Metatron leaves in his place—still talking with Cardozo—Sabbatai Zevi, who wears a turban, and also "Roshi, my spirit-guide," who is "wearing the kind of hat that is called *sombrero*."[39]

Sabbatai Zevi's turban is symbolic of his Muslim identity. Surely the sombrero symbolizes, in a similar way, Roshi's Spanish identity. With his choice of headgear Roshi reveals who he essentially is—namely, *the young Spanish Miguel Cardozo*, whom Abraham Cardozo had left behind him many years before when he sailed off to Venice and became a Jew.

80

6.

Roshi does not seem to have been among the celestial beings who assured Cardozo over and over throughout the summer and autumn of 1681 that Redemption would arrive the following Passover. They were an impressive enough crowd, nonetheless. Sabbatai Zevi was among them. So were the prophet Elijah and "numerous saints in the Academy On High." These spiritual beings spoke the promise in God's name. They wrote their message of salvation on paper, on walls, on Cardozo's forehead.[40]

In the summer of 1681 Cardozo was granted a particularly dramatic sign, not unlike that once given the prophet Samuel (1 Sam 12:16–18). Cardozo prayed that there be a great storm over the Bosporus, such that rain and hail would pour down on the European side at Istanbul. Yet, on the Asiatic side at Uskudar, not a drop was to fall. And so it happened.

The rabbis of Constantinople got wind of these doings. Rumor had it that Cardozo, anticipating Redemption, had abolished the four fasts commemorating the destruction of the Temple. (This was exactly what Sabbatai Zevi had done back in 1666.) Cardozo was later to protest vehemently that it was all a slander. The leaders of the Constantinople community, however, believed the report, and they went for Cardozo's blood.

They excommunicated him. They bombarded him with threats. They wanted (says Elijah Kohen, perhaps with some exaggeration) to bring him before them and smash his head open. They declared his life to be legitimate prey for anyone who might choose to take it.[41] Constantinople became a lion's den for Cardozo, who did not much want to be devoured. He withdrew to Rodosto.

That was where, at the very end of 1681, he received the unsettling news that Sabbatai Zevi's widow was on her way to see him with a proposal of marriage.

Chapter 6
Cardozo
the Wanderer

1.

...right before he died, [Sabbatai Zevi] told his wife that she must seek me out and speak to me of esoteric matters, which should serve me as proof that I am to marry her. When I learned of this, I left Rodosto for Constantinople....[1]

Cardozo was already married, of course.[2] Given his penchant for multiple marriages, this was hardly an obstacle for him or for Esther Zevi. Still, he seems to have been seized by a fit of uncharacteristic shyness.

The thought of performing the ultimate *tiqqun* of lovemaking, in bed with the Messiah's wife, must have seemed more than a little frightening—given, especially, that the Messiah was presumably about to return to this world for the impending Redemption, now only a few months away. Esther herself must have seemed more than a little frightening. Cardozo must have grasped that she had plans of her own for her new Messianic consort and may have intuited that she would be more than his match. The lions' den of Constantinople suddenly seemed a haven.

Esther did not give up quite yet.

> She got to Rodosto three days later....When she did not find me
> there, she was in tears. She sent a courier to Constantinople, to
> ask me whether she might not come there to tell me all that
> the Messiah [Sabbatai Zevi] had enjoined upon her. Or, per-
> haps, I might come to Rodosto, to hear what she had to say?
> For these were matters upon which depended the beginning of
> our Redemption.[3]

Cardozo put her off till after Passover. Redemption would by
then have arrived. There would then be "love and brotherhood,
peace and affection," he wrote to her, quoting a traditional wedding
benediction. In other words, wedding bells were in their future, if
only the lady would have patience.

The lady would not have patience. She left Rodosto, apparently without another word to Cardozo, and went back to
Adrianople. We meet her again a year or so later in her hometown
of Salonica with a new Messianic partner.

2.

Passover arrived on the evening of April 22, 1682. It ended
eight days later. It was a disaster. Of course there was no
Redemption; of course Sabbatai Zevi did not return from the dead
or from beyond the River Sambatyon or from wherever it was he
had gone. All the promises of all the spiritual entities, from Elijah
on down, had come to nothing.

Cardozo was baffled. He was also discredited, humiliated,
dreadfully vulnerable. His life was again in danger. A band of
Jewish vigilantes (according to Elijah Kohen) planned to lynch him
and "throw his carcass into Devils' Valley."[4] More important,
Solomon Galimidi's faith in him was now shattered. There was no
longer any home for him in Constantinople.

He again left the city. This time, he did not stop in Rodosto but traveled on to the Dardanelles, where he seems to have spent the next few years shuttling between Gallipoli and Canakkale.[5]

For Solomon Galimidi, he had a few final words before departing:

> Our Redemption is far off. I am going wherever the spirit takes me. You may believe what you please about the Messiah and the Redemption. But be very careful indeed about the Deity whom I have made known to you, and make sure that you are not seduced from His faith by Yom Tov Romano or others of that ilk.[6]

Galimidi, perhaps touched for the moment by the melancholy sincerity of this plea, promised to keep the Faith.

3.

A bad time now began for Cardozo and his family. There was poverty. There was disease. Once again, as in Izmir, there were deaths. Elijah Kohen can hardly contain his glee as he tells how five of the family died during this period, including Cardozo's "old wife" and her son.[7] Cardozo sent the Galimidis a stream of futile letters, begging their forgiveness and their generosity. These letters—or at least those that Elijah Kohen is pleased to pass on to us—do not show Cardozo at his most dignified. "My daughter Ruhamah died thanks to you," he wrote the Galimidis at one point, "because on the fourteenth day of her illness I wasn't able to buy chicken for her and she died of hunger, and now she is in heaven condemning you."[8] The accusatory whining is repellent. The suffering is real.

There were other, stranger afflictions. On July 5, 1683, Cardozo and several others saw four human-like shapes on the moon.[9] Cardozo recognized three of them as Isaac Luria, Sabbatai Zevi, and Nathan of Gaza. (Nathan had by now been dead for more than three years.) The fourth was a woman.

Cardozo never tells us who the woman was, and, indeed, she vanishes from the story after the very beginning. (Unlike her three companions, she never comes down from the moon.) It seems likely to me that he himself did not know who she was. Yet, thanks to a suggestion of my colleague Professor Lance Lazar, I think we can make a fair guess at her identity.

Seventeenth-century Spain was filled with paintings—visual propaganda for the doctrine of the Immaculate Conception—that showed the Blessed Virgin as Queen of Heaven, *standing on the moon*. (Velazquez did a particularly fine painting of this genre about ten years before Cardozo was born; there are others by Zurburan and Murillo.)[10] It is easy to imagine a tiny Miguel Cardozo standing, open-mouthed with awe, before some artistic representation of the mysterious Lady who rules the night sky.

The image penetrated Cardozo's unconscious. Decades later—when he had come to believe that the Christians' Mary is in fact a supreme she-devil, the demonic counterpart to the Shechinah[11]—the image reemerged in a powerful hallucination. He did not remember or understand its source. It had perhaps become fused in his mind with the image of Esther Zevi, whom Cardozo had no doubt begun to see as a mysterious and tantalizing "queen of the night" who had teased his hopes for a few weeks and then vanished.

The other three entities—the male figures on the moon—are much friendlier and more loquacious. They visit Cardozo in his home. They discuss Kabbalah with him. Only gradually does he come to realize that they are not quite the departed saints they seem to be. Exposed at last, they protest their good intentions. They had taken on the shapes of the deceased holy men in order, out of pure love for Cardozo, to disabuse him of any false beliefs he might happen to hold. They patiently explain that, as Cardozo well knows, "it is the First Cause that decides, of Its own will, who is to be the reigning Deity." Now, sad to say—they tell him—"the sins and disbeliefs of the Jewish people have brought it about that the Deity in Whom you believe, and Whom it is your goal to proclaim the world over, has been stripped of His power."

Cardozo knows by now that he is dealing with demons. It is too late. He cannot get them out of his bedroom. On and on they go in their sweet, sinister tones. Cardozo's God has become helpless, and "that is why you are doomed to a life of harried wandering, deprived of all repose, persecuted and scorned; why you cannot succeed at anything. You have seen that, in YAHVEH's name, you were promised Redemption. Yet that promise turned out to be a fantastic lie. The truth is that it is Samael [Satan] who now holds the power, and that is why the Gentiles dominate the world."

This is a crude, demonic caricature of Cardozo's theology. Later he will explain to himself, in his measured scholastic prose, why it cannot be true, why Samael can *never* become Deity as the real God has.[12] But now the devilish voice speaks with all the authority of the unconscious and the repressed, and Cardozo cannot banish it.

Sabbatai Zevi—or rather, the demon in Sabbatai Zevi's shape—is the one who speaks most powerfully.[13] Was it not Cardozo's God, he asks, who smote Pharaoh, Sennacherib, and Nebuchadnezzar because they had scorned and blasphemed Him? Well now! we shall blaspheme Him worse than any of them—and here the demons spew out a string of vile blasphemies—and if He still has any power, let Him burn us up!

It is not the three demons who get burned up, but Cardozo himself. He is feverish, "gravely ill," as he says, with *fiebre ardiente* ("burning fever"). One of the evil three stands by his sickbed. They will torment him, the demons promise, till he is dead. "For it is our God's pleasure to do to you as the Lord did to Pharaoh."

Eventually they leave. Their parting words, according to one version of the story, are in Spanish: "Gran hakham eres, muncho sabes" ("you are a great sage; you know much").[14] "Off with you to Salonica!" Cardozo cries to the demons, and off to Salonica they go.

This was in July 1683. Before many months had passed, hundreds of Sabbatian believers in Salonica had converted en masse to Islam, and the anguished Cardozo was sure that his demons were behind it.

4.

We cannot be sure precisely what happened in Salonica in 1683.[15] A large proportion of our information on the event is from

Cardozo himself, who mentions it repeatedly, in a tone of pained and baffled outrage, but never gives a clear account of it.

The strange drama had four principal actors. There was Solomon Florentin, one of the most distinguished rabbis of Salonica, who was a believer in Sabbatai Zevi. There was his colleague Joseph Filosoff, who had become Sabbatai's father-in-law. There was Joseph's son, Jacob Filosoff, who was to become better known as Jacob Querido (Jacob the Beloved). There was Querido's sister, Esther Zevi.[16]

Strange stories were later told about Esther and how she had managed at one stroke to make herself sister and mother of a new Messiah.[17] She sequestered herself, it was said, for three days and three nights with her fifteen-year-old brother. When she emerged, she told how her brother had died in the room that they had shared. Sabbatai Zevi had come to her, then, and they had made love, and she had become pregnant with Querido and had borne him anew and had nursed him and raised him till he had grown to be fifteen years old again. Querido had died, in other words, and after three days had been resurrected. He was now the son of Sabbatai Zevi. He was now Messiah ben Joseph.

Visions followed. Filosoff and Florentin saw them. So did others in Salonica. Mysterious beings of light—demons or rebel angels, Cardozo was sure—manifested themselves. The theophany at Mount Sinai, the divine chariot of the prophet Ezekiel—all were seen anew. A new Messianic movement, with Querido at its center, was born. Before many months had passed, the four leaders of the new movement had all converted to Islam, and their followers, who by now numbered in the hundreds, "took the turban" after them.

The news reached Cardozo amid the poverty and misery of his life by the Dardanelles. It left him outraged and appalled. True enough—what the Sabbatians of Salonica had done, in abandoning their Judaism, was hardly different from what Sabbatai Zevi had done in 1666. Cardozo had defended and justified Sabbatai's apostasy. That had been a special act of Messianic self-sacrifice, however. Its purpose had been to *spare* other Jews, by an act of vicarious atonement, from having to live the kind of Marrano nightmare that

Cardozo had fled Spain in order to escape. Now the Salonicans inexplicably had entered into that very same nightmare.

For Florentin and Filosoff, Cardozo felt a kind of baffled pity. How was it possible, he wondered, for two scholars so distinguished to have fallen into Satan's trap? (He was later to imagine that they repented on their deathbeds.) For Querido—"the vile and damnable Querido," he calls him[18]—Cardozo felt mostly rage and loathing. He hated the boy, perhaps because he knew that Querido had become not only an apostate but also a persecutor who had driven rabbis faithful to Judaism into exile in Italy.[19] If Cardozo had also heard the rumors about Querido's habit of sleeping with his followers' wives, the information can hardly have sweetened his feelings for the new young Messiah.

There was perhaps a deeper and more painful grudge, too. Cardozo had once himself had the chance to become Esther Zevi's Messianic consort. Once he had been invited to climb, as it were, into Sabbatai Zevi's nuptial bed. He had hesitated then, and it was all lost. Now this pup—this adolescent *Messiah ben Joseph!*—was in the place where the real Messiah ben Joseph ought to have been. (For who knew what Esther Zevi had done with him in that room, three days and three nights, hidden from every eye but God's?)[20]

Perhaps worst of all, Querido, and not Cardozo, had become the adoptive son of Sabbatai Zevi.

5.

The double trauma of 1682–83—the failed Redemption, the great apostasy—would haunt Cardozo for the rest of his life. He would poke at it and probe it, again and again, the way one pokes with one's tongue at an aching tooth.

In the meantime his "life of harried wandering," of scorn and persecution, dragged on and on. He left the Dardanelles in 1686 and tried to settle in Adrianople (Edirne). He was promptly expelled.[21] Back he went, this time to Constantinople. (He was now almost sixty years old.) Once more he taught the Mystery of

Divinity. He accepted women, now, among his students, and Elijah Kohen is sure that he did this solely in order to seduce them.[22] He performed his *tiqqunim*. He was reconciled with Samuel Galimidi, whose father had died in a gruesome accident while Cardozo was in Gallipoli.[23]

His enemies made his life unpleasant with nasty rumors. The most wounding of these, perhaps because it triggered some of the most shame-filled memories of his past,[24] was that he had never been circumcised. (One woman, evidently insane, became obsessed with Cardozo's foreskin and went through the streets screaming about it to anyone who would listen.)[25] Meanwhile, the Jewish authorities in Constantinople subjected him to an unending stream of abuse and harassment.

Most of the "persecution," as Cardozo calls it, was fairly petty. But it took its toll, and at one point Cardozo decided he had had enough. He closed his doors to his students. All his efforts to teach God's Divinity had yielded him, and them, nothing but persecution and ridicule. From now on he would keep silent and let God do what He pleased. As in Izmir, plague struck. Four of Cardozo's young sons died. As in Izmir, Cardozo saw in this the hand of God. He opened his doors to his students once more. They would never again be closed.[26]

For a time the officials of the "Christian Carabusa"—evidently a corporation of some sort representing European Christians resident in Constantinople—took Cardozo under their powerful wing. On at least one occasion they kept him out of jail.[27]

His relations with them soured. He was accused of having tried, at the instigation of the Venetian Senate, to poison their leader. He had allegedly given the man medicine, which was fed to a dog, which thereupon died.[28] Nothing seems to have come of the accusation, and we may hope that, as Cardozo seems to imply, it was a fabrication by his Jewish enemies. (Elijah Kohen, always eager for any story that might be used against Cardozo, does not even mention it.) Disturbingly, though, Cardozo never actually denies the charge. One comes away with the uneasy feeling that, as

in Tripoli in 1672, he may have allowed himself to get caught up—
to his immense discredit—in the conspiratorial politics of his time.

The last ten years of Cardozo's life are mostly a blur of chaotic
wanderings. He leaves Constantinople in 1696, shadowed by scandal.[29] From there he goes to Rodosto. Daniel Bonafoux invites him
to Izmir, but the local rabbis prevent him from entering.[30] He tries
again to settle in Adrianople. He is again expelled. He goes back to
Rodosto. He drifts back and forth between the island of Chios and
Candia (modern Iraklion) on the island of Crete, and eventually
goes to Alexandria. He supports himself by his medical practice,
which is apparently fairly successful.[31]

He is in his seventies now. His hearing is failing, but his sex
drive, says Elijah Kohen, is as strong as ever.[32] Kohen entertains us
with a string of stories on this theme. All of them are grotesque; all
of them are fairly disgusting. Whether any of them is true, we do
not know.

He writes letters and treatises on the Mystery of Divinity.
Always, until the very end, he writes.

6.

One episode, at once pivotal and emblematic, stands out from
those final years. This was Cardozo's expulsion from Edirne
(Adrianople) in the fall of 1697.[33] He had tried to make his home in
Edirne some months earlier but had run afoul of one of the city's
leading rabbis.

Elijah Kohen's enthusiasm knows no bounds as he pours out
praise upon this rabbi—this pious zealot, this defender of the faith,
this pillar of orthodoxy whose passion for Judaism's purity would
not allow him to tolerate the presence of so foul a heretic as
Cardozo. "A holy guardian-angel," was this rabbi; "his seemly
grace beyond compare, even with purest gold; no mystery, even of
Kabbalah, beyond his capacities…expert in every kind of wisdom;
a man whose words are few, but always true."[34] His name? Samuel
Primo.

We must pause here to ask: Is Kohen being disingenuous, or merely naive? Does he not know that Primo had once been Sabbatai Zevi's personal secretary? Has he never heard of Primo's noxious responsum from the summer of 1666, which promised Sabbatai's Messianic blessing to any thug who might take it upon himself to brutalize an "unbeliever"?[35]

Primo in his later years was still a Sabbatian believer. He did not limit himself to thinking that Sabbatai was Messiah. As far as Primo and like-minded individuals were concerned, Sabbatai was now God Himself. The Blessed Holy One, the God of traditional Judaism, was no longer a figure of any real importance; He had "withdrawn into His root above," and Sabbatai Zevi had become the effective Deity.[36] Primo's religious ideas, and those of Querido and the Salonican apostates, were not much different. What differed was the mask behind which they hid their beliefs. For Querido and his followers, the disguise of choice was a superficial Islam. For Primo, it was traditional Judaism.

The explanation for Kohen's open-mouthed adoration of Primo seems to be this: In writing *Sefer Merivat Qodesh* (the Cardozo biography) Kohen was unwittingly taking part in the tangled sectarian infighting among the Sabbatians. He was young in 1707, when he wrote the book,[37] and doubtless naive. He had no visible reason to hate Cardozo. He was put up to writing the biography by another man, whose grudge against Cardozo was old and deep.

That man's name was Yom Tov Romano. Once, in Constantinople at the beginning of the 1680s, he had been a student of Cardozo's—or at least under Cardozo's influence.[38] But he "backslid," which seems to mean that he moved from Cardozo's orbit into Primo's.[39] Cardozo complains, accordingly, that Romano had "Christianized" his religion.[40] Like Primo, he taught a doctrine of a divine Messiah.

For a time, it would seem, Cardozo saw Romano as a particularly dangerous menace. You must beware, he told Solomon Galimidi in 1682, of being seduced away from God's Faith "by Yom Tov Romano, or others of that ilk."[41] In the years that followed, Romano waged a bitter pamphlet war against Cardozo and his disciples. Cardozo responded in kind. He pointed out to his students, among other damning facts, that the name *Yom Tov Romano* has the same numerical value in Hebrew as does *Esau*. He composed a ferocious prayer for Romano's destruction and sent it to his students, with instructions for them to recite it.[42]

Sefer Merivat Qodesh was Romano's vengeance. It was the last assault in Romano's pamphlet war, waged by proxy, against a man who was now dead. Elijah Kohen actually wrote the book, but it was Romano who encouraged the project and perhaps sponsored it. He supplied Kohen with his information on the Sabbatian movement from the Romano family archive.[43] When the book was completed, Romano wrote the preface.[44]

No wonder, then, that Samuel Primo—Romano's ally and fellow-traveler, and Cardozo's arch-nemesis—appears in *Sefer Merivat Qodesh* as a pure and unblemished saint. He was a shining knight of faith, indeed, who slew the dragon Cardozo in the presence of Edirne's rabbis and community leaders, and the congregation of the children of Israel.

7.

Primo summoned Cardozo twice to appear before him at his *yeshiva*, the institute of higher learning of which Primo was master.[45] The second time, Cardozo came.

The war between the two men had been declared even before their public confrontation. Primo had taken copies of *Abraham's Morn* and had them burned. Another of Cardozo's treatises, *The Lord Is Good to All*, would later go up in flames.[46] No doubt Primo would have been pleased to burn the writer along with his books. But this was impossible. He had to content himself with discrediting and humiliating Cardozo in full public view, and then driving him from the city.

We have accounts of the episode from Kohen and from Cardozo himself.[47] Both agree that a huge throng was in attendance, including all or nearly all the Jewish notables of Edirne. "There thrones were established for judgment," Kohen says pompously,[48] and he adds that Cardozo's judges sat in a semicircle, like the Sanhedrin of old.

Cardozo began his defense on what he evidently supposed to be an assertive note. "I stand in the presence," he thundered, "of a man who considers me to be uncircumcised!" The rumors of his incomplete conversion to Judaism, first spread against him in Constantinople, had followed him to Edirne. They were making his life miserable. He could not lay them to rest, could not get them out of his head. He may have thought that Primo was responsible for circulating them. He now demanded that three circumcisers be selected from the crowd to examine him in a private room. *Then* they would see how false the rumors were.

The outburst seems to have taken Primo aback. Perhaps he had never heard the rumors and had no idea what Cardozo was talking about. Perhaps he had heard them but had not taken them seriously. In either case, he was not interested. He had no intention of allowing his inquisition to be derailed so they could go off and scrutinize this lunatic's genitalia. He answered sternly that it was not the uncircumcision of Cardozo's *flesh* that concerned him but the uncircumcision of his *heart* and of his *lips*. He then returned to his questioning.

Yet Primo himself had difficulty keeping his inquiries above Cardozo's waist. He took particular offense at Cardozo's multiple wives. What a lust-crazed voluptuary we have here! he proclaimed, indicating the seventy-year-old Cardozo. "Care you nothing," he demanded of Cardozo, "for the ban of Rabbenu Gershom?"

Primo was playing to the crowd, of course. He must have known that a Sephardic Jew like Cardozo would have had little reason to govern his life by Gershom of Mainz's ban on polygamy. Cardozo tried to explain, to justify himself. But one of the dignitaries cut him off. "Enough of this talk!"[49] the man roared. Let Cardozo get to the point! Let him produce the books of his so-called wisdom!

Cardozo brought forth his manuscripts. Perhaps he had hoped for this. Perhaps he had imagined that even these blind rabbis could be brought to the truth once they saw his proofs of the Divinity set down on paper. But all they cared about was to hunt through his books for references to Sabbatai Zevi. When they found none, they supposed it was because Cardozo had erased or torn out the crucial passages.

The Ladder of Jacob. The Two-edged Sword. This Is My God.... One after another Cardozo handed over his precious writings to the scrutiny of a court whose presiding judge secretly believed that God had withdrawn from the universe and handed over His power to Sabbatai Zevi. These men had already burned *Abraham's Morn.* At least one of Cardozo's other treatises was soon to follow.

Cardozo fought back as best he could. "You are the adherents and enthusiasts," he cried out, "of a man [Primo] who denies the Torah! I can promise you to bring, within a fortnight, solid proofs from Istanbul that he believes the Messiah to be divine. But me, who believes in God and in Moses His servant, you have repudiated!"[50]

It was useless. Primo was the one with the power in Edirne, not Cardozo. The demons by the Dardanelles had been right: Satan does indeed rule the world. Cardozo was banned from the city. By rabbinical decree all were henceforth prohibited from studying with him. The next morning seven wagons stood by his door,[51] waiting to carry the Cardozos and their belongings back into exile.

It took them a few days to get ready to leave. Cardozo spent much of this time delivering public proclamations of Edirne's doom. God would have His revenge for the way His faithful servant had been treated! All the Jews' houses, all their synagogues, would go up in flames! In the meantime one of Cardozo's wives stationed herself outside Primo's *yeshiva,* shrieking out insults and curses against the tyrant.

It was still no use. None of it was any use. The seven wagons were at last packed. They rumbled off, toward Rodosto.

Cardozo's life of harried wandering had begun once more. No one could imagine how it might end.

Chapter 7
Who Was This Man?

Here lies a doughty Knight,
Who, bruis'd, and ill in plight,
Jogg'd over many a Track
On *Rozinante's* Back....
  —Cervantes, *Don Quixote*

1.

I am no Messiah. But I am the man of whom the Faithful
Shepherd spoke...: "Worthy is he who struggles, in the
final generation, to know the Shechinah, to honor Her
through the Torah's commandments, and to endure
much distress for Her sake."[1]

Cardozo came to the end of his road in 1706. That year, like so
many of its predecessors, was supposed to be a Messianic year.
Forty years would then have elapsed since Sabbatai Zevi had become
an apostate, an event that had taken place when Sabbatai was forty
years old. This was important, because the Jewish people's First
Redeemer, Moses, had fled Egypt at age forty. He had returned forty
years later, to rescue the Israelites from bondage. The life story of the
Last Redeemer (the Messiah) is patterned after that of the First

Redeemer. In 1706, therefore, Sabbatai Zevi might be expected to return from his "flight"—into Islam and afterward into death.[2]

Perhaps anticipating this Messianic denouement, Cardozo had tried a few years earlier to settle in Palestine. The Jews of Jerusalem had kept him from getting much beyond the port at Jaffa. So Cardozo had drifted into Egypt, first Alexandria, later Cairo. He earned his living, in good times, as a physician. In bad times, he was a wandering fortuneteller.[3]

"But Bramblebush"—Elijah Kohen's pet epithet for Cardozo[4]—"did not realize that his day of doom was near; that the time of reckoning was at hand....Criminal! wounds shall wipe him away—and a blow to the inside of the gut—on that day, known to God, when He avenges Himself and His Unity."[5]

Cardozo had a nephew named Shalom, says Kohen, whom he had apprenticed to himself and trained as a doctor. And one day, says Kohen, Cardozo went out to pay a house call on a certain Egyptian official in the company of his nephew and a certain one of his disciples—"Weepingwillow," Kohen calls him—who was also Cardozo's son-in-law.[6] And Cardozo received payment in gold coins, and he "gave only a tiny bit of money to Shalom, while being doubly generous to Weepingwillow." And so they quarreled, and Shalom drew his knife, and he drove it into Cardozo's belly.

"And on the third day Bramblebush died," Kohen gloats, "all thanks to his treachery against God, his claiming that God is something other than what He really is."

He was seventy-nine years old.

2.

Who was this man?

"I am no Messiah," he wrote, a few years before his death—a strange denial, coming from a man who had proclaimed over and over, in speech and in writing, that he was Messiah ben Joseph.

In his last years, he was no longer even a Messiah-bearer, at least, not consistently or with very much conviction. He never quite ceased to believe in Sabbatai Zevi. But his feelings for him had grown tepid. Thirty years earlier, when Cardozo had poured out his Messianic faith before the judges of Izmir, he had allowed himself no doubt "that the true Messiah is Sabbatai Zevi, for whom I am obliged to sacrifice my life."[7] Matters were no longer so clear. One remark or another might slip now from Cardozo's pen, betraying his skepticism. He might complain, for example, that Querido and his followers had not only abandoned the Torah, but had even "taken as Deity a man [Sabbatai Zevi] who is only doubtfully Messiah."[8]

Part of the problem was that the versions of Sabbatianism that Cardozo had kept hearing, from the likes of Querido and Primo, had slowly worn away his trust. Could it be, he found himself wondering, that Sabbatai Zevi had indeed taught these vile heresies? Had Sabbatai become another Jesus the Nazarene, befouling the world with his self-deification? Had Cardozo escaped Christianity, only to fall into the clutches of a new and even worse version of Christianity?

Cardozo eventually managed, with a little help from the Heavenly Academy, to reassure himself that Sabbatai was legitimate Messiah, that he was innocent of the evil doctrines that his followers had spread in his name. Sabbatai even came to visit Cardozo, accompanied by Roshi—Sabbatai in his turban, Roshi in his sombrero—and the three of them chatted for nearly half an hour. Sabbatai confided to Cardozo, in Spanish, his personal opinion of Samuel Primo: "Es un mal hombre."[9]

This was comforting, of course, but Cardozo's disillusionment went deeper. Sabbatai Zevi had utterly failed to do what a Messiah was supposed to do: spread the knowledge of God's Divinity throughout the Jewish public. He might be Messiah, but he had not been very good at the job. Cardozo himself had done better.

Yet Cardozo denies that he is Messiah. He is prepared to swear, most vehemently, that he is *not* Messiah:

> I swear, by the existence of the Blessed Holy One whose name is THE LORD, that *I am not Messiah ben David; nor am I Messiah ben Ephraim. And if I believe that I am Messiah, may God*

never forgive me. And may I have no share in the God of Israel, in this world or the next.[10]

Cardozo wrote these words in his treatise *Ani ha-mekhunneh (I Am the Man They Call...)*, which he composed in his last years, reflecting back on his youth. Is this the same man, we wonder, who wrote the treatise *Israel, Holiness to the Lord*, in which he took completely for granted that he *was* Messiah ben Ephraim?[11] Is he even the same man who wrote the opening words of *Ani ha-mekhunneh*? "I am the man they call...*mem-bet-aleph*," he says there, and it is completely obvious to anyone familiar with Cardozo that *mem-bet-aleph* are the initials of *Messiah ben Ephraim*. (Yet in the very next breath he reverses himself and claims that *mem-bet-aleph* do not stand for *Messiah ben Ephraim* after all, but only...*Michael ben Abraham!*)[12]

The contradictions are not relieved, but rather compounded, by the manner of Cardozo's death. It has a weirdly Messianic quality to it, as though it were foreseen, perhaps even planned, by its victim.

Zechariah, we remember, had uttered a cryptic prophecy that "they shall look upon him whom they have pierced, and they shall mourn for him, as one mourns for an only child" (12:10). The Talmud had understood this mysterious person to be Messiah ben Joseph, doomed to die violently in the course of Redemption.[13] The Hebrew verb *daqaru*, "pierced," can also mean "stabbed"—as Cardozo well knew. A passage that Cardozo wrote, not many years before his death, can accordingly be read as a foreshadowing of that death: "...Messiah ben Ephraim was doomed to worship idols, and to be pierced [or stabbed] in the war of Gog and Magog."[14]

Let us put ourselves in the old man's mind and imagine some of the thoughts that may have occupied his last days. Cardozo knew that he had worshiped idols during his youth in Spain. *That* part of Messiah ben Joseph's doom had already been fulfilled upon him. He knew that, as Messiah ben Joseph, he must be "pierced" in the course of the great conflict of the end-time, the "war of Gog and Magog." Yet he knew also that he was old and soon must die, that the end-time had not yet begun, that the Messianic year 1706 was turning into one more disappointment.

Sabbatai Zevi had not returned to initiate the Redemption. Left to his own devices, Sabbatai Zevi would never return. The burden of setting the redemptive events into motion lay upon Cardozo himself. And so Cardozo, to enact what he was sure was his Messianic destiny, picked a quarrel with a nephew—whom he knew to be hot-tempered and handy with a knife.

3.

So who was this man who said he was Messiah and then swore he was not, and at the end threw away his life that he might die a Messiah's predestined death? In the venerable Kabbalistic text *The Faithful Shepherd*, Cardozo found his own answer to this question:

> Worthy is he who struggles, in the final generation, to know the Shechinah, to honor Her through the Torah's commandments, and to endure much distress for Her sake.[15]

A certain man—so Cardozo interpreted the text—would appear at the end of the Jewish people's exile. Boldly, without fear of any being in heaven or on earth, that man would "struggle to know the Shechinah, and to communicate knowledge of Her to the broad public. For Her sake, moreover, that man will take upon himself much suffering, hardship, persecution."[16] Cardozo said: I am that man.

Cardozo had discovered, many years before in Venice, that a profound and impenetrable mystery shrouded the subject of God's femininity.[17] The rabbis of Venice, questioned about it, were left baffled and speechless. So Cardozo went off to Egypt, his head swirling with doubts, to learn from the great Kabbalists of his generation the solution to Her mystery. But (he wrote, many years later) "nothing they could tell me gave me any relief whatever."[18] Everything that the Kabbalists had said, supposedly to exalt the Shechinah, in fact disparaged Her.

The Shechinah is indeed a divinity, the Kabbalists had assured Cardozo. God has ten *sefirot*, and the tenth and final *sefirah*, *Malkhut*, is the female part of Him. It is this *sefirah* that the rabbis call by the name Shechinah. All ten *sefirot*, the Shechinah included, are "divine in the full sense of the word; because they cling to and are united with the Deity."

For the young Cardozo, this answer was no answer at all.[19] It reduced the Shechinah from a female Divinity who "couples with the Blessed Holy One as a woman couples with her husband," to a single *sefirah*, a mere vessel for divinity—one vessel among ten, at that.

Cardozo set off on his own to find a way to conceive the Shechinah as a full Divinity, no less God than Her Husband, the Blessed Holy One. Eventually, he thought he had found it. He came to believe that the Shechinah is God in Spirit, God in body, just like the Blessed Holy One. She and He emerge from the same divine Root. She and He, together, are One God, nourishing themselves, in their union, from the First Cause that shines within them. They are distinguishable, yet they are One, much as we humans are distinguishable as mankind and womankind, yet together are one humankind.[20]

Everyone had known the male God. The Jews of Cardozo's time, along with the Muslims, had made the dreadful mistake of confusing Him with the First Cause, but at least they had preserved the recollection that there *was* a male Deity. The female God had been disparaged, abandoned, misunderstood. She had been made "small" by human sin, reduced to only one of the ten *sefirot* that ought to constitute Her body. The other nine *sefirot* had been taken over by the demons, who fattened themselves off Her body and made themselves powerful through Her light.[21] She had been left, by human ignorance and inaction, to languish in Her "smallness."

Knowing all this, what must Cardozo do? He must rescue the Shechinah and defend Her. He must proclaim Her greatness to the Jewish people. He must restore Her to Her proper glory: dedicate his life and his *tiqqunim* to "enlarging" Her, such that She become "a complete Person, fit to couple with Her Husband and fully to unite with Him."[22]

In his famous description of a certain would-be knight-errant, a few generations before Cardozo, Miguel de Cervantes has his hero reflect:

> ...that a Knight-Errant without a Mistress, was a Tree without either Fruit or Leaves, and a Body without a Soul. Should I, said he to himself, by good or ill Fortune chance to encounter some Giant, as 'tis common in Knight-Errantry, and happen to lay him prostrate on the Ground, transfix'd with my Lance...would it not be proper to have some Lady, to whom I may send him as a Trophy of my Valour? Then when he comes into her Presence, throwing himself at her Feet, he may thus make his humble Submission....[23]

Did the elderly Cardozo see himself as having been a knight-errant, of sorts, who had dedicated himself to the Shechinah as his "Lady"? For Her sake, he has endured much distress. In Her honor, he has observed the Torah's commandments. The *tiqqunim* he has performed (a Kabbalistic counterpart to knightly combat?) were done for Her benefit.[24]

Eventually, thanks to these *tiqqunim*, She will be free and whole. Eventually, in the Messianic time that Cardozo has struggled to inaugurate, the vanquished Gentile nations will come into the Shechinah's presence, throwing themselves at Her feet, making their humble submission to Her Divinity.[25]

4.

None of this, of course, ever happened. The lifelong crusade of the Shechinah's knight ended sadly, in futility and failure. Cardozo died at the end, to no effect.

His death, in itself, is not particularly sad. We all die—we are lucky if we live as long as Cardozo did—and very few of us accomplish anything by the act of dying. But it is melancholy to see the entire life of a gifted and brilliant man dedicated to an enterprise founded on delusion.

Cardozo's deludedness did not consist, essentially, in his belief in Sabbatai Zevi. His Sabbatian Messianism, important as it was to him, did not lie at the center of his convictions. His tragic, incorrigible blindness lay in his absolute trust in the Kabbalah. He would not allow himself to see that the scholastic principles of Kabbalah are something different from the laws of empirical reality. He would not abandon the fantasy that Kabbalistic ritual can control events in the real world.

Pondering Cardozo's life, one is tempted to compare him not only with Don Quixote, but, by way of contrast, with Solomon Maimon (1754–1800). Maimon was born in Poland, yet left his native land to resettle in Germany, there to become an "enlightened" Jewish philosopher. Like Cardozo, he was much attracted in his youth to the Kabbalah and thrilled by the accomplishments that Kabbalah promised to make possible. Accordingly, he learned rituals for making himself invisible, and, having performed them,

> believed with all confidence that I was now invisible. At once I hurried to the *Bet Hamidrash*, the Jewish academy, went up to one of my comrades, and gave him a vigorous box on the ear. He was not indolent, and returned the blow with interest....Sorrowfully I was obliged to give up entirely the hope of making myself invisible.[26]

Cardozo, unlike Maimon, never gave up the hope of using Kabbalistic magic to accomplish impossible feats. He therefore poured away his life, and the lives of his family and his followers, into what we can recognize as an unending string of futilities.

Was Cardozo, then, a lesser man than Maimon—less courageous, less honest with himself? Before we make this judgment, let us recall: Maimon's sense of reality had not been warped and attenuated, as Cardozo's had, by a childhood of deception, concealment, and terror in the dismal shadow of the Spanish Inquisition.

5.

Cardozo was forgotten, but not quite immediately. He remained important enough, the year after he died, to have a biography written about him. This is impressive. It is not made any less impressive by the fact that the guiding principle of the biography is relentless, mind-numbing hatred for its subject, and that its only effect was to befoul the dead man's memory.

None of Cardozo's books was printed during his lifetime or for more than a century and a half after his death. It is not clear whether he himself wanted them to be printed. In 1713, his disciples tried to publish *Abraham's Morn* in Amsterdam. Their effort accomplished nothing, except to provoke the rabbis to a fresh burning of Cardozo's manuscripts.[27] One of Cardozo's writings, *The Mystery of Faith*, appeared in print the following year. Ironically, nobody knew that Cardozo had written it. He had passed it off, all too successfully, as the work of Sabbatai Zevi.[28]

In 1713 and 1714, much of the Jewish world was convulsed by a controversy surrounding the figure of Nehemiah Hayon, a peripatetic and somewhat disreputable preacher and Kabbalist who created a scandal with his Kabbalistic publications.[29] It is not easy to get a clear picture of what the scandal, or the controversy, was about. Hayon's enemies repeatedly accused him of being a disciple and continuator of Cardozo, and, indeed, the ideas in Hayon's writings often have a very Cardozan ring to them.[30] But Hayon himself preferred, once the brickbats and then the excommunications had begun to be thrown about, to distance himself from the man who had inspired his thought.[31]

The Hayon controversy soon faded. The memory of Cardozo faded with it. Who, after all, would have cared to keep Cardozo or his ideas alive? The orthodox traditionalists detested him. In his ideas of Redemption, indeed, he had foreshadowed the eighteenth-century Jewish emancipation.[32] But the leaders of the emancipation could have had little use for this Kabbalist, who not only saw the core of religious devotion in the most bizarre, magic-style *tiqqunim*, but who hammered across in every one of his writings the unwelcome truth that the God of Judaism and the God of philosophy cannot be the same.

Yet one circle of admirers did preserve—indeed, venerate—Cardozo's name and some of his teachings. These were the Dönmeh, the descendants of the apostates of Salonica, the followers of Querido, who had abandoned Judaism for Islam in 1683 and whom Cardozo cursed and despised until the day of his death.

The Dönmeh sect survives today in modern Turkey. It is the last living offshoot of Sabbatian Judaism, preserved intact, under a thin veneer of Islamic practice, for more than three hundred years after the sect's founders imitated their Messiah by "donning the turban" of Islam.[33] It was these sectarians who remembered and revered not only Sabbatai Zevi, but also his partner-Messiah, a man named Abraham Michael Cardozo. It was they—these mosque-attending children of the Salonican apostates—who remembered and cherished the most fundamental of the teachings to which Cardozo had dedicated his life: that it is the Divine Androgyne, and not the First Cause, who is the true God of Israel.[34]

6.

Shall we say Cardozo was a thinker ahead of his time? Quite the contrary. Like Don Quixote, he was an unusual and striking figure at least in part because he was an archaic figure. He normally gives the impression of being anywhere from seventy to one hundred years behind his times. This is not to say that he was narrow or insular. His mind and his spirit were by no means confined within the boundaries of Judaism. Given his life history, there is no way they could have been. He was a cosmopolitan intellectual, very much part of the wider world. Only, he belongs to the wrong century. Cardozo's "wider world" was that of the 1500s, not the 1600s.[35]

It is not easy to think of men or women, in Cardozo's time or in our own, who are quite like him. Yet, if we had to think of some individual close to his own period with whom he might be compared, surely our minds would run toward the enigmatic *magus* of Elizabethan England, John Dee.[36]

Like Cardozo, Dee was a powerful, original, and unconventional thinker. Like Cardozo, Dee combined a brilliant, rational intellect with fantastic credulity. Like Cardozo, Dee put his trust in magic as a solution to human problems. Like Cardozo, Dee treated the world of ghosts and demons and angels as though it were as real as the ordinary human world, and in most ways more important. If Dee and Cardozo had been contemporaries, we might take the two of them as symptomatic of a peculiar trend among the finer minds of their time. Yet Dee was born in 1527, exactly one hundred years before Cardozo, and he died in 1608, ninety-eight years before Cardozo's death.

7.

If Cardozo cannot be claimed as a thinker *ahead* of his time, it is beyond question that he was *out of step* with his time. He moved from city to city, from culture to culture, alien in them all. He did not fit with the religion in which he grew up, nor with the religion to which he converted and which for the rest of his life received all his dedication and loyalty. His perspective is always that of the perceptive outsider, thinking through old issues afresh. It is in this, Cardozo's unconventionality, that his enduring importance lies.

Out-of-step people, as Don Quixote's admirers will recognize, often have insights that those who are in step tend to miss. For his own time, Cardozo may have been something of an anachronism, peculiar and quaint. At the end of the twentieth century, we may often find his thoughts and his pains and his spiritual conflicts mirroring our own. They do so in ways that are startling and sometimes healing.

Do we sometimes look around us and see God as helpless or comatose, and the world ruled by Satan? Do we find ourselves yearning for God's recovery, for His rebirth, and, through that, for our own recovery and rebirth?

ABRAHAM MIGUEL CARDOZO

Do we find ourselves identified, unbreakably, with a religious tradition, yet alienated from the people who ought to be our fellow-believers? Does this alienation extend, at times, to the content of the tradition, and we yearn for a way to redefine that content or to see it in fresh perspective?

When we look within ourselves, do we sometimes have a sense of some inner, personal destiny that we can barely define, in which we believe only intermittently and hesitantly, and yet that we can deny only at the cost of being false to our nature?

In these respects, and in others, Cardozo's intuitive perceptions—and his dedication to pursuing his perceptions wherever this might lead him—seem often like a familiar face, unexpectedly glimpsed.

"You must not be astonished," says Cardozo—in the treatise in which he speaks of the impending rebirth of God—"to find us using the language of resurrection in connection with the [divine] vessels of the World of Emanation."

> Our ancient rabbis have ordained that we are to recite the blessing of Him "who resurrects the dead" when we see a beloved friend after a year's absence, even though what is involved is neither death nor resurrection, but only delightful surprise. Similarly, now that God's faith is coming to be revealed, we must give thanks as though we had come back to life, and as though God, too, were being resurrected among us....[37]

In meeting Cardozo, at the dawn of the twenty-first century, we may easily feel as though we were seeing an old, long-absent friend.

Blessed be He who resurrects the dead.

Part Two
CARDOZO SPEAKS

Chapter 8
Scenes from
the Youth of a
Maverick Theologian

"I Am the Man They Call..."[1]

I am the man they call, at times, *mem-bet-aleph*, which are the [Hebrew] initials of *Michael ben Abraham*. At other times I am called *aleph-mem-koph: Abraham Michael Cardozo*.[2] I am of the Marranos of Spain. I was born in the town of Rio Seco, which means "dry river."

Our blessed God, in His grace, gifted me with knowledge and a formidable memory. In consequence, I was able to engage in any study and to master any book. When I was six years old, my parents made known to me that I was a Jew. When I was twelve, difficult problems presented themselves to my mind. I would wander about the countryside, meditating, seeking God. I took to reading the Scriptures in Latin, despite the tremendous danger that this entails everywhere in Spain.

I had found written in the books of Cadmus and of Hermes,[3] who lived before the Torah was revealed—and, subsequently, in all the books of the Greeks, the descendants of Japheth and of Shem as well—that *the First Cause has no name whatever. It has no charac-teristic, nor is there any epithet that is suitable for It.* All the world's sages and philosophers, it seemed, were in agreement on this point.

I thus began to have my doubts about religion, and I posed to my father the following question:

> You affirm, do you not, that the First Cause has no name? Surely it is something quite evident, proven conclusively, that the Infinitely Simple can have no name or epithet? Well, then, how do you make sense of the fact that the Torah, the Prophets, and the Holy Writings all call the First Cause by the name YAHVEH and by other names and epithets as well? He Himself told Moses that He has a name: "This is My Name for ever" [Exod 3:15].

To which my father responded:

> The very passage you quote, actually, proves that the First Cause has *no* name. For, if It had one, Noah's descendants would necessarily have known it. So would Abraham and all his offspring. The name of the First Cause, indeed, would have been common knowledge, familiar to all human beings. Moses would have had no need to ask what it was. What Moses wanted to know was this: Suppose the Israelites were to ask him, "What is His name?" What should he say to them?
>
> He had learned by oral tradition from his father Amram, without having any textual authority for it, that the God of Abraham, Isaac, and Jacob is named YAHVEH. However, being a great expert in every branch of wisdom, Moses thought that the First Cause has no name. His father's tradition, that Its name is YAHVEH, could not mean that that is Its name in the strict sense of the word, that is, something unique to the particular defining essence of the First Cause. [YAHVEH] must, rather, be a sort of remote epithet, to be used as an indicator when one wants to allude to the First Cause or talk about It.
>
> God answered Moses that "My name is YAHVEH. This is My name for ever," He said, indicating thereby that "I am He who brings [*mehavveh*] all things into existence."[4] "This is how one makes mention of Me, in all generations": it is an indica-

tor, which "people shall use in all generations to make allusion to Me." The name, consequently, does not relate to God's essence. It is simply an epithet, an indicator used to designate Him, and Him alone.

And, with that, I was satisfied.

Why, you may ask, did I put myself to all this trouble? Let us grant (you say) that all the Gentiles, all the sages of this world, have believed that the First Cause has no name—and yet the Torah tells us that He does! The human intellect, with its human reasonings (you say), has no ability to set aside the words of God. Why, then, did I not simply put my faith in the Torah?

We know—we can take for granted—that there can be no contradiction between Truth, on the one hand, and our pure Torah on the other, inasmuch as it *is* the Truth. We call by the name *Truth*, moreover, any doctrine that is solidly grounded and has been convincingly demonstrated by way of Reason. If, therefore, anything be found in the Torah that contradicts the Truth known to us through rational demonstration, we must interpret the Torah's words in such a way that reason's Truth remains intact.[5]

The Torah says that "the Lord went down," that "He went up," that "He repented Himself." It talks about "the eyes of the Lord" and "the ears of the Lord" and "the finger of God," and so on and so forth. Short of heresy, we cannot take such passages literally, for Reason teaches conclusively, as does our true tradition, that God neither undergoes change nor possesses limbs. We must suppose, rather, that the Torah employs human expressions.

The same applies to our present case. By a thousand proofs do we know that the First Cause has no name. We *must*, therefore, interpret the Torah in such a way that this Truth is not abandoned.

I came afterward to the city of Leghorn.[6] I learned Scripture, Mishnah, and Gemara. My teachers were the flawless scholars Rabbis Abraham Valensi, Samuel Aboab, and Moses Zacuto.

In the course of studying the Bible commentators, the Geonim, and the midrashim, I saw how our ancient rabbis interpreted the biblical passage, "When they shall say to me, What is His name? what am I then to tell them?" [Exod 3:13]:

> Do you seek to know My name? In accord with what I do, so am I called. At times I am *El*, at other times *Elohim*. When I have mercy on My world, I am called *YAHVEH*, for the name *YAHVEH* specifically designates the divine Attribute of Mercy.[7]

"Well spoke my father!" I said when I had read this. He was right: the First Cause has no name. Even the name YAHVEH, it seemed, did not correspond to the divine essence. It was only an epithet, corresponding to a specific action, an indicator, special to God and used for the purpose of speaking about Him.

I subsequently began my study of Gemara. I found there, in tractate *Berakhot*, statements that left me appalled: that God prays, for example, that He wears phylacteries, that He studies the Torah and performs the commandments.[8]

At that time, a certain monk in the city of Venice preached a sermon in which he challenged all the scholars of the *yeshiva* to tell him the true nature of the God of Israel. He propounded the problem of the Shechinah. Is She a created being? he asked. (For such was the opinion of Saadiah Gaon in his *Book of Beliefs* in the section treating of the divine unity, of Ibn Migash and of Maimonides in his *Guide to the Perplexed*, and of many other scholars, all of one accord.)[9] He opened all these books and read aloud from them before us and before the Christians.

But he went on: Nachmanides rejects this view, in his commentary on the Torah portion *Vayyiggash*,[10] affirming that the Shechinah is not a created being but rather a Creator. Countless arguments have been offered, by countless scholars, proving that *this* was the real teaching of Moses.

Well then! it must be that we do not truly know God. For let us say that the Shechinah is a created being. We then commit idolatry when we prostrate ourselves to Her in the prayers of the

'Amidah.[11] But suppose She is a deity? We then have *two* gods: the Blessed Holy One, and the Shechinah.

[The monk] went on to sharpen this dilemma, with arguments solidly grounded in the teachings of our ancient sages. And there was no one, among all the rabbis of Venice, who could answer him.

My head swirled. I found myself once again caught in a web of doubts. To escape them, to find for myself some kind of spiritual equilibrium, I set out for Egypt. There I spent five years. I wanted medicine to heal this wound of mine, and I sought it from Rabbi Hayyim Kohen, from Rabbi Iskandrani, and from Rabbi Samuel Vital, the son of Rabbi Hayyim Vital. There, too, I found the aged pietist Rabbi Benjamin Halevi.[12]

To put the matter in a nutshell: *nothing they could tell me gave me any relief whatever....*

> [Disappointed in his teachers, Cardozo turns to books of Kabbalah. There he finds confirmation of his belief, that names and qualities are utterly incommensurate with the First Cause. He also finds hints that the God whom these names designate is not the First Cause, but something emanated from It, who incarnates Himself within the Kabbalistic *sefirot* "like a soul within a body."]

Once I had discovered these preliminaries, I applied myself continually to the project of knowing the God of Israel: recognizing Him, making Him known to others. Through unceasing investigation, I would discharge my duty [to seek knowledge of God], and I would enter into the chambers of wisdom.

I pored over the words of our ancient sages: the *Sifra*, the *Sifrei*, the *Mekhilta*.[13] I pored over the wisdom of the early Kabbalists and of the more recent ones as well. I did not leave the study of the Zohar by day or by night—till God, in His grace, granted me to understand the Mystery of the Unity of His Shechinah. I knew truly then that God is One and His Name One,[14] and that He is *our* God and not the God of the Gentiles....

I returned, moreover, to my reading of the Gentile books, for my brother [Isaac] had six thousand books in the city of Venice. I learned that the Chaldeans wrote about the loftiness of the First Cause, yet had nothing but contempt for the God of Abraham….All the Gentiles [of antiquity] believed that the First Cause is the Supreme Deity, that through Its will It exalts some god or other to a rank above the other gods, and, correspondingly, some earthly king or another to a rank above all the others.

We, however, who are God's servants, holding fast to His truth, know the following to be true:

—that God is continually and eternally graced with effluence from the First Cause;

—the He is God of gods and Lord of lords, through the will of the First Cause (which is absolutely Simple and has no second, inasmuch as It is Its Will and Its Will is Itself);

—that it is *God* who grants dominion to all the gods of the nations, who uplifts and degrades all the celestial princes, who gives power to all earthly monarchs and grants dominion over the world to whomever He pleases….

[Cardozo advances a few of his standard proofs that the true God is a being inferior to the First Cause, who requires "blessing"—that is, effluence—from the First Cause. God requires, moreover, human assistance in procuring that "blessing."[15] The medieval Jewish philosophers, like Maimonides, went dangerously wrong when they supposed that He is identical with the First Cause.]

It follows that Maimonides was quite mistaken [in that he identified God with the First Cause, and consequently] was compelled to embrace the shocking doctrine that the Shechinah is a created being rather than a deity.[16]

When the Bible says that "Israel shall spend many days without a true God" [2 Chr 15:3] and that "the wisdom of its sages shall perish and the perceptions of its enlightened men shall become hidden" [Isa 29:14], it is prophesying of Maimonides and all his sort—who lived after the time of the Geonim. It is *not* speaking of the Tannaim, the Amoraim, or the Geonim.[17] All these men knew God truly. They recorded their knowledge in texts open and esoteric, presenting their theological observations in a scattered fashion, such that God's Mystery would become known to those who fear Him, close to the time of the End. For thus, at the End of Days, would they begin to seek out that which they had once rejected.

We must now respond to an objection that some raise against us on the basis of a rabbinic passage:

> Four individuals have arrived, on their own, at a knowledge of God: Abraham, Job, Hezekiah, and King Messiah.[18]

—*Four*, and not five.

We are thus compelled to admit that this deity whom I reveal is *not* truly the deity that was recognized by Abraham, Job, and Hezekiah, and that will in future time be proclaimed by King Messiah to the Jewish people and to the entire world, after he shall have recognized Him on his own. It would indeed seem to follow, from the rabbis' words, that no one will recognize God at the end of the exile until the Redeemer comes.

Or, alternatively, that I am the Messiah.

I should like to ask these critics: Suppose Messiah ben Joseph should come first [before Messiah ben David]?[19] Will he recognize the Creator, or will he not recognize Him? If they say, "he will not recognize Him," then it appears that the Jewish people will be redeemed without having any knowledge of God. This is in contradiction to all the Jewish sages, who say that we will not have Redemption until we begin to know the Lord. But suppose they say: "He must necessarily recognize Him"—then, lo and behold! there are five.

We may therefore resolve this problem by supposing that the rabbis were speaking of whichever Redeemer should arrive first, or, perhaps, the two Messiahs are considered as one. This is why people take me to be Messiah ben Ephraim, in accord with what I say: in order that this God [that I preach] may be true.

ABRAHAM MIGUEL CARDOZO

Yet I swear, by the existence of the Blessed Holy One whose name is THE LORD, that *I am not Messiah ben David, nor am I Messiah ben Ephraim.*
And if I believe that I am Messiah, may God never forgive me.
And may I have no share in the God of Israel, in this world or the next.

Chapter 9
Defending the
Fallen Messiah

INTRODUCTION

1.

The late 1660s were a bad time for the Sabbatian faithful. Their Messiah was a professing Muslim. Early attempts to deny that fact had been exposed as wishful thinking. Their prophet, Nathan of Gaza, had become a wanderer. Episodically, he found himself at the receiving end of interrogations by rabbinic tribunals, in places like Ipsola and Venice. "Time after time," Cardozo wrote, "was he put to the test....It was discovered each time that there was no truth to his dreams or his speeches...for not one of his predictions came true."[1] Rumor had it that he was dead.

The rabbinic court at Izmir, meanwhile, circulated a lengthy epistle demonstrating that Sabbatai Zevi was a vile scoundrel and the "prophet" Nathan a fraud. Some time early in 1669, the Jews of Tripoli—where Cardozo was then living—received their copy. In June 1669,[2] Cardozo stepped forward to defend the faith.

Cardozo had, by this time, plenty of opportunity to rehearse his arguments. He had earlier set them forth, in much shorter and rougher form, in a Hebrew letter preserved for us in Jacob

Sasportas's collection of documents on the early Sabbatian movement, *Zevi's Fading Flower*.[3] Cardozo apparently wrote this letter some time in the spring of 1668.[4] Sasportas assumed that the intended recipient was Cardozo's brother Isaac and that this letter constitutes Abraham's answer to a "witty," jocular letter he had received from his brother earlier that spring, in which Isaac had "made a great joke of him, his dreams, and all that he said."[5] The internal evidence of Abraham's Hebrew letter, however, does not support Sasportas's assumption, and it seems at least as likely that it was a circular letter, intended for several of Cardozo's admiring correspondents.[6]

Cardozo *did* write his brother a letter—appropriately, in Spanish—several months later, in October 1668.[7] Here the tone is entirely different. Cardozo is no longer haughty, self-assured, and condescending, as he is in the Hebrew letter. Instead, he is haughty, vituperative, and abusive. As might be expected, he does not much appreciate his brother's jokes at his expense, or the reminders of how in his youth he had "played guitars, sang *villancicos*, and composed comedies, and that it was only through the merit of my fathers that I didn't disgrace them completely."[8]

Both of the letters of 1668, the Hebrew and the Spanish, repeat many of the same arguments for the Messiahship of the "Man Profaned," as Cardozo calls Sabbatai Zevi. Both may be seen as rough drafts for Cardozo's masterpiece of Messianic propaganda: *The Epistle to the Judges of Izmir*.

2.

In its structure and its argumentation, the *Epistle* is lucid, methodical, and compelling. In its tone, it is calm, reasonable, and conciliatory. Cardozo begins by professing the deepest respect for the "judges of Izmir." They are absolutely right, he says: Sabbatai Zevi *has* done foul deeds. They are right again: Nathan of Gaza is not a prophet.

The Bible, after all, tells us how we are to know the true prophet, the true messenger of the Lord. A prophet could be expected to perform a "sign or wonder," an evidentiary miracle that would vouch for his prophethood (Deut 13:2–3). As we learn from Maimonides, this evidentiary miracle does not have to be some dramatic alteration of the course of nature. A fulfilled prophecy is sufficient to demonstrate a prophet's genuineness. An unfulfilled prophecy, by contrast, will prove the prophet is false. Such an unfulfilled prophecy "is the word the Lord has not spoken. The prophet has spoken it in deliberate rebellion. You must not fear him" (Deut 18:21–22).[9]

Nathan obviously fit into this latter category. His prophecies, always of imminent redemption, went wrong with monotonous regularity. Cardozo admits forthrightly that Nathan is no prophet in any sense that the writer of Deuteronomy would recognize. "Unbelieving" readers of his *Epistle* must have been disarmed by this admission—which, it would have seemed, cuts the ground out from under all Sabbatian belief. Only later would they realize how cunningly the concession had been made.

When Sabbatai Zevi had first appeared on the horizon at the end of 1665, his advocates declared that the four fasts commemorating the destruction of the Temple were abolished, turned into festivals. After all, that was what the prophet Zechariah (8:19) had said would happen when the Redemption came. The gravest of these fasts, that of the Ninth of Av (which can fall anywhere from July 14 to August 13), was turned into a celebration of the Redeemer's birthday: "the Feast of Consolations." In the heady days of 1666, Cardozo had joined in making the fasts into holidays. Not any more. "Not merely do I believe, I *know* that you have correctly admonished us to maintain our holy Torah and the words of our blessed sages by observing the fasts....I have myself resumed that practice."

If Sabbatai Zevi has split the Jewish community into traditionalists and innovators, Cardozo implies, he himself is solidly in the traditionalist camp. He stands shoulder to shoulder with the "judges of Izmir." It is as their ally and partner, in the defense of Torah and tradition, that he undertakes to clear up a few of their misapprehensions about "the momentous event that has occurred in our time."

3.

The *Epistle* may reasonably be divided into three parts. (These are my divisions and my titles, not Cardozo's.) The first is the *argument*: a careful step-by-step demonstration of what is to be expected of the Messiah, summed up under six headings, followed by proof that Sabbatai Zevi perfectly fits the profile sketched by the ancient Jewish prophets and rabbis. The second is *testimony* to Cardozo's own experiences with the supernatural, which he represents as the essential ground for his personal conviction that "the true Messiah is Sabbatai Zevi, for whom I am obliged to sacrifice my life." Of course, his readers must take his word for all that he says in this section, but they have surely already been persuaded by the rational argument that has preceded the testimony. The third part (omitted from the translation) is a string of afterthoughts: a miscellany of topics that do not fit easily into the tightly organized structure of parts one and two.

Nearly half the *Epistle* is devoted to the first step of the argument: the six "characteristic markers" of the Messiah, which Cardozo documents exhaustively from biblical and rabbinic sources. (It is indicative of Cardozo's care and patience in building his structure that he does not so much as mention Sabbatai Zevi until after his demonstration of the "characteristic markers" is complete.) We learn from this demonstration that the Messiah (1) must be an ordinary human being; (2) must be humiliated, tormented, and abused; (3) must perform deeds that are strange and dreadful; (4) must become profaned, after having once been holy; (5) must *not* be revealed to the world through the agency of a "prophet by consensus" (a person, that is, who is acknowledged as prophet by the consensus of the Jewish people, and whose words must therefore be regarded as authoritative).[10]

To these five criteria—of which all but the first would have seemed entirely fantastic to most Jews of Cardozo's time, or indeed of any time—Cardozo adds what he thinks of as a sixth "marker": we are under a religious obligation to believe in the Messiah, even before we have certain knowledge that he is the Messiah.

With the last three of the five criteria, we see where Cardozo was leading with his opening concessions to the "judges of Izmir." Sabbatai Zevi has indeed, *as they have said*, done awful things. This is because he is the Messiah, and, as Cardozo now demonstrates, this is the Messiah's preordained fate. For this same reason, he has become "profaned." Once a Jew, he is now a Muslim. He would not be the Messiah otherwise. Nathan of Gaza is no prophet, *cannot* have been a prophet because, if he were a prophet in the proper biblical sense of the word, the man whom he announced could not possibly have been the Messiah. In other words, *all the time the "judges of Izmir" thought they were proving that Sabbatai Zevi could not be the Messiah, they were in fact proving very effectively that he is the Messiah.*

4.

The Messiah must suffer. This is the core of Cardozo's argument. We will not forget, as we read it, that Cardozo was brought up within a different faith, which obviously and demonstratively claimed a suffering Messiah.

Almost since the very beginning of Christianity, believers in the Crucified Lord had drawn support from a mysterious prophecy in the Book of Isaiah (52:13—53:12). In cryptic language, the prophet tells of a "servant" of God who was "crushed on account of our iniquities…and through his wound we found healing…and the Lord inflicted upon him the sin of us all." The ancient rabbis (the sages of the Talmud and midrash) normally ignored this passage, perhaps because of the Christians' fondness for it. Challenged, they might reply that the "servant" was in fact a collective representation of the Jewish people, which suffers dispersion for the benefit of the nations of the world.[11] This position became, in the Middle Ages, the normative Jewish interpretation of Isaiah 53.

121

Cardozo will have nothing to do with this so-called Jewish interpretation. It is an innovation of modern writers, he tells us, who are too eager to ward off Christian thrusts—and also, perhaps, "to show off their own superlative acuity." On this subject, he affects a pose of starchy orthodoxy. Will anyone refuse the (alleged) consensus of the ancient rabbis, that Isaiah 53 speaks of the Messiah?[12] "Well then: let us ask this fellow why he believes in Isaiah at all!" We believe in the prophets, in the last analysis, on the authority of the rabbis. The rabbis' interpretations of the prophets' words, therefore, must also be taken as authoritative.

Does Cardozo protest too much? Is he distancing himself here from the Christian faith of his childhood, which nonetheless has profoundly influenced his understanding, not only of Isaiah 53, but of the entire subject of the Messiah?[13] Sasportas, passing judgment on Cardozo's letter of spring 1668, insists that Cardozo's thinking is saturated with Christianity, and we have seen numerous examples in the preceding chapters of how very right Sasportas was.

Writing in February 1668, Nathan of Gaza had interpreted Isaiah 53:5 in a way similar to Cardozo's.[14] Nathan barely touches on the idea that Cardozo made his central theme, that the Messiah of Isaiah 53 suffers in order to atone for the sins of the Jewish people, and it seems very likely that Cardozo's Christian upbringing is responsible for the difference. Yet, in exploring the roots of Cardozo's doctrine of the suffering and "profaned" Messiah, we must not neglect an essential Jewish source, albeit one that shows its own traces of Christian influence. This is the Kabbalistic text called *The Faithful Shepherd (Ra'ya Mehemna)*, written by an unknown person early in the fourteenth century and incorporated into the Zohar.

The Faithful Shepherd of the title is Moses, who is a prominent speaker in the text. So is the prophet Elijah, and the second-century sage Rabbi Simeon ben Yohai. This last individual, as we saw in chapter 2, had been the central character of the Zohar. His exegetical and theosophical conversations with other Palestinian rabbis had been the Zohar's staple material. In *The Faithful*

Shepherd, which was evidently written as an imitation and continuation of the Zohar, the action takes place in the "Heavenly Academy," and Simeon ben Yohai, now deceased, meets and exchanges ideas with the greatest figures of biblical antiquity and with God Himself.[15]

The pertinent passages from *The Faithful Shepherd* are translated among the Background Texts to this chapter. In these texts, all the speakers—Elijah, Simeon ben Yohai, Moses himself—take for granted that Moses is the Suffering Servant of Isaiah 53. He suffers in that he is buried outside the Holy Land (Deut 34:6), in the unhallowed realms of sin and profanation. It is not, of course, for his own sin that Moses suffers. "'He was profaned on account of our sins' [Isa 53:5].[16] Through your burial, you were made profane on account of the sin and the iniquity of the Jewish people." By this profanation, this willingness to be cut off from the land of Torah, Moses brings healing to the Jewish people. More specifically, he saves, or at least attempts to save, the future Messiah ben Joseph from the profanation and bloody death that are his own destiny.

"He was profaned"? Christian readers of Isaiah 53 will perhaps be surprised by this translation of verse 5. The Hebrew word *meholal*, here rendered "profaned," is normally taken to mean "wounded," or, referring more specifically to Jesus Christ, "pierced." Yet the anonymous author of *The Faithful Shepherd* has understood the biblical text in a way that is entirely reasonable, if perhaps unusual. Cardozo, confronting the devastating paradox of a Messiah "profaned" by conversion to Islam, was only too happy to read Isaiah through the eyes of *The Faithful Shepherd*.

Cardozo was not the only one. Nathan of Gaza, in the letter mentioned above, quotes the same texts from *The Faithful Shepherd* that underlie Cardozo's argument. As Sabbatian writers tended to do, Nathan treats Moses as a foreshadowing of the Messiah—a "type" of the Messiah, to use Christian language. What *The Faithful Shepherd* says about Moses, therefore, really applies to Sabbatai Zevi. Cardozo is a bit more hesitant than Nathan about the use of typology. Yet, like the rest of the Sabbatians, he saw the First Redeemer and the Last Redeemer as intimately linked.[17] What is true of Moses is *also* true of Messiah ben David, that is, Sabbatai Zevi. It is true, as we shall see, of Messiah ben Joseph as well.

5.

There are other Messiahs besides Sabbatai Zevi in *The Epistle to the Judges of Izmir.* Jesus puts in a brief appearance as one of those "sneaks and scoundrels" who claimed Messiahship in the past, and who hypocritically pretended—unlike Sabbatai Zevi—to be the Torah's devout adherents (cf. Matt 5:17–20). Cardozo is more interested, however, in another would-be Messiah of Jewish antiquity. This is Simeon Bar Kokhba, whom Cardozo calls, following the rabbinic tradition, Ben Koziba.

The historical Bar Kokhba was a fighting man, a rebel leader. He may or may not have claimed to be Messiah. For three years he and his soldiers held out against the Romans in a bloody and ultimately catastrophic Palestinian-Jewish uprising (132–35 C.E.). Subsequent rabbis, understandably nervous at the whole idea of political Messianism, did their best to slight Bar Kokhba's memory.[18] Only a few scanty passages in Talmud and midrash speak of him. He was a mighty man, indeed, but a harsh and godless tyrant, whom the rabbis themselves—not the Romans!—executed for his Messianic pretensions (BT Sanhedrin 93b). Yet the rabbinic midrash on the Book of Lamentations remembers that Rabbi Akiba, the most prominent of the rabbis (Tannaim) of the early second century, had proclaimed that this false Messiah was the true Messiah.[19]

Cardozo will not deny that Ben Koziba and his claims were false. But, following in the footsteps of Maimonides (see the Background Texts), he stresses that Akiba believed in him nonetheless. Why was so great a scholar so drastically wrong?

The answer, says Cardozo, is that Akiba was mistaken as to the *fact* of Ben Koziba's Messiahship. But Akiba saw clearly, and correctly, where his duty lay. Given the evidence available to him, it was Akiba's religious obligation to put his faith in Ben Koziba, even though he had no certain knowledge that Ben Koziba was really the

Messiah. The case for Sabbatai Zevi, Cardozo argues, is stronger than the case for Ben Koziba ever was. Akiba believed in Ben Koziba. How much more is it our duty to believe in Sabbatai Zevi! And what of the other true Messiah—Messiah ben Joseph?[20] He peeps out only sporadically in this text. His relation to Messiah ben David (=Sabbatai Zevi) is never clearly defined. Yet Cardozo speaks of this second Messiah's becoming profaned "among the uncircumcised"—among the Christians, that is—and amid the temples of (Catholic) "idolatry." Surely Cardozo hints, however faintly, at what he will later both state explicitly and deny explicitly: that he is himself Messiah ben Joseph.[21]

BACKGROUND TEXTS

King Messiah is destined to arise, to restore the kingdom of David to its ancient dominion, to build the Temple, and to gather Israel's exiles. In his time, all the laws [of the Torah] will regain the force they once had. Sacrifices will be offered; Sabbatical and Jubilee years will be observed, exactly as prescribed in the Torah....

You must not imagine that King Messiah is under any obligation to perform evidentiary miracles: to do things outside the regular course of nature, resurrect the dead, or anything of that sort. This is certainly not the case. Consider Rabbi Akiba—the greatest of the Mishnah's sages. He was armor-bearer for Ben Koziba the king; he used to call him King Messiah; he, and all his contemporary sages, believed that he *was* King Messiah, until (for our sins) he was killed. Only after he was killed did they realize he was not the Messiah. And the sages never asked him to perform an evidentiary miracle....

If a king should arise from the house of David who studies the Torah, applies himself to the commandments as did David his ancestor...compels the Jewish people to obey and to maintain [the Torah], and fights the Lord's battles—he is to be presumed the Messiah. If he proves successful, and he builds the Temple in its proper place and gathers the exiles of Israel—he is certainly the Messiah. He shall mend the entire world, such that all serve God together. So the Bible says: "Then I will turn to the nations a pure language, so that all shall call upon God's name, and serve Him in unison" [Zeph 3:9].

—Maimonides, *Code of Jewish Law, Laws of Kings and Their Wars*, chapter 11

*52:13*Behold My servant shall prosper. He shall be exalted, lifted up, raised very high. *14*Just as many were appalled at you, in the same way his appearance is disfigured from that of a man and his form from that of humanity. [15]Thus shall he triumph over many nations. Kings shall shut their mouths because of him, for they have seen that which had not been told to them and that which they had not heard have they come to understand.

[53:1]Who has believed our report? Upon whom has the Lord's arm been revealed? [2]He sprang forth like a young plant, like a root out of parched earth. He was without form and without beauty, that we should look at him, and had no appearance, that we might consider him handsome.

[3][He was] despised, abandoned by men, a man of pains, schooled in sickness. [He was] like one who hides his face from us—despised, and we thought nothing of him. [4]Indeed, he carried our sicknesses and endured our pains, whereas we thought him to be afflicted, smitten by God, tormented. [5]He was profaned on account of our sins, crushed on account of our iniquities. For our benefit was he punished, and through his wound we found healing.

[6]All of us, like sheep, had gone astray. Each of us had wandered his own way. And the Lord inflicted upon *him* the sin of us all. [7]He was harassed; he was tormented. Yet he did not open his mouth. He was brought like a lamb to slaughter. And, just as a ewe is silent before those who shear her, he did not open his mouth. [8]From imprisonment, from judgment was he taken. Who shall speak of his generation? For he was cut off from the land of the living. On account of my people's sin, they had the plague. [9]He placed his grave with criminals, with the rich, in his death. Yet he did no violence, and he spoke no deceit. [10]But the Lord wanted to crush him, to make him sick.

Will he offer himself as a guilt-sacrifice? Then he shall see offspring, live a long life, and, through him, the Lord's wish shall prevail. [11]He shall see and be satisfied with the reward of his own labor. By his knowledge shall this righteous servant of Mine justify the many and carry their iniquities. [12]Therefore I will grant him a portion with the many, and with the mighty ones shall he divide the spoils—because he poured himself out unto death, and with transgressors was he counted, and he carried the sin of the many, and he intercedes for the transgressors.

—Isaiah 52:13—53:12 (translated as Cardozo understood it)

Elijah said: O Faithful Shepherd [Moses]! The hour has come for me to ascend on high. Speak! impose an oath upon me. For it is for your sake that I seek to ascend. The Blessed Holy One granted me permission to reveal myself to you in your prison-house, in your place of burial, to do you kindness. For you have been profaned through the sins of the people. So it is written: "He was profaned on account of our sins" [Isa 53:5].

The Faithful Shepherd said: I adjure you by the Name YAHVEH! Do all in your power not to delay, for I am in dreadful suffering. I looked everywhere and found no one to help me, to bring me out of this pain; in this burial of which it is said concerning me: "He placed his grave with criminals" [Isa 53:9]. They do not recognize me. As far as the wicked Rabble[22] are concerned, I am like a dead dog, stinking in their midst....

—*The Faithful Shepherd* (a Kabbalistic
work of the early fourteenth century, printed
as part of the Zohar), on the Torah portion
Naso' (Zohar, III, 125b)

Elijah rose, and all the Masters of the Academy with him, and they blessed [the Faithful Shepherd]. "Sinai! Sinai!" they said. "It would be proper for us to hear your words and be silent. Yet, with the permission of the Blessed Holy One and His Shechinah, I [Elijah] should like to tell you something, to your honor."

He said to him, "Speak."

[Elijah] began his discourse: "O Faithful Shepherd!...Because [the patriarchs]...behaved kindly toward you, you have suffered many afflictions for their sake, in order that Messiah ben Joseph not be slain...and in order that he and his offspring not be profaned amid the idolaters. As punishment for the sin of idol-worshiping [King] Jeroboam, he was doomed to be profaned through idol-worship, he and his offspring. For Jeroboam ben Nebat was of his [Joseph's?] offspring. And on his account it is said concerning you:

'He was profaned on account of our sins...and through his wound we found healing'" [Isa 53:5].
—*The Faithful Shepherd*, on the Torah portion *Ki Teze'* (Zohar, III, 276b)

O Faithful Shepherd!...The Bible says of you, "No one knows his burial-place to this day" [Deut 34:6]. Woe to those deaf-hearted, blind-eyed people who do not know your burial-place! You begged the Blessed Holy One not to bring you into that burial-place, in which you would be called *dead*...and these idiots say, "Was Moses really afraid of death?"...They have no idea what your burial-place was, what your death was....

For [Moses] was buried within an image that was unworthy of him; a "parched and exhausted land, without water" [Ps 63:2]; meaning, "without Torah." In that place, he is "without form and without beauty" [Isa 53:2]. Whoever sees him in that image thinks "he has no appearance, that we might consider him handsome" [Isa 53:2]. Thus it is that Isaiah's prophecy, [which begins] "Behold My servant shall prosper" [52:13], alludes to him.

This was the burial that made [Moses] beg that he not die there, outside the Holy Land, for it was a parched, hungry, exhausted, thirsty land, devoid of the "water" that is Torah....Buried in a place unworthy of you, naked, without the skin and flesh that are your clothing, wandering adrift from your home, exiled, tramping from place to place—had you not been buried outside the Holy Land, outside your Bride [the Shechinah]—Israel could not have gone forth from exile.

It was of you that it was written: "He was profaned on account of our sins" [Isa 53:5]. Through your burial, you were made profane on account of the sin and the iniquity of the Jewish people....Thanks to you, all that is low and cast down—the Jews, that is, who are the lowliest of all nations—shall be exalted....This is how "through his wound we found healing": through his being joined to us[23] in our exile, we found healing.
—*The Faithful Shepherd*, on *Ki Teze'* (Zohar, III, 280a)

The Holy Lamp [Rabbi Simeon ben Yohai] stood up and said: Master of the world! Here is the Faithful Shepherd...the equal of six hundred thousand Israelites....Of him it is said, with reference to the generation of the Last Exile: "The Lord inflicted upon him the sin of us all" [Isa 53:6]....Yet the rabbinic scholars have no awareness of the Faithful Shepherd.

I adjure you, Elijah, by the sacred name of YAHVEH: reveal him to all the leaders of the rabbinic scholars, that they may be aware of him, that he be profaned no more. For so it was said of him: "He was profaned for our sins...."

—*The Faithful Shepherd*, on *Ki Teze'* (Zohar, III, 282b)

EPISTLE TO THE JUDGES OF IZMIR[24]

[Preface]

Addressed, in the week of the Torah portion *When you come to the land IN WHICH YOU ARE TO DWELL, which I am giving to you* [June 9–15, 1669],[25] to the flawless rabbis and splendid judges—

Rabbi Hayyim Benveniste (God save and protect him!)
Rabbi Solomon Algazi (God save and protect him!)
Rabbi Solomon ibn Rabbi Abraham Kohen
Rabbi Isaac de Alba

—may God watch over them forever! Amen.

I begin by acknowledging that we have received Your Worships' letters. I have seen the solemn warnings issued by you, about belief in the man abused and reviled [Sabbatai Zevi]. I have digested the narrative, composed and signed by you, of all the foul deeds he perpetrated from the day he was born until the day he appeared before the Turk. And I have pondered the arguments by which you convincingly demonstrate that his deeds are devoid of substance.

Still more convincingly do you show that there is no substance in Nathan Benjamin [Nathan of Gaza]. Time and time again was he put to the test: in Your Worships' presence, in Adrianople, in Venice.[26] It was discovered each time that there was no truth to his dreams or his speeches. These proved to be empty and vain lies, the work of a deluding spirit, for not one of his predictions came true. It was the same, they assure us, in Alexandria.

The flawless Rabbi Joseph Dayyan, emissary of Hebron, has now visited our town and told us very much the same thing. It must therefore be acknowledged that Nathan Benjamin was *not* sent by God to reveal the Messiah. Virtuous and trustworthy men, moreover, have written to me that they heard Nathan Benjamin himself admit that whatever visions he saw were for his own private edification. That was why he was nowhere able to perform any evidentiary miracle that might establish him as a prophet.

I am myself aware of acts performed by the Man Profaned [Sabbatai Zevi][27] that are yet more bizarre than those about which you wrote us. Nothing, therefore, could be farther from my purpose than to call into question the verdicts reached by the courts in Ipsola, Adrianople, and Venice. These verdicts are certainly true. Every Jew must believe that they have rightly ruled that, in accord with the Torah and the commandment, there is no substance in Nathan Benjamin.

Nor is it my intent to dispute Your Worships. Not merely do I believe, I *know* that you have correctly admonished us to maintain our holy Torah and the words of our blessed sages by observing the fasts[28] as occasions to cry out to the Lord. I have myself resumed that practice. God forbid that I should be among the stubborn dissenters who in each town separate themselves from the holy congregations! I have cast my lot with them,[29] and in cooperation with them do I act.

My purpose, rather, is to resolve certain problems relevant to the momentous event that has occurred in our time and to relate, without the slightest falsehood, what the heavenly beings have taught me and what I have myself learned from my study of Scripture and Gemara. My goal therein is to bring to public awareness the manner in which the Redeemer is to come, and what it is that he must do. Finally, I shall take up the question of Rabbi Nathan Benjamin, and demonstrate precisely what we are to believe about him.

[Part One. The Argument]

[Step 1: Cardozo demonstrates, on the basis of sources that most Jews of his time would consider authorita-

132

tive—Bible, Talmud and midrash, Kabbalah—that the Messiah must possess six characteristic markers.
His first marker: he is to be an ordinary human being.]

Let us begin with the question of *whether the Messiah is to be, like Moses, a human being born of a woman.*

I raise this issue, because I have seen certain fools claim that the Messiah is going to descend from heaven or emerge from Paradise. They invoke certain passages in the rabbinic literature and in the Zohar that speak of King Messiah as sitting in the heavenly study hall, and in Paradise as well. It is evident, however, that these remarks apply to the Supernal Radiance, and to the holy spirit that is destined to enclothe itself within the levels of King Messiah's own soul, so that he can perform those wonderful and terrible acts that are needed to bring us out of exile.

This is the secret meaning of the biblical passage, "The spirit of the Lord shall rest upon him: a spirit of wisdom and understanding, [a spirit of counsel and might, a spirit of knowledge and fear of the Lord"; Isa 11:2]. When our ancient rabbis tell us that the Messiah was born on the day the Temple was destroyed and that he is in Paradise,[30] they are obviously referring to the descent of that spiritual portion from the higher realms to the lower. It must be in Paradise in a state of readiness, garbed appropriately, so that the Messiah will be able to receive it in any generation that proves worthy of consuming the two Messiahs.[31] The rabbis have said, accordingly, that "in each generation there is a person suitable to be Messiah, if that generation is only worthy of it";[32] from which it follows that the Messiah is to be a human being born of a woman.

So, too, the Gemara: "If he is alive, he is to be someone on the order of our holy rabbi" [Judah the Patriarch][33]—who was woman-born, and indeed endured great suffering. Rabbi Eliezer the Great, moreover, has written that Messiah ben David is to be born within Ishmael [Islam].[34] And the clearest proof of all lies in the fact that Rabbi Akiba and the greatest of the Tannaitic sages believed that Ben Koziba, who had been born in their midst, was the Messiah.

133

[The Messiah's second marker: he is to be tormented, humiliated, abused.]

Our second topic of inquiry, then, must be *the characteristics of the Messiah*.

The Messiah's greatness and his dignity require no discussion. Bible and Gemara have made them familiar even to schoolchildren. Our ancient rabbis, indeed, have gone so far as to say that the Messiah will be greater than the patriarchs, greater even than the angels.[35] What *does* demand our attention is the torments and the profanation that he is to suffer.

Our ancient sages made a great point of telling us that King Messiah is to endure more suffering than any human being. God, they assert, is to bring upon him torments and dreadful ills the like of which neither the patriarchs nor David had to endure. They say in another place that "God divided sufferings into three equal parts: one part he gave to the patriarchs and David, one to the Jewish people, and the third to King Messiah."[36]

When the Bible says that the Messiah's "delight shall be in the fear of the Lord" [Isa 11:3], the rabbis [read *hariho*, "delight," as though it were from *rehayim*, "millstones," and] explain: "This teaches us that God loaded sufferings upon King Messiah as though they were millstones."[37] Rabbi Yohanan, Rava, and Ulla are all quoted (in tractate *Sanhedrin*) as saying, "Let the Messiah come, but let me not see him. Why not? Because of the agony of the Messiah."[38] The phrase is to be taken literally: the "agony" is indeed experienced by *him*. And, in the same passage, our holy rabbi [Judah the Patriarch] is likened to King Messiah, on account of his having endured suffering for many years.

Commenting in the same vein on the text "I will surely have mercy on him" [Jer 31:20], the rabbis teach that the Messiah must suffer imprisonment.[39] Commenting on the verse "they mocked the footsteps of Your Messiah" [Ps 89:52], they tell us that "the Jews will sing a hymn at the Messiah's coming. But they will not sing it until after the Messiah shall have endured mockery."[40] This is confirmed by the Zohar, which says that among the Jews the Messiah will be considered "like a dead dog."[41]

In summary, *that which the rabbis taught in the Gemara and the midrashim and the Zohar, in accord with the traditions they inherited from the prophets and the elders, and in accord with the fifty-third chapter of the prophet Isaiah, has all been fulfilled in King Messiah.*

[Chapter 53 of Isaiah, with its "suffering servant of the Lord," is key to Cardozo's demonstration of Sabbatai Zevi's Messiahship, as it had long been key to the Christians' argument for Jesus. But surely the Christians are wrong in their basic premise? Surely the chapter does not speak of the Messiah?

Ah! says Cardozo. Surely it does!]

Recent commentators, to be sure, have interpreted [Isa 53] as applying to the Jewish people, or, perhaps, to Jeremiah or Josiah or some righteous man.[42] Their purpose in all this is to evade the objections that the Christians are perpetually raising against us and to show off their own superlative acuity as well. Yet Rabbi Moses Alsheich has returned to the exegesis of our ancient sages, from whose waters we drink and from whose words we live. And these sages have taken great pains to record for our benefit many indicators by which we may easily recognize how the Messiah must be: mocked and insulted, profaned and accursed by the entire Jewish people.

Rabbi Simeon ben Yohai thus cries "Woe!" upon anyone who happens to live in the Messiah's time, on account of the danger to his faith, for well did the ancients know that only a tiny minority would believe in him. This is why it was all the sages' habit to say, "Let the Messiah come, but not in our time."[43]

Will anyone tell us that "I prefer not to believe our ancient rabbis when they assert that the fifty-third chapter of Isaiah speaks of the Messiah"? Well then, let us ask this fellow why he believes in Isaiah at all! For, were it not for the authority of our ancient rabbis who fixed the Book of Isaiah in the canon, we would have no way of knowing that Isaiah and his utterances are truthful. We do not, in the last analysis, believe in our rabbis on the prophets' authority.

On the contrary, it is on our rabbis' authority that we believe Isaiah and Ezekiel to have been true prophets.

The conclusion follows inevitably. *Anyone who denies that the fifty-third chapter of Isaiah speaks of the Messiah has thereby denied the words of our rabbis in the Gemara and the tradition.* I do not choose to address such people, who reject the traditional consensus that our predecessors have received and have, with one accord, handed down to us. This tradition can hardly be toppled by invoking proofs from modern writers!

Our ancient rabbis, moreover, have expounded Psalm 22 and Psalm 89 with reference to Messiah ben David, in such a way as to show with absolute clarity that the Messiah is to be mocked and insulted, abused and scorned, precisely as declared by Isaiah. I need say no more.

Now, *glorious greatness* and *abysmal humiliation* are polar opposites. They cannot conceivably coexist in one and the same subject, and therefore must succeed one another. It is, moreover, self-evidently impossible that the Messiah's greatness and glory should come first, to be followed by humiliation and profanation. We are therefore compelled to admit that he must experience shame and humiliation immediately upon his appearing, or, perhaps, that after he appears he will enjoy some limited measure of greatness, followed by suffering and profanation. However this may be, he will eventually enter into his great glory, and into the state of sanctity that he never truly abandoned.

[The Messiah's third marker: though essentially righteous, he must perform deeds that are strange and dreadful.]

We must now give our most sober consideration to the question of how it might be possible for so virtuous a folk as the Jewish people to abuse and insult a wise man, a man righteous and humble, such as the Messiah is destined to be. What could possibly bring them to designate him a scoundrel and transgressor, as Isaiah [53:12] declares it his fate to be "counted with transgressors"? The problem is truly overwhelming, inasmuch as our ancient rabbis and the Zohar do attest that the insult and humiliation is to take place in its entirety *after* the Messiah has been revealed as such—however this process is to be conceived. Our reason confirms that this must be the case.

We have no alternative but to admit that King Messiah must do many things that are not in accord with the Torah and its commandments. His deeds shall be strange, alien, most unspeakably repugnant—"for alien is his working, strange his deed"[44]—and on account of those deeds shall he be rejected. For, if this is not so, how might we imagine the words of Isaiah and of our rabbis finding their fulfillment?

There is yet another condition that must be satisfied. *The Messiah must in one way or another have the power to act contrary to the commandments.* He must be able forcibly to resist the Jews' efforts to injure or kill him when he does the acts that have brought down upon him their insult and curse. This in spite of the fact that they are supported by the Torah itself, which they see him violating.

It is beyond all question that the Messiah will be doing his Creator's will, obeying God's direct commands as well as the dictates of his own wisdom and knowledge, for the purpose of justifying the multitude. Isaiah says as much: "He did no violence. He spoke no deceit. [...] By his knowledge shall this righteous servant of Mine justify the many and carry their iniquities" [53:9, 11]. Which is to say, the Messiah shall be regarded as "smitten by God and tormented, plagued, profaned, wanting in appearance and handsomeness" [53:4, 5, 2] on account of the strange acts and alien utterances that he is destined to do and to speak. Yet in all this speech and all these acts there is no violence, no deceit.

An apparent superfluity in the biblical text yields the clue. The Messiah is unquestionably God's servant, and a God-fearing man. Once Scripture has spoken of "My servant," why must it add that he is "righteous"? Why must it inform us that he will do no violence and speak no deceit? The intent must be to communicate, as plainly as possible, that *the Messiah will perform actions that are beyond the Torah's limits and that break the commandments.* He will say things that must seem violent and deceitful to all who see him or hear about him. They will repudiate him; they will declare him loathsome and contemptible, scoundrel and criminal; they will refuse him all credence. That is why the Scripture must assure us that "he did no violence," and all the rest of it. He is "righteous"; he did exactly what the Lord told him to do.

In tractate *Sanhedrin*, our ancient rabbis interpret the verse, "his delight shall be in the fear of the Lord" [Isa 11:3], to the same effect. "This teaches," they say, "that God loaded blows and sufferings upon King Messiah."[45] God commanded him, in other words, to do things that would naturally bring upon him suffering and insult.

[The Messiah's fourth marker: having once been holy, he is to become profaned.]

All who are schooled in the Zohar's wisdom, all who are expert in the simple meaning of the biblical text as set forth in the Gemara and the midrashim, will be compelled by this and by other evidence of the kind to acknowledge *the very close attention devoted to the profanation of the Messiah*. And no wonder: our whole knowledge of the Redeemer and of his characteristics turns on this one point.

"He was profaned on account of our sins, crushed on account of our iniquities" [Isa 53:5]. In the Gemara and other texts, as well as in the Zohar and the *Tiqqunim*, this verse is applied to Moses, to Messiah ben David, and to Messiah ben Ephraim.

[It is not exactly self-evident that the Hebrew word *meholal*, used in Isaiah 53:5, means "profaned." (Most modern translations give it as "wounded.") Cardozo therefore must demonstrate this point.]

The word *meholal* ["profaned"] turns out, under close examination, to be derived from *hol* [the state of being non-holy]. So the rabbis tell us in tractate *Sanhedrin*, in connection with the verse "if a priest's daughter profane herself by whoring" [Lev 21:9],[46] and in many passages in which they expound the verse "do not profane your daughter to make her a whore" [Lev 19:29].[47] Similarly in Ezekiel: "...for the sake of His name that is profaned among the

Gentiles. And I will sanctify My great name that you have profaned."[48] His point is that "I will again make My name holy, you
having profaned it among the Gentiles." In like manner, "whoever
profanes it must be executed" [Exod 31:14]: the Sabbath is holy,
and anyone who makes it non-holy deserves execution.

Now, our rabbis have interpreted "he was profaned on
account of our sins" as referring to Moses, who was buried, not in
the Holy Land, but in a non-holy location beside Beth-peor.[49] This
was done for the sake of the sinful generation of the desert, its purpose being to make atonement for them and to allow them to enter
the land of Israel at the time the dead are resurrected. They apply
it also to Messiah ben David.[50] For, like Moses, he is destined to be
"profaned" like a corpse in a criminal's grave, this being the secret
meaning of the words "he placed his grave with criminals" [Isa
53:9]. From having been holy, in other words, he is to be made
non-holy.

Elijah speaks of Messiah ben Ephraim in a similar vein.
Jeroboam, son of Nebat, worshiped idols and led Israel into sin;
Messiah ben Ephraim is Jeroboam's offspring; he and his own offspring must therefore become "profaned" amid idolatrous temples,
in order to make atonement for Jeroboam's sin.

[Cardozo is referring to a passage in *The Faithful
Shepherd*, in which the prophet Elijah is the speaker.[51]
"Idolatrous temples," in Cardozo's usage, can easily be
Christian churches—of the sort that he must have
attended Sunday mornings during his youth in Spain.
This will lead us to suspect that the "Gentiles" in the
next paragraph are specifically the Muslims, while the
"uncircumcised" are the Christians.[52]]

Rabbi Moses Cordovero fully accepted this doctrine. So did
Rabbi Hayyim Vital. And the distinguished, indeed inspired
Kabbalist [Hayyim Kohen of Aleppo], author of *The Scholar's
Torah*,[53] declares that Messiah ben David is to be profaned among
the Gentile nations. From having been holy, that is, he is to become

non-holy among the Gentiles, and Messiah ben Joseph similarly, among the uncircumcised. This much is certain, beyond all doubt.

A fresh point now requires elucidation. The profanation of Moses consists in his having been buried outside the Holy Land. But what is the precise nature of the process by which the Messiahs,[54] having been holy, come to be non-holy?

Elijah's statements prove that Messiah ben Joseph is destined to become profaned among idolaters. In other words, just as Jeroboam son of Nebat was profaned through idolatry of his own free will, thus Messiah ben Joseph will be profaned through idolatry *not* of his own free will—for otherwise he would be a very wicked person, which God forbid—but under duress. This is why Isaiah did not use the [reflexive] verb *mithallel*, which would mean that "he profaned himself," but the passive *mehullal*, meaning that "he was profaned."

How otherwise could he become non-holy? "Israel," after all, "is holy to the Lord" [Jer 2:3], "a holy people" [Deut 7:6]. A Jew may sin, but he does not thereby become non-holy. Were it otherwise, every single one of the righteous would become non-holy, "for there is no righteous person on earth who does good and never sins" [Eccl 7:20]. Achan, say our ancient rabbis, committed grave iniquities [Josh 7]. Yet, sin though he did, he was a Jew: he was still included among the holy people, not among the non-holy. For, as we well know, all the Gentile nations are designated *non-holy*.

From all of this, it is overwhelmingly clear that *the Messiahs are to be removed from the sphere of holiness*—that is to say, the Jewish people—*to that of non-holiness*. They must, in other words, enter the realm of Gentile-dom, and that under duress. For, if we should suppose them to be doing this willingly, they could hardly be called righteous.

Now, Isaiah says of the Messiah: "His appearance is disfigured from that of a man; his form, from that of humanity" [52:14]. "A man" means a Jew; "humanity" means the holy people. It is plain to see that Israel—in exile, without king or prince or priest or altar—is not in the form of a people. Through their sins, in other words, they have become disfigured, so that they are not in the form of a people. In precisely the same way the Messiah, compelled against

140

his will to be among the Gentiles, without Torah or observance of the commandments, shall be "disfigured [...] from humanity," which is to say, the Jewish people. This will explain why Scripture says, "Just as many were appalled at you"—["you" referring to] Israel— "in the same way his appearance" [—"he" being the Messiah—] "is disfigured from that of a man" [Isa 52:14].[55]

This is all most horribly shameful. Hence the cry, "Who has believed our report?" [53:1]. "Who could possibly believe?"—the prophet intends to say—"and who could possibly accept the report I am delivering to future generations, telling them that the Messiah is destined to be without form and without beauty" (by which he means the Torah), "that he must spring forth like a root out of parched earth" [53:2].

A root that has dried up has no hope of ever bearing fruit. What hope then can it have if it is planted in "parched earth" where there is no water, which our rabbis understood to mean a place where there is no Torah? It follows that the Messiah is to "spring forth" after he shall have been like a dry root. He must first become, in other words, like one planted in "parched earth," where there is not even a drop of Torah.

> [He must, in other words, first be in the "parched earth" of Gentile-dom, and afterward emerge in his Messianic glory.]

This seems to be how we are to understand the statement of Rabbi Eliezer the Great, that Messiah ben David is destined to be born among Ishmael [Islam]. What possible advantage could there be in our knowing among whom he is to be born? Had Rabbi Eliezer's point been merely to convey that the Messiah is to be born of woman, there would have been no need to specify among what people he is to be born.

When he speaks of the Messiah's birth, however, he means his *manifestation in actuality*, in accord with the secret meaning of the verse "I have this day begotten you" [Ps 2:7]. And he intends to convey this marvelous mystery: *While the Messiah is still among Ishmael, he shall be like an unborn child. He shall then come forth from among them.* When Rabbi Eliezer says that the Messiah shall be born among them, the meaning is that *he shall be profaned among Ishmael,* like an Ishmaelite [a Muslim, that is]. Afterward he shall manifest himself with enormous power in Ishmael's midst, and all shall know that he is the Messiah.

The Jews will not recognize the Messiah, in consequence of his having been thus profaned. That is why Scripture says, "He was like one who hides his face from us" [53:3]. People who look at his face, his head, or the clothing he wears will not be able to tell whether he is Jew or Gentile—much less that he is the Messiah. And suppose that we do know him, from having seen him in his original status as a Jew? We will then count him among transgressors, as the Bible says, "With transgressors was he counted" [53:12]. (For a "transgressor" is essentially a person who leaves his proper domain, as in the sentence "Moab transgressed against Israel" [2 Kgs 1:1].)[56]

The Gemara says, in the name of Rabbi [Judah the Patriarch], that the Messiah's name is Leper,[57] and a leper is someone who "dwells outside the camp" of Israel [Lev 13:46]. Hence the Scripture: "We thought him to be afflicted, smitten by God, tormented" [Isa 53:4].

It is plain, moreover, that the Torah is called "life"; and, in Kabbalistic usage, "the land of life."[58] Anyone who leaves it may be called *cut off.* Because the Messiah is destined against his will to depart from it, Isaiah says that "he was cut off from the land of life" [53:8]. He is thus like a dead man, like one buried among criminals; and this death is as severe for him as though he were to die a thousand times each day.

The Messiah, our ancient rabbis tell us, is to suffer to the point of saying, "My God, my God, why have You forsaken me? You are so far from saving me! from my words of anguish" [Ps 22:2]. In that very passage it is written, "They have divided my garments among themselves. They have cast lots over my clothing" [22:19]. The Gentiles, in other words, will strip off his "garments" and dress him in a different mode of "clothing."

The text speaks first of "my garments," and afterward of "my clothing." It implies thereby that the Jews will "cast lots" over this "clothing," each in his own mind; pondering, that is, whether [the Messiah's clothing implies that] he is Jew or Gentile, apostate or apostate only under duress. The same point is made in the eighty-ninth psalm. "You have enwrapped him in shame, selah" [Ps 89:46]: they are to dress him in the clothing of shame.

Isaiah says the same. "We have heard songs from the end of the earth: Glory to the righteous!" [24:16]. "The righteous" is a designation for the Redeemer.[59] Isaiah has thus begun by proclaiming the good news of salvation. Why, then, does he go on at once to cry out, "My secret is mine! my secret is mine! woe is me! The betrayers have done their betrayal, and, with the garment, the betrayers have done their betrayal"?[60] He evidently knew, but was not permitted to reveal, that the Gentile "betrayers" were destined to dress the "righteous"—the Redeemer, that is—in the "garment," which is to say the clothing, of the betrayers.

The question is bound to arise *why* all of this needed to befall the two Messiahs. The simple explanation is plain from the Torah. Of our own free will we abandoned God's Torah, and, while dwelling in our land, performed idolatry. We are therefore condemned to depart from the Torah under duress, to perform idolatry against our will. God has imposed upon the Messiahs the iniquity of the entire people,[61] and it is they who pay our debt. This is the hidden meaning of the text, "For our benefit was he punished, and through his wound we found healing" [Isa 53:5].

From the perspective of Kabbalah, there is here a mystery that is great and evident.[62] I shall not record it, inasmuch as I do not know whether Your Worships are conversant with this domain of learning. I judge that I have solid reason to keep the mystery concealed, in that it is plain to me that in all our Diaspora there are hardly three or four people who truly know the Kabbalah, albeit many do study it. It requires ten years of study merely to become a physician. Consider, then, how much it must require to become a Kabbalist! Most especially so, in that the human intellect, pure and lucid though it may be, is bound to stumble in comprehending so divine a science, save that its principles and its mysteries have been communicated to the inquirer from above.

Yet I shall say this much.[63] Once one has grasped who it is among the supernal ranks to whom these words apply—"For our benefit was he punished, and through his wound we found healing"—then one will know the mystery. And he will know why, for our sins, the Temple has been built into a Gentile prayer-house.[64]

The prophet Isaiah has recorded for us, in chapter 49, three further distinguishing marks of the Messiah. "Thus speaks the Lord, Israel's redeemer and holy one, to the despised of soul, the loathed Gentile, the rulers' slave: Kings shall see him and they shall arise; princes, and they shall prostrate themselves" [49:7]. The prophet, according to the Zohar, is speaking of Messiah ben David.[65] He calls him "despised of soul," meaning that he is despised on account of some matter that relates to the soul. He is "loathed," and the prophet does not say, using either the active or the passive form of the verb, that he is loathed *by* Gentiles.[66] The implication is rather that, on account of his Gentile characteristics, he is loathed *by Jews* who suppose him to be a Gentile. And he is a "rulers' slave": prior to his phase of greatness, before the time when all the kings shall prostrate themselves before him, he must be a "rulers' slave."

The conclusion is this: I have come to grasp the knowledge that the Messiah—whoever he may turn out to be—*is destined, under compulsion, to enter an alien religion.* This is beyond all doubt, beyond all error, beyond all misunderstanding.

> [The Messiah's fifth marker: however it is that he is to be revealed to the world, it is *not* to be through the agency of a prophet whose legitimacy has been established and publicly acknowledged by the Jewish people ("prophet by consensus").
>
> The skeptics, such as the "judges of Izmir," made a great point of Nathan of Gaza's having failed all the tests by which he might show himself a legitimate prophet. Cardozo now embraces this argument and turns it

against the skeptics. The very fact that Nathan is *not* a prophet by consensus, he says, is itself evidence that Sabbatai Zevi *is* the Messiah.

Cardozo's argument at this point is particularly subtle and difficult. It turns upon a close analysis of the rabbinic responses to the claims of the second-century Messianic pretender Bar Kokhba (Ben Koziba). Since some at least of the ancient rabbis—notably, the great Akiba—found Ben Koziba's claims plausible, it follows that their traditions cannot have led them to expect anything of the Messiah that Ben Koziba did not provide. Ben Koziba was never proclaimed as Messiah by a consensus-prophet. Q.E.D.: the rabbinic tradition cannot have taught that a consensus-prophet would proclaim the Messiah.

Cardozo supports his inferences by arguing from the silences in Maimonides's description of the Messiah (translated in the Background Texts).]

We must now turn our attention to the problem of *the manner in which the Messiah is to be revealed.* On this subject, our ancient rabbis had no reliable tradition. This we learn from Maimonides: they had no tradition of how the sequence of events was to unfold.

Many hold the misconception that Maimonides says that our blessed rabbis had no knowledge whatever of the Messiah. Absolutely false! Our rabbis taught, on the basis of the traditions they had received, that the Messiah shall be esteemed by the Jews as contemptible, worthy of insult and abuse, accursed and profaned. They knew by tradition that, in him, the fifty-third chapter of Isaiah would find its fulfillment. They had trustworthy traditions also concerning his greatness and glory. They found themselves uncertain, however, just how his *manifestation* would transpire.

Most scholars assert that Elijah must precede the Redeemer, to bring us the good news and to reveal him. This, however, is mere opinion. It cannot claim to be consensus. Proof for this lies in the fact that Rabbi Akiba and his contemporary sages believed Ben

Koziba to be the Messiah. Were it essential that Elijah or some other prophet precede the Redeemer, Rabbi Akiba and his colleagues could not have maintained this belief.

"Should one arise from the house of David"—says Maimonides—"who studies the Torah, applies himself to the commandments [...] and fights the Lord's battles, he is to be presumed Messiah."[67] If anyone has these characteristics, the presumption is that he is the Messiah. Plainly enough, Maimonides did *not* believe that Elijah or any other prophet would come to reveal him.

We may reasonably suppose that the ancients had a tradition to the effect that the Messiah's manifestation would *not* take place through any prophet by consensus, or through Elijah—in any public and universal manner, that is. Those who *did* believe that the Messiah would be revealed by Elijah supposed that this would not take place in public. Rather, [Elijah] would come to the Chamber of Hewn Stone [in the Temple],[68] or the Mount of Olives or some other private location and communicate the Messiah's identity to those present. They would afterward write to all Jewry that the Messiah had been revealed by Elijah.

Rabbi Akiba and his colleagues, however, were of the opinion that the Messiah [would not be revealed by Elijah, but] would reveal himself through his own triumphant deeds. *All* the sages evidently shared a tradition that the Messiah would not be revealed by a consensus-prophet. The Gemara thus says that Ben Koziba made inquiry declaring himself the Messiah, whereupon the sages sent to investigate if he could judge by his sense of smell. They told him, according to another passage, that he could not be the Messiah because it is written of the Messiah that "he shall slay the wicked with the breath of his lips" [Isa 11:4], which Ben Koziba could not do.[69] Had they believed that Elijah must come first, and only afterward the Messiah, what would have been their point in demanding these signs?

This variety of opinions must have its roots in the following situation: The rabbis had received and transmitted a tradition that asserted the Messiah would be scorned and cursed, insulted and profaned, and that the Jewish people would regard him as a transgressor—all of this to take place *after* his manifestation. They did not know just how these things might happen. Assume for the moment that Elijah or some other consensus-prophet, well known to all Jewry, were to come and reveal the Messiah. How could the Jewish people afterward insult and curse him?

Shall we imagine that the Messiah might, after his manifestation, perform strange and alien acts that are not in accord with the Torah or the commandments and for this reason become the object of insult? It is quite impossible. Even the most minor Jewish prophet, once certified by the Torah's criteria, becomes immune to all suspicion, even if he violates every single one of the Torah's commandments (idolatry excepted). He may order us, moreover, to violate on a temporary basis any commandment but the prohibition of idolatry; we must obey. It goes without saying, then, that King Messiah may break the commandments and do things we consider strange, once he has become revealed. Death is the penalty for all who resist him or disbelieve him.

Once the Messiah has been revealed by a consensus-prophet, then, there is no place for abuse or insult. The unlettered mob might conceivably abuse and insult him. The scholars, who know the Torah and its rulings, certainly could not. Yet, it appears, it is precisely the learned men of the Messiah's time who are destined most cruelly to abuse him.

Can we suppose, alternatively, that the Messiah is to reveal himself while in a state of lowliness? But who would ever believe some contemptible fellow, on his own recognizance, to be the Messiah? He would instead be judged criminally insane! No, this could not constitute a manifestation, by which the Messiah's identity might become known.

It was this that led Rabbi Akiba to believe that the Messiah would reveal himself through some great and triumphant deeds he would do. Afterward, he supposed, the Messiah would fall from his greatness; then would come the torments, the scorn, the insult that the Messiah is obliged to suffer to secure atonement for the Jewish people. He would in the end return to his promised greatness and would gather in the Jewish exiles and rebuild the Temple.

[This was why Akiba was ready to accept Ben Koziba as Messiah. But why did most of Akiba's fellow rabbis reject him? Cardozo explains:]

The other sages, however, denied that greatness of the sort that Ben Koziba demonstrated could serve as proof of his Messianic status. His kingship, they thought, was purely natural. Instead, they believed, the Messiah was to be revealed through one of the prescribed Messianic signs, for example, ability to judge by his sense of smell or to slay with the breath of his mouth. The torment and insult would come afterward. God would hide His face from him— "as though hiding His face from him," Scripture says [Isa 53:3][70]— and he would no longer possess this special ability. It would thus become possible for insult and abuse to be visited upon the Messiah, till such time as he would emerge from them. He would then rise to his proper rank, conceivable only to God, from which he would never more fall. The Messiah could not possibly, in consequence, be revealed by a consensus-prophet.

[Still] other sages believed that it was Elijah who would reveal the Messiah, and that this would take place in private, in the Chamber of Hewn Stone [in the Temple]. This view was the most solidly established, and therefore won the allegiance of most of the early sages, and the later ones as well. It was a common occurrence in those days for Elijah to appear to the rabbis, and they consequently supposed that he would make an appearance of that sort to tell them who the Messiah was. But this must be done in a private place, to a small number of sages, and not in full public view.

This for the following reason: *the possibility must exist for the Jewish people to believe in him, then afterward to reject and insult him.* The sages to whom Elijah had revealed himself would [according to this hypothesis] dispatch messengers and letters to convey this information to the entire Jewish people. Elijah, they would say, had revealed himself and borne witness that So-and-so was the Messiah. Most of the Jews would believe. But afterward, when King Messiah's troubles and his strange deeds would have come upon him, they would be able to withdraw their faith from him. "Villain and transgressor," they would call him. The sages who wrote them about Elijah's revelation, they would say, were lying. Or, perhaps, it was a demon that had revealed itself to them. Or maybe they were drunk or dreaming.

All the sages of Israel, however, had this in common: *They believed, and had learned by tradition, that the Messiah was not to be revealed by a consensus-prophet.* This much is entirely evident from what they have said.

Maimonides himself wavered. In his legal writings, he refrains from affirming that the Messiah would be revealed by a consensus-prophet. Hence he says that "if a king [...] should study Torah [...] and fight the Lord's battles...the presumption is that he is the Messiah." In his letters, he expresses the opinion that there is to be prophecy in Israel prior to the Messiah's coming.[71] He does *not*, however, say that it is by a consensus-prophet that the Messiah will be revealed.

There is, moreover, solid reason to insist that the Messiah cannot be revealed by a consensus-prophet. For, should he be revealed by a consensus-prophet, this in itself would (God forbid!) topple the entire Jewish people into the most grievous sin.

Consider: once the word of the Lord has been spoken to us by a consensus-prophet, we are compelled on the Torah's authority to believe in it. The penalty for denying any part of it is death by supernatural agency. God, moreover, is aware that King Messiah must unavoidably do strange deeds on account of which the bulk of the people must inevitably deny him. He consequently did not wish that the Messiah be revealed by a consensus-prophet. The sages knew this, and that was why they agreed that, however the Messiah was to be revealed, it would *not* be by a consensus-prophet.

Isaiah shows most plainly that such is the case. This is why, on the subject of the Messiah's greatness, he has so very little to say. "Behold My servant shall prosper. He shall be exalted, lifted up, raised very high" [Isa 52:13]. Yet he goes on for an entire chapter about how the Messiah is to be profaned, degraded, ridiculed! Prophets will never speak in vain. For every word they write there is some necessity, some benefit for the Jewish people. What necessity, what benefit is there in all the markers of the Messiah's insult and ridicule that are recorded by Isaiah and by the rabbis? If he is to be revealed by a prophet, after all, no sooner will the prophet's word come true than we will recognize it is he.

Why, moreover, does Isaiah [53:1] cry out, "Who has believed our report? Upon whom has the Lord's arm been revealed?" When a consensus-prophet comes to reveal the Messiah, many will be able to say: "I have believed! And the Lord's arm"—signifying the Messiah, and exalted prophecy as well—"has been revealed upon So-and-so." But Isaiah well knew that the Messiah will *never* be revealed by a consensus-prophet. That is why he piled detail upon detail, so that by their aid we might be able to recognize who the Messiah is.

For it is necessary to know the Messiah, even while he is scorned and loathed and profaned. It is necessary to come to his aid through Torah study and repentance, through prayer and charity, through fasting and good deeds. And it is *most highly beneficial* to anticipate salvation and to believe in the Messiah, as I shall explain presently, with God's help. This is why Isaiah says, "Who has believed our report?" Who could possibly believe, he means to say, that such a man could be the Messiah? given that he was not revealed by a consensus-prophet. This is why he says, "Upon whom has the Lord's arm been revealed?" No, indeed; it was not in vain that Isaiah inscribed all the ways of the Messiah during the time of his abasement.

"Surely"—some may object—"these markers might fit many people. In vain, then, did the prophet write them!" But the fact is that, much as Nachmanides has said with reference to the signs of Moses,[72] God well knew that the *ensemble* of these markers could not fit anyone but King Messiah. And so He informed Isaiah.

We are thus compelled to the belief that all these characteristic markers are laid out in just such a way that anyone in whom we observe them is to be presumed King Messiah. All who have precise knowledge of the prophecy will grasp how convincingly it gives us knowledge of the Messiah, and how unequivocally it demonstrates that the Messiah cannot possibly be revealed by a consensus-prophet. Had God intended to send the Jewish people a prophet to reveal the Messiah, He never would have had Isaiah inscribe for us all these details. Nor would our blessed sages have expatiated at length on the details of the Messiah's humiliation.

[The Messiah's sixth marker: we are obligated to believe in him, even before we have certain knowledge that he is the Messiah. (This is not exactly a "marker," but Cardozo chooses to treat it as such.)]

We must now launch our inquiry into the question of *whether, during the time the Messiah is being abased and ridiculed, we are obligated to believe in him, and whether this belief is in some way meritorious.* For here, as well, a cardinal principle is at stake.

Some claim, on the basis of Maimonides's statements, that we have no obligation to believe in the Messiah until he gathers Israel's exiles and builds the Temple. How perfectly childish! If this were so, there would no longer be room to speak of *faith* but rather of *knowledge.* As Maimonides says, "Then it will be a matter of certainty that he is Messiah." [That is, once he has gathered the exiles and rebuilt the Temple.]

What Maimonides meant is that we are obliged to believe in the Messiah *before* it becomes clear beyond any shadow of doubt that he is indeed so. Thus Maimonides writes: "When a king arises from the house of David who studies God's Torah [...] and fights the Lord's battles, he is to be presumed Messiah." He obviously cannot be "presumed Messiah," as far as we are concerned, unless we believe in him. According to Maimonides, therefore, we are obligated to believe he is the Messiah, just as we would believe anything else on the basis of presumption. And if this king should die or be slain without having gathered the exiles? Then it will be clear that he was not the Messiah after all, but only a testing that God has willed upon us. We will have done our duty, in other words, by *believing* that he is the Messiah. If he actually turns out to *be* the Messiah—well and good.

The ancients taught us our duty to believe, and the considerable merit thereby obtained, through their having believed in Ben Koziba. Why otherwise would they have testified that they had believed in him? It would have been far better for them to have kept silent about the whole matter, to prevent it from becoming a second source of error. (The leprous plague provoked by the Nazarene, who had been executed for declaring himself Messiah, had begun to infect the world only a short time before.) But we must interpret the conduct of Rabbi Akiba, and of the rest of the Tannaim, in the most favorable light. We must say they would never have proclaimed Ben Koziba to be the Messiah, lacking (as they did) absolute certainty on the matter—had they not known that belief in the Messiah, *prior* to the confirmation of his Messiahship by the miraculous signs he must eventually perform, is itself an obligation and a source of benefit.

Such was the opinion of Maimonides. This is why he tells us we are obligated to believe and to presume that the righteous and Torah-studying king who rises to fight the Lord's battles is indeed the Messiah, even though it remains possible he may *not* be the Messiah! In this dispute, it seems, Maimonides has taken our side.

And, in truth, the proof is in Isaiah. Imagine for a moment that we are not under absolute obligation to believe in the Messiah, until he has achieved his state of greatness. Why then did Isaiah so multiply the details that characterize him? Why does he cry out, "Who has believed our report?" He must intend that we be capable of recognizing the Messiah even in his state of abasement, such that we believe in him and thereby assist him with our belief.

Taking as our premise that *all who have need of Redemption, need to have faith in the Redeemer*, we may draw an analogy from the First Redeemer to the Second.

When it was God's will to send Moses to Pharaoh, to bring the children of Israel out of Egypt, Moses sought to evade his mission. He did not protest that he was afraid of Pharaoh or in dread of the Egyptians. His essential argument was rather that *the Israelites would not believe in him*. This is obviously problematic. What possible difference could it have made to Moses whether they believed in him or not? The exodus would depend upon Pharaoh's decision. Pharaoh was the opponent against whom Moses must battle until, at length, the Israelites would leave Egypt over his resistance. But Moses was well aware that, absent the faith of those to whom salvation was promised, this promise could not easily be brought to fruition. It would rather demand terrible sufferings and immense exertion. This is why Moses had no fear of Pharaoh's sword or of any other danger. He was afraid, rather, of the people who lacked faith and of the possibility that the Israelites might not believe in him.

The Second Redeemer is dependent upon faith in precisely the same way. This is the hidden meaning of the text, "Righteousness shall be a belt round his waist, and faith a belt round his loins" [Isa 11:5].[73] A belt, once buckled on,[74] strengthens the loins of the man wearing it; in the same way faith augments the strength of the Redeemer. The verse conveys, as well, that the believer ought to cling to [the Messiah] just as a belt clings to a man's waist.

> [How does this work? Cardozo turns to the Kabbalah for an explanation. The Messiah/Redeemer, in his current status, is associated with *Malkhut*, the lowest of the *sefirot*. In this status, his radiance is feeble and obscure. "Faith" is associated with the same *sefirah*. Therefore, faith is necessary if the Messiah is to be successful.[75]]

The mystery is this: The "redeemer-angel" [Gen 48:16] is the *sefirah Malkhut*.[76] The Messiah is similarly called *Malkhut*, as is evident from the Zohar and the *Tiqqunim*, which assign "the kingdom *[malkhut]* of the house of David" to the lowest [sefirotic] level and declare it to be in need of effluence from the superior ranks.[77] The *sefirah Malkhut* is also called "faith," and "mirror that does not shine." As long as the Messiah is in this status of *Malkhut*, he will not shine with the radiance of the "shining mirror," which is called "Torah."[78] He will not radiate the sort of prophecy that, like sunlight, is clear to everyone, but only some meager visionary experience [like Nathan of Gaza's]. *As long as this condition obtains, faith is necessary.* For, if his prophecy were to shine like sunlight, we would not speak of *faith* but rather of *knowledge*.

This yields the following consequence. If we were dealing with a clear case of prophecy, in which evidentiary miracles vouch for the prophet's having been sent by the Lord to tell us who the Messiah is, *the believer would obtain no merit for his faith*. The Torah obligates us to believe every prophet whom the Lord has truly sent. The believer in the Messiah would then not really believe in the Messiah! He would, instead, believe in the prophet, and, in so doing, would fulfill one of the Torah's affirmative commands.

Suppose now that the Messiah were in his state of great glory. Suppose he were already enjoying the inspiration of "the spirit of the Lord, a spirit of wisdom and understanding" and so forth [Isa 11:2]. By believing in him, one would have no merit whatsoever for one's faith! Where something is clearly known, faith has no relevance. No one would speak of *believing* that twice times three is six; we would not call anyone a *believer* that he is an animate being or that the pillar he can see with his eyes is really a pillar. It is precisely where there is no clear light, no clear proof from Torah or from reason, but only faint illumination, that *faith* comes into play. For faith is the "mirror that does not shine," knowledge the "shining mirror," and anyone who wants to rise to the level of *knowledge* must first enter through the portal of *faith*, which is "the gate of the Lord."[79]

This provides an additional reason why the Messiah cannot possibly be revealed by a prophet who appears on the Lord's mission, as demonstrated by evidentiary miracles in accord with the Torah's requirement. There must be opportunity for Jewry's faith to be put to the test and for us thereby to acquire merit. This is no less essential than the requirement that the Messiah suffer torments, by means of which he makes atonement for the Jewish people and brings them out of exile.

Of this most recondite mystery, I shall say no more.

[Step 2: Cardozo sums up the results of the inquiry so far and points forward to the next step.]

We may say, in conclusion, that our knowledge of the Messiah rests upon six principles:

First, he is unquestionably to be born of woman.

Second, he must suffer torments following his manifestation.

Before he can rise to his lofty station, he must be insulted, cursed, and reviled.

Third, he must perform strange actions and must say things that will cause the Jews to lose faith in him. Yet, for all this, he will be righteous, for God will command him to do many things.

Fourth, he must be profaned. That is to say, he must be transformed from a state of holiness to a state of non-holiness, and he must do this, not of his own free will, but under duress.

Fifth, he is not to be revealed by a consensus-prophet. The sages of Israel have been unanimous on this point. They consequently formulated various hypotheses to explain how he *would* be revealed, such that all that is said about him might be maintained.

Sixth, we are obligated to believe in him *prior* to his truth's becoming clearly established. Faith is meritorious; it is beneficial; it is necessary.

Our task is now to consider whether Rabbi Sabbatai Zevi might conceivably be the Messiah. We must consider, also, what presumption we ought to hold with respect to him. Are we obliged to believe in him? Or, perhaps, is the very act of claiming him to be Messiah an act of iniquity?

[Step 3: Cardozo measures Sabbatai Zevi against the characteristic markers of Messiahship and finds that they all suit him perfectly.]

Our *first* condition in no way contradicts his Messiahship: the Messiah must be woman-born.

Our *second* provides clear indication that he *is* the Messiah. He has indeed suffered. He has twice been imprisoned; the second time, enjoying dignity and fame. (He was kept in a place where, in the past, no Jew had ever been imprisoned, but only viziers and generals and the like.)[80] Since his manifestation he has been the subject of innumerable insults and taunts. There was opposition to him even at the beginning of his manifestation, even though we who were far from the scene of events had been under the impression he had been revealed by a consensus-prophet. Great rabbis subsequently attacked him, even though all who had gone to examine the prophet Nathan agreed that he was deserving of credence.

What of the *third* condition? Your Worships have already borne witness, and affixed your signatures to that testimony, that he has fulfilled it. In full public view, he has done and spoken the strangest things. The world could hardly have borne a man who so shamelessly violated the Torah—who publicly[81] and for a full twenty years dared to speak the Sacred Tetragrammaton—if he were not the Messiah.

Is it thinkable that any Messianic pretender, actuated by any motive whatsoever, would ever try to win acceptance as Messiah by perpetrating such bizarre actions and gross transgressions? and that in full public view? This would hardly bring him to his goal! On the contrary: all would lose faith in him. Anyone who sought to deceive the people would surely represent himself as a saint, would surely uphold the Torah and the commandments and all the teachings of our rabbis. Thus did Jesus the Nazarene, claiming he had not come to violate a single commandment.[82] Thus did all the sneaks and scoundrels who have launched Messianic careers on some seven or eight occasions, pursuing the strategy of outward piety and uprightness and thus duping the people into believing in them.

On this supposition, Sabbatai Zevi would have destroyed himself body and soul for no purpose. He is without any worldly power, remember, yet he acts in such a way as to make himself obnoxious to the Jews, who will naturally want to kill him in their zeal for God's Torah. Who will be his protector? He well knows the practice of the Turk; he is not ignorant of the danger he incurs.[83]

Shall we say, then, that he is insane? If this were so, he surely would have stopped claiming to be Messiah once he had been put in prison. He did the very opposite. While in prison, he decreed to the entire Jewish people that they treat the Ninth of Av as a full festival.[84] We may find some indication of this (albeit not conclusive proof) in the defense he was able to offer on his own behalf, such that the Turk did not kill him but rather exalted him.[85]

As for the *fourth* condition—well, everyone knows that he has satisfied it. The Turk has brought him out from a state of holiness and into a state of non-holiness. Your Worships have heard (so you have written) that he petitioned[86] the Turk to accept him into his religion. I beg to assure you that this is false. The Turk twice pressured him with threats to abandon his faith, and they hurriedly dressed him in alien garb, yet he did not so much as open his mouth.[87] "Well, then," some say, "he should have become a martyr for the faith." But if he knew beyond doubt that he was the Messiah, it was his duty to follow wherever God might lead him, for good or for ill.

As for the *fifth* condition, the circumstances of his manifestation are all but conclusive proof that he is Messiah. The sages' conjecture, that Elijah would reveal the Messiah in a private locale and *not* in plain view of the whole Jewish people, has in him become solid reality. Rabbi Nathan Benjamin saw and heard, in a fully valid prophetic experience, that Sabbatai Zevi is the Messiah. From the very beginning he told all the rabbis who came to examine him that the Lord had *not* sent him to the Jewish people, that he could not provide any evidentiary miracle. But, in view of his marvelous wisdom, all the rabbis came to realize that they must believe he had seen the message of God.

> [Cardozo here takes up the task he promised at the end of his preface: of defining the prophetic status of Nathan of Gaza.]

We may take it as wholly certain that they did not frivolously put their trust in him! True, he may have erred in that he revealed the Messiah without having God's warrant or commission; we shall address this presently. And they may have sinned who wrote to all the Jewish people that "there is a prophet," without any qualification. We shall presently see that they really should have defined the situation with full accuracy.[88]

But we must stick to the issue [of the rabbis' absolute trust in Nathan], for here we have a clear proof. Consider: when the rabbis were on their way from Gaza to Constantinople with Rabbi Nathan, while they had stopped in Aleppo, they received the awful news that the Turk had clothed Rabbi Sabbatai Zevi with disgrace. Yet they did not fear for their lives, nor did they waver in their support. *They went with him.* Well they knew the danger they were in: all the Jews would persecute them and would hand them over to the Turkish authorities. *Yet they went with him,* just as they had at the beginning. I do not speak of one rabbi, or of two, but of a full thirty rabbis! If they had not regarded Rabbi Nathan as trustworthy, they certainly would not have involved themselves in a business so hazardous, so fraught with risks to body and soul and faith. Dreadful events, to be sure, may have taken place, but truth is not therefore wanting.[89]

Rabbi Nathan spent more than two months in Leghorn.[90] All who spoke with him privately have conceded his wisdom and his righteousness and have come to believe that what he says is true in the sense that he has received a prophecy *for himself.* It is true that the rabbis of Venice found no substance in him. But there was a particular reason for this. All of us who were far removed from the scene of events simply assumed that Rabbi Nathan was a prophet in the sense that he had received the Lord's commission and was equipped with evidentiary miracles, as the Torah says a prophet ought to be. This assumption, the Venetian rabbis discovered, was incorrect. When Rabbi Nathan saw and heard the message, "Thus saith the Lord: Your savior is come, Sabbatai Zevi his name," it was *for himself* that he saw and heard it.

The rabbis consequently ruled that, by the Torah's criterion, there was no substance in his words. This, after all, is the definition of a prophet to Israel: someone whom the Lord has truly dispatched and who carries with him (as it were) the Lord's seal, that is to say, evidentiary miracles, which must be performed over and over again by any worthy person who wishes to be acknowledged as prophet by the consensus of the Jewish people. Measured against this definition—so Your Worships and the Adrianople rabbis have testified—he has indeed been examined and found without substance. The prophet must provide a sign; he has no sign. This I do indeed believe, with absolute certainty: *he is no emissary-prophet.*

"Why then," someone may say, "will you not believe us when we write above our signatures that Sabbatai Zevi is not the Messiah?" To which I reply that the Messiah [unlike the prophet] is under no obligation to provide evidentiary miracles. Therefore, inasmuch as he is destined to be abused and insulted by the rabbis of Israel, the more these rabbis insist that he is *not* the Messiah, the more do they prove that he *is* the Messiah! For this is one of his signs; it is an essential distinguishing characteristic of him.

In conclusion, then: *Your Worships' assertion that the prophet* [Nathan] *is no prophet is a statement of certain knowledge. Your parallel assertion with regard to the Messiah is pure conjecture.*

God further helped the Messiah to be revealed[91] by sending into every place sparks of spiritual holiness that proclaimed in a thousand different ways the glad tidings that Sabbatai Zevi is the Messiah. "Demons' work all!" you will say. But this is pure conjecture; wanting any scrap of evidence, it does not deserve the name even of conjecture. How, in truth, did Your Worships succeed in establishing the fact (to which you signed your names) that all these spiritual entities were lying? How could all of them, from east to west, have agreed without divergence on the single message that Sabbatai Zevi is Messiah? Demons and evil spirits will lie, to be sure, but they will not be able to lie unanimously. This is the hidden meaning of the verse, "All the workers of iniquity shall be divided" [Ps 92:10].

I may add that I have a thorough knowledge of history and can aver that spiritual testimony of a public character, such as we have seen in our own time, is attested for *none* of the Messianic outbreaks of the past. I would query, moreover, whether demons and spirits have the power to act of their own will, without God's permission, or whether they do not. If one should say that they do, then why have they not already destroyed the world? It is our credo, truly, that the spirits cannot do anything of this kind absent God's permission. How could we possibly believe that, after this bitterly cruel exile of ours, spirits might [be given leave to] deceive us and injure the Messiah? (God has warned us, after all, to "lay no hand on My anointed ones" [Ps 105:15].) It is surely more plausible to think that they came to bring the good news of Redemption! To claim that the spirits revealed in our time were all liars is simply putting ideas into one's adversary's head[92]—and who could bring himself to do that?

159

[These arguments, as Scholem has pointed out, were to become inconvenient for Cardozo after 1683, when "lying spirits" seduced the Sabbatians of Salonica into mass conversion to Islam.[93] But, when Cardozo writes this, 1683 is still fourteen years away.]

"Still," you will retort, "we have no clear evidence that all the spirits were holy. There were indeed things revealed that proved to be true—but many were deceiving." Yes, but this was all so that the Messiah's manifestation should not become *absolutely* plain. God gave permission to some lying spirit to manifest itself along with the true spirits, in order to make possible the fulfillment of everything, trials included, that is destined to befall after the Messiah is revealed.

If, then, we are to take prophecy, rabbinic tradition, and the conditions we have established to be our criteria, it will follow that *Sabbatai Zevi has a greater presumption of being Messiah than Ben Koziba had*. We have a greater duty to believe that he is the Messiah than we do to believe in the man of whom Maimonides wrote that "he is to be presumed Messiah." If, Maimonides said, a wise and righteous king should "arise [...] and fight the Lord's battles," we are obligated to believe he is Messiah even though this has not been established beyond all doubt. Ben Koziba fitted this description, as we have seen, and the sages therefore believed in him. And yet, as things turned out, he was *not* the Messiah.

Up till now, however, we have seen no one who revealed himself as Messiah, and who had all the distinguishing characteristics [found in Sabbatai Zevi], who nevertheless turned out *not* to be Messiah. The markers of *this* Messiah, therefore, seem to be more accurate than those of either Ben Koziba or of the Messiah sketched by Maimonides. Those of Ben Koziba and Maimonides have proven deceptive, while the markers of *this* Messiah have so far not betrayed a single flaw. From the qualitative distinction between the former and the latter, therefore, the nature of our obligation clearly emerges.

One may well ask why Maimonides did not indicate the markers of the Messiah's abasement, as he indicated those of his greatness.

The answer is that Maimonides was uncertain how the Messiah was to be revealed. He came to the conclusion that abasement and insult would in no way serve to reveal the Messiah's identity, and therefore excused himself from writing about them. Rather, he decided, the Messiah would be revealed by some great triumph which would induce the Jews to believe him to be the Messiah. The insults and the abuse would presumably come afterward. But, since they would not serve to reveal the Messiah, he would leave them to one side.

I need say no more. We have seen already that all has been fulfilled. The Messiah has been revealed. His fame has spread as far as the Spanish Indies. He has been profaned. All Scriptures are fulfilled.

[Part Two. The Testimony]

I shall now tell Your Worships the absolute truth. But I must first provide a preface.

God, in His mercy, has given me honor and high station in this country [Tripoli]. I have slaves and servant-girls. I have horses to ride.[94] I have no obligations to the state beyond making calls upon the commander of the country's army, two or three times a week, at my own convenience. All my food and clothing is provided me from his house. I do not need to attend to the sick of the town, and therefore have all my time free for the study of Torah.

Keep in mind, as well, that I am far distant from both Gaza and Izmir. I could not possibly have conspired with Nathan Benjamin for the two of us to announce in unison that Sabbatai Zevi is the Messiah. What, moreover, can be supposed to motivate my yearning for the Redeemer's advent? Certainly not my being in exile, for I experience no exile.[95] It cannot be the need to struggle for a living, for I am at my ease. Nor can it be the wish for time to study Torah, for I have both time and preparation. I am indeed among those who long for our salvation. But this is not for the sake of any material gratification. No: it is because I seek to fulfill the

161

injunction that we must look with eagerness toward our salvation.[96] It will be wholly evident from this that my purpose is not, God forbid, to seduce the Jewish people into false worship, and that anyone who suspects me of this crime is a devilish villain. What can I possibly gain by revealing these matters?

Let me begin by taking a solemn oath, by the existence of the Cause of all causes and the Occasion of all occasions,[97] whose name is the Lord. *Never, in all my life, have I exercised power over any angel or spirit of a deceased saint, or over any spirit whatsoever, to compel that entity to reveal itself to me or to answer any question of mine on any subject at all. I have never employed any of God's holy names to accomplish any effect or to summon any creature whatsoever.* Always, from my youth down to the present, have I been innocent in this respect with the Lord my God.

I swear, moreover, that from the day that the lights first began to reveal themselves to me—as I shall describe in detail presently—they have told me nothing that was false. It may possibly be that rumors have circulated in your town to the effect that my spirit-guides have on occasion lied. I now share with Your Worships the true facts; namely, that I have twice erred in understanding my visions, and only afterward came to realize their true meaning. It has also happened that I have begun to initiate certain people into these truths and then found them unworthy, whereupon I deliberately got them muddled so they would come away with the impression that my revelations were false.

And now I will speak the truth.

[Many of the stories that follow had already made their appearance in Cardozo's Hebrew letter of 1668 (see the introduction to this chapter). There are sometimes interesting variations between the two versions; see the endnotes to the following material.]

In the year 5409 [1648–49] I was studying Torah in Venice. That was where I began my studies at the age of twenty-two, having left Spain when I was twenty-one. I had a dream that the Messiah had appeared and that the people of Venice did not believe in him. But

God gave me strength, and I seated him on my shoulders and proclaimed through the marketplaces, "This is the true Messiah!"

One night, some eight and a half years ago,[98] I saw the entire Jewish people ingathered to the holy land, their king with them. They were distributing estates, and the Temple was built up in the most splendid way. Another night, I saw in my dream the heavens opened and God hurling fire from heaven upon this city. I fell on my face; I prostrated myself; I said, "Lord my God! Do You intend wholly to eradicate this town?" They responded, "For the sake of three persons, I shall not destroy the entirety." He then showed me who the three persons were. Two of them were in this town; the third was a member of my household who was still in Leghorn.

I told people about this dream, so that they would repent. Not long after that, my entire household arrived in this city. The plague began afterward. Little boys and girls died, as did women. But, with one exception, no adult male perished. I normally take little account of dreams. But this time it occurred to me that I might combine the two dreams of the two nights,[99] and take this as a hint that, the [latter dream] having been fulfilled, so would the [former].

After the year 5423 [1662–63] had begun, moreover, I saw in a dream the following words written out: "The Redeemer will come in the year 5425" [1664–65]. The last digit was mutilated, however, as though worms had been eating at it and only the bottom hook had survived. The dream must mean, I concluded, that the Messiah would be revealed either in 5425 or 5429 [1668–69]. (The hook of the letter that marked the digit did not protrude beneath the line, and therefore could have indicated only 5 or 9.) When I compared the hook of the mutilated digit with that of the first digit, I found them to be similar. Hence I concluded that his manifestation would take place in 5425, and so it happened.

A great and mysterious event befell me another night. My head was filled with ideas as I lay in bed,[100] yet I was not dreaming but was fully awake. The next morning I told the people of my household that a baby boy was going to be born to me, and that he would prove to be a lamp for the Messiah. But they should not rejoice over him till ten days had passed, I told them, for before the tenth day he would suddenly die. And so it happened! The boy was born, and on the day of his birth this town received the good news that the Messiah had been revealed. He then died suddenly on the eighth day, before he could be circumcised. This is all true as the Torah of Moses.

Subsequently, in the month of Shevat 5426 [January 7–February 5, 1666], during the predawn hours, a light appeared in my house to an old lady.[101] For thirty-one years now the woman has been ill with the disease called *paralyza*, such that her left arm is emaciated like a dead limb and she cannot move it at all. The disease recurred nine years ago, with the effect that the bone of her upper leg became dislocated, the tendons contracted, and the entire leg was left as immobile as the arm.

When she saw the bright light, she assumed the sun had risen. She then went back to sleep and woke to find the whole house dark. She became alarmed. "Master of the universe!" she said. "Is it not enough that I am like a dead woman? Must I go blind as well?" (For she thought she had suddenly lost her vision.) But then the lunatic [the Muslim muezzin, that is][102] sounded his customary call [to prayer], and she was relieved, for she knew it must still be night.

When she told us her story the next morning, we laughed at her. Over the next fifteen days, the lights appeared to her three or four times more. But I still did not take her seriously.

One night I was given the premonition that a star, big as the full moon, was going to appear in the sky. The lady told me the next morning that, in the predawn hours, she had seen a star like the sun and the moon, which had illuminated the entire house. It was then that I realized that what she had been saying was absolutely true. I thereupon begged God for an explanation of these events, and He heard my prayer.

I was given yet another premonition of the star's appearance during the month of Adar [March 8–April 5, 1666],[103] and a third time, with greater clarity, on the night of the Great Sabbath [April 16].[104] And on Saturday, the twenty-fifth day of the Omer of the year 5426 [May 15, 1666], the star appeared in the eastern sky half an hour past sunrise, to the right of the sun. It was the size of the moon; people saw it shining with a clear, brilliant light. God covered the sun with a thick cloud, so that the witnesses would be able to gaze at that star as it rose along with the sun. They watched it for about half an hour, till the sun had risen further and left the cloud behind. The witnesses' vision then began to suffer, and the star gradually faded from their view.

I myself did not see it. I had contracted an eye disease and had not yet gotten out of bed. But I could hear the sounds of great amazement from those who did see it from the upper story of my house. These were Samuel Alluf, son-in-law of the judge Rabbi Joseph Agiv; Abraham Nunez, now resident in Leghorn;[105] and Joseph ibn Sheshet. Other Jews saw it from the wall.

Why this sign was granted me cannot be explained. Inasmuch as I did not see it, I prayed God to tell me if it was indeed the star of which I had had the premonition. Now, the old lady was by the courtyard entrance late that Tuesday afternoon, and she began yelling that she had just seen for the fourth time[106] a star as big as the sun, which had all but blinded her by its sheer brilliance. Wednesday I kept on praying, and it was seen yet again in the late afternoon, in the middle of the courtyard.

In the month of Shevat [January 7–February 5, 1666], and in First Adar [February 6–March 7], I dreamed that I saw seven Tannaim sitting studying the Torah, Rabbi Simeon ben Yohai and Rabbi Hiyya the Great among them. In my presence, the Patriarch ordered them to summon a certain man. I heard the Patriarch say to the seven Tannaim, "Give honor to the king." They all stood up, and the Patriarch gave a loud shout, "Bring a throne for the king, bring a throne for the king!" And the man said, "No need; sit down; sit down and busy yourselves with a profound *halakhah*."

I woke up then, and immediately the dream came back to me. The ceiling of the room opened, and I saw the Lord sitting on a throne high and exalted. I had previously been composing an original hymn about the Shechinah's having gone back up to Her proper place,[107] and now God said to me that "I have received this hymn." He assured me, moreover, that "salvation is now at hand, so give the Jewish people a message of great consolation and honor." That morning the old lady had told me that she had been shown, within the light that had appeared to her, a throne white as snow. So I said, "May it be Your will, Lord my God, that I be shown who is going to sit on this throne," whereupon a cloud appeared and covered the throne. I thus began to be entirely convinced that the old lady had been speaking the truth.

On one occasion afterward, I spent the entire night begging and pleading with God to grant me a trustworthy token by healing the old lady. When I got up in the morning, the token and the wonder turned out to be in the healing of my own eyes.

Your Worships must know that, a year and a half earlier, I had contracted (for my sins) a grave eye disease called *cataratas* [cataracts]. I had tried every cure known to man, but to no avail. My blindness actually grew progressively worse, till I had despaired of my vision. Now I praised and thanked God for the grace He had shown me. Yet I nevertheless resumed my prayers and my pleas. This, I said, was an inner sign that people would never believe if I told them about it. But if God would only do me the very great favor of restoring the old lady's arm and leg to their former condition, then the people would surely become firm believers upon seeing the great miracle, would surely turn themselves to repentance and good deeds!

Sure enough: a light was revealed to her shortly before dawn. Her arm relaxed. Her big toe stretched itself out, and the bone of her upper leg went back into its socket. Her mouth and her left eye were healed; her right eye did indeed wobble a bit, but not as badly as before. Her left shoulder went back up to its proper place, and the arm came away from her body. Her leg extended itself, though not such that she could stand on it. This was because God did not wish to publicize the sign, but only granted it to me so that I might believe in the mission He had given me.

The lady remains well to this day. After three days, alas, my own illness began to come back, and my cure did not last. Perhaps this was because I had asked for the second sign.

I asked God's favor on yet another occasion. I was suffering greatly, in intense and enduring pain. I asked that He allay my doubts by letting me have an answer to the question that I would formulate in my mind. I thought upon the kingship and wondered to whom it would belong—and hardly had I finished when a heavenly voice proclaimed: "It is Sabbatai Zevi who is destined to reign!"

One day, moreover, I was in some perplexity over the interpretation of two visions I had seen during the night. In came my four-year-old daughter, named Rachel. She told me—speaking not in ordinary language, but, as though teasingly, in a marvelous manner—she told me my innermost thoughts, and, in a few words, revealed to me what I had kept locked up inside me. Then out she went again. We ran after her and asked her about the things she had said. But she had not the slightest recollection of them, and would not reply on the subject, just as though nothing had ever happened.[108]

One night, also, the most terrific thing happened to me. I announced to my entire household, and to other people as well, that "through this immersion [which one of Cardozo's wives was to undergo, in preparation for lovemaking][109] I am about to beget a baby boy whose name is to be Ephraim." I said quite explicitly that he would be born on a Sabbath. And all of this came true.[110]

After this I received the good news that a baby boy named Asher was to be born to me. On the day of his birth there would be princes in Israel, and even beforehand the words would be spoken: "Happy are you, Israel! [Who is like you, people saved by the Lord?" Deut 33:29].[111]

I call heaven and earth to witness that, on one single day, I saw two or three extraordinary signs and tokens, each of them indispensable. Oh, I could go on like this endlessly! but I have written only the tiniest fraction. And through all these experiences I have come to know that the true Messiah is Sabbatai Zevi, for whom I am obliged to sacrifice my life.

Chapter 10
In Quest of the
Hidden God

INTRODUCTION

1.

...it would seem inevitable, from the very nature of our
exiled condition, that this [Jewish] people—poor and
oppressed, tormented by hordes of dreadful calamities—
could not hope to acquire wisdom of any kind. The
wonder and the miracle is that we, lacking ease and tranquility, nevertheless have some measure of sagacity and
wisdom.

Cardozo might have been writing about himself in this passage.
The treatise from which it is taken, *This Is My God and I Will
Praise Him*, was composed in 1685 or 1686.[1] At that time, Cardozo
was in his private exile by the Dardanelles, and "ease and tranquility" must have seemed a remote and heartbreaking memory.

Cardozo and his family had been forced out of Constantinople
in the spring of 1682. He was humiliated, disgraced. The
Redemption, which he had so confidently predicted for Passover of
that year, had not materialized. His patron, Solomon Galimidi, had

lost faith in him. Sabbatai Zevi's widow, Esther, once so eager to marry him, had turned her back on him forever. His enemies were ready to lynch him.

The next four or five years were a time of poverty and misery for Cardozo and his family. Hunger, disease, and death were regular visitors to their household. There were spiritual afflictions as well. Demons, descending from the moon, settled themselves into his home. They stayed with him for days on end, tormenting his body with fever and his soul with blasphemies.[2] The twin traumas of that decade—the failed Redemption of 1682, and the mass apostasy at Salonica in 1683—were to cast their shadow over the rest of his life. When he set about writing *This Is My God*, the pain of them must still have been fresh and raw.

One could not guess any of this from reading *This Is My God*. Of all Cardozo's theological writings—he was to write something like sixty treatises, some of them voluminous, in explication of his ideas—it would be hard to find one that is more calm and self-assured in its tone, more lucid and methodical in its presentation. The chaos and unhappiness of Cardozo's life in the mid-1680s have left hardly a trace in the text. Nor could one imagine, from reading it, that only a few years earlier his faith and self-confidence had been all but devastated.

The treatise's ideas, to be sure, were hardly new. Those who had read *Abraham's Morn*, at the beginning of the 1670s, would have found practically nothing in *This Is My God* that they did not already know. Cardozo had been making essentially the same points and advancing many of the same arguments in their support for the past fifteen years. He would keep on making these points and arguments, in different sequences and with minor variations, until his death twenty years later.

He did not, however, always write for the same audience. Many of his treatises are intended for the specialist in Kabbalah. He consumes page after page with extended quotations from the Zohar, and even more extended discussions of these quotations. He describes and analyzes God and His component elements with all the precision of a physicist discussing subatomic particles. *This Is*

My God, by contrast, is Cardozan theology for the layperson. To the extent that he can, Cardozo keeps himself clear of Kabbalistic technicalities. More than three-quarters of the treatise (chapters I–X, XII–XIV)[3] can be understood with only the most minimal Kabbalistic background. In chapter XI, Cardozo provides what he evidently intends to be a novice's introduction to Kabbalah, so that even the untutored reader will understand the unavoidable Kabbalistic discussions in the final chapters.

This simplicity has its disadvantages. Cardozo's solution to the question he poses throughout the treatise—Who is God?[4]—emerges here far less precisely than it does in some of his other writings. (It could not be otherwise. Cardozo could not count on the reader of *This Is My God* to have mastered the technical vocabulary in which the specifics must necessarily be stated.) Yet this same simplicity gives *This Is My God* its enormous value as Cardozo's primer to his own theology. A reader of the twenty-first century, no less than the lay Jewish reader of the seventeenth, can turn to it for a first encounter with what Cardozo regarded as his deepest and most precious insights. The obstacles to comprehension are relatively few. They may be surmounted with relative ease.

2.

It is not entirely clear how long a book Cardozo intended to write. The fullest surviving manuscript of *This Is My God* contains seventeen chapters and the beginning of an eighteenth. The first sixteen of these chapters are a self-contained, coherent, and well-structured unity; the closing of chapter XVI may be well understood as a conclusion to the entire treatise;[5] and it seems reasonable to assume that the first sixteen chapters are the treatise as Cardozo originally conceived and composed it.[6] (Chapter XVII and the fragmentary chapter XVIII are both appendices, afterthoughts.) The sixteen chapters may usefully be grouped into three approximately equal divisions of the treatise. I have marked them parts one, two, and three, but the reader must keep in mind that, unlike the chapter divisions, they have no basis in the manuscripts. They are entirely my own.

In **Part One** (chapters I–VI), Cardozo establishes the overwhelming importance, for the Jewish individual and the Jewish community, of knowing God's true identity and the nature of His Divinity. He demonstrates that the Jewish people have long since lost that knowledge. He explains, in terms of divine justice and providence, how it was that this extraordinary—indeed, preternatural—act of "forgetting" came about. **Part Two** (chapters VII–XI) is a survey of contemporary religious belief, non-Jewish and Jewish, which illustrates, for Cardozo, the range and variety of contemporary ignorance of religious truth. In **Part Three** (chapters XII–XVI), Cardozo leads the reader on the uphill path out of this ignorance toward what he regards as the essential intellectual achievement of recognizing God's true identity.

Cardozo tacks on to the end of this treatise, first, a technical appendix discussing some of the Kabbalistic implications of his theory of Divinity (chapter XVII), and then a fragment of a second appendix, in which he rehearses his familiar argument that the Jewish liturgy represents God as the recipient rather than the source of blessing, and therefore an inferior and dependent being (chapter XVIII).[7]

I translate chapters I–XVI in full, omitting only three brief passages[8] that complicate the understanding of the text far out of proportion to any contribution they make to the argument. I leave the "appendixes" untranslated. (Chapter XVII, in particular, would mean little to those without background in Kabbalah.) But I do translate the conclusion to chapter XVII, in which Cardozo conveys, in a really elegant and moving way, his sense of indebtedness to those who came before him to the investigation of Divinity.

3.

How best to approach the reading of *This Is My God*? I suggest that the reader first review the account of Cardozo's theology I have given in chapter 4, and, before tackling Cardozo's discussions of Kabbalah (chapters IX, XI, XV–XVI), review what I have said about Kabbalah in chapter 2. (Cardozo seems to have regarded *This Is My God*, chapter XI, as an entirely adequate introduction to Kabbalah. Modern readers are unlikely to agree.) The following synopsis of the argument can serve as the reader's road map, for what lies ahead:

Part One: Cardozo begins by defining the essential religious obligation of Judaism as *intellectual*. We Jews, Cardozo says, are required to *know* the Lord, that is, to possess a clear intellectual awareness of Who that Deity is that we worship. This is demanded by the First Commandment. "I am the Lord your God, who brought you out of the land of Egypt" (Exod 20:2), means, *know* the existence of the true God. Similarly, the *Shema*'—the fundamental credo of Judaism, stated in Deuteronomy 6:4—constitutes a demand for an intellectual understanding of God's Divinity and His Unity (chapter I).

Individually, it is the life's task of each of us to seek this awareness while we live on this earth. The successful attainment of this goal is our only legitimate source of pride. It is a rare achievement: only four human beings have attained it or will attain it through their own, unaided intellectual powers. These are Abraham, Job, Hezekiah (a king of ancient Judah, described in the Second Book of Kings), and the Messiah (chapter II).

Collectively, the entire Jewish people is obligated to know who God is and to grasp the nature of His Divinity, so that they may serve, as Isaiah says, as His witnesses. (You cannot witness to a truth that you do not yourself understand.) The ancient rabbis emphasize how essential this service is: when the Jews do not witness to God's Divinity, they say, God is not truly God (chapters I, III). Yet, tragically, the Jews *cannot* witness to Him because at present they do not know Him, and they do not know Him because He has hidden Himself from them and caused them to forget the knowledge of Him that their ancestors (in biblical and Talmudic times) once possessed (chapters I, III, IV). The doom, pronounced upon them in ancient times, therefore continues to be fulfilled upon them: "Israel shall spend many days without a true God" (2 Chr 15:3).

Why did God hide Himself? Cardozo gives two answers. The divine self-concealment was a punishment on the one hand, an act of mercy on the other. A punishment because the Jews in ancient times had perversely spurned and deliberately forgotten the God whom they knew, and He punished them, appropriately, by compelling the Jews to forget Him against their will and in spite of their best efforts (chapter III). An act of mercy because, once the Jews know Who it is to Whom they pray, they will be able to force with their prayers an end to their exile, and a premature end to the exile would, in the long run, have harmed them (chapter IV).

This last point has a corollary, which Cardozo announces at the end of chapter II and continues to refer back to throughout the first stage of his argument. In order for the Jews to leave their exile, they must recover the lost knowledge of God. It is therefore the Messiah's essential role to discover this knowledge on his own and to reveal it to the Jewish people. This act, of discovery and publication of the saving knowledge, is the essence of his redemptive task. As Cardozo puts it, perhaps in unconscious allusion to John 1:49:

> That person, therefore, who has struggled successfully to recognize the Creator and who has communicated the knowledge of His Divinity to the public, is to be called the *Son of God* and the *Redeemer of Israel*. (chapter II, end)

Cardozo *may* be referring here to Sabbatai Zevi. But Sabbatai does not appear in *This Is My God*, apart from a vague allusion to him in an entirely non-Messianic context (chapter XI). We have seen, moreover, that Sabbatai bitterly disappointed Cardozo, in that he did *not* discharge the Messianic task of communicating the knowledge of God's Divinity to the Jewish public.[9] It therefore seems more likely that the Messianic "Redeemer" to whom Cardozo here refers is none other than himself.

Near the end of chapter IV, Cardozo first alludes to the key error that has blinded the Jews to God's true identity. This is their

173

belief, which they share with the Gentiles of modern times, that God and the First Cause are one and the same. Now, the Bible teaches that the Gentiles *cannot* know the true God, prior to the Messiah's coming. So, if the Gentiles do not know God, contemporary Jews—whose doctrine of God is essentially that of the Gentiles—cannot know Him either (chapter V).

Cardozo illustrates the consequences of the false identification of God with the First Cause by pointing to the Jews' utter inability satisfactorily to define the identity of the Shechinah. We know the Shechinah exists, because our ancient rabbinic sources speak of Her. But, proceeding as we do from false theological premises, we cannot explain who She is without falling into either idolatry or ditheism.[10] Contemporary Jews, it would seem, do not know the God of Israel (chapter VI).

Part Two: Having made this point, Cardozo leaves the question of the Shechinah—he will never actually resolve it in *This Is My God*, apart from a few oblique hints—and embarks upon a survey of world religions. (He thereby fills out the picture that he had sketched, in the most general terms, in chapter V.) He finds that *all* religions, ancient and modern, agree that there is a Supreme Being who is the First Cause, and that that Being is to be loved and venerated. Christians and Muslims identify that Being with the God of Israel, who gave Moses the Torah. So do the Deist philosophers of modern times, who, however, reject the Torah itself as Moses's fabrication (chapters VII–VIII). So do contemporary Jews (chapter IX).

Jews, however, are split into two camps, the Kabbalists and the "literalists." The literalists insist on God's pure and absolute Unity. The Kabbalists, by contrast, believe in a multiplicity of divine entities (the ten *sefirot*) that have emanated from God and are necessary for His worship (chapter IX). On this question, Cardozo comes down solidly on the side of the Kabbalists (whose beliefs he sketches in chapter XI), providing clear demonstrations of the existence of the *sefirot* from the Bible and the rabbinic literature (chapter X). Yet, on the issue of the relation of God and the First Cause, the Kabbalists are hardly less deluded than their literalist opponents (chapter XI).

So far, Cardozo's survey of comparative religion has revealed a sort of contemporary "universal consensus" that God and the First Cause are one and the same. Yet, since the Gentiles cannot possibly have true knowledge of God until the Messianic era (chapter V), *the very fact that the Gentiles believe in this equation is itself evidence that it is false* (chapter X). We must take a different path toward a true knowledge of God.

Part Three: Cardozo takes as his starting point the premise—which he establishes on the basis of natural reason, Bible, and midrash—that the Creator of the world is God by definition. It does not matter if there are other creators besides Him; it does not matter if they are superior to Him; it does not matter whether or not He is the Supreme Being. All that matters is that it is He who has created us, and it will follow that He is the God whom we must worship (chapter XII). This point is important for Cardozo's argument. Otherwise, we might be tempted to argue that, if there is a "God" who is inferior to and derivative from the First Cause, we ought to pass Him by and worship the First Cause. This is precisely where Cardozo does *not* want us to go.

Cardozo now turns to the ancient sources (mostly, but not exclusively, Jewish), to establish that there was an ancient "universal consensus" concerning the God of Israel, quite different from the modern consensus that he has discussed in chapters VII–IX. This consensus was that the God of Israel is *not* the First Cause, but something distinct from and inferior to It. Such was the belief of the ancient pagans before the time of Abraham, of the Greeks and the Romans (chapter XIII), of the ancient Jews whether or not they were loyal to God (chapter XIV). It was the belief also of the angels, as Cardozo demonstrates through a brilliant analysis of the rabbinic tradition according to which the angels wanted to worship the newly created Adam (chapter XIII). *This* consensus, universally held until the end of the Talmudic period, conforms to the truth. The error of the pagans was not their distinction between the First Cause and the God of Israel—on this point, they were entirely correct—but their belief that the First Cause and not the God of Israel was Creator of the world.

In chapter XV, Cardozo's argument takes a strange turn, which seems to undermine everything he has said so far. After having insisted, for pages, that God and the First Cause are not the same, he now seems to turn around and say that they *are* the same. Why does he do this? The answer is that he has become distracted into polemic against his fellow Sabbatians. Some of them have claimed, supposedly on Sabbatai Zevi's authority, that the God of Israel is identical with the *sefirah Tif'eret*.[11] This is wrong, says Cardozo: God is not any one *sefirah*, nor even the totality of the *sefirot*, but a higher Spirit that incarnates itself within them all. In order to pound this point across, Cardozo allows himself—at a considerable sacrifice of clarity—to speak as though this indwelling Spirit were the First Cause.

In the very last sentence of chapter XV, Cardozo's argument gets back on track. In chapter XVI, it rolls to its triumphant conclusion. God is not the First Cause after all, but a Spirit emanated from the First Cause, inferior to the First Cause and dependent upon It.

The "tainted texts" of Talmud and midrash, which had so troubled Cardozo when he began his studies years earlier,[12] now find their explanation. The Talmud says that God prays. To whom does He pray? To the First Cause, from which He emerged and which dwells continually within Him. The "tainted texts" speak of Him as limited and dependent, because in a sense He *is* limited and dependent.

Cardozo has thus rediscovered and revealed the ancient and authentic Jewish doctrine of God. The "many days," for the duration of which Israel was to be "without a true God," are drawing to their close. Redemption is at hand.

BACKGROUND TEXTS

¹The spirit of God came upon Azariah the son of Oded. ²He appeared before Asa and said to him: "Listen to me, Asa, and all Judah and Benjamin! The Lord is with you, as long as you are with Him. If you search for Him, He will allow you to discover Him. But if you abandon Him, He will abandon you ³and Israel shall spend many days without a true God, without a teaching priest, without Torah.

⁴Then [Israel] shall return, in its troubles, to the Lord God of Israel. They shall seek Him, and He will allow them to discover Him. ⁵In those times, no one shall have security, for great tumults shall befall those who dwell in all lands. ⁶One nation shall be crushed against another, and one city against another, for God will have vexed them with troubles of every kind.

⁷You be strong, though, and do not relax yourselves. For you will be rewarded for what you have done."

—2 Chronicles 15:1–7 (translated as
Cardozo would have understood it)

The biblical text "Who has anticipated Me, that I may reward him?" [Job 41:3] is spoken of Abraham, who arrived on his own at a recognition of God. So it is written: ..."And from himself the good man shall be satisfied" [Prov 14:14]: this was Abraham, who recognized God on his own. No one taught him how to recognize God. He did so on his own, and thus became one of the four individuals who have arrived, on their own, at a recognition of God.

Job arrived on his own at a recognition of God. How do we know this? From the biblical text "I have stored up, from my own dictation, the words of His mouth" [Job 23:12]. Hezekiah king of Judah also arrived on his own at a recognition of God. How do we know this? From the biblical text "Butter and honey shall he eat. Of

177

his own knowledge shall he reject the evil and choose the good" [Isa 7:15]. King Messiah arrived on his own at a recognition of God. And thus also did Abraham.

God said to him: "Abraham, the upper and the lower realms all belong to Me....You made My Name known throughout the world. By your life! I am granting to you the upper and the lower realms....'Who has anticipated Me, that I may reward him?'"

—*Midrash Numbers Rabbah* 14:2

How do we know that God wears phylacteries? From the biblical text "The Lord has sworn by His right hand, and by His mighty arm" [Isa 62:8]. "His right hand" refers to the Torah...while "His mighty arm" refers to the phylacteries....How do we know that God prays? From the biblical text "I will bring them to My holy mountain, and I will gladden them in the house of My prayer" [Isa 56:7]. The text does not say, "their prayer," but "My prayer." It follows from this that God prays.

What prayer does He pray?..."May it be the will from within Me that My mercies overcome My anger, and that My mercies dominate My attributes, and I deal with My children in accord with the Attribute of Mercy; and, on their behalf, I go beyond the requirements of justice."...

Rabbi Ishmael ben Elisha said, "Once I entered the Holy of Holies to burn incense, and I saw Akhtariel Yah, Lord of Hosts, sitting on a high and exalted throne. He said to me: 'Ishmael, My son, bless Me!' I said to Him: 'May it be the will from within Thee that Thy mercies overcome Thine anger, and that Thy mercies dominate Thine attributes, and that Thou deal with Thy children in accord with the Attribute of Mercy; and, on their behalf, Thou go beyond the requirements of justice.'

"And He nodded to me, with His head."

—BT Berakhot 6a–7a

"You are My witnesses, says the Lord; and I am God" [Isa 43:12]: whenever you are My witnesses, I am God. But, when you are not My witnesses—if one dare to say it—I am not God.

—*Sifrei* (Tannaitic midrash) on Deuteronomy, para. 346

THIS IS MY GOD, AND I WILL PRAISE HIM[13]

[Part One]
Chapter I
Human Beings Are Under the Obligation
to Recognize Their Creator

It is a well-known fact that humans have been created with intelligence and free will in order to serve their Creator. It is, moreover, impossible truly to serve a Being while remaining ignorant concerning that Being's existence. God therefore endowed humans with an innate knowledge by which His Divinity might be apprehended, in order that they might conduct themselves wisely.

He went even further. Through His faithful servant Moses, He communicated His existence to the Jewish people. He gave them the Torah and its interpretation in order that they might serve Him perfectly in accord with its dictates. He desired not only their belief in Him, but also their recognition and *knowledge* of His true reality, through principles immovably rooted in wisdom, understanding, and knowledge.

Such was the case with the generation that possessed knowledge [who crossed the wilderness with Moses].[14] "You have been shown," Scripture says of them, "in order that you might *know*, that the Lord is God; there exists none beside Him" [Deut 4:35]. And again: "You must *know*, and keep firmly in mind, that the Lord is God in the heavens above and on the earth beneath. There exists none other" [Deut 4:39]. And again: "I will choose you as My people and I will be your God; and you shall *know* that I am the Lord" [Exod 6:7].

That is why the essence of the whole Torah is contained in the words: "I am the Lord your God, who brought you out of the land of Egypt" [Exod 20:2]; meaning, that we are obligated to *know* that the Lord exists. This is the First Commandment, and it is to be performed with the mind.

Thus David commanded his son Solomon: "Know the God of your father, and serve Him" [1 Chr 28:9]. Solomon said: "Know Him in all your ways" [Prov 3:6]. Compare also Isaiah, chapter 43[:10], "You are My witnesses, says the Lord, and My servants whom I have chosen, in order that you may know and believe Me, and understand that I am He," etc.; and Jeremiah, chapter 9[:23], "But if anyone wants to take pride, let him take pride in this: that he understands Me and knows Me. For I the Lord am maker of goodness and justice and righteousness on earth; for these are the things I desire, says the Lord." The prophet further says, "What wisdom have you?" [Jer 8:9]; thereby rebuking those who, without any knowledge of God's Divinity, parade themselves as wise. He means by this to indicate that *knowledge of God* and *wisdom* are one and the same.

True virtue, then, consists in the recognition of God's Divinity and the knowledge of His commandments, to the end of serving Him, and absolute evil consists in the absence of this perception.

That is why God imposed upon the Jews, as penalty for their having abandoned and disobeyed Him, that which is described in Isaiah: "I shall proceed to deal with this people in the most extraordinary manner. Their sages shall lose their wisdom; perception shall be hidden from their enlightened folk" [Isa 29:14]. For "Israel shall spend many days without a true God" [2 Chr 15:3].[15]

What was the sin that provoked this extraordinary penalty? Isaiah defines it as the Jews' having honored God with their mouths, while their hearts were far from Him [29:13]. He further writes: "The ox knows its owner, and the ass knows his master's manger. But Israel has not known; My people has not understood" [1:3]. They had refused, in other words, to know the Lord.

The entire Talmud is filled with this obligation we have[16] to devote our energies to investigations that will bring us to recognize the God of our fathers. The rabbis wrote in the Zohar, [in that section of the Zohar that comments] on the Torah portion *Terumah*

[II, 161b],[17] that God requires each soul to swear an oath before it descends to put on mortal flesh: that it will labor to know His true nature, for this is the mission upon which it has been sent. Interpreting the verse "Please let me taste a little bit of water from your pitcher" [Gen 24:17], they declared that the Prince of the Presence asks of each soul when it leaves the flesh and returns to heaven: "Please let me have a little bit of the knowledge of God you obtained while you were in the world you have just left." And, if the soul has no knowledge, it is ejected, even though it may possess merits and good deeds.[18]

We may say, in conclusion, that all the world's thinkers are agreed that all created entities, with their properties and their powers and their functions, exist for one purpose. From them, and for their sake, all intelligent beings are to recognize the existence of a Deity, and God's greatness and wisdom. (So we read in Isaiah [43:7]: "All that is called by My Name, it is for My glory that I created it, fashioned it, made it.")

All branches of knowledge that treat of physical and spiritual entities are essential means for attaining a conception of the Creator. We do not learn them as ends in themselves. Their purpose, rather, is the assistance they provide us toward this goal.[19] One does not light a candle in the darkness solely in order to light it. It is, rather, a means by which he may see that which he ought.

Anyone unwilling to contemplate what God has wrought in His creations, will have no ability to form a conception of His greatness. Of such people, the Bible says: "They do not contemplate the Lord's deeds, or what He has fashioned. He will destroy them; He will not build them up" [Ps 28:5]. Thus also Isaiah, chapter 5[:12–13]: "They will not look at what the Lord has done, and they have not seen what He has fashioned. For that reason—their want of knowledge—My people has been exiled."

We are obligated to know His Divinity, for we are witnesses that He is God. "You are My witnesses," the Bible says, "and I am God" [Isa 43:12]. Our ancient rabbis interpret this: "Whenever you are My witnesses, I am God. But, when you are not My witnesses—

181

if one dare to say it—I am not God."[20] He who recognizes God, has a God.

"Hear O Israel," says the verse, "the Lord is our God, the Lord is One" [Deut 6:4], which means: "Understand and know God's existence, His Divinity, and His unity; for He is One, and His Name is One."

Chapter II
Advantages That Accrue from the Striving to Know One's Creator

The wise must take no pride in their wisdom; the powerful must take no pride in their power; the rich must take no pride in their wealth. But if anyone wants to take pride, let him take pride in this: that he understands Me and knows Me....

[—Jeremiah 9:22–23]

It could have gone without saying that external wisdom, bodily strength, and the wealth that is measured in silver and gold are neither relevant nor comparable to the knowledge of God. The text, therefore, must mean something else. Those who are wise in Torah, Mishnah, and Gemara must "take no pride" in that. "Take no pride": even if they are also powerful in the sense of restraining their impulses, subduing the wicked, or rescuing the oppressed. "Take no pride": even if, on top of all that, they are rich in money, knowledge, acts of charity, good deeds.

For all the many plaudits he receives, the possessor of these qualities must himself take no pride in them. It was God, after all, who gave him intelligence and the power of comprehension and who provided him with an instructor. It was He who gave him strength when He fashioned him, who assisted him when he wanted to subdue his impulses, who helped him rescue the poor from those who would take advantage of them. It was He who endowed him with wealth and knowledge, who cooperated with him in performing charities and works of mercy. That is why the biblical text concludes: "For I the Lord am maker of goodness and justice and righteousness on earth" [Jer 9:23].

Only one person may legitimately take pride in himself. This is he who, like Abraham and Job and Hezekiah,[21] has striven on his own to recognize his Creator, and who has arrived at this awareness through his own knowledge and inquiry. The Bible says of such a person: "It was Me that he desired. I will therefore rescue him from danger and exalt him, because he has known My Name. When he calls Me, I will answer him," etc. [Ps 91:14–15].

The Zohar, on the Torah portion *Bereshit* (page 69 [of the Mantua edition of the Zohar]),[22] says that anyone who struggles toward recognition of the Creator—even if he fails to attain his goal, even if his understanding is erroneous—is nonetheless deserving of universal praise. Similarly, page 73 [of the Mantua edition]:

> How greatly is one obliged to recognize his Creator's glory, and to know how he ought to praise that glory! Whoever knows how to praise his Creator in the proper manner, God will fulfill that person's wishes. Indeed, that person multiplies blessings above and below [...] and God Himself takes pride in his honor. The Bible calls him "My servant Israel, in whom I take pride" [Isa 49:3].[23]

On page 128, the Zohar says that if anyone shatters his body in pursuit of the knowledge of his Creator, that person's soul is called "daughter of God," "daughter of the world's ruler."

> "The servant ran to meet her" [Gen 24:17]. This [servant] is [the angel] Metatron [who runs to meet the devout inquirer after God, symbolized in Genesis 24 as Rebecca].[24]

Page 130 says that

> there is no place that is concealed from those who know the Mystery of their Creator, and who know how to attach themselves to Him. Of them the Bible says: "No eye but Yours, God, has seen what He will prepare for the one who waits for Him" [Isa 64:3] [...] who knows how to find reasons that will

serve toward recognizing Him. The Creator takes pride in such people every day. They enter all the celestial gates, among the holy heavenly beings.[25]

And, on page 182 [Zohar, I, 182a], we read that all those souls that devoted their energies in this world to the recognition of their Creator and the mystery of the higher wisdom are granted a rank above that of all other souls, and they will be the first to rise at the resurrection.

Our rabbis' words, quoted in the Zohar, will lead us to this conclusion: Until the knowledge of how God is to be recognized begins to spread among the Jewish people, they will not be able to leave their exile.

*That person, therefore, who has struggled successfully to recognize the Creator and who has communicated the knowledge of His Divinity to the public, is to be called the **Son of God**, and the **Redeemer of Israel**.*[26]

Chapter III
Whether the Jewish People, in Exile,
Have Forgotten the Existence of the True God

The sinfulness of the ancients had reached such a pitch that, by Elijah's time, the Jewish people were no longer certain whether the Lord was God, or Baal. They subsequently claimed that "the Lord has abandoned the land" [Ezek 8:12], improperly denying His knowledge of their doings.[27] They spurned His laws and His covenant, and abandoned all of His commandments. Thus He spoke through Hosea (chapter 7[:13]): "I would have redeemed them, but they spoke lies about Me."

By King Hezekiah's time, nearly all of the Jews had forgotten the Divinity. It was Hezekiah who struggled successfully to recognize God, as our ancient rabbis have taught us.[28] "Whoever among you fears the Lord, let him listen to what His servant has to say!" [Isa 50:10].[29] That is to say, one should listen to the words of Hezekiah, who proclaimed Him as God in Israel.

By Jeremiah's time, they had come to disbelieve in the Lord. Thus he says, chapter 5[:11–13]: "The house of Israel and the house of Judah have wholly betrayed Me, says the Lord. They have denied the Lord, claimed that He is something other than what He is, and that 'evil will not come upon us, nor shall we see the sword or famine.' The prophets shall be so much wind, without any divine word; thus shall it be done to them."

Although they had abandoned Him and worshiped idols, and had performed every conceivable abomination, He still did not send them into exile until they had denied the existence of the deity named YAHVEH. So we learn from our ancient rabbis, and from the Zohar on the Torah portion *Terumah:* "The Jews did not go into exile until they had denied the Lord," and they will not leave their exile until they confess Him.[30] For this reason, God and His celestial court imposed upon them a punishment to fit their crime: that the faith in His Divinity be concealed from them and sink into oblivion. (This is the meaning of Jeremiah's words, "thus shall it be done to them.")

2 Chronicles, chapter 15[:3], tells us that "Israel shall spend many days without a true God, without a teaching priest, without Torah." Our ancient rabbis explain, on the authority of tradition, that this prophecy is to come true in this final exile of ours.[31]

Compare Hosea, chapter 3[:4–5]: "Many days shall the children of Israel remain without a king" (meaning, God) "and without a prince" (meaning, the Davidic dynasty), "without sacrifice" (meaning, the Temple) [...] "without an ephod" (meaning, the Urim and Thummim) "and without teraphim" (meaning, idols). "Afterward shall the children of Israel return and seek the Lord their God" (whom they had forgotten while they were in exile) "and David their king" (whose dynasty they had repudiated). "They shall turn trembling to the Lord and to his goodness" (meaning, the Temple) "in the end of days"—at the end of the exile....[32]

Our rabbis interpret the words of Scripture [2 Chr 15:3], "without Torah," to mean, "without a Sanhedrin."[33] For, as long as no Sanhedrin exists, our only norms are those deduced in each generation from the principles of the Gemara, and our legal rulings are as diverse as the reasoning that underlies them.[34] The rabbis say elsewhere, moreover: "The Jews are destined to forget the Torah" [BT Shabbat 138b].

Yet it is written in Isaiah [59:21]: "My spirit that is upon you, and My words that I have placed in your mouth, will never cease to be spoken by you and your descendants, says the Lord, for all time." God tells Moses, similarly, that "their descendants will not forget how to utter it" [Deut 31:21]![35] We find ourselves, therefore, faced with a contradiction. [Are the Jews destined to forget the Torah, or are they not?] But [the contradiction is resolved if we assume that] the texts have a hidden meaning:

The Torah's essence is knowledge of God. It instructs us about His Divinity, and how He is to be worshiped. One must obey the Torah for its own sake [literally, "for its own name," *lishmah*], that is, for the sake of the Name YAHVEH, inasmuch as the entire Torah *is* God's Name. Anyone who has forgotten God's Divinity has forgotten the Torah.[36] (This follows from the reason why it is called Torah. Its purpose is to *instruct* us [*le-horot*; from the same root as *Torah*]: who God is—"you have been shown in order that you might know that the Lord is God" [Deut 4:35]—and how we are to worship Him, bless Him, do Him obeisance, and invoke Him in truth.) If one forgets the true God, therefore, there remains with him only the Torah's body, devoid of spirit. This, and this alone, is what the Jews are promised they will never forget.

> [Cardozo now moves to the heart of his argument. The Jews have indeed forgotten the true God, and therefore have lost the spirit of the Torah.]

God revealed to Moses that He had pronounced this doom [of forgetting the true God] upon the Jewish people.

> This people will go whoring after the alien gods of the land they are entering. They will abandon Me and break the covenant I made with them. I will grow angry with them on that day; I will abandon them and hide my face from them. [...] I will surely hide my face on that day [Deut 31:16–18]

—like a man who conceals his face, so that no one can recognize him. Thus Moses writes: "You forgot the Rock that begot you, the God who gave birth to you...so that He said, I will hide My face from them" [Deut 32:18–20].

Thus also Isaiah, chapter 29[:13–14]:

> The Lord said, This people draws near to Me with its mouth and honors Me with its lips, yet its heart is far from Me; their fear of Me is no more than a human precept in which they have been instructed. For that reason, I shall proceed to deal with this people in the most extraordinary manner. Their sages shall lose their wisdom; perception shall be hidden from their enlightened folk.

The root *pl'*, "extraordinary," has a double meaning. It can refer to something *miraculous* (as in: "he did an extraordinary/ miraculous deed" [Judg 13:19]; "acting extraordinarily/miraculously" [Exod 15:11]). Or it can bear the implication of concealment (as in: "if some case should be extraordinary for you / *concealed from you*" [Deut 17:8]; "is anything extraordinary for Me / concealed from Me?" [Jer 32:27]).

Now, the essential *wisdom* and *perception* of the Jewish people is their knowledge of the Divinity and of the Torah. That was Isaiah's point: once they have no knowledge of God, what *wisdom* can they possibly have? Solomon says, in the same vein, that "the beginning of wisdom is the fear of the Lord" [Ps 111:10][37] and "the fear of the Lord is the beginning of knowledge" [Prov 1:7], meaning that *fear* and *wisdom* are one and the same, as are *knowledge* and *fear*. Indeed, one cannot *fear* God unless one recognizes Him.

The Jews' punishment thus fits their crime. They had honored God with their lips while secretly disbelieving in Him in their hearts. He therefore declared that He would do a most *miraculous* act, an act of *concealment* for which there exists no parallel. The sages—and, it goes without saying, the multitudes—would lose the *wisdom* of the knowledge of the Divinity, while the enlightened folk should have no *perception* of His existence.

187

Let us consider, now, that we have not forgotten the number of years that has elapsed since the Creation or since the beginning of our exile. Scattered though we are over all the world, we all agree nevertheless that the current year is 5446 [1685–86] as reckoned from the Creation, 1616 as reckoned from the destruction of the Second Temple.[38] Given that we are continuously writing letters and legal documents [which require dating], there is no way the chronology could possibly be forgotten.

By any rational consideration, it is a yet greater impossibility that our mouths and our hearts should forget the faith of the God of Israel. Do we not day and night think upon His name, make mention of His Shechinah, pray to Him and study His Torah? That is why Isaiah speaks of this disappearance of the knowledge of God's Divinity from the Jewish sages as something "most extraordinary." Indeed, a more extraordinary act of concealment would be beyond our power to imagine.

But might we suppose that, when the prophet says that "their sages shall lose their wisdom," he does not after all mean that they will lose the knowledge of Divinity? Perhaps he intends the natural or spiritual sciences? geometry or astronomy? or, perhaps, the sagacity and cunning required for day-to-day existence among the Gentiles?

But this is absolutely out of the question. Throughout all our history down to the present day, the Jewish people have not lacked people who were *sage* and *enlightened* in all of these varieties of wisdom. And even supposing that at some time it has befallen or should befall that we be lacking in *wisdom* of this sort—what would be *extraordinary* about such a thing? What would be the *concealment*? On the contrary: it would seem inevitable, from the very nature of our exiled condition, that this people—poor and oppressed, tormented by hordes of dreadful calamities—could not hope to acquire wisdom of any kind. The wonder and the miracle is that we, lacking ease and tranquility, nevertheless have some measure of sagacity and wisdom.

Anyone, moreover, who closely examines the preceding and following context in Isaiah, must necessarily admit that it is

Divinity of which the prophet speaks, saying that it is to be concealed from the sages of Israel.

We are called *witnesses* to God's Divinity. Our ancient rabbis teach that the Gentiles have never been and can never be His witnesses. "Whenever you are My witnesses," they have said, "I am God. But, when you are not My witnesses—if one dare say it—I am not God." It will follow from this that He has no other witnesses. Our rabbis knew that in our exile we would become deaf and blind, knowing nothing, witnessing to nothing. They therefore said: "When you are not witnesses, I am not God." This time would come to pass—they intended to say—during the exile.

This is why Isaiah says that our eyes and ears will be opened when the Messiah comes, that we will again become witnesses to God's deity, and that He will again become known to us. So it is written:

> You are My witnesses, and My servant whom I have chosen, in order that you might know Me and believe Me, and comprehend that I am the One: before Me no god was created, and after Me none will be [Isa 43:10].

See Isaiah, chapters 35, 42, 43, 49.

God promises through Jeremiah (chapter 31[:32–33]) that, when salvation arrives, "I will be their God and they shall be My people. No longer shall they instruct one another: 'Know the Lord.' For all of them shall know Me, from the least to the greatest, says the Lord."

The matter stands thus: First, the Jewish people will be in exile, "without a true God…without Torah" [2 Chr 15:3]. Then the Messiah will come. Like Abraham, Job, and Hezekiah before him, he will come to recognize through his own inquiry who the God of Israel truly is. So the rabbis have written, in the midrash on the Torah portion *Naso'* [*Midrash Numbers Rabbah* 14:2]. He will open the eyes of the blind and the ears of the deaf. Not only the Jews will experience enlightenment. He will reveal even to the Gentiles the mystery of the God who has concealed Himself. For thus we read in Isaiah [45:15]: "You are a God who has concealed Himself—the saving God of Israel!"[39]

It will by now have become clear that the Jews, in their exile, were to have forgotten the faith of God.

Chapter IV
The Reason for the Divine Concealment, and the Benefit Procured Thereby

Our ancient rabbis, of blessed memory, have taught that Father Abraham was given the choice whether his children should expiate their sins by going into exile, where they would be enslaved to all the nations, or by entering hell. He chose exile, and God confirmed his choice.[40] On the basis of this text, and of many other texts and arguments as well, it may be established that the exile was an absolutely necessary means for providing speedy expiation for the sins of the Jewish people. We could not possibly have survived without it.

Now, there was no way the Temple might have been destroyed and the Jews exiled without God's Name (which had become widely known among the Gentiles) suffering profanation. "These are the Lord's people, and yet they have gone forth from His land" [Ezek 36:20]. This must, the Gentiles reasoned, have been the result of God's weakness. If He had had the power, would He not have punished His people on His own soil? Would He have needed the Gentiles as His agents? And would He have destroyed His own house? They could only conclude that the Gentile gods were more powerful. Thus it is that God complains that the Jews have profaned His Name among the Gentiles.

We are obliged to confess that, thanks to our sins, God's Name is subjected to unremitting, unending contempt. This much is evident from the abuse directed against Him by Sennacherib, Titus, the Romans, and all of the Gentile nations. Yet, as the rabbis teach in many places, the Temple's destruction and the scattering of the Jewish people among the nations was essential for the Jews' own benefit. In His love for the Jewish people, therefore, God took no thought for His honor and had no care for the holiness of His Name. For the expiation of our sins, an exile of long duration was necessary.

Now, the Bible says that "the Lord is near to all who invoke Him, to all who invoke Him in truth" [Ps 145:18]. To which the Zohar (on the Torah portion *Ha'azinu* [III, 297a]) raises the question: "Is there anyone who invokes Him in falsehood?" And it answers: "Yes, any person who invokes without knowing who it is he is invoking."

So it was in the days of the judges. When the people abandoned God, He would give them into the power of the Gentiles. In their distress, they would cry out to Him—and "in truth" would they cry out to Him, as those do who know His Divinity. He would then at once come to their rescue. If He did not, they would plead with Him until He Himself began to suffer on their account. Thus the Bible tells us: "His soul was pained by reason of Israel's suffering" [Judg 10:16].

Suppose now that we, in this bitter and savage exile of ours, possessed knowledge of Him and could invoke Him in truth. Would not the sheer multitude of our sorrows and woes—not to mention the open profanation of His name that our exile has occasioned—bring Him to suffer all the more on His children's account? The effect would be that this exile would last only a few years, and that we would leave it before its punishment had sufficed to expiate our sins. We would then require a fresh exile! all the more so, in that we habitually incline toward sin whenever we lead a life of liberty in the Holy Land.

Our ancestors abandoned the God of truth, denied Him, and declared He did not exist. In punishment for this, we were condemned to an exile of long duration, "without a true God" [2 Chr 15:3], without king or Temple. For this reason, God was obliged to "deal in the most extraordinary manner" [Isa 29:14], hiding Himself from the Jewish people until He had fallen into oblivion among them. Thus they would not know Him and would not be able to invoke Him in truth. Only thus would it be possible to effect the expiation of their crimes, purge them of their sins, and bring the Holy of Holies.[41] Only thus would the exile last the time required to mend that which the Jews had deformed and blemished in the supernal spheres.

> [The concept of the "Mending" *(tiqqun)* of the cosmos is crucial for Kabbalah, and doubly so for Cardozo.[42]
> Cardozo here provides an explanation for one of the most painful dilemmas of his contemporary Jews. In biblical times, God heard His people's prayers and jumped to their defense. Why does He nowadays seem so deaf to prayer?]

Our sins and crimes were yet aggravated by the profanation of God's Name and by the gross insult that the Gentiles endlessly heaped upon the God of Israel—all on our account. Divine Justice blamed us for this; the Enemy [Satan] demanded that His Severity[43] punish us for it with the most stunning catastrophes. For this reason, God ordained that we no longer recognize Him, that we no longer be able to invoke Him in truth.

Wishing that His Divinity no longer be insulted by the Gentiles, He concealed Himself from them as well. Hence the dissemination and establishment of the Gentile religions, the essential premise of which is that *the God of Israel is the First Cause, creator of everything that exists.* The Gentiles accepted Him as God; no longer would they insult the God of Israel or profane His Name. On the contrary: all declared Him to be God, worshiped Him, and feared Him. By invoking our sins, they justified His having destroyed the Temple and scattered us among them. The cause was no longer His impotence. It was, rather, His just judgment and His free will.

The evil opinion that the philosophers and the pagans had held about the God of Israel, therefore, disappeared. The vicious remarks they had made about Him were voided. The effect was that the Jewish people were relieved of the heavy guilt of having profaned God's name and of the punishment that the Accuser had demanded the divine Justice to exact from them.

This will explain why God ordained that the Christian and Muslim peoples never abandon the faith in the First Cause that they had accepted, each in accord with their particular religion. To this day they have taken no other deity in Its place, nor have they left their religion for another. The First Cause, they declare, is their God and the God of Israel.

The result is that all of us today—Jew, philosopher, Muslim and Christian alike—know and worship the First Cause. The exile, meanwhile, goes on and on. We endure the punishment that it *must* go on, and that, in fitting retribution for our sins, we remain in ignorance of God's Divinity.

Thus will it continue, until the End. Or perhaps, through penitence, prayer, and observation of the Torah's commandments, we may succeed in speeding the time of our redemption. This will be the time when the faith of the Hidden God—God of our fathers, Abraham, Isaac, and Jacob—will be revealed, when the Messiah will arrive, recognize Him through his own efforts, and make His Divinity known to all the Gentiles.

Thus He says in Ezekiel, chapter 38[:23], describing what will happen after the war of Gog and Magog: "I will be magnified and sanctified in the view of many Gentiles. And they shall know that I am the Lord."

Chapter V
Whether, in Exile, the Jewish People Have Already Experienced the Fulfillment of the Prophecy That We Would Be Without a True God

We have, then, been condemned to the just and necessary punishment that we spend, before we can leave our exile, "many days without a true God" [2 Chr 15:3]. It necessarily follows that, as long as this sentence has not yet been executed upon us, our salvation must still be remote.

If it can be demonstrated that we now possess a true knowledge of God, even the passage of many years will hardly suffice for us to abandon and to forget this belief, given that the Gentile religions that share our belief in the First Cause have themselves adopted it. And even when this situation shall have come to pass, and our knowledge of the Divinity have fallen into oblivion, we must remain thus in exile for "many days." Anyone, therefore, who maintains that our Redemption is near, must concede that we are presently "without a true God." Or else, if he claims that we now have a true God, he must abandon his opinion [concerning the Redemption].

But the truth is this: *The God of Israel has never been God of the Gentiles, nor has He ever been called so.* The Gentiles indeed had witnessed and had heard about the mighty miracles He performed in Egypt, at the Red Sea, and in the desert; all that He did among His people, in His land, and in His Temple; and that which he spoke to the prophets. Yet not a single Gentile community was willing to acknowledge Him as God.

Ezekiel prophesied, and our ancient rabbis have taught, that it will be after the war of Gog and Magog that all the Gentiles are to recognize that the Lord God of Israel is God. It cannot happen before then.[44] *Then* it will be that "they shall say, Come, let us go up to the mountain of the Lord, to the house of the God of Jacob, so that He may teach us His ways," etc. (Isaiah, chapter 2[:3]). In Micah, God says that "at that time, I will transform the nations' speech to a pure one, so that they can all call upon God's Name and serve Him all together."[45] We find stated clearly in Joel chapter 1, and in Ezekiel chapter 37 to the end of the book, that it will be after the war of Gog and Magog that the Jews and all the Gentiles will know that the Lord is the true God, that they will acknowledge the holiness of His great Name and the glory of His Shechinah. It will be after the Messiah's coming, say the prophets, that "the earth will be filled with the knowledge of the Lord" [Isa 11:9], that "His name alone will be exalted" [Ps 148:13], that "He shall be called God of the whole earth" [Isa 54:5].

The prophetic tradition, and that of the Jewish sages, is unanimous: it will be after we emerge from exile that the true faith, with the knowledge of the Divinity, will be revealed to all the Jews and all the Gentiles. It is written in the Zohar (on the Torah portion

Vayyera'),[46] in the *Idra*,[47] and in many other places that the biblical prophecy—that people will no longer tell one another to learn to know the Lord, since everyone will know Him [Jer 31:33]—will at that time be fulfilled.

It follows that one can distinguish three epochs:

1. *the exile*, when the Jewish people have no knowledge whatever of the Divinity;
2. *the end of the exile*, when the Messiah comes to a recognition of his Creator and communicates the faith to a few of the Jewish people, who then tell a few others[48] in secret, out of fear of the Jews[49] (and, it goes without saying, of the Gentiles!);
3. *after our salvation*, when the revelation of God's faith is proclaimed throughout the entire world.

Shall we suppose that the faith in God we currently profess is the same true faith that was known to our patriarchs and our prophets, to our Tannaitic and Amoraic rabbis? that it is the very faith that the Messiah's investigations will bring him to recognize and to proclaim among all the Gentiles? If so, it must follow that all the Gentiles possess an accurate knowledge of God! No less than our contemporary Jews do they believe that the First Cause is the God who created everything. They, no less than we, are witnesses to His Divinity.

What, then, will have become of the Bible's assertion that "you are My witnesses" [Isa 43:12]? meaning, *you*, and not the Gentiles. What will have become of its testimony that God "has communicated His matters to Jacob"—that is, those matters that concern His Divinity—but "has done nothing of the kind for any Gentile nation," who "have not known the judgments" [Ps 147:20–21]? How, in other words, could the Gentiles possibly have known the Mystery of Divinity? What would become of "the Lord's mystery belongs to those who fear Him" [Ps 25:14]? namely, the mystery of His Name and His Being?

How could we possibly claim that the Torah and its scholars have spoken the truth? "You have this day sworn to the Lord," says the Torah, "that He will be your God, and the Lord has this day sworn to you that you will be His own special people" [Deut 26:17–18]. And the rabbis say, in the Talmudic tractate *Berakhot* [6a], that God wears phylacteries containing the words, "Who is like Your people Israel, one nation in the earth?" [1 Chr 17:21]. He means thereby (say the rabbis): "You declare My absolute uniqueness when you say, 'Hear O Israel, the Lord is our God, the Lord is One' [Deut 6:4]. I, too, will declare your absolute uniqueness: Who is like Your people Israel, one nation in the earth?"

What will have become of the Lord's covenanted promises to our patriarchs, that He will be God of Israel and not God of the Gentiles? that His Shechinah will repose with the seed of Jacob and not with alien nations? that the Jews are His people and His special possession, whom He will never abandon or forsake? Can the enemies of His Torah, the murderers and persecutors of His children, enter into the mystery of His Divinity no less than the holy seed of Israel, who devote themselves to His Torah and are martyred for His sake? Where, then, is His justice?

If the Gentiles have recognized Him truly, it will follow that they have become His people and He their God! To maintain, however, that any Gentile community now professes or ever can profess (prior to the end of the current exile) true belief regarding His Divinity, is to contradict and to deny the Torah and the Prophets, the rabbis and the Zohar. These sources declare, one and all, that the truth of God cannot be revealed to the Gentiles until after the Messiah has come. Our enemies, in fact, offer precisely this argument for the Messiah's already having arrived: that the Divinity (i.e., the First Cause) is now known to the entire world.

It follows that anyone who credits the Muslims, Christians, and philosophers with possessing the true faith has in effect abandoned his Judaism. For it must be acknowledged that they will not recognize the true God until the Messiah has come and we have emerged from that exile in which we still find ourselves.

The conclusion is inescapable. We must acknowledge, and indeed insist, that the Gentiles have no true God. Inasmuch as we share with them the belief in the First Cause—which cannot have been the faith of our patriarchs and prophets, the faith that will be revealed at the end of the exile—we are now just like them, as far as the Divinity's faith is concerned.

It is thus clear, beyond any shadow of doubt, that the sentence has been executed upon us, and upon the Gentiles all the more: "Many days without a true God" [2 Chr 15:3]. And so it shall remain, until the time that we come forth from our exile.

Chapter VI
How It Is That the Jews Presently Have No True God

We must now engage the opinions of the contemporary scholars of literalist bent, who are expert in Gemara and midrash and who want nothing to do with Kabbalah.

The fundamental principle of Judaism, as everyone knows, is that the Lord our God is One. He is One and His Name is One, not two, not more than two. Yet Mishnah and Gemara, midrashim and commentaries, all speak continually of "the Blessed Holy One *and* His Shechinah." The Blessed Holy One, everyone agrees, is none other than the Creator of the world, the God of Israel, the Lord of Hosts. What, then, is this [female] entity we everywhere call Shechinah? Is She a divine being, or one that has been created? If the former, we shall need to determine whether or not She is the Blessed Holy One Himself.

Saadiah Gaon, in the section of his *Book of Beliefs* that treats of the Redemption,[50] arrives at the conclusion that the Shechinah is an entity that was at some point brought into existence. She is a *creation* in the full sense of the word, created by God for His greater glory. Maimonides maintains the same position in many passages of *The Guide to the Perplexed*.[51] That which the Torah and Prophets call "Glory of the Lord," he says, and which the rabbis call "Shechinah," is in fact a mighty creation, awe-inspiring to the highest degree. Rabbi Joseph ibn Migash,[52] and other scholars of Torah distinguished for their learning and holiness, say much the same.

Their essential argument is the pure and simple unity of the First Cause. They assume, of course, that the First Cause and the

God of Israel are one and the same. Given this premise, it must be agreed that anything that exists apart from the First Cause must have at some time been brought into existence, must have been a *creation* in every sense. Prophets and rabbis alike testify that the Blessed Holy One and the Shechinah are not the same. Q.E.D.: the Shechinah's existence must have had some beginning in time.

There is, indeed, considerable evidence that the Blessed Holy One and the Shechinah are distinct entities. Our ancient rabbis, for example, tell us that the Shechinah has suffered exile, that She descended with the Jews into Egyptian exile and was sent away with them into Babylonian exile. That is what the Bible means when it says, "For your sakes I was sent away to Babylonia" [Isa 43:14];[53] and, again, "For your sins was your Mother"—the Shechinah, that is—"sent away [...] where is your Mother's bill of divorce, by which I sent her away?" [Isa 50:1].[54] The Shechinah, then, has been *sent away*, while the Blessed Holy One, who rules Her as a man rules his wife, has done the *sending*.

Our sages also assert that the Shechinah cries out to the Blessed Holy One on Her children's behalf,[55] that, moreover, a supreme necessity is served by the Shechinah's presence in these nether regions.

The [medieval] rabbis [like Saadiah and Maimonides][56] therefore could not maintain that Shechinah and Blessed Holy One are two designations for the same entity, which is sometimes called by the one name and sometimes by the other, depending on the functions it performs. They were left no choice but to insist that the Shechinah is a created being, since the alternative, that She is Herself a creator, would carry with it the unacceptable implication that the Creator is no longer unique.

The testimony of our ancient rabbis, however, makes plain that the Shechinah is in no sense a created being. On the contrary, She is a divinity in the full sense of the word. The reader may consult on this point Nachmanides's commentary on the Torah portion *Vayyiggash*, which refutes the view of Maimonides and his adherents.[57] The tradition of prophets, Tannaim, and Amoraim attests the Shechinah's absolute divinity. All the Kabbalists treat it as axiomatic.

Anyone who denies this is the case must suppose us all to be idol worshipers! After we have completed the *'Amidah* prayer, according to the Gemara, we must move three paces and prostrate ourselves to the Shechinah.[58] Yet anyone who prostrates himself in prayer to a created being is an idolater.

The Talmudic tractate *'Avodah Zarah* contains the following passage:

> "Until thrones were placed" [Dan 7:9]. Said Rabbi Akiba: "There were two thrones: one for the 'Ancient of Days,' one for the son of David." Rabbi Eleazar sent him the message: "Akiba, how long are you going to profane the Shechinah?"[59]

Rabbi Akiba "profaned the Shechinah," explains Rashi, by imagining a being of flesh and blood seated beside the "Ancient of Days." It will follow that the Shechinah is a divinity in an absolute sense, that, in fact, She *is* the "Ancient of Days."

Our rabbis comment as follows on the biblical demand that one "cling to" God [Deut 10:20]: "Is it really possible for a human being to cling to the Shechinah? Is She not a blazing fire? as it is written, 'The Lord your God is a blazing fire'" [Deut 4:24].[60] Similarly, in reference to the verse "On the day the Tabernacle was erected" [Num 9:15], Rabbi Simeon asserts that the Shechinah was on earth with Adam in the Garden of Eden. He offers as his proof-text: "They heard God's voice" ["walking in the garden"; Gen 3:8].[61] And, in the verse "Thus says the Lord…for your sakes I was sent away to Babylonia" [Isa 43:14], the holy name YAHVEH itself is used to designate Her. (Cf. also the midrash on the "ten descents of the Shechinah.")[62]

> [The midrash of the "ten descents" repeatedly applies to the Shechinah verses from the Bible that speak of "the Lord" (YAHVEH). It therefore completes Cardozo's demonstration that the rabbis will quote, with reference

to the Shechinah, biblical texts that speak of YAHVEH or of "God." Q.E.D.:]

From all that has preceded, it will be evident that our rabbis considered the Shechinah a divinity in the full sense of the word.

Gemara and Kabbalah, therefore, require that we give absolute credence to the following three propositions:

First, that the Shechinah exists.
Second, that She is a divinity in the full sense of the word.
Third, that She is *not* identical with the Blessed Holy One.

And yet the most fundamental truth of our religion is that the Divinity is One, and not two! The First Cause, moreover, possesses a unity that knows neither limitation nor second.

On the one hand, from the viewpoint of Saadiah Gaon, Ibn Migash, Maimonides, and their many partisans, it is heresy to say that the Shechinah is a divinity. For this will contradict the unity of the Creator, whom they identify with the First Cause. But if, on the other hand, we are to rely upon our rabbis (the Tannaim, Jonathan ben Uzziel, Onkelos,[63] and Rabbi Simeon ben Yohai) and upon the Kabbalists (Nachmanides, Rabbi Abraham ben David, Rabbi Bahya)[64]—to whom we may add Rashi, the Tosafot,[65] and many of the commentators—anyone who claims that the Shechinah is a created being is, however unwittingly, the heretic. The faith of our patriarchs and prophets has vanished from his mind.

Such people have *profaned the Shechinah*, and have thereby profaned the divine Name. For the Shechinah is just that: the Name of the Blessed Holy One. So the Bible tells us: "My Name is in him" [Exod 23:21],[66] from which we may infer that every angel in existence is nourished from the Shechinah's glow. When the Bible says that "the Lord is One," this refers—say our rabbis—to the Blessed Holy One. When it adds, "and His Name is One" [Zech 14:9], this refers to the Shechinah. ("He and His Court," similarly, [are the Blessed Holy One and the Shechinah together].)[67]

It is clear what conclusion we are to draw. Of all the Talmudists who are now alive—these being the "sages" of our time—there is not a single one who can be said to possess a true knowledge of God.

God's threat, understood in its plainest sense, has been carried out. Our sages have lost their wisdom. Perception has been hidden from our enlightened folk. Gemara and prophecy have come true. We are without a true God. And so we will remain, until a righteous teacher[68] shall arrive to recognize that true God and to make His Divinity known.

> [Cardozo has by now thoroughly disposed of "the contemporary scholars of literalist bent...who want nothing to do with Kabbalah." They are certainly "without a true God."]

But what of the Kabbalists? Can it be said that they have a true knowledge of the Divinity? We shall see presently that, for the past thousand years, *not a single Kabbalist has known the identity of the God of Israel*. The Jewish masses, of course, have known even less, and it is entirely evident from this that the Gentiles cannot possibly have had a true God.

The next stage of our inquiry must be to elucidate the belief of the contemporary Gentiles. Only then can we turn to examine the Jewish belief, which will bring us to the essential purpose of our study.

[Part Two]
Chapter VII
What the Philosophers and the Muslims Believe

We may classify, under the rubric *philosophers*, the immediate offspring of Noah, along with the Chaldeans and the Egyptian sages, the Greeks and the Latins. We may include, as well, all those moderns who believe in a single First Cause, simple in Its nature and infinitely exalted, unlimited and eternal, creator of all that exists. They call It "the necessarily existent," and the "Cause of all causes." The best among them add that one is obliged to love It, to worship It, to stand in awe of It.

Thus it was that Plato's teacher Socrates was executed at the ripe age of one hundred and ten: he refused to pay honor to any of the Greek gods, declaring that there was no god other than the First Cause, the world's Creator. Aristotle, Plato's disciple, nearly suffered the same fate. But, defeated by him in public disputation, the Greeks found themselves unable to put him to death. They instead sent him into exile, where, impressed by the wisdom of Simeon the Righteous, he became converted to Judaism.[69]

With regard to the various religions, the philosophers maintain that the First Cause has never given and will never give a Torah to any nation, has never spoken and will never speak with any living human. Prophecy do they deny. The Torah, they say, is only that which has been decreed by the human intellect, in accord with the right reasoning that is imprinted in the human soul. The First Cause, they say, cannot be the private God of Israel or of any other nation, for It is a deity common to all souls and all bodies.

No kingdom, nor indeed any civilized people, has ever denied the existence of the First Cause. Hermes Trismegistus, who was teacher to Pharaoh, wrote with truly marvelous insight about the First Cause, as one may see from reading his books.[70] Pharaoh therefore was familiar with the First Cause and acknowledged Its existence. So did all the Egyptian sages, as Nachmanides points out in his commentary on the Torah portion *Shemot*.[71] But the philosophers, from the time of Noah's sons down to the end of the Amoraic period, supposed the Jewish God to be an entity created by the First Cause, just as were those other heavenly powers whom the Gentiles called gods.

I derive my knowledge of this doctrine from the books of the philosophers, and of the *poetas*,[72] writers of verse, that is. It is confirmed by the testimony of the Gemara and the midrashim. Thus we find the Gentiles asking: "Having created the world, what does your God do now?"[73] The inquirers suppose that the

First Cause is Creator of all that exists, and that the God of Israel is one of Its creations. They suppose, further, that the Jews have advertised their God as Creator of the world in order to puff up His prestige. They consequently ridicule the Jewish God, and, if the Jews insist that their God *is* the First Cause, they turn their contempt away from the God of Israel and direct it toward the lying Jews themselves.

The same point was made by that noble lady who said, "My god is greater than yours: your god is fire and mine is the snake; Moses your master fled from the snake and drew near to the fire."[74] She did not believe that the God of Israel is identical with the First Cause, and thus allowed herself to speak of Him in a facetious manner. The Talmud is filled with exchanges of this sort.

The more recent philosophers, however, have for the past thousand years (and down to the present) held a different belief. It is indeed the First Cause, they say, whom we have taken as our deity. They consequently cannot mock our God, nor can they ridicule us for believing in Him. They themselves, after all, believe in the First Cause no less than we do. But they reject the Torah, declaring it to be Moses's own fabrication. I had frequent debates with adherents of this position while I was in Italy.[75]

The *Muslim* doctrine of God is the same as that of the philosophers. The First Cause, they say, is the God of Israel, and He it was who created all that exists. They acknowledge the reality of prophecy; they grant that a divine Torah was revealed through God's prophet Moses at Mount Sinai. But (they say) God has spurned us and abolished the Torah, on account of our sins. He has instead chosen them and has revealed to them, through the Ishmaelite [Muhammad], a new Torah.

Philosophers and Muslims thus share one and the same doctrine of God, while differing with regard to the Torah. The former reject prophecy and revealed religion, while the latter insist that Torah and prophecy both derive from the First Cause.

Chapter VIII
What the Christians and the Pagans Believe

The *Christian* belief is as follows: The First Cause is God, and He it is who has created all that exists. He is the God of Israel; He has revealed prophecy; He gave Moses the Torah.

The First Cause, they say, is one Deity in three Persons.[76] The first of these Persons is called "Father." He recognizes Himself, and He begets the Second Person, which is called "Son." This latter remains in a perpetual state of recognizing and loving the Father, who in turn recognizes and loves the Son. The Third Person, called "Holy Spirit," is emanated from this love.

The Christians' error lies in this: They believe that the three Persons are equal in essence, in existence, and in power. They are eternal, moreover, none of them having any temporal beginning, such that the Father is in no way prior to the Son or to the Spirit. They have only one intellect and only one nature, so that they are three distinct Persons yet a single Essence; the First Cause is thus not three gods but One.

The Son, they say, created all that exists through the power of the Father and the agency of the Spirit. The mystery is that of the "Who" from the "Who," in [the biblical verse] "Who created these?" [Isa 40:26].[77] And [the Christians] permit no one, who is without training in logic, physics, psychology, and metaphysics, to discuss this mystery.[78]

> [Cardozo here states the "mystery" of the Trinity in terms that sound more Kabbalistic than Christian. I am not certain what he has in mind. See the notes to the preceding and the following paragraph.]

Their doctrine—I have objected to them—necessarily requires either that we make three gods of the First Cause, or else that we concede the existence of only one single Person. Otherwise, there is no way the Spirit can have been emanated. Consider: If the Son loves the Father because He begets Him; and if the Father loves the Son because He is begotten from Him; and if the Spirit owes Its existence to their love—it must follow that the Father and the Son possess distinct intellects, in order that they can recognize and love one another. If there are two intellects, then the Christian faith will require that there be two gods. If there is only one intellect, then love and recognition cannot exist between Begetter and Begotten, and there is no possible way for the Spirit to be emanated. None of the Christian thinkers has found a way to answer my objection, and the source from which they have derived their false belief will be readily apparent to any Kabbalist.[79]

The crucified Jesus, according to Christian belief, had a body of flesh and blood. His soul was a mere created entity, of no more inherent importance than any sinner's soul. But the Second Person (the Son) incarnated Itself in him, the Divine Nature unified itself with the human, and the man Jesus thus became a deity and a human being at the same time. When he was executed (they say) the Torah of Moses lost all validity. When he died, Adam's sin was expiated. And, when his soul left his body, it gathered up those sparks of holiness and those souls that had come into the power of the demonic.[80]

Lies, every word.

Pagans, of the present time as well as of the past, believe in a First Cause that is Creator of all that exists, and that is infinitely hidden from human beings.

So exalted is this First Cause, they say, that no blessing, praise, prayer, or worship can possibly be relevant to It. Rather, It has created certain supernal spiritual and physical entities for the purpose of overseeing the inferior creatures. These entities are called gods, inasmuch as they receive effluence from the First Cause and transmit it to the creatures under their dominion. They thus function as intermediaries between the First Cause and human beings. It is they whom one must invoke, and who must receive sacrifice, worship, and blessing. These actions enhance the benefit and illumination that they receive from the First Cause, which they in turn pass on, as needed, for the welfare of all creation.

This much is evident from the behavior of those people, drawn from among the seventy peoples of the world, who traveled in the ship with Jonah. Faced with danger, "each one cried to his gods" [Jonah 1:5]. When Jonah told them that he feared "the Lord...who made sea and dry land" [1:9], their reaction (say our rabbis) was as follows: "This god of yours, we understand, is a great one. So call upon your god; perhaps God"—by which they meant the First Cause—"will give thought to us."[81] But they themselves invoked only their own gods.

This will explain why the pagans construct temples, statues, and icons for all their pseudo-deities; yet, in the house they built in honor of the First Cause, there was no statue or portrayal whatever: the First Cause is without any form. We can also understand how it was that Pharaoh and Hiram, king of Tyre, were able to claim divinity for themselves.[82] The effluence from the First Cause, they supposed, would descend upon them; other humans would receive it from them by doing them worship and obeisance.

The pagans comport themselves in a just and ethical manner, and carry out their business dealings in good faith, for the sake of the First Cause, for that, they suppose, is Its wish. All the rest—blessings and professions of faith, obeisance and invocations, all the pagan cultic acts and ordinances—go to their gods, to each according to his proper cult. We may see this even today, among the pagans of India, China, and Japan. They believe there exists a First Cause, Creator of all. But they worship the other gods.

We may thus conclude that philosophers and Muslims, Christians and pagans, all believe that there exists a First Cause, a hidden supreme God.

Chapter IX
What the Jews Have Believed for the Past Thousand Years

Jewish theology teaches that the First Cause is the God who, through His will and desire, created all that exists. He is One; He is unique; He is not composite. He is eternal and of unlimited duration. Nothing like Him or equivalent to Him could possibly exist, even if He wanted to bring it into being, for His essence and His existence could not extend outside Himself.

The Torah that God gave through His servant Moses will never (Jews believe) lose its validity, as long as the world exists. He will not replace it with anything else, nor will He ever abrogate it.

It is He whom the Jews invoke, to whom they give obeisance and worship, to whom they direct their blessings and praise. He has various names, they say, in accord with the various ways in which He treats His creatures: punishing them, or showing them mercy; it is all one. He himself, without any mediation, created all that exists and now administers it. What we call His *attributes* are not entities that emerge from Him, but rather His very essence. They are designations that indicate His powers, in accord with His actions.

Such has been the doctrine, for the past thousand years down to this very day, of all Jewish thinkers—apart, that is, from those who know the Kabbalah.

The *Kabbalists* believe that ten pure and spiritual Intelligences have been generated by and from the First Cause. These Intelligences are infinite; they are unified with one another; their end is firmly rooted in their beginning and their beginning in their end. The First Cause incorporates Itself within these Intelligences, forming with them a more true union than that which the soul has with its own will and intellect. Through the Intelligences, the First Cause created and sustains everything. Without them, neither creation nor providence would be possible.

These, say the Kabbalists, are God's *attributes*. They are also His names. We make use of them when we designate the First Cause as *El, Elohim, YAHVEH, Zeva'ot*, or the like, and it is on their account that we do so. Apart from them, the First Cause has no name or appellation whatever. It is wholly impossible to invoke, bless, or worship the First Cause [directly]; rather, it is through them that we make our invocations. Without them, it is absolutely forbidden even to conceptualize the First Cause, much less to offer It a blessing.

According to the ancient philosophers, Plato maintained this doctrine. Those entities that we know as the *sefirot*, he called "divine Ideas." This is why Plato was called, even by Jewish thinkers, the "divine philosopher."

These *sefirot* are not created beings. A *creation* is necessarily delimited and distinguished from the essence of its creator, like a stone that is carved out from a mountain. (The Hebrew word *bara*, "to create," literally means "to carve," as in the biblical passage "Carve out for yourselves from the mountain....")[83] But the *sefirot*, say the Kabbalists, are *emanated* from the First Cause, much as light and heat are emanated from the sun. The word *emanation* indicates a reality that has emerged from the inner being of that entity that has caused its existence. The emanation remains perpetually with its cause, albeit outside it; unified with it, and not distinct.

It will follow that [at least] one of these two approaches must, by their own accounting, be without a true God. The Kabbalists believe that the *sefirot* are divine in every sense of the word. Without them, one cannot worship or invoke the God of Israel, that is, the First Cause. Without them, there would be no way for created beings to have come into existence. The literalists, on the other hand, insist that nothing that exists can be considered divine, apart from the First Cause in all Its simplicity.

How true it is, then, that we have spent the past thousand years "without a true God" [2 Chr 15:3]! The advocates of each of the two contrary positions consider their opponents deluded heretics, and there seems no way to bridge them. One might, indeed, suppose that the truth is with the Kabbalists, but this view will not survive the examination of Kabbalistic doctrine that is to follow.

There is no doubt as to the conclusion we must draw. The prophecy, that "Israel shall spend many days without a true God" and without a Sanhedrin,[84] has been fulfilled upon us. Yet anyone who believes that the Gentiles have a true God has erred as surely as though he were a Gentile himself. For the Mystery of Divinity has been granted to the Jewish people alone.

Chapter X
Which of These Two Beliefs May Be Regarded as True

The literalists offer an argument on their own behalf, which turns out in fact to demonstrate the contrary. Muslims, Christians, and philosophers, they say, unanimously maintain the belief that the First Cause is the Creator. To create *ex nihilo*, after all, requires infinite power; such power is the very essence of the First Cause and of no other being. The First Cause alone, therefore, is the Creator. It, and not some entity emanated from It, is the true God.

But it can only be the fearers of the Lord who possess His Mystery[85] and the knowledge of Divinity. The Gentiles who refused the Torah cannot possibly have this knowledge. *So this very fact, that the literalists believe precisely as the Gentiles do, is itself compelling evidence that they are wrong.* It is hardly conceivable that the Gentiles recognize Israel's God more clearly than do His servants the Kabbalists!

For the truth is that our ancient rabbis have indicated as clearly as might be desired that God possesses *sefirot*—divine attributes by means of which He created the world and by means of which He administers His creations. Anyone who denies this must be incurably blind.

Thus the midrash on the Torah portion *Naso'* attests to the existence of ten [entities, which it calls by the name] *"sefirot belimah."*[86] The rabbis say, in Talmud and midrash, that God used the Attribute of Judgment to create the world; then, realizing that it could not thus survive, He mixed in with it the Attribute of Mercy.[87] They use expressions like, "the Attribute of Judgment said in God's presence";[88] or, "the Attribute of Judgment lodged an accusation";[89] or, "sinners transform the Attribute of Mercy into the Attribute of Judgment, while the righteous do the reverse."[90] They speak of a "higher Attribute of Judgment" and of a "lower Attribute of Judgment."[91] They tell how "God descended from the Attribute of Grace to the Attribute of Judgment."[92] They call Him "King who sits on a throne of Judgment and Mercy."[93] They tell us that, "wherever the Bible puts 'and' before God's name, it means to indi-

209

cate 'Him and His [celestial] Court' [that is, the Shechinah]."⁹⁴...All
of this is attested by our liturgy: "May it be Your will, Lord our
God, to treat us with the Attribute of Grace and the Attribute of
Mercy."⁹⁵

In the *Sifrei* [an ancient midrash on the Books of Numbers
and Deuteronomy], the rabbis say:

> "...like the Lord our God, whenever we invoke Him" [Deut
> 4:7]. It is *Him* that we are to invoke—not His attributes.⁹⁶

This is clear evidence that God has attributes that are outside
Himself, that are not the same essence as Himself. Why, otherwise,
would the rabbis forbid us to pray to them? Why would they
require us instead to invoke the Master of these attributes, the Lord
of the *sefirot*?

> [Up to this point, Cardozo has presented rabbinic evi-
> dence (or pseudo-rabbinic; see n. 96) for the existence of
> divine attributes that are themselves divine beings, which
> the Kabbalists called *sefirot*. He now turns to the Bible,
> where "Wisdom" appears as a more or less autonomous
> being who assisted God in creating the world.⁹⁷]

Solomon says in Proverbs [3:19]: "The Lord, making use of
Wisdom, established the earth." And Wisdom itself speaks as follows:

> The Lord brought me into being first of all,
> Prior to anything He then did.
> I was selected from among the primordial entities, from the very
>   beginning of eternity.
> Before the primeval chaos, I had come to be [...]
> Before the mountains were fixed in place [...]
> Before He had made the earth and its habitations [...]
> I was there, nurtured with Him [Prov 3:22–30].⁹⁸

David says much the same [in his Psalms]: "How manifold are
Your works, Lord! Using Wisdom, You have made all of them" [Ps

104:24]. It will follow that God created the world by making use of *Wisdom*, that this *Wisdom* is an entity that was brought into existence prior to all creation, and that it is *not* God Himself, but something that He brought into being, within which He incorporated Himself, and by means of which He fashioned His creation.

This will serve as proof that the First Cause [sic!] has attributes, *sefirot*, instruments, and that all that exists was created by means of these instruments. We are obliged, moreover, to admit that these *attributes* are superior to created beings. It is obvious, after all, that the worship of any created being is idolatry. So, if the *attributes* were some sort of created entity, the rabbis would have had no need to warn us against worshiping or invoking them [as they do in the supposed passage from the *Sifrei*, which Cardozo has quoted above]. Yet it is also clear that the *attributes* are not God's essence. For, if they were, why should invoking them have been forbidden at all?

> [Cardozo has not yet established, as he later will, that God and the First Cause are two distinct beings. He therefore speaks provisionally in the preceding paragraph, as though the First Cause were the possessor of the *sefirot*. (So Cardozo's Kabbalistic contemporaries believed; see the preceding chapter.)]

We thus have no alternative but to believe:

that *sefirot* exist;
that the world was created by means of them;
that, by their agency, the Creator continues to administer His entire creation;
that they themselves are *not* creations but divine entities adhering to the Creator Himself (which is why the rabbis were obliged to preserve us from error by telling us to invoke "Him, and not His attributes").

Philosophers, Muslims, and Christians, to be sure, continue to insist upon their dogma that there is no such thing as *sefirot*, or attributes. But they only show themselves thereby to be witless ignoramuses. Those Jews, similarly, who share their belief in the First Cause and their denial of the existence of the *sefirot* have forgotten the faith of the patriarchs and the prophets.

It is much the same as in the case of the Shechinah.[99] The Jews lack the fundamental principles that would enable them to solve Her Mystery; it therefore remains hidden from them. They thus propound the shocking doctrine that She is a created being—so greatly do they dread to encroach upon the Unity of the First Cause, believing as they do that the First Cause is the God of Israel, Creator of the world.

Chapter XI
The Belief of the Post-Talmudic Kabbalists

The Kabbalistic tradition—to provide the preliminaries necessary for the understanding of this subject—asserts that, from the First Cause (which the Kabbalists call *Ein Sof*, "the Infinite"), there emerges a single pure spiritual entity: a holy Intelligence, simple in its nature. This entity emerges by a process of *emanation*, like the light that emerges from the sun and yet remains unified with its source, such that the power of the Emanator perpetually inheres within the Emanated. This First Emanation, whose source is the First Cause, is therefore wholly unbounded and infinite. The Kabbalists call this First Emanation *Keter* ["Crown"] and ascribe to it the divine name *Ehyeh* ["I Am"].[100]

> [In chapter IX, Cardozo spoke of the *sefirot* in general terms. Now we are introduced to them individually. Each *sefirah* has a name of its own; each *sefirah* is associated with one of the Bible's sacred names for God.
>
> This chapter is likely to prove very difficult for the modern reader. It should be read in conjunction with chapter 2, above. (Alternatively, the reader may prefer to skip this chapter; the rest of the treatise can be understood without it.)]

From the First Cause and *Keter*, a second Intelligence is emanated. This is the *sefirah Hokhmah* ["Wisdom"]. The divine name associated with it is *Yah* ["the Lord"].[101] Through the power of *Keter* and the will of the First Cause, *Binah* ["Understanding"] is produced from *Hokhmah*. This is a *sefirah*, a third Intelligence; the name one associates with it is *YHVH* [the consonants of the sacred Tetragrammaton, the four-letter Name of God], vocalized with the vowels of the name *Elohim* ["God"].[102]

From *Binah* comes *Hesed* ["Grace"], with the divine name *El* ["God"]; from *Hesed* comes *Gevurah* ["Power"], with the divine name *Elohim* ["God"];[103] from *Gevurah* comes *Tif'eret* ["Splendor"], with the divine name *YAHVEH* [the Tetragrammaton]; from *Tif'eret* comes *Nezah* ["Eternity"], with the divine name *YAHVEH Zeva'ot* ["Lord of Hosts"]; from *Nezah* comes *Hod* ["Glory"], with the divine name *Elohim Zeva'ot* ["God of Hosts"]; from *Hod* comes *Yesod* ["Foundation"], with the divine name *Shaddai* ["Almighty"]; and from *Yesod*, by the power that flows forth from the superior entities, comes *Malkhut* ["Kingship"], with the divine name *Adonai* ["Lord"].

These entities are more closely unified with one another, and the entire collective with each individual member, than the human intelligence and will are with the human soul. They constitute, with the First Cause, a single tightly knit unity. The First Cause incorporates Itself within them, as though It were their soul. Correspondingly, one may speak of the ten *sefirot* as "body" [for the Divine], in comparison with the First Cause. But they are, nonetheless, Intelligences of infinite purity.

When "embodied" in *Keter*, the First Cause is called *Ehyeh*, like the *sefirah* itself. In *Tif'eret*, It is called *YAHVEH*; in *Malkhut*, It is called *Adonai*. When "embodied," in like fashion, in any given *sefirah*, It is called by the name of that *sefirah*. "Above" the *sefirot*, however—which is to say, apart from them—the First Cause has no name or appellation whatsoever. It is forbidden even to think about the First Cause, other than through the *sefirot*; impossible to give It worship or blessing, other than through them. This is why the rabbis say: "It is Him [that we are to invoke]—not His attributes."[104]

In the creation and administration of the world, the First Cause reveals Itself in *Tif'eret*—like a human soul within that individual—more than in any of the other *sefirot*. Like *Tif'eret* itself, therefore, the First Cause is always called YAHVEH; or, "the Blessed Name"; or, "the Blessed Holy One." And, inasmuch as it is through *Tif'eret* that the First Cause reveals Itself to created beings, *Tif'eret* is called "Blessed Holy One," "Blessed Name," or *YAHVEH*; and designated Its throne and Its chariot.

> [So far, Cardozo has described the doctrines of the medieval, pre-Lurianic Kabbalah. He now turns to the far more elaborate system developed in the sixteenth century by Isaac Luria. (See above, chapter 2.4–5.)]

Now, it was Rabbi Isaac Ashkenazi Luria who revealed anew to the world the doctrine of the ancients: the Tannaim and Amoraim, the authors of *Sefer Yezirah* and the *Bahir*, the *Zohar* and the *Tiqqunim*.[105]

Luria taught that one simple, infinite entity, designated "Primordial Adam *[Adam Qadmon]* of Creation,"[106] is produced from the First Cause; and that from this entity the ten *sefirot* were produced in the order indicated. It was then that there occurred the "Shattering," hinted at in the rabbinic statement that God "created worlds and destroyed them"; this is the "Death of the Kings."[107]

The First Cause's effluence within Primordial Adam afterward became greater than it had been previously. Ten more *sefirot*, consisting of vessels and lights [contained within the vessels], were thus generated. Through them, Primordial Adam repaired the vessels and the essences of the prior *sefirot*. From all this was constructed the World of Emanation *['olam ha-azilut]*, with its Five Persons *[parzufim]*.[108]

The [1] "Patient One" is identical with the *sefirah Keter*. *Hokhmah* and *Binah* are [2] "Father" and [3] "Mother." Father and Mother then coupled, uniting with one another. Through the power of *Keter*, the effluence from Primordial Adam, and the will of the First Cause, they thus gave birth to the two Persons called [4] "Irascible One and [5] His Female," that is, *Tif'eret* and

Malkhut. The Male consists of nine *sefirot (Hokhmah, Binah, Da'at; Hesed, Gevurah, Tif'eret; Nezah, Hod, Yesod),* while the Female consists of the single *sefirah Malkhut.*[109] These ten *sefirot* [of the Male and Female combined], which emerged from Father and Mother, are what is meant by the "ten *sefirot belimah.*"[110]

The Persons are both *essence* and *vessel* containing the essence; both body and soul. The First Cause extends Itself within them. We are obligated to invoke and worship the First Cause, through the Irascible One and His Female. By so doing, we draw light, effluence, and intelligence from *Keter, Hokhmah,* and *Binah* to the two Persons *Tif'eret* and *Malkhut,* which correspond to Male and Female. For it is from their coupling that all creation takes its origin. When they are in union, moreover, the First Cause reveals Its Name and Its sanctity in that locus [of their union],[111] to an ever-increasing degree, and these become revealed to the entire World of Emanation.

[Menahem] Recanati has propounded an alternative doctrine, which, it would seem, has been advocated by Nachmanides, Rabbi Abraham ben David, and many others.[112] We are obliged, according to this view, to believe that YAHVEH exists, and that He is the *sefirah Tif'eret.* We must accept Him as deity.

Nachmanides writes to this effect in his Torah commentary, on the passage "I am the Lord your God" [Exod 20:2]. And in another passage, he writes:

> The Bible says, of anyone who believes only in the First Cause, that "the Lord will be unwilling to forgive him" [Deut 29:19], just as he was unwilling to believe in Him.[113]

Tif'eret, these thinkers say, is the Great Name by which all existence came to be and by which the Torah was revealed. Certain passages in the Zohar may be invoked in support of this position. This belief—that one must direct worship and invocation, blessing and praise, to the *sefirah Tif'eret* (it being the God of Israel)—has recently attained some measure of popularity. Yet the disciples have wholly failed to grasp their teacher's intent.

[The "teacher" in question is Sabbatai Zevi.[114] His followers have represented him as equating the God of Israel with the *sefirah Tif'eret*. But, Cardozo thinks, they have taken his remarks out of context or, perhaps, mistaken his early, unripe opinions for his mature views.[115]

Cardozo will devote much of chapter XV, below, to demolishing this false belief of his Sabbatian colleagues.]

The Kabbalists, we thus find, are divided into the following schools:

1. those who say that the First Cause is God, whom we must worship in the ten *sefirot*;
2. those who say that we worship the First Cause in *Tif'eret* and *Malkhut*—not, however, *qua sefirot*, but as full Persons, constituted of Essence and the Vessels that contain it—that is, in the Irascible One and His Female;
3. those who insist that the First Cause is to be worshiped within *Tif'eret*, meaning by that the sixth *sefirah*;
4. those who believe that it is *Tif'eret* itself that is to be worshiped, that we direct our blessings to *Tif'eret* with the aim of drawing upon it the effluence from Father and Mother that will permit it to unite with *Malkhut*.

It is plain enough that no true God is to be found among any of the Kabbalists of the past thousand years! Rather, they are split into opposing camps on the matter of the Deity's very essence and on the essentials of worship and faith.

We must draw from this the following conclusion: *Not one person in the entire world knows the God of Israel. Not a single one of our contemporary thinkers recognizes who God truly is.* And this is the extraordinary act [prophesied by Isaiah] that God has performed. He has hidden Himself entirely from the knowledge and the perception of the entire Jewish people.

[Part Three]
Chapter XII
That the World's Creator Must, Under Any and All Circumstances, Be God

We may count it an obvious truth that the man who has begotten a given individual must be that individual's father. The son owes him honor and recognition and, under biblical law, would commit a capital offense if he were to strike or to curse him [Exod 21:15–17].

We may thus consider it yet truer, and more fundamental, that the world's Creator is the God of all created beings. Nature, reason, and learning alike do compel us all to acknowledge Him as God and, with our full capacities, to love Him, fear Him, worship Him, and send Him our blessings and prayers. The Torah commands the same.

Jews, philosophers, Christians, and Muslims are thus in accord: Anyone who worships or admits to the existence of any god other than the Creator is an unbeliever and an idolater. Inasmuch as there is only one Creator, it is impossible that there should be two Gods. If there were multiple creators, however, each created being would be obligated to acknowledge as God that creator who had created *him*, and not any other creator.

Many men, after all, have begotten children. Yet I am not obliged to honor and recognize any of these men as "father," aside from the one who has begotten *me*. He may be just as much a human being as my father, but that is not the point. I do not honor and serve my father because he is a human being, but because he is the specific human being who has begotten me.

Created beings, similarly, do not worship the Creator on account of what He inherently is, but because it was He who created them. Justice, reason, and nature dictate that we acknowledge Him who created us as God, even if there were to exist some other being equal or superior to Him. Justice demands, after all, that we honor our father, even though there exist others like him, and even one—God, that is—who is superior to him.

Just as the begetter is *father*, so the Creator is *God*; this proposition is self-evident. I undertake nonetheless to advance proofs on its behalf.

"In the beginning *[be-reshit]* created *[bara]* God *[elohim]* the heavens and the earth" [Gen 1:1, following literally the order of the words in Hebrew]. Surely it would seem more appropriate to begin by saying "God *[elohim]* in the beginning *[be-reshit]* created *[bara]*." King Ptolemy's translators, accordingly, put the word *elohim* at the very beginning of the Torah.[116]

The rationale [of the original biblical sequence] is this: The word "God" designates *the possessor of a power incorporating all powers*. The magnitude of a power is known by the greatness of the action it effects, and it is impossible to conceive any action more imposing than a creation *ex nihilo*, which demands a power that is infinite. The Creator therefore must possess unlimited power, which necessarily incorporates all powers. Q.E.D.: the name "God" should and must, in theory and in practice, belong to the Creator.

How is the Creator to be recognized? From His actual creations. That is why the Torah does not begin "God in the beginning [created]," but rather "In the beginning created God," as if to say: from the fact that He *created*, it is evident that He is *God*. One might usefully formulate it this way: A being that has the potential to create has the possibility of being called "God." A being that actually has created is unquestionably God. And a being that lacks the power to be Creator cannot possibly be a true God.

So says Isaiah [45:18]: "The Creator of the heavens is the one who is God." We read in Jeremiah, chapter 10[:11]: "Thus you shall say to them, The gods who did not make the heavens and the earth"—meaning to say, "He alone is God who created the heavens and the earth. How then can you give the name 'gods' to these beings who did not create the world? who, on the contrary, are themselves creatures?" Our ancient rabbis claim that God left one of the northern regions in an imperfect state, as if to say, "Does anyone else wish to call himself God? Let him come and perfect it; then will I concede his divinity."[117] Isaiah, chapter 44[:7], speaks in the same vein: "If there exists any like Me, let him proclaim aloud, let him give an ordered narrative, of how I established the orders of creation."[118] The Prophets and the Writings are filled with passages of this sort. And all the world's thinkers are prepared to admit that the Creator must be the God to whom all rational beings owe worship and recognition.

But note well: The Torah, Prophets, Writings, and the ancient Jewish sages do not say that the *First Cause* is God, but that the *Creator Himself* is God. We recognize Him as such, not on account of His inherent properties, but on account of His Creation.

It will follow from this that the world's Creator, *whoever He may be*, is God. If one should become convinced that the Creator and the First Cause are identical, then he must accept the First Cause as God. But, if he becomes aware of the existence of some Being superior to the Creator, *this will have no effect whatever upon his obligation to recognize his Creator as God.*

All the philosophers and the Gentiles maintain the dogma that the First Cause alone is Creator, and that the Creator has neither second nor superior. Literalist Jewish thinkers have maintained the same for the past thousand years. They have assumed that such was the doctrine of the patriarchs, prophets, Tannaim, and Amoraim. Moreover, the foundational principle of Moses's Torah, and of the tradition of the ancient Jewish sages, is that the Creator is God, and that it was He whom Father Abraham, on the basis of independent contemplation of His creations, came to recognize as such.

Reason demands that we grant two propositions:

First, that there exists a Necessary Existent that is eternal, that is the First Cause, and that admits of no more primary cause;
Second, that there exists a Creator and Sustainer of all created beings.

But reason does not demand that this Creator and the First Cause be identical. Rather, it permits two options: (1) that the Creator is an emanation from the First Cause, as laid out by some of the ancient philosophers;[119] or (2) that the First Cause *is* the Creator, without any intermediary.

It is a fundamental principle of the Torah that the worship of any deity other than the Creator is idolatry. Hence: "I am the Lord your God, who brought you out of the land of Egypt. You shall have no other god beside Me" [Exod 20:2–3]. The Israelites had personal experience of the Exodus from Egypt; they had no such experience of the Creation. The point of the miracles that accompanied the Exodus was to demonstrate that the God who brought the Israelites out of Egypt was none other than the Creator, that, therefore, He alone was God.[120]

We must conclude that these miracles were *not* intended to prove that the being who brought them out of Egypt was the First Cause, but rather, that He was the Creator of the world. It will follow that the prohibition of idolatry is directed against the worship of anything but the One who created heavens and earth, who brought the Israelites out of Egypt—*whoever that One may happen to be*: perhaps the First Cause or perhaps some being emanated therefrom.

The thinkers mentioned above had as their purpose, no doubt, to exalt the First Cause above all blessing and praise. Creation *ex nihilo* requires infinite power; infinite power is a necessary property only of the First Cause; therefore—so runs their argument—the First Cause must Itself be the Creator.

But suppose that Adam's son Seth were to have begun by believing that the Creator had fashioned him, just as He had fashioned his father, and that he had acknowledged the Creator's greatness by so believing. Suppose, again, that he were to have come to realize that Adam had begotten him. Surely he would do right to abandon his initial belief. *For the Creator's power would be more evident through Seth's being Adam's son than through his having been, like Adam, the Creator's own handiwork*. Not only was the Creator able to create Adam; He was able to imprint in him the ability to reproduce his own image.

Suppose now that a person begins by believing that the First Cause created everything and subsequently grasps that the Creator is in fact a being emanated from the First Cause. *This latter doctrine is infinitely and incomparably more deserving of acceptance*. More fully does it reveal the power of the First Cause, that has produced a Being capable of Creation *ex nihilo*.

The importance of the Cause, after all, may be known from the magnitude of its Effect, and the creation of existing beings is a matter disproportionately trivial for the First Cause. If a being that emerged from the First Cause has power to create the world, the First Cause Itself is yet more deserving of the title of Creator. For the Cause of the agent must also be the Cause of that agent's action.

We must draw the following conclusions: *The world's Creator is God. Attribution of deity to any created being is idolatry. Blessing and praise of the First Cause is indeed worship of God, but a worship that is devoid of truth*:

> **First,** because the worshiper has attributed to It the act of Creation in order to magnify Its power;
> **Second,** because he offers blessing to an Entity for which blessing, and the additional benefit conferred thereby, are irrelevant,[121] and for which expressions of praise—designed as they are for acknowledging the existence of the God who emerges endlessly from the First Cause—are wholly inadequate;
> **Third,** because he denies God's lofty rank and shows Him no respect.

> [In chapter IV, Cardozo had raised a question inspired by Psalm 145:18. What does it mean to invoke the Lord in some way other than in truth? He has now given the answer.]

Our next step must be to investigate, by every means available to us, whether the First Cause is the Creator or whether the Creator has been emanated from the First Cause. We shall thus arrive at the answer to our question: Who is God?

Chapter XIII
What the Pagans Have Believed About the God of Israel

It must be clearly understood that no one of sound mind can possibly deny the existence of the First Cause. All the nations have known the First Cause; all their thinkers have paid homage to It. Even the disbeliefs expressed by one or another of them have had as their purpose, not the disparagement of the First Cause, but Its exaltation.

Those who maintain the eternity of the world, for example,[122] do not intend thereby to say that it is eternal *in and of itself*, in the absence of a First Cause. When they write that the Cause of all causes has brought the world into being, what they mean is that the world emerges from It by a process of emanation that has no beginning in time. (The Kabbalists hold the analogous belief that the First Emanation comes into being, without any beginning, from the power of the First Cause.) Their aim is to avoid any suggestion that the will of the First Cause might be subject to alteration, or that Its power might since primordial times have remained inert. Such was the opinion of Aristotle, until, upon hearing the wisdom of Simeon the Righteous, he abandoned it.

The philosopher who asserts (as did Plato) the existence of a Prime Matter is seeking to distance himself from the notion that any dead bodies such as the elements might have emerged from a simple Being of infinite oneness and purity. He who denies (as did Epicurus) that there can be any individual providence governing the lower realms of creation, argues that it is beneath the dignity of the First Cause to busy Itself with creatures so lowly and so sordid.

Pagans do not now, nor have they ever, worshiped their false gods with the intent of denying or degrading the First Cause. On the contrary, they seek to exalt Its greatness. No blessing or worship can be suitable for It, they say, nor can It be grasped other than by means of its garments.

[The pagans, Cardozo thinks, conceive their gods as the "garments" of the First Cause.]

With this in mind, we shall readily comprehend that which is asserted by Scripture, rabbis, and Zohar: The descendants of Adam and Noah, down to the time of the Tower of Babel, were great sages who recognized the Creator. (Adam, one may discover, served as Methuselah's teacher for three hundred years, while Noah was Methuselah's pupil for six hundred.) The wisdom of these ancient folk led them into evil ways, both generally and specifically. They refused to worship the Creator; they spoke contemptuously of Him; they took to performing forbidden acts that drew them away from holiness and brought them near to the demonic. "What is Shaddai," they said, "that we should worship Him? What good will it do us to make our requests of Him?" [Job 21:15].[123]

Notice that they did not say, "Who is Shaddai?" for they knew perfectly well who He was. Their point was to express their contempt: "What is Shaddai?"—as the Bible says elsewhere, "What are human beings, that You keep them in mind?" [Ps 8:5]—an expression that is wholly unthinkable if applied to the First Cause.

The hidden meaning of the passage is this: They knew, or at any rate believed, that the Creator is called *El Shaddai*, having been the one who said *dai* ["Enough!"] to the world;[124] that, moreover, He had been emanated from the First Cause, which used Him as a mere instrument. Prayer and worship are appropriate, not to the First Cause in Its pure simplicity, but only to some intermediate being; all powers possessed by created beings, furthermore, have devolved upon them from the First Cause, which Itself cannot be said to originate from anything else.

Given all this, they reasoned, why should they be obliged to render worship and blessing to El Shaddai alone? Was He not, like any other god, begotten of the First Cause and graced by Its efflu-ence? "What is Shaddai," they therefore said, more than any other god? "What good will it do us to make our requests of Him," and not of some other being? And these sinners concluded that each of them might worship whatever took his fancy.

This will hardly seem astonishing, once one recalls the teaching of our ancient rabbis that the angels, upon seeing Adam's majesty, were about to receive him as a deity, prostrate themselves to him, and cry out "Holy!" before him.[125] How would it have been possible—on the supposition that it is the principle of our faith that the First Cause is God—for the angels to have proposed to worship Adam as God? They cannot conceivably have deluded themselves into thinking he was the First Cause—he who had been fashioned at the very end of the process of creation, after them and with their consent, and in full view of them all! How can it have entered their minds to rebel against the First Cause with such an act of idolatry? Or (we might rather ask) how could our sages of blessed memory have brought themselves to write such strange things, were it not that they possess some benefit for us that far outweighs their repulsiveness? We have no choice but to inquire what that benefit is, or why it is beneficial.

> [We see here, once again, Cardozo's theory that the *aggadot shel dofi* ("tainted texts") are the key to the rabbinic literature. The blessed sages would never have taught such weird things, unless they were crucial.]

The angels had both faith and knowledge that every existent has its beginning in the First Cause, and that the Creator, who brought all created beings into existence through His power, was emanated from that First Cause. The Creator sustained the angels, granted them the benefits of His effluence, directed their actions. The angels concluded from this that they were obliged to acknowledge the Creator, to bless Him, to declare His holiness. But now they saw that this human being had been assigned a rank higher than theirs, so closely bound to the Creator that it was the human who would first receive the effluence; they would receive it only afterward, from that human himself. It thus occurred to them that it would be proper for them to receive the human being as their deity. Adam, they thought, would grant them the divine effluence, in its proper measure. He himself would worship and bless the Creator as *his* God, from whom *he* drew the effluence. And they, Adam, and the Creator would alike recognize the First Cause as Supreme Deity.

To this proposal, Adam made wise reply. It is not the being who grants effluence that is God, he warned the angels, but rather the One who created and fashioned everything. It was not I who created you, he said, and we are obliged to acknowledge that the One who made us is God. (The sages have related, accordingly, that Adam said to them: "Come, let us bend the knee and prostrate ourselves; let us kneel before the Lord who made us" [Ps 95:6].)[126] Holy beings that they were, the angels took Adam's advice and made his opinion their own. Sinful humans, however, were inclined otherwise, preferring to worship other gods.

Thus it is that the rabbis and the Zohar interpreted the word *qedem*, in the biblical passage "As they journeyed from *qedem*" [Gen 11:1],[127] to mean that "they journeyed away from the Primordial One of the world." They said, in other words, "We do not want Him and we do not want His godhood. Is He not content with taking the upper realms for Himself and leaving the lower realms for us? and will He now compel us to worship Him?"[128]—and, in consequence, they abandoned the Lord. Anyone with a brain in his head must perceive that they cannot have spoken thus about the First Cause, nor would they ever have rebelled against It.

There is a great deal more of this sort in the Zohar, on the Torah portion *Noah*.[129] The Chaldeans, moreover, threw Abraham into the fire for this reason alone: that he asserted there to be one Divinity above all others, who had created the world, who was emanated from the First Cause; that he proclaimed that this Divinity alone must be worshiped; and that he ridiculed those who worshiped any deity or celestial power other than the Creator.[130]

The midrash says of Lot that "he journeyed from *qedem*; that is, away from the Primordial One of the world. 'I do not want Abraham,' he said, 'and I do not want his Deity.'"[131] Beyond all doubt, Lot knew who it was who was Abraham's God. Had it been the First Cause, he could not possibly have said that he did not want It.

Laban, similarly, knew the God of Abraham, Isaac, and Jacob, and he did not care to worship Him.[132] When he made Jacob swear an oath by Him, this is how he phrased it: "May the God of Abraham and the God of Nahor judge between us" [Gen 31:53]. Which our ancient rabbis interpreted as follows: "'God of

225

Abraham' refers to the holy; 'God of Nahor' refers to the profane," to the [demonic] "Other God."[133] If the "God of Abraham" were the First Cause, how could Laban have coupled Him with the "God of Nahor," whom he himself regarded as a created being? Laban obviously did *not* believe that Father Abraham's God was the First Cause.

When Pharaoh said, "Who is the Lord, that I am to obey Him? [...] I do not know the Lord," and Moses answered that He is "the God of the Hebrews" [Exod 5:2–3], Pharaoh went on to ask "whether He is old or whether He is a young fellow; since when has He been king? and how many provinces has He conquered?" He asked his wise men whether they knew of Him. "We have heard," they replied, "that He is the Son of the Wise, the Son of Ancient Kings."[134] This is clear proof that they believed the Lord, God of the Hebrews, to be just one among the deities originating from the First Cause. Nor did Moses, Aaron, or the elders of Israel ever tell Pharaoh that the Being who had sent them was the First Cause. (Pharaoh and the Egyptian sages, as I have already said, were perfectly aware of and ready to acknowledge the First Cause.)

Jethro was a great scholar and a man of sound judgment, conversant with all the deities and their cults. When he saw what God had done to the Egyptians, he said: "Now I know that the Lord is greater than all the gods!" [Exod 18:11]. He could not have been speaking of the First Cause, for that would already have been self-evident.

Upon the entrance of the Ark of the Covenant into the Israelite camp, the Philistines exclaimed: "Woe is us! Who can save us from these powerful gods? the very same gods who inflicted every plague upon the Egyptians in the desert" [1 Sam 4:8]. In Elijah's time, uncertainty prevailed with regard to who the God of Israel might be.[135] The Arameans declared the God of Israel to be "a god of hills...not a god of the valleys" [1 Kgs 20:28].

Gentiles spoke of the Lord as "the god that is in Jerusalem."[136] "Truly," said Nebuchadnezzar, "your god is the god of gods, the master of kings" [Dan 2:47], and, on a subsequent occasion, "I decree that any people, nation, or tongue that speaks ill of the god of Shadrach, Meshach, and Abednego shall be torn into pieces, his house made a dungheap" [Dan 3:29]. Thus Darius: "I decree that folk throughout my royal dominions tremble and stand in dread of the god of Daniel" [Dan 6:27]. Who could be so stupid as to believe that all these great kings and sages were speaking of the First Cause?

The fact is that *all pagans have believed that the God of Israel is something other than the First Cause.* They have written quite explicitly, in the books of the Greeks and the Latins, that the God of the Jews is the private god of this nation, emanated, like all the rest of the gods of the various nations, from the First Cause. One writer might speak of Him in a respectful vein; another, to the contrary—each in accord with the contemporary fashion.[137]

Yet no Gentile community has ever been willing to accept Him as a god; although they had many other gods, they did not want Him. For each and every one of their gods they built temples. Indeed, they constructed a building in honor of the First Cause, inscribing on its walls that "this structure is dedicated to the Hidden God, the Unrecognized."[138] But they never built any structure in honor of the Lord, the God of Israel.

The reason for this is plain. Once one has acknowledged a deity and built a temple in his name, one is obligated to worship him in accord with the particular ordinances he has laid down.[139] The Gentiles did not care to subject themselves to the heavy burden of God's Torah. They therefore would not acknowledge His divinity or build Him a temple, for they did concede that it was possible [and therefore would become obligatory, once they had acknowledged Him] to offer Him cultic service. They built a temple for the First Cause precisely because they thought it impossible to worship the First Cause and forbidden to offer It blessing.

One may conclude from this that all the pagan Gentiles believed that the God of Israel is to be equated neither with the Creator nor with the First Cause.

Chapter XIV
What the Idolatrous Jews Believed About the God of Israel;
the Opinion and the Faith, Also, of Those
Who Served the Lord

It is evident that the Israelite idolaters shared the Gentiles' belief that the God of Israel is a being distinct from the First Cause. They consequently built the golden calf, intending it to be their guide in the desert. "They said, 'These are your gods, O Israel, who brought you up from the land of Egypt'" [Exod 32:4]; meaning, These can serve you as guides just as well as the One who brought you up from there.

When, in Elijah's time, the people were uncertain "whether the Lord is God...or Baal" [1 Kgs 18:21], their uncertainty did not concern the First Cause. Nor was it an issue of nomenclature, whether the First Cause was properly called YAHVEH or Baal. Rather, the point at issue was which of those two gods was bearer of effluence from the First Cause; which, therefore, might appropriately be worshiped and blessed as the true God.[140] For never did the Gentiles, far less the Jews, forget the existence of or entertain any doubts about the First Cause—a point requiring no further elaboration.

Manasseh, king of Judah, abandoned the Lord and worshiped all the other gods. When troubles came upon him, he prayed to them and found they had no reality; he then looked to the God of his ancestors. "Manasseh said"—in the words of our ancient rabbis—"I have already called upon all the gods and found them to be unreal. Now I am calling upon You. If You save me, I will know that You are God. If You do not, I will say that You too are unreal."[141] Manasseh surely knew that the Lord was God.[142] A remark like Manasseh's will make no sense if applied to the First Cause. Its existence is a logical necessity whether or not an individual's prayer is answered, and all that exists attests to the infinity of Its power. It was precisely because the idolaters held unanimously that the God of Israel was *not* the First Cause that some of them were prepared to deny His existence, while others doubted it. And none wished to accept Him as God.

When we ask, "What then was the belief of the Lord's servants?" we find that they had learned, from tradition and from their own powers of comprehension, that He is *not* the First Cause. He is, rather, a certain infinite Being, holy and awe-inspiring in the highest degree, which was emanated from the First Cause.

All will concede that the proposition that there exists one Primordial Entity, Cause of all causes, requires no wonders or miracles to demonstrate its truth. The intellect can grasp this without any such aid. There can be no action without an agent to perform it; the chain of causation cannot extend itself infinitely, and nothing that exists can have brought itself into existence.

The miracles that Moses performed in Egypt, therefore, [cannot][143] have been intended to compel Pharaoh and the Israelites to believe that Moses was an emissary of the First Cause or to communicate that the First Cause was the Creator of the world and God of the patriarchs. This is wholly unthinkable. God sent Moses to Pharaoh with the message that he "must learn that there is none like Me in the whole earth" [Exod 9:14]; or, as Moses puts it, "that the earth belongs to the Lord" [9:29]. "The purpose," Scripture says, "is to demonstrate to you My power, so that people the world over may tell of My Name" [9:16]. Pharaoh himself (say our rabbis) confessed at the Red Sea, "Who is like You, Lord, among the gods?"[144]

Pharaoh, as we have seen, believed in the First Cause. So did all his sages. They maintained that the First Cause exercised providential supervision over the Egyptian divinities—the land, the river, the Nile[145]—and that It bestowed Its effluence upon Pharaoh, who represented himself as a divinity. "This is the finger of God" [Exod 8:15], said the Egyptian wizards, supposing It to act even upon the very dust.[146] What could it possibly mean to demand "that you recognize that I am the Lord, in the midst of the earth" [Exod 8:18] of someone who already granted all this to be true with regard to the First Cause?

The truth, however, is this: Moses's message was that the God of Israel is the world's Creator, its incomparable Guide, Overseer of the upper and lower realms—*even though He is not the First Cause, but rather a being emanated from It*—and that He has the power and the freedom of action to save His people in accord with His will. All the wonders and miracles were necessary to inspire Pharaoh and his servants, as well as the Israelites, with the conviction that He is the God of gods. This message was a novel one and difficult to accept. That was why the people could not believe in the Lord or in Moses His servant, until He had split the sea for them.

Moses's words, similarly, are unintelligible if applied to the First Cause. "The Gentiles from whom You liberated us are bound to say, 'The Lord had no power to bring the people into the land He had promised them; that is why He slaughtered them in the desert.'"[147] Who would ever think of saying that the First Cause had executed judgments on all the gods of Egypt, yet somehow lacked the strength to destroy or to subdue the kings and gods of Canaan?

Joshua's speech, in chapter 24[:15], points in the same direction. "You must choose this day who it is you are going to worship. The gods your ancestors worshiped on the other side of the Euphrates? Or perhaps the gods of the Amorites, in whose land you now live? I and my family, at any rate, will worship the Lord!" The people respond that they want the Lord. To which "Joshua said, 'You cannot worship the Lord: He is a holy God, He is a jealous God'" [24:19]. Each and every syllable of this is inconceivable, if spoken about the First Cause, the deity of which is in no way dependent upon human choice.

Of that Elisha who is designated "the Other One" [the heretic rabbi, Elisha ben Abuyah], the Talmud says: "Return, backsliding children—apart from Elisha, the 'Other One,' who recognizes his Creator yet rebels against Him."[148] Who could possibly fail to recognize the First Cause? Why, then, should Elisha have been given any credit for this awareness?

"Well do I know," says King David, "that the Lord is great; our Lord is greater than all the gods" [Ps 145:5]. Who could possibly be ignorant that the First Cause is greater than any of Its creations? Why should David congratulate himself on possessing this information? One might just as well say, "Well do I know that a father is older than his son!" What King David congratulates himself upon, however, is his knowing the greatness of that God who is emanated from the First Cause, which *does* indeed require exceptional intelligence.

One must consider, moreover, that no nation in the world has ever forgotten the First Cause. No one could ever possibly forget It. For the intellect recognizes It and has the ability to discover It. If, then, the God of Israel is the First Cause, what can have moved our ancient rabbis to say that in King Hezekiah's time people had forgotten the God of Israel?[149]

If the Creator is the First Cause, how can Abraham have come to recognize Him on his own? His parents, brothers, and all the Chaldeans would have been perfectly aware of the existence of the First Cause, perfectly ready to grant Its reality. How might we justify our rabbis' claim that "four individuals have arrived, on their own, at a recognition of the Creator"?[150] Many people are capable of arriving at a recognition of the First Cause without any instructor. Many have in fact done so.

Jews, philosophers, Muslims, and Christians are not merely aware of the existence of the First Cause, but actually worship It. How then can it be possible for the Messiah among us to arrive, through some process of contemplation, at an independent recognition of the First Cause? He must inevitably receive some instruction from his teacher. And when he comes to announce the divinity of the First Cause to Israel and to all the Gentiles—they will one and all have recognized it beforehand!

The conclusion is inescapable: *The Lord's servants maintained the belief that the God of Israel, currently in concealment, is an emanation of the First Cause whose existence remains altogether unknown to the Gentiles.*

[Cardozo now begins to move toward a solution of the problems raised in the earlier parts of the treatise.]

When Moses came to rescue them—so the Zohar tells us in its sections on the Torah portions *Va'era* and *Terumah*[151]—the Israelites knew nothing of the reality of their ancestors' God. In

231

their exile, they had forgotten His faith. Moses therefore instructed them as follows:

There exists one supreme Deity, Creator of all, judge and ruler of the Gentiles;
which is God of the patriarchs;
which has both male and female aspects, namely the Blessed Holy One and the Shechinah;
which is *not* the First Cause—to which the categories of "male" and "female" are alien—but rather an emanation from It.

Evidentiary miracles were required of Moses, to prove that this was indeed the true God. Miracles yet more striking and more notorious will be required nowadays, to demonstrate the reality of that God whose Faith we, in our exile, have forgotten.

Commenting on the Song of Songs, our rabbis explain that "King Solomon" is the Blessed Holy One, while his "Bride" is the Shechinah. "My sister, bride," He calls Her [Song 4:9, etc.], while She says to Him, "If only You were My brother, sucking My Mother's breasts!" [Song 8:1]. It is also written, "Go out, you daughters of Zion, to see King Solomon in the crown with which His Mother crowned Him" [Song 3:11].[152]

[The point of these quotations is not altogether evident here. But, in other writings, Cardozo explains that we learn from them that God is a gendered being who, at least in His/Her "bodily" aspect, may be spoken of as having a "Mother."[153] This Deity can hardly be the genderless First Cause.]

The Faith of the Lord's servants—attested by Torah, Prophets, and Writings, rabbis and Zohar—is consequently that *the Blessed Holy One, God of Israel, is not the First Cause Itself, but an emanation from It.*
We may conclude with the following observation: If we take as our standard the opinion that had been universally held[154] until

the time of the completion of the Gemara, we shall find that not one of our contemporaries knows the identity of the God of Israel.

Chapter XV
Whether the First Cause Is the God of Israel, Creator of the World

It is, as we have said, a distinctive characteristic of the First Cause that It is a simple Unity, independent, which does not incorporate Itself within any *sefirah*. Such, at any rate, is the opinion of the philosophers and the Muslims. It is also the belief held by those Jews, living after the time of the Talmud, who know nothing of the Kabbalah.

One might hold, alternatively, that the First Cause is distinguished through Its being united with and incorporated within the *sefirot*; it having already been shown [in chapter X] that the world's Creator possesses [sefirotic] attributes. Our current task must be to inquire whether the First Cause, *qua* "spirit of the *sefirot*," is the God of Israel, as believed by the Kabbalists mentioned in chapter [...].[155]

By way of preface, we must remark that the Messiah is to come for the purpose of investigating the problem of achieving recognition of the God of Israel, who has been forgotten in the course of the exile. The secret must necessarily be concealed within the words of the Torah, the Prophets, and the Writings. The Messiah will arrive at an understanding of the Divinity from these sources and will make use of them to communicate it, in such a way that not a single text, biblical or otherwise, will be found to contradict his interpretation.

We have previously determined, furthermore, that *the world's Creator must, under any and all circumstances, be God.* If, therefore, we wish to know who God truly is, we must investigate the question of who the Creator is.

From the words of our sages, it will appear that the First Cause is the Creator.

233

[This proposition is, of course, entirely contrary to the trend of Cardozo's argument. In chapter XVI, he will turn around and decisively refute it.

Cardozo's argument, for the duration of the present chapter—up until the very last sentence—is provisional. Cardozo adjudicates between the first and the fourth of the Kabbalistic theories of Divinity summarized at the end of chapter XI: the doctrine that "the First Cause is God, whom we must worship in the ten *sefirot*"; vs. the doctrine that the *sefirah Tif'eret* is itself the God of Israel. (The latter view, as we have seen, was held by many of Cardozo's fellow Sabbatians.)

Speaking, provisionally, as though these were the only two alternatives, Cardozo decides in favor of the former. Only at the end of the chapter does he remind us that there is a third option: that there may exist a "Spirit of the *sefirot*," distinct from the *sefirot* themselves, and distinct also from the First Cause.]

"I am the first and I am the last, and besides Me there is no God" [Isa 44:6]. The sages interpret this to mean: "I am the first, in that I have no father. I am the last, in that I have no son. Besides Me there is no God, in that I have no brother."[156] Not one of the divine attributes or *sefirot* could say such a thing; all have been emanated,[157] and thus have fathers and sons and brothers. The biblical verse and the rabbinic comment can properly apply only to the First Cause.

Midrash Exodus Rabbah supports this conclusion:[158]

God said to Moses: "Do you seek to know My name? I am named only in accord with My deeds. When I act in accord with My grace, I am called *El*. When I execute judgment, I am called *Elohim*. When I have mercy on My creatures, I am called *YAHVEH*. Therefore: *ehyeh asher ehyeh*, 'I will be that which I will be' [Exod 3:14]—through whichever place or attribute I act, by that name I will be called."

When He acts through the *sefirah Hesed*, in other words, He is called *El*. When He acts through *Gevurah*, He is called *Elohim*. When he acts through *Tif'eret*, he is called *YAHVEH*. And (says God) inasmuch as I invariably act toward you through [this last] attribute,[159] it "will ever be My Name"; that is, the name *YAHVEH*, which is *Tif'eret*. "And that will be My designation for all time" [Exod 3:15], says God; "yet not of My essential being, for names are appropriate only to created entities." All the *sefirot*, as we know, have names that are fixed permanently in accord with their natures. It follows that not one of them can be the Creator.

The rabbis also interpret *ehyeh asher ehyeh* to mean: "I am He who was; I am He who is; I am He who will be."[160] It cannot be truthfully said of any emanated being that "he was, he is, he will be." This can be said only of the First Cause, an eternal and primordial entity, without either temporal or existential beginning.

The *Zohar Hadash*[161] asserts that Abraham knew the Creator and that he subsequently ascended to the *sefirot Binah, Hokhmah*, and *Keter*, and arrived at a recognition of Him on their behalf. We are there told that the "Ancient of Days" [= *Keter*], *Hokhmah, Binah*, and the rest of the *sefirot* are the Creator's names, by which He is called. It will follow that the God of Abraham is superior to *Keter*; that He is the Creator; and that we are obliged to concede He is the First Cause.

The *Sifrei* declares that "the distinguishing mark of this faith of ours is that we worship and invoke the Creator, and not His attributes."[162] The *Sefer Yezirah* speaks of "ten *sefirot* that have no end, all of them governed by a single Lord."[163] The Zohar, on the Torah portion *Aharei Mot*, tells us that "the Blessed Holy One emitted ten *sefirot* and incorporated Himself within them."[164] It follows that the Creator cannot be a *sefirah*, but must function as a spirit for the *sefirot*. That is to say, He is the First Cause.

Tiqqunei Zohar Hadash, page 23: "Before the creation of the world"—[this "creation" including] even the [sefirotic] World of Emanation—"He and His Name were within the *sefirah Keter*." He subsequently emitted the *sefirah Hokhmah*, and descended into it; He similarly produced *Binah* and the rest.[165] Now, if the Blessed

Holy One (God, that is) was initially in *Keter* and only subsequently emitted *Hokhmah*, this will confirm that the Blessed Holy One who created the world is the First Cause, and that *this*—not the totality of the *sefirot*, nor yet any one among them—is God.

From the seventieth of the *Tiqqunei Zohar*, we learn that the "vessels" and the "limbs" (i.e., the external and internal aspects of the *sefirot* of the World of Emanations, from *Keter* on down) function as a body for the Blessed Holy One. He, correspondingly, is their spirit. This text calls Him by the proper name YAHVEH, and it designates Him as the "Cause of causes," which is within and among all of the *sefirot*.[166] The *Tiqqunei Zohar Hadash* say in several places that we direct our prayers toward the One who is within the *sefirot* as the spirit is within the body, and that we invoke Him sometimes in *Hesed*, sometimes in *Gevurah*, sometimes in *Tif'eret*.[167]

It would be quite gratuitous—and would moreover exhaust our paper as well as our time—to record each and every one of our ancient rabbis' remarks to the same effect. It would seem from all this evidence that it was the First Cause, incorporated within Its attributes, that created the several worlds,[168] and that this is the true God.

If this is so, those Kabbalists who hold this position [that is, the first of the four Kabbalistic "schools" summarized at the end of chapter XI] will be found to maintain the faith once professed by our ancestors, our prophets, and our sages. By contrast, close examination of all that has been said above will show that the alternative proposition [maintained by the fourth "school"]—that the *sefirah* *Tif'eret*[169] is the world's Creator and the God of Israel—is absolutely untenable.

We must, rather, identify God as a single Entity who is *possessor* of the attributes and who functions *as their spirit*, who is in His essence infinitely more important than all of them, and who is their sustainer and their guide. It was He who used them in His act of creation. It is He who is the God of Israel.

Anyone who says that the God of Israel *is* an attribute—whether one *sefirah*, or several taken together—is grossly mistaken. The truth is that the *sefirot* are "vessels" and "limbs"[170] for that Spirit that is the essential Divinity. Even schoolchildren have enough knowledge to demolish this theory. Everyone, after all, has learned that the patriarchs served God through the *sefirot Hesed, Gevurah*, and *Tif'eret*, which together constituted the Chariot ridden by the Deity.[171] This Deity cannot therefore have been *Hesed* or *Gevurah* or *Tif'eret*.[172] Those who believe that the *sefirah Tif'eret* can be, independent of everything else, the hidden essence of Divinity have not penetrated to the truth at its deepest level. It is as if they had claimed the true essence of a human being to be his body, whereas it can be only his spirit....[173]

The evidence marshaled above, we may conclude, convincingly disproves the notion that the world's Creator can be identified with any one of the *sefirot* (or attributes). He is, rather, a Being who is the Spirit within the *sefirot*.

[And now Cardozo overturns everything he seems to have been saying in this chapter, up to this point:]

But it will by no means follow from this that the First Cause is the Creator—until, at least, we have been able to establish that the "Spirit" of which we speak is the First Cause.

Chapter XVI
That the Blessed Holy One, God of Israel, Is the Spirit of the *Sefirot;* That He Is Not the First Cause

The rabbis say in the Gemara (tractate *Berakhot*) that God prays; that He enwraps Himself in a fringed garment; that He wears phylacteries; and that He studies Torah.[174] They relate how the serpent told Eve that God ate from the Tree, and thus created the world.[175] [He therefore requires something outside Himself, in order to be Creator.] They write, in their story of how the moon's stature came to be diminished, that God told the Jews to "bring a sin-offering on My behalf, to atone for My having diminished the moon."[176] [He therefore requires human cooperation, in His own "Mending."] And there are many more passages of this sort.

237

These same rabbis declare, unanimously,[177] that God is possessor of the attributes. He is too lofty, too much concealed, to have any name beyond those of His attributes, and in accord with the actions He performs. Yet He *prays*, and these passages were therefore spoken of Him—passages from which *it is clear that He cannot be the First Cause*.

Anyone who dares attack Him, on the basis of these passages, will pay for it dearly.[178]

We read in the *Yalqut* that, when God says, "Let Us make humanity in Our image, after Our likeness" [Gen 1:26], He means: "Not male without female, nor female without male, but rather like Us."[179] The commentators explain [this combination of male and female in the Deity] as referring to the Blessed Holy One and His Shechinah.

[God is an androgyne, Cardozo thinks—this being the clue to understanding the nature of the Shechinah's divinity—and we are created in God's image in that, like Him/Her, we are gendered beings.]

Now, it was the Creator who said, "Let Us make humanity." He therefore cannot be the First Cause, who has neither image nor likeness, who is neither male nor female. (The Shechinah, I have already demonstrated, is a divinity in the full sense of the word.) How is it even conceivable that this is the First Cause?

The twenty-second of the *Tiqqunei Zohar* [65a] introduces the Divinity in all its aspects. The *sefirot* are there declared the "body," while the Blessed Holy One is the "spirit" shining within that body. Inside it all shines that concealed entity that binds it all into one, yet concerning which there is not the smallest hint—the First Cause, in other words. The passage thus states explicitly that the Blessed Holy One is a Spirit within the *sefirot*. He is not the *sefirot* themselves. Nor, on the other hand, is He the First Cause.

From the treatise on the "Secrets of the Letters" (in *Zohar Hadash* [4b]), we learn that the *sefirot* are the sacred names used for the Blessed Holy One. They are pure, lofty Intelligences, whose

essential being cannot be known even to a prophet. Yet they function as His body, and He is called the "inner spirit" within them,
which human knowledge has no capacity to attain. All the more
unattainable is the mystery of the Infinite. The Zohar on the Torah
portion *Vayyera'* (commenting on the verse "Her husband is known
by means of the 'gates'" [Prov 31:23]) says much the same; so also
[in its commentary] on the Torah portion *Vayyehi*.[180]

Commenting on the Torah portion *Terumah*, the Zohar
speaks of the Blessed Holy One's ascending to the Infinite, then
coming back down again.[181] *Tiqqunei Zohar* 50 [86a-b][182] says that
the Blessed Holy One (who is husband to the Shechinah) nourishes
Her at times through the *sefirot Hesed, Gevurah,* and *Tif'eret,* at
times through *Nezah, Hod,* and *Yesod.* At times He climbs to the
Father and the Mother, or even beyond *Hokhmah* and *Binah,* and
procures Her sustenance from there. At times, indeed, He ascends
as far as to the Infinite. And *Tiqqunei Zohar* 70 [127a] describes the
King, who sits on the throne of Severity and of Mercy, as having
ascended to a higher plane.

The preface to *Tiqqunei Zohar*, page 13,[183] speaks of the First
Cause as maintaining and sustaining the ten *sefirot* by means of that
Spirit. It declares, further, that the First Cause has nothing in com-
mon with either Spirit or *sefirot.*

Zohar, to the Torah portion *Har Sinai*, says that the Blessed
Holy One and the Shechinah must be coupled together, His elements to Hers, if the First Cause is to reveal Itself there. For, if the
Blessed Holy One is not united with the Shechinah, "the Cause of
causes will not reside there." Moses thus prays as follows: "May it
be Your will, O Cause of all causes, to bring together the Shechinah
and the Blessed Holy One."[184] And, in *Tiqqunei Zohar Hadash*, the
First Cause commands the Blessed Holy One to descend from Its
presence, and to couple with the Shechinah.[185]

These passages, and a thousand more like them, speak plainly
and leave no room for doubt. They declare that *the Blessed Holy
One, God of Israel, Creator of the world, is not the First Cause.* Rather,
He is a certain entity, in His essence unfathomable, who developed
out of the First Cause by a process of emanation—or, perhaps,

evolved by some more august process that we call "emanation" because the Hebrew language has no proper word for it. He is not any one *sefirah*, but a Spirit to all the *sefirot*, embodied within them. Making use of the *sefirot*, and drawing upon the power of the Infinite [First Cause], He created and administers everything that exists. In the *sefirah Yesod*, He appeared to the patriarchs. In *Tif'eret*, He appeared to Moses and revealed the Torah. All of this was and is accomplished through the Shechinah.

It will now be evident that *the ancient philosophers and pagans spoke the truth.* So did the Jews: the Tannaim and the Amoraim, the Zohar and *Tiqqunei Zohar*, the books *Yezirah* and *Bahir* and *Berit Menuhah*.[186] All agreed that the Blessed Holy One, God of Israel, is not the First Cause, but rather an emanated being. He is not a *sefirah* or an attribute, but rather the maker of the attributes and the Spirit of them all. It is He whom we worship, He, and not His attributes, whom we invoke.

"He is first": prior to any of the *sefirot*. "He is last, and there is no God beside Him": in that He has no father or brother or son, as do the *sefirot*.[187] Nor is He the "Son" of the First Cause. Father and son must necessarily be the same sort of being, sharers of a common essence, whereas His essence is unlike that of the First Cause. (We shall presently elaborate.)[188]

The Blessed Holy One, furthermore, has no name, other than in accord with His actions or in accord with the attribute through which He manifests Himself. He prays to the First Cause, which is *within* Himself,[189] the purpose being to benefit His children and to accomplish His own unification with the Shechinah. I shall presently reveal, as well, the meaning of His "fringed garment" and His "phylacteries."[190]

It is certain, likewise, that the [modern] philosophers, the [Jewish] scholars of the past, and the Muslims as well, have no true God, inasmuch as the Creator and the First Cause are not identical. The Christian religion is false, down to every last detail. The Kabbalists, too, are wrong. The First Cause, even as embodied within the *sefirot*, is something other than the Blessed Holy One,

God of Israel, and It did not Itself create the world by using the *sefirot*.

Finally, it can now be grasped how it is that the Shechinah is a true divinity, along with the Blessed Holy One. He and She are two aspects—certainly not two gods—but one single and unified Deity.[191]

Blessed be He [the Blessed Holy One], **and blessed be His Name** [the Shechinah],[192] **for all eternity! Amen, amen, selah! Forever!**

> [I understand this to have been the original ending of the treatise. I assume that chapter XVII (published by Scholem), and the fragmentary chapter XVIII (in ms JTS 1677), are Cardozo's subsequent additions. (See the introduction to this text.)
>
> Of these supplementary chapters, the only passage that demands translation is the conclusion to chapter XVII. Here Cardozo nobly conveys his debt to his predecessors, and his sense that he is "standing on the shoulders of giants."]

...Nowhere do we find, among all the *sefirot* and spirits of the Lurianic hierarchies, any one entity precisely identical with that being whom we call Blessed Holy One: the world's Creator, Israel's God. From Rabbi Simeon ben Yohai's time down to Luria's own, no one had ever discussed the subject of the emanations in terms of "body" and "spirit" as Luria did, in precise detail as well as general principle. Yet never did he speak of this one Spirit whose existence we have now discovered, and whose divinity we now proclaim.

Yet how might it have been possible for anyone to have discovered the identity of the God of Israel, if Luria's scholarship had not paved the way? From the end of the Amoraic period onward, it would seem, generation after generation of Jewish thinkers have investigated the Kabbalah, each scholar adding his fresh discoveries to those of his predecessors. Little by little, bit by bit, piece by piece, they built up our understanding of Divinity. In holiness, in purity, with the most tireless effort, they laid the foundations for the achievement that is at last within our grasp: *comprehension of God's identity and of the Shechinah's divinity, which we had forgotten in our exile.*

Surely our predecessors, ancient and modern, deserve to be credited as though they themselves had made this discovery! It was through their labors and by dint of their efforts that God's faith has now come to be understood, and that it has begun to be communicated to the wider public, thereby effecting the Redemption of the Jewish people.

Unless we know the mystery of Divinity, which our ancestors first denied and then forgot, we will have no possibility of leaving our exile. All of us moderns—Jews, Muslims, philosophers, Christians—believe in the First Cause. We worship the First Cause; we give It our blessings. But *it was through God and the Shechinah* that the First Cause created us and gave us the Torah, and, accordingly, it is only by invoking Him that we may find salvation.

It will thus be seen how thoroughly necessary it is for us to know God, to worship Him, and to bless Him truly and rightly.

Chapter 11
Mending a
Disfigured Deity

INTRODUCTION

1.

The rambling text entitled *Israel, Holiness to the Lord*, starts off as a treatise on the two Messiahs and their relation to one another. At its midpoint, the document reveals itself for what it most essentially is: a script for a Cardozan "Mending-rite" *(tiqqun)*.[1] It is written for Cardozo's disciples in Izmir—Elijah Kohen, Daniel Bonafoux, and four other men—and provides instructions for a ritual to be carried out in Cardozo's absence.

The text gives no indication as to where it was written, beyond that Cardozo was obviously not in Izmir at the time. But it mentions the "failed Redemption" of April 1682,[2] in a context that suggests this is a fairly recent event. We may reasonably suppose that, like *This Is My God*, this text dates from Cardozo's Dardanelles period, some time in the middle 1680s.[3]

As usual in Cardozo's *tiqqunim*, the ritual acts prescribed are simple and sparse. More important than the acts themselves are the biblical texts and prayers to be recited during their performance. Most important of all are the *kavvanot* (mental intentions) that are to accompany the recitations. Not only must the actors know what to say and what to do, they must fully understand the theory behind it all. That is why the bulk of the text is given over to theoretical discussions, normally couched in the most recondite concepts of the Kabbalah and supported by the standard, highly eccentric (as they now seem) modes of Kabbalistic argumentation.

A text like this is a problem for the translator. What it has to say—about Cardozo's perceptions of himself and Sabbatai Zevi as co-Messiahs, about the flaws in the Divinity and the process of "mending" them, about the demonic powers that stand in opposition to the "Mending"—is so fascinating and important for understanding Cardozo that it can hardly be omitted from a volume of this sort. But its argumentation is complex and difficult, and alien to most modern categories of thought. Without background in Kabbalah, and without at least some knowledge of Hebrew, much of the treatise will be unintelligible.

I have chosen, therefore, to omit nearly all of the theoretical argument that constitutes the first half of *Israel, Holiness to the Lord* and to begin the translation very shortly before Cardozo begins prescribing for the ritual. I have also abridged, sometimes very considerably, the theoretical portions of the second half and have retained only the least abstruse and confusing of Cardozo's Kabbalistic allusions and ruminations.

2.

Cardozo takes the title of his treatise from Jeremiah 2:3: "Israel is holiness to the Lord, the beginning of His yield." Inspired by this verse—or, more accurately, by an ancient rabbinic midrash that quotes this verse[4]—he embarks upon a complex Kabbalistic meditation (not included in the translation) on the first and last words of the Five Books of Moses. The very first word of the Torah is *bereshit*, "in the beginning" (Gen 1:1). Its very last word is *yisra'el*, "Israel" (Deut 34:12). The two words can be shown in various ways—most of them utterly forced and unconvincing to any but the most committed Kabbalist—to be essentially one. The Torah is thus revealed as a marvelous unity, "its end rooted in its beginning and its beginning in its end."

Contained within these two words that are one are the two Messiahs who need to become one. These are Sabbatai Zevi as Messiah ben David and Abraham Cardozo as Messiah ben Joseph. (Cardozo leaves no doubt in this treatise that he regards himself as Messiah ben Joseph.)[5] Both Messiahs, Cardozo reveals, are present at the beginning and the end of the Torah: Sabbatai under his own name; Cardozo under the name of Roshi, the spirit-guide who figures prominently in this text as Cardozo's Messianic *alter ego*.[6]

The two Messiahs manifest themselves in the biblical text in different ways.[7] These differences are symptomatic of the tensions that presently exist between them. And these tensions have not been eased but rather exacerbated by the fact that Sabbatai Zevi is now dead.

The Messiahs ought to be in harmony, but they are not. "Jealousy over power," Cardozo writes, "is psychologically inevitable...and this principle extends itself to Messiah ben David and Messiah ben Ephraim, who will struggle against one another and envy one another until the very end."[8] This state of affairs is crippling for both Sabbatai and Cardozo. "The son of David cannot be a complete Messiah in the absence of Messiah ben Ephraim, nor can the son of Joseph be a complete redeemer in the absence of Messiah ben David."[9] A man and a woman are a complete human being only when they are together. Just so, "Messiah ben David and Messiah ben Ephraim are called *Messiah* when the two of them are together. Each of them is a half Messiah."[10]

It is no accident that Cardozo uses a sexual image to convey the relationship of the two Messiahs. Throughout the treatise, Cardozo returns again and again to the point that the Messiahs correspond to—or, perhaps, are manifestations of—the two lowest *sefirot* in the Kabbalistic system. *Yesod*, the divine phallus, corresponds to Messiah ben Joseph. *Malkhut*, the receptive female genital with which *Yesod* copulates,[11] corresponds to Messiah ben David.

There is a remarkable consequence to these equations. Sabbatai Zevi, considered as a historical person, was obviously

male. Yet, in Cardozo's Messianic scheme, he is the "female" partner. Like the *sefirah Malkhut* that he manifests, Sabbatai is "the
mirror that does not shine." He is "poor and desolate and withered,
his spirit having left him once and for all. He consequently…will
not be able to provide any clear and detailed explanation of the
Mystery of the Divine Faith." Over against this ineffectual,
"female" Messiah, who cannot perform what for Cardozo is the
essence of the redemptive task, stands the phallic, "masculine"
Messiah ben Ephraim. *Here* is a Messiah who, unlike Sabbatai Zevi,
can find the truth and communicate it effectively.[12] He it is who
"will come to grasp the Faith of the First Cause, through the
Blessed Holy One and His Shechinah, and will be able to provide
the Jewish people with a detailed theology."[13]

Hostility between the two Messiahs, Cardozo has told us, is
inevitable. Yet it must be brought to an end if Redemption is to be
achieved: if Sabbatai Zevi is to rise from the (literal) dust in which
he is buried; if Cardozo is to rise, with him, from the (figurative)
garbage pile to which he has been consigned by the ridicule and
disbelief of his contemporaries.[14] The world-redeeming fusion
between the two must be brought to reality. This is one of the goals
of the "Mending-rite" prescribed in *Israel, Holiness to the Lord*.

3.

Cardozo's disciples are engaged in the "Mending," not only of
the two Messiahs, but also of the God they serve. To understand
the nature of the divine flaw, and the means Cardozo chose to
mend it, we must have recourse to the Kabbalistic conception of
"effluence" *(shefa')*. This is the life-giving essence, envisioned
sometimes as light and sometimes as fluid, that flows down from
the higher levels of divinity in order to nourish the lower.[15]

The Kabbalists' favorite prooftext for their image of *shefa'* as
a liquid was Genesis 2:10: "A river goes forth from Eden to water
the garden…." "Eden," according to the Zohar, stands for the
higher *sefirot*; "the garden," for the lower. The "river" is the effluence from which the lower *sefirot* draw their sustenance.[16] When

times are as they should be, this "river" flows plenteously. But at times, due normally to human sin, the Divinity's relations with Itself will be disrupted. The river then "becomes waterless, all dried up" (Job 14:11).[17]

For Cardozo, the source of the "river" lies in the realm above the *sefirot*, among the abstract, mysterious entities that are the "soul" of God. It is these entities that animate and grant divinity to God's "body," that is, the Lurianic "Five Persons," most especially the Irascible One.[18] The "effluence," symbolized by the river, flows from God's "soul" to God's "body," from the super-sefirotic beings to the "Five Persons." When the effluence fails for whatever reason, the "Five Persons" become like five beached stones, deprived of the nourishment they need in order to function as a living Deity. God then lies comatose and helpless. "Wake up! why do You sleep, O Lord?" the Psalmist frantically demands (44:24). There is really nothing God can do about it, any more than a drought-withered tree can turn itself green again. Like that tree, God is no longer quite Himself. As Isaiah says (52:14), He is "disfigured in appearance...and in form."

Isaiah spoke these words about the mysterious "Suffering Servant." For Cardozo, as we have seen (in chapter 9), the Suffering Servant is the Messiah. But the relevant passage of Isaiah has a deeper Kabbalistic meaning as well. The Servant is God Himself, and His "suffering" is His diminishment when the *shefa'* is withheld from Him.[19] And there is worse. Even as the five divine "Persons" lie helpless, removed from the life-giving "river," their demonic counterparts have somehow managed to insinuate themselves into the precious waters.

Cardozo had learned from the Kabbalah that there exists a developed hierarchy of the demonic, mirroring that of the Divine. (The demonic sphere, says the Zohar, "imitates the Holy, as an ape imitates human beings.")[20] There are "Five Persons" in Divinity; there are, correspondingly, "Five Persons" in the demonic. Both divine and demonic spheres, for example, have their Irascible One and His Female. But the divine male-and-female are the Blessed

Holy One and His Shechinah, while their demonic counterparts are Samael (Satan) and the Snake.[21]

We need not go into the details of Cardozo's theory of the demonic. The essential point, for the understanding of the text before us, is this: *The sustenance that ought to go to nourishing the Divine now nourishes the demonic.* This is why, Cardozo thinks, his time is out of joint. It is the task of Cardozo, and of his faithful band of disciples, to set it right.

4.

Once the reader has grasped the problems that must be "mended"—within the Divinity, and between the two Messiahs—it becomes a fairly simple matter to understand the "Mending-rites" that Cardozo prescribed for them. The use of the plural, "rites," is appropriate. The text really sets forth two *tiqqunim*, rather loosely connected to one another. We may call the first, for convenience, "the mending of the stones"; the second, "the mending of the rods."[22]

The "mending of the stones" proceeds as follows: The disciples are to go together to a body of water, variously described as "river" and as "brook." There they are to perform a series of operations with stones. Sometimes they are to put stones in the water. Sometimes they are to remove stones from the water and throw them as far away from the water as possible. They are to recite, as usual in a Cardozan *tiqqun*, a long string of biblical passages, each with the appropriate "intentions." The central passage for this *tiqqun* is Genesis 2:10–14: the river that goes forth from Eden to water the garden and then divides into four streams.

From what we have earlier seen, the symbolism of the rite is entirely transparent. "Stones" may stand for the divine Persons or they may stand for the demonic Persons. (Of the biblical texts that Cardozo prescribes for the ritual, some use the word "stone" in a positive sense, others in the negative.) The divine Persons must be placed securely within the flow of effluence. The demonic Persons must be banished, far away from it.

For the "mending of the rods," the central text is Ezekiel 37:15–28. In imitation of the prophet Ezekiel, Cardozo's disciples are to take two rods and symbolically make them into one. For Ezekiel, the two rods stand for the kingdoms of Judah and Israel (the latter called "Joseph" or "Ephraim," after the supposed ancestor of its people). For Cardozo, they represent Messiah ben David[23] and Messiah ben Joseph. The essential point of the symbolic act remains the same. Two entities that belong together have somehow become separated. The ritual actions of the prophetic *magus*, or of his delegated disciples, can unify them.

For this purpose, the disciples are to go to "the well that is above Messiah ben David's fountain," near the Jewish cemetery in Izmir.[24] Daniel Bonafoux takes the two rods and dips their ends into the water of the well. Elijah Kohen then holds the rods while reciting Ezekiel 37 and other significant biblical texts. Finally, Bonafoux prays "that the Blessed Holy One grant one spirit to the Messiahs, and that He unite Himself with His Shechinah." The unification of the Messiahs thus mirrors the internal unification of the Deity.

5.

We must touch upon two more points before we turn to the text itself.

The first concerns the Messianic quaternity that appears near the end of the treatise. The four streams into which the river from Eden divides itself are said to represent (among other things) four Messianic figures. The first two are, of course, Messiah ben David and Messiah ben Ephraim. The third is Moses, whom Cardozo regards as an important actor in the Messianic drama. (He calls Moses "the essence of the ultimate Redemption," the "body" of which the two individual Messiahs are the arms.)[25] The fourth, says Cardozo, *may* be the prophet Elijah, whom Jewish tradition had normally represented as forerunner and herald of the Messiah. Or— and here he delivers a real surprise—the fourth may be a woman: the *Mevasseret Ziyyon*, "She who brings the good news to Zion."[26]

This woman, who slips so easily into Elijah's traditional role, seems to be entirely without precedent and without context. Yet Cardozo seems to take her for granted and makes no attempt to explain who she is. We are left to grapple with the mystery of her identity.

Perhaps we are to seek her origin in Cardozo's biography. Meir Benayahu has suggested that she is none other than Sabbatai Zevi's widow, Esther.[27] The overtures that Esther Zevi made to Cardozo at the end of 1681 seem indeed to have stirred him deeply. It would not be surprising if they found their way into his Messianic fantasies. But, as we have seen, *Israel, Holiness to the Lord* must have been written at some time after the failed Redemption of April 1682, months or years, that is, after Esther had turned her back on him. Cardozo was later to speak of Esther Zevi with the most intense bitterness.[28] Would he still have been fond enough of her, when he wrote this treatise, to cast her in a redemptive role?

Or perhaps we are to make sense of the Messianic quaternity, with its female "fourth," in the context of Jungian psychology. For the Jungians, the quaternity is an "archetype of wholeness" that crops up—spontaneously and without direct influence by individuals or cultures on one another—in dreams, mythology, and art. A common feature of the quaternity is that *the fourth member of the group is in some way different from the other three*. The "fourth" may be a demonic figure in the company of three divine entities (like Satan, taken together with the Christian Trinity). Or the "fourth" may be a female in the company of three males.[29]

It is striking that the Messianic quaternity of the present text has its mirror in the demonic quaternity that visited Cardozo, from the moon, in July 1683.[30] (This may, indeed, have been about the time that Cardozo wrote *Israel, Holiness to the Lord*.) In both of these foursomes, there are three male figures, plainly and specifically identified, plus a female "fourth," her identity left mysterious.[31] If this is indeed the key to understanding the "woman who brings good news to Zion," we must suppose that her essential reality is not historical but psychological. She will then have emerged, unbidden and uncomprehended, from Cardozo's unconscious. He does not explain her identity for the reason that he himself does not consciously know it.

6.

The second point concerns what is surely one of the most alienating features of this treatise for modern readers. This is Cardozo's penchant for building his arguments upon *gematria* and upon other artificial games—we can hardly regard them otherwise, nowadays—that he plays with Hebrew letters and words.

The starting point of *gematria* is the fact that every Hebrew letter can serve also as a number. (*Aleph*, the first letter of the alphabet, is 1; *bet* is 2; and so forth.) Add up the numerical values of the letters of any word, and you will get the *gematria* value of that word. Find some other word that has the same *gematria* value, and you may conclude, if you are a Kabbalist, that the two words (and the concepts they represent) are mystically linked.

Even when the method is followed strictly and rigorously in its own terms, it is bound nowadays to seem silly and irrelevant, and *gematria* is seldom used with any rigor. Its manipulators have all sorts of devices to make their numbers come out the way they want,[32] these devices are applied in the most arbitrary way, and Cardozo himself makes full (and arbitrary) use of the entire bag of tricks. How seriously can we take any argument that claims to rest upon such "evidence"?

The answer is, not at all seriously, and also, very seriously indeed. Of course *gematria* does not prove anything. To believe that it does, one would first have to accept the premise that the Hebrew language and all its peculiarities are God's own personal invention, designed for the specific purpose of communicating the Torah's mysteries. Cardozo took this premise for granted. Few modern people will do the same.

Gematria will appear in a different light, however, once we grasp that its essential purpose is to provide rationalizations for associative links that have already been sensed intuitively. These links may sometimes be very profound. For example: Many of the early Sabbatians (Cardozo not included) venerated Sabbatai Zevi as "holy serpent," ostensibly on the ground that the Hebrew word for "serpent" *(nahash)* has the same *gematria* value as "Messiah" *(mashiah)*. The *gematria* equation is obviously coincidental, without significance. Yet it masks a deep and perhaps not fully conscious awareness of the numinous power of the figure of the serpent.[33] When we read Cardozo, similarly, we may think what we like of his numerical manipulations. It is the intuitive link, not the numbers, that is important.

BACKGROUND TEXTS

*15*The word of the Lord came to me, saying: *16*Son of man, take you one stick and write upon it, "For Judah, and for the children of Israel his companions." And take one stick and write upon it, "For Joseph: the stick of Ephraim, and all the house of Israel, his companions." *17*And bring them near to one another, till they are one stick; and the two become one in your hand.

*18*When your people say to you, "Will you not tell us why you are doing these things?" *19*you must speak to them as follows: *20*"Thus says the Lord: I am taking the stick of Joseph, which is in the hand of Ephraim...with the stick of Judah; and I shall make them into one stick, and they shall be one in My hand...." *22*I shall make them one nation in the land, among the mountains of Israel. There shall be one king for them all. They shall no longer be two nations, nor shall they be divided any longer into two kingdoms....*24*And My servant David shall be king over them...*26*forever.

—Ezekiel 37:15–26

*10*A river goes forth from Eden to water the garden. From there it divides and becomes four streams. *11*The name of the first is Pishon; this is the one that encircles the entire land of Havilah, where there is gold. *12*The gold of that land is good; bdellium is there, and the onyx stone. *13*The name of the second river is Gihon; this is the one that encircles all the land of Kush. *14*The name of the third river is Tigris; this is the one that goes eastward toward Assyria. And the fourth river is Euphrates.

—Genesis 2:10–14

The waters have failed from the sea;
The river becomes waterless, all dried up.

—Job 14:11

ABRAHAM MIGUEL CARDOZO

I am the man they call, at times, *mem-bet-aleph*; which are the initials of *Michael ben Abraham* [or, alternatively, *Messiah ben Ephraim*]....I am of the Marranos of Spain. I was born in the town of Rio Seco, which means "dry river."...

—Abraham Miguel Cardozo[34]

ISRAEL, HOLINESS TO THE LORD[35]

[1. Preamble]

[In this passage, Cardozo uses images of light, rather than of liquid, to describe the divine "effluence." He uses the terms "Adam of the World of Emanation" and "Primordial Adam" to speak of the super-sefirotic beings that function in his theology as the "soul" of God.[36]]

You must know, now, that when the Temple was destroyed the light of the [higher] *sefirah Hokhmah* was withdrawn from the *sefirah Tif'eret*.[37] The light of "Adam of the World of Emanation," too, was reduced. The *sefirot* of the Irascible One and His Female were thus left in the state of being "disfigured in appearance from that of a man, in form [from that of humanity," Isa 52:14]; the reference being to *Tif'eret* and *Malkhut*.[38] The Blessed Holy One,…[which is] the rational soul of the Irascible One, had withdrawn Itself into the heights, leaving the Irascible One diminished, and as though He were asleep.[39] (This is the secret meaning of the verse, "Wake up! why do You sleep, O Lord?" [Ps 44:24].)

If this situation is to be mended, there must be a revelation of the light of "Adam of the World of Emanation" in conjunction with Primordial Adam, as there was at the time of the original "Mending."[40] This is why I have been able to obtain permission to unveil the reality of "Adam of the World of Emanation," the purpose being to seat the King on His throne.

The Five Persons of the World of Emanation are as follows:
[1.] the Patient One,
[2.] Father,
[3.] Mother,

[4.] the Irascible One, and
[5.] His Female;

also known as:

[1.] *Keter,*
[2.] *Hokhmah,*
[3.] *Binah,*
[4.] the Irascible One,[41] and
[5.] *Malkhut.*

All emerged from the Holy King, and it is He who sustains them and waters them.[42]

[2. The symbolism of the brook and the stones]

You must begin the Mending-rite by proceeding, in secret, to the brook. Rabbi Elijah Kohen is to substitute for Messiah ben Ephraim [Cardozo], and he is to be accompanied by Roshi. Rabbi Daniel is to be accompanied by Rabbi David Habillo and Rabbi Nathan; Shem Tov Shemaiah by Rabbi Isaac Luria; Moses Nahum by Rabbi Asher Kohen; Hananel by Rabbi Abraham Yakhini; and Benjamin Curial by the prophet Samuel.

> [Each of the six disciples has one or more spirit-guides with him.[43] Elijah Kohen, who serves as Cardozo's stand-in, has for his guide Roshi—Cardozo's Messianic, or celestial, *alter ego.*]

The brook symbolizes Primordial Adam. Rabbi Elijah must take from it, in accord with the full instructions that I shall provide presently, five stones the size of a fist or greater. These stones represent the Patient One, Father, Mother, Son, and Daughter [=the Irascible One and His Female].

The word for "stone," *even,* suggests the *building* activities engaged in by the Primordial Adam.[44] The word *even* itself stands for the *sefirah Malkhut*....The demonic powers are called "stumbling stone" and "obstacle stone" [Isa 8:14]...[while] the holy *sefirot* are called "smooth stones."[45]...

Now, when you take up these stones, your purpose is not to separate or to distance them from the brook, to distance, that is, the Persons from the Primordial Adam. God forbid! These are our portion and our heritage; it is our task fully to mend the flaw inflicted upon them by our ancestors' sins and by our own, and it is for this purpose that you are taking them up. For it is he who has true knowledge of God who is able to do the "Mending."

While standing at the river bank, recite the following passage:

> A river goes forth from Eden to water the garden. From there it divides and becomes four streams. The name of the first is Pishon; this is the one that encircles the entire land of Havilah, where there is gold. The gold of that land is good; bdellium is there, and the onyx stone. The name of the second river is Gihon; this is the one that encircles all the land of Kush. The name of the third river is Tigris; this is the one that goes eastward toward Assyria. And the fourth river is Euphrates [Gen 2:10–14].[46]

The "river" is Primordial Adam....He perpetually "goes forth from Eden," this being "Adam of the World of Emanation." The "garden" is that vacant space, which, according to Rabbi Isaac Luria, was left when the Infinite initially contracted Itself into Itself....This is, in the truest sense, that "garden," and it is for the purpose of watering it that the river—Primordial Adam—goes forth from the primordial Eden,[47] which is "Adam of the World of Emanation," our portion and our heritage....[48]

After you have done this, put the five stones of the realms of holiness into the river's waters, and afterward recite the following prayer:

> [The prayer that follows is addressed, at least initially, to the Divinity that is the "soul" of the ten *sefirot*. One need

257

not decipher all the prayer's Kabbalistic allusions in order to get a feel for what Cardozo envisions his "Mending-ritual" as accomplishing. The lower aspects of the Divine are to be reconnected with the exalted source of the holy liquid "effluence" from which they have their origin, and from which they have become detached. This is symbolized, of course, by the placing of the stones within the waters of the stream.]

Open my lips, O Lord, and my mouth shall declare Your praise.[49]

O Master of all the worlds, You who necessarily exist! O God, above whom there is no God! O Lord over all the lords, King over all the kings! Like the soul in the body and in its clothing, You shine within the ten *sefirot* of the World of Emanation, the ten *sefirot* of the World of Creation, the ten *sefirot* of the World of Fashioning, the ten *sefirot* of the World of Making. You join together all the worlds: the *yod* to the *hei*, the *hei* to the *vav*, and the *vav* to the *hei*.[50] You give life to them all, and the host of heaven prostrates itself to You before Your honored throne. You it is who unites the Blessed Holy One and His Shechinah. In the light of the manifest faces, Your face [is latent].[51]

May it be Your will to bring the Shechinah near, from You, to the Blessed Holy One. For, as seen from Your perspective, there is no separation or dissociation, no banishment or distancing.

Please, O Master of the worlds!
let the benevolent forehead of that Holy Ancient One make itself visible to the Irascible One, the Glory of Israel the holy people [that is, the *sefirah Tif'eret*], through that light of Primordial Adam that is poured forth from "Adam of the World of Emanation," Your honored throne;
let the Supreme Grace spread out from the Hidden Wisdom of the Patient One, through His glorious beard;
let the three heads [of the Patient One], along with the supreme head of the Ancient of Days, radiate plenteous effluence and mighty light, and let them grant blessing and lofty grace to the holy Dispenser;

let that effluence and light and blessing and Supreme Grace descend, from that incomparably holy Dispenser, down to Father and Mother;

let [Father and Mother] be joined in perfect union through the Supreme Knowledge, so as to grant the brains of maturity to *Tif'eret* and to *Malkhut*;

let the effluence and light and blessing and grace and severity be drawn forth from Father and Mother to the Irascible One and His Female (for the King's head is perfected by both grace and severity);

and let the Blessed Holy One and His Shechinah be united body to body, soul to soul, through that Foundation of the World [the divine phallus: the *sefirah Yesod*], in the powerful light You shine there, from the following names:[52]

Crown of the Patient One
YOVADA HAYA VAYAVA HAYA
Membrane of the Patient One
YOVADA HAYA VA'AVAHEYA
Hidden Wisdom of the Patient One
YOVADA HE'A VA'AVA HE'A
Father and Mother
Y'HH VYHH
Tif'eret and Malkhut
Y'HDVNHY

Now, O Lord our God, rescue us for the sake of Your Name! You are our Father; You are our hope; it is You who will save us through Your servant Sabbatai Zevi and Your beloved Abraham Michael Cardozo. "The spirit of the Lord shall rest upon him; a spirit of wisdom and understanding, a spirit of good counsel and power, a spirit of knowledge and fear of the Lord" [Isa 11:2, referring to the Messiah]. Then will the prophecy be fulfilled: "Israel shall be saved eternally through the Lord. Never again shall they be shamed or humiliated" [Isa 45:17]. "The Lord shall be King over all the earth. On that day the Lord shall be One and His Name One" [Zech 14:9].

May it be the will from within You,[53] Lord our God and God of our ancestors, to pour forth the light of Your presence, through the unity of Your Shechinah, to Your honored throne and the World of Creation, to the seraphim and all the pure and holy Spirituality that is there. May Your light, Your grace, Your severity spread from there to the World of Fashioning: to Metatron prince of the presence, to Michael the great prince, to Gabriel the mighty prince, to Uriel and to all the pure and holy angels who serve You, and to Roshi and to the prophet Elijah and to Her Who Brings the Good News to Zion.

[We shall presently hear more about this mysterious lady, the "Mevasseret Ziyyon."

Cardozo goes on to quote a series of biblical passages that use the Hebrew word *roshi*—normally translated as "my head."]

And speedily let the prophecy be fulfilled: "You have anointed Roshi with oil; my cup overflows" [Ps 23:5]. "You have protected Roshi on the day of battle" [Ps 140:8]. "Now let Roshi be exalted over my enemies round about me; and, trumpeting, I will offer sacrifices in His tent" [Ps 27:6].

[3. The symbolism of the two rods]

Now take two rods.

One of them must be of the wood of the date-palm. You must concentrate on this rod's being Messiah ben Ephraim: the *sefirah* *Yesod*, the "Righteous One."[54] Recite the verse, "The Righteous shall blossom like a date-palm, flourish like a cedar in Lebanon" [Ps 92:13]. As you do that, concentrate on the words "righteous like a date-palm," which have the same numerical value as *Abraham Cardozo*.

The word for "date-palm," *tamar*, has moreover the same numerical value as shemesh, "sun," which stands for the *sefirah* *Yesod*.[55] The point is that the date-palm bears fruit through its being male and female together: *Yesod* and *Malkhut*. It thus alludes to the combination of the two Messiahs.

260

[Cardozo is the phallic male in this partnership, while Sabbatai Zevi is the female.]

You must take the other rod from the wood of a pomegranate tree. And you must recite: "They set forth from Ritmah, and they encamped in Rimmon-perez" [Num 33:19]. Concentrate on this: that the exile is bitter as a broom-plant [*retem*, as in the place-name *Ritmah*], while the Redemption and the ingathering of the exiles is sweet as a pomegranate [*rimmon*], for all the Jewish people will then be under their king's rule, the Pomegranate crowned king, and all his people contained within him. So what the verse means is that "they set forth" from exile "and they encamped" in Messiah ben David [Sabbatai Zevi], who is the Pomegranate, son of Perez, son of Judah.[56]...

> [In a passage omitted from the translation, Cardozo demonstrates that Messiah ben Ephraim, as representative of the *sefirah Yesod*, is also a "pomegranate." Yet the two "pomegranates" are not quite the same. Messiah ben David is a sweet pomegranate. Messiah ben Ephraim is a sour pomegranate—perhaps Cardozo's allusion to the bitterness of his own life. Moses, a third Messianic "pomegranate," is intermediate between the two.]

Then recite:

Come, my love, let us go out into the country. Let us spend the night in the villages. Let us get up early in the morning and go to the vineyards. We will see if the vines have budded, if the blossoms have opened, if the pomegranates are in blossom. There I will give you my love [Song 7:12–13].

The blossoms have appeared in the land, the time for singing has arrived, the voice of the turtle-dove [*tor*] is heard in our land [Song 2:12].

Concentrate on this: that the "pomegranates" [of the first passage], which are the "blossoms" [of the second passage], "are in blossom." And, inasmuch as they have already "appeared in the land" [that is, both Messiahs have appeared on earth], the pomegranates' "time for singing has arrived." "The voice of the *tor*," the "turtle-dove," "is heard in our land" and below it.[57] For now that the *Tor*ah is being revealed—and the Torah is the *sefirah Tif'eret*[58] and the Blessed Holy One, for He is the "voice of the Torah," it having been revealed in His voice—God's divinity is being "heard in the land."

All this is thanks to those "pomegranates," who proclaim the Mystery of the Faith so that all the ends of the earth may turn to God and find salvation. In the same way, the sound of the "pomegranates'" song induces the Jews to turn their attention to the task of studying and understanding the Torah. Hence: "there I will give you my love." The Blessed Holy One and His Shechinah will become united, as one.

Now, you must understand that during exile times it is not possible that any prophet should formally be dispatched on God's mission.[59] Outside the Holy Land, this is all the more impossible. What *can* happen is that deceased saints and angels reveal themselves. Thus it was in the generation of Rabbi Simeon ben Yohai, concerning which it was said that there would be no generation like that one till the generation of the Messiah [Zohar, III, 206a]. It will follow that, when such a generation *does* make its appearance—in that the knowledge of the Lord is revealed, and the saints reveal themselves on earth as well—we are left in no doubt that that is the Messiah's generation.

Moses will then reveal himself. So will Messiah ben David, the pious folk, and the angels. Then God's faith will become known; then wisdom will increase. So says Solomon, speaking in the person of the Shechinah as She secretly converses with the Blessed Holy One: "Come, my love [...] we will see if [...] the pomegranates"—the Messiahs, that is, who reveal the Divinity—"are in blossom in the land." She then tells Him that "the blossoms have appeared in the land": Moses, Messiah ben David, and the saints have already made their appearance on earth.[60] And, if so, there can be no doubt that "the time for singing has arrived" to our land, along with "the voice of the *tor*," which is the *Tor*ah.[61]...

The "time for singing," to be sure, has arrived....But, if [the Redemption] is to happen, some "Mending" is required for the two Messiahs: they must be brought into union. For they are natural opposites, corresponding respectively to the *sefirot Hesed* ["Grace"; Sabbatai Zevi] and *Gevurah* ["Judgment"; Cardozo]....Yes, the "time for singing" has arrived. But so long as the Messiahs remain, as "pomegranates," two distinct entities, [Redemption] is not possible....

[The two Messiahs are not only two "pomegranates." They are also two "Zevis." ("Zevi" is the Hebrew word for "gazelle.") Sabbatai is obviously a "Zevi." Cardozo demonstrates, through a complex biblical argument (omitted from the translation), that he himself is a "Zevi" also.]

Once there were two *qav*s [= two *Zevi*s].[62] One is the "ruined *qav*" [=*Zevi*], an esoteric hint at the Kings Who Died, who derived from the aspect of *Malkhut*. But there is also another *qav* [=*Zevi*], a *qav* of "Mending," which comes from the aspect of *Yesod*. Messiah ben David is the *qav* [=*Zevi*] that was fated, from its very root, to leave the sphere of holiness for that of impurity, and even to die. This was in order to purify and to mend those sparks of holiness that had remained mixed in with the "ruined *qav*."

Messiah ben Ephraim, by contrast, is the *qav* [=*Zevi*] that derives from the aspect of the Living One [the *sefirah Yesod*], which pours forth light from the *sefirah Hokhmah*. His fate it was to be born among the Christians. This was in order that the sparks that had descended from holiness might be saved from the demons, those, too, that fell from *Yesod* [which is the divine phallus] in a sort of seminal emission.

Now, it is the way of the gazelle *[zevi]* always to look back toward the place from which he came.[63] This is fine and proper for Messiah ben David, who left the Jewish community and went out from Torah and holiness into the realms of the profane. (He also left his body, and he will need to return to it, in order to speed the ingathering of the exiles.) That is why he is "Zevi."

Messiah ben Ephraim, by contrast, went out from impurity and entered into holiness, and therefore ought *not* to look back toward the place from which he came. The Christians claim that Jesus is like God. It is therefore appropriate for Messiah ben Ephraim to say "Who is like God?" *[mi ka-el]* meaning by this that "there is no one like God, O Jeshurun" [Deut 33:26], for "there is no deity other than the Lord" [cf. Ps 18:32]. That is why his name has always been *Michael, mi ka-el,* "who is like God?"...as if to say, I am the kind of *Zevi* who is always saying, "Who is like God?" and who will never, God forbid, look back to the place from which I came.

On the basis of these remarks, you will understand how it is that Messiah ben David has been profaned. You will understand, too, how the prophecy of Elijah has been fulfilled, that Messiah ben Ephraim is fated to be profaned among the idolaters to atone for the sin of his ancestor Jeroboam. Not only that: Elijah prophesied that Messiah ben Ephraim's offspring would be profaned as well. And so it has come to pass....

> [Cardozo took the name Abraham upon his return to Judaism, but had been baptized Miguel. The literal meaning of the name is, as he says, "Who is like God?" From the very baptismal font, therefore, the infant Cardozo implicitly denied the lie into which he was baptized.
>
> The prophecy of "Elijah" is found in *The Faithful Shepherd*, Zohar, III, 276b. It is translated among the Background Texts for chapter 9. I do not know what Cardozo means by the "profanation" of his offspring.]

[4. The four rivers of Eden]

[Cardozo returns, after a long delay, to the four streams into which the river, flowing from Eden, was divided (Gen

2:10–14). The locus of division, he says, is the *sefirah Keter* (which corresponds to the "Person" called the Patient One). The four streams—Pishon, Gihon, Tigris, Euphrates—stand for the four "Persons" of Father, Mother, Son, and Daughter. They stand for something else as well: four Messianic figures. The first three of these are Messiah ben David, Messiah ben Ephraim, and Moses. The fourth, as we shall see, is something of a mystery.]

"The name of the first is Pishon" [Gen 2:11]. This is the *sefirah Hokhmah* [=Father]...."The name of the second river is Gihon; this is the one that encircles all the land of Kush" [2:13]. This is *Binah* [=Mother]...[whose] role is to cover and to protect....The roots of the two Messiahs' souls derive from Father and Mother. This is why the numerical value of the words "the name of the first is Pishon," when the number of its letters are counted in, is equivalent to the value of "Sabbatai Zevi" (when the totality of that name is counted in).[64] And it is why the phrase, "the name of the second river," has the same numerical value [965] as "Abraham Michael Cardozo"!...

Now, at Messiah ben David's coming...the *sefirah Hokhmah* withdrew itself....Messiah ben David was then left "a waterless river, all dried up" [Job 14:11]....He was unable to reveal the Divinity in any explicit fashion, and he withdrew himself to the heights. Messiah ben Ephraim, by contrast, is the *sefirah Yesod*. He derives from the Mother's genital, which is called "the broad places of the river."[65] He is thus able to spread doctrine throughout the world, and the divine effluence along with it, to make known the faith of the Cause Above All Causes, through the Blessed Holy One and His Shechinah. This is why the numerical value of "the broad places of the river" (plus an extra "one" for the entire phrase) comes to 877, which is the numerical value of "Abraham Cardozo," plus the number of the letters in that name.

[There is a paradox here. Cardozo is the man from Rio Seco, "dry river";[66] yet it is Sabbatai Zevi, and not Cardozo, who proves to be the "waterless river, all dried up." But Cardozo has given us the key to resolving the paradox. The "dry river" (Christianity) is in his past, not his future. Unlike Sabbatai Zevi, whose transit is from the "watered places" of Judaism into the parched desert of Gentile-dom, Cardozo will not look back to the place from which he came.]

"The name of the third river is Tigris" [Gen 2:14]. This is the Irascible One, which is called the *sefirah Tif'eret*....[It corresponds to Moses, who] incorporates the roots of both Messiahs.... "And the fourth river is Euphrates" [Gen 2:14]. This is the *sefirah Malkhut*, which is the source of all that is produced.[67]...The Bible does not speak here about "the name of the river" [as opposed to the first three rivers, where the *name* is mentioned explicitly]. This is because *Malkhut* takes on various names, in accord with whatever effluence this *sefirah* receives [from the *sefirot* above it]....

The fourth [Messianic figure] is the Man Who Brings Good News *[ha-mevasser]*, and this is Elijah. Yet it remains unclear whether Elijah is really the one who will announce the Redemption. It is possible also that this will be done by a *woman— Mevasseret Ziyyon*, "She Who Brings Good News To Zion"—and *this* is why the text leaves the "name" unmentioned.[68]

[5. The mending of the stones]

In the exile, the river that goes forth from Eden has been reduced to a trickle. The "Five Persons" of the World of Emanation are left as beached stones, at least as far as the outer aspects of the *sefirot* are concerned. In their interiors, to be sure, there is still living water. This is the hidden meaning of the passage, "You shall speak to the rock and it will yield its water" [Num 20:8]. The *sefirot*, after all, are the moist Stones from which the waters emerge.[69]

Yet nowadays, thanks to our transgressions, the demonic Stones have nourished themselves from the divine effluence. They must be separated from this river and distanced from it as far as they possibly can be.

Therefore:

You must first take five stones from the river bank, corresponding to the five demonic Persons: Patient One, *Hokhmah*, *Binah*, Irascible One, and *Malkhut*.

Stand you at the river's edge, and, in one single action, hurl three stones—which you must take from a higher spot, farther removed from the river—into a distant place, where the river cannot water them any more.

Then set the remaining two stones, corresponding to the demonic Irascible One and His Female, at a greater distance from one another.

Throw the one with all your strength to the other side of the river. Throw the other...[70] in the place where you stand, far away, so that the two stones are separated by the river.

Before taking up the stones, recite the passage from "A river goes forth from Eden" up to the word "Euphrates" [Gen 2:10–14].

Then recite:

> I am sending an angel before you, [to protect you on the way, and to bring you to the place that I have prepared. Beware of him, and be obedient to him. Do not rebel against him; for he will not forgive your sin, for My name is in him.
>
> If you indeed obey him and do all that I say, I will be an enemy to your enemies and war against those who are hostile to you. For my angel shall go before you, and bring you to the Amorite, the Hittite, the Perizzite, the Canaanite, the Hivite, and the Jebusite; and I will destroy them.—Exod 23:20–23]

And so on, to the end of the chapter [Exod 23].

As you recite this passage, concentrate on the following: The "angel" in question is Messiah ben Ephraim. (The initial letters of *anokhi sholeah mal'akh*, "I am sending an angel," stand also for *Abraham Sabbatai Moses*.) Of the six nations mentioned, "the Canaanite" is a collective term for the entire group. The other five—"the Amorite," "the Hittite," and so forth—are the five stones, the "Five Persons" of the demonic World of Emanation, all of them comprised in the term "Other God" [Exod 34:14].

267

And afterward recite the text from "Behold I am making a covenant," through the word "Egypt" [Exod 34:10–18]....
After this, you must take the five stones from the river bank and recite: "Your enemies, Lord, Your enemies shall perish, all the workers of iniquity shall be scattered" [Ps 92:10]. Keep in your mind, as you recite, that the "Five Persons" of the impure World of Emanation are always God's enemies. They indeed destroy the effluence of the river. But they shall then be scattered, they and all those bands[71] of theirs who are responsible for perversions, wickedness, iniquity.

Then throw the stones, and say: "Water wears away the stones, it washes away the earth's dust, and You have caused human hope to perish" [Job 14:19]—"and the Gentiles must grasp that they are only human!" [Ps 9:21].[72] The water, the effluence of the river, has indeed been swallowed up by those "stones."[73] But that very same water shall wear them away and fragment them—them and all their bands.

"He has put an end [qez] to darkness. He is the Searcher-out, on behalf of every Extremity, of the Stone of darkness and the shadow of death" [Job 28:31].[74] "Darkness" is a term for the demonic forces. The Infinite One has set a boundary to this darkness, and an "end" to its dominion and to its nourishing itself from the river. This "end" has come about through Cardozo and Zevi, who are qof-zadde [qof, the initial letter of "Cardozo" + zadde, the initial letter of "Zevi"], qez, "end."

When shall the end come for the dominion of darkness? When the Infinite One hands Cardozo and Zevi over to that darkness! He has put Messiah ben David outside the Torah's light, and now has buried him. He has put Messiah ben Ephraim in the darkness of the failed Redemption and has subjected him to endless trials....

[Sabbatai Zevi has left Judaism and is now dead. Cardozo must struggle with the conundrum of the "failed Redemption" of 1682, and the trials and humiliations that have followed in its wake. Why did all this happen? Because God must sacrifice the two Messiahs to the

Darkness, in order to destroy the power of that Darkness.]

Our entire purpose now is to destroy the structure of the impure *Binah*, *Tif'eret*, and *Malkhut*, which are "darkness and the shadow of death," Samael and the Snake....

Then you must say, "There is a time to throw stones!" [Eccl 3:5]—and throw them!

Hurry, now, and take five more stones from the dry areas by the river bank, and say, "There is a time to gather stones together" [Eccl 3:5]. Concentrate on this phrase having (once its three [Hebrew] words are included in the count) the same numerical value as *Sabbatai*, and, thanks to his merit, you will succeed.

[The demonic "stones" (=*sefirot*) are cast away. The divine "stones" are gathered together, and presumably—although Cardozo does not explicitly say so—placed in the life-giving waters.]

Then recite: "For your covenant is with the stones of the field, and the beasts of the field have made peace with you" [Job 5:23]. For we have a Covenant; [and] these are the stones of the Shechinah.[75] Consequently, we do not need to do anything more to arouse the Blessed Holy One, till His love shall desire [Song 2:7]....The task of arousing the supernal desire belongs to Messiah ben Ephraim [=the *sefirah* *Yesod*, the divine phallus] and to no one else....

[The souls of the departed, Cardozo explains, have no power to perform the necessary "Mendings." Only the living—Cardozo and his disciples—can do that.]

The prayers of the saints in heaven are indeed of assistance to the living. But it is performance of the commandments—and study and good deeds, and prayers uttered with the proper intentions—that brings about "Mending" and effluence in the supernal realms. The souls of the saints have no way to effect this, except by joining and attaching themselves to people who are currently alive on earth. This is the reason why the spirit-guides are so active nowadays. You must understand it well.

[6. The mending of the rods]

Once you have completed all these recitations and all these actions in the field and the garden [?], then proceed to the well that is above Messiah ben David's fountain, where I have gone in your company.[76]

Rabbi Daniel [Bonafoux] must take the two rods [described above, section 3], bound together, and dip their ends into the water that is within the well. Let him recite:

> Then let Israel sing [this song: Rise up, well! answer her! Well that the princes have dug, that the nobles of the people have cut out, with a scepter, with their staff. And from the desert to Mattanah, and from Mattanah to Nahaliel, and from Nahaliel to Bamoth, and from Bamoth to the valley that is in the field of Moab, the top of Pisgah which looks out upon] the desert [Num 21:17–20].
>
> Hear O Israel, the Lord is our God, the Lord is One [Deut 6:4].[77]
>
> The Lord has reigned [Ps 93:1], and the Lord shall [be king over all the earth; Zech 14:9].

At this point Rabbi Elijah must take the rods in his hand and recite the passage from the thirty-seventh chapter of Ezekiel that begins "take you," plus the eleventh and twelfth chapters of Isaiah, and the passage from the Zohar on the Torah portion *Vayyiggash*, page 207 [of the Mantua edition], that ends with the words "with songs and praises."

> [In Ezekiel 37:15–28, the prophet is told to take two sticks, one for Judah and one for Ephraim, and to combine them into one. For Cardozo, this represents the unification of the two Messiahs, himself and Sabbatai Zevi.

270

The "eleventh and twelfth chapters of Isaiah" include a prophecy of the reign of the Davidic Messiah (11:1–10), a promise that Judah and Ephraim will live in harmony and cooperation (11:13–14), and the words—relevant to the ritual's locale—"you shall draw water with joy from the fountains of salvation" (12:3). The Zoharic passage[78] describes the beneficent reunion and reconciliation of the two quarreling "kings," Judah and Joseph, by which Cardozo surely understands Sabbatai Zevi and himself.

Daniel Bonafoux is now to pray that the two Messiahs become united, and that the male and female elements of Divinity—which are apparently parallel to the two Messiahs—do the same.]

Then let Rabbi Daniel stand off at a distance from you. Let him pray that the Blessed Holy One grant one spirit to the Messiahs, and that He unite Himself with His Shechinah, for the purpose of disseminating knowledge of His Divinity and revealing the exaltation of the Cause Above All Causes.

The spirit-guide will then instruct you, and will ask the Lord of Wonders to provide some miraculous token that the "Mending-rite" has been found acceptable.

[7. Conclusion]

From the time that you set forth to perform the "Mending-rite" until you have completed it, you must be careful to avoid any quarreling or dissension. If there is anger or bad feeling among you, you must put it off for another day.

You alone, humble folk, are to go on this errand. No one who has doubts about the faith of God and His Messiahs may accompany you. And make sure you thoroughly understand the "Mending-rite" among yourselves.

As you perform the ritual, recite it in such a way that the million saints' souls who will be there can hear you, understand you, and help you.

"By the power of the faith of Abraham Michael Cardozo, Messiah ben Ephraim"—so let Rabbi Daniel say—"I command all who hear the words of this Mending-rite to show themselves so they can be seen!" Whatever spirit he can recognize, or whatever spirit has his name written upon him, you are to write down and send to me as soon as possible. Give details of place, date, time; of the miracle; of the sequence of events; and of the people who were present.

And be you well.

Chapter 12
Reminiscences of the Shechinah's Knight

INTRODUCTION

1.

Sometime near the beginning of the eighteenth century, the aged Abraham Cardozo received from one of his admirers a book of Zohar interpretation for his opinion and comment. The author of the book was one Mordecai Ashkenazi, a man of Polish origins and somewhat limited academic background. Ashkenazi had published the book in 1701, with the assistance of his devoted teacher, the Italian Kabbalist Abraham Rovigo. He titled the book, in Rovigo's honor, *Abraham's Tamarisk.*[1]

Few readers of *Abraham's Tamarisk* are likely to have known that both Rovigo and his protege were devoted Sabbatians, faithful to the fading memory of their Messiah. Still fewer were aware that the Zohar interpretations in the book were inspired, if not actually dictated, by a spirit-guide *(maggid)* who appeared to Ashkenazi in his dreams and revealed to him Kabbalistic mysteries.

Cardozo was among those who were in the know concerning the book's supernatural origin. It did not impress him. At age seventy-five, he had come to understand the world of ghosts and demons, better, perhaps, than he ever understood the real world through which he had spent his life wandering. He had come to be aware that even the blessed dead are not necessarily reliable guides to those mysteries that really count. The psalmist had written, long ago, that "truth shall spring forth from the earth" (Ps 85:12). Cardozo had learned from these words—as the seventeenth century itself had begun to learn, in very different ways—that the truths that redeem humanity come from our own earth and not from Beyond. Spirits cannot teach us these truths. We must find them ourselves, through our own intellectual powers and labors. Cardozo had devoted his life to this quest, and that life, if not the quest, was nearing its end.

Cardozo explained all this to the person—we do not know who it was—who had sent him the book. He may have intended to write a brief response, an epistolary "book review," as it were, of *Abraham's Tamarisk*. But a remark of his correspondent's, apropos of his old enemy Samuel Primo, set Cardozo to reflecting on the trials and setbacks of his long quest. He was reminded of a story, and then that story reminded him of another, and so on. By the time he was finished, he had penned an extraordinary document that fills more than thirty pages of printed Hebrew text and that reveals Cardozo as few humans have ever been revealed.

2.

Isaac Molho and Abraham Amarilio, who published the letter in 1960 from a manuscript preserved by the Dönmeh (secret Sabbatians) in Salonica, speak of it as "a sort of long autobiography."[2] Scholars have come to designate it Cardozo's "autobiographical letter," and I follow this convention. Yet anyone who reads the letter expecting an autobiography in the normal sense of the word is bound to be disappointed. There is nothing in it like a clear, orderly narrative sequence. It is instead a rambling chain of anecdotes, held together by free associations, the tales of an old man looking back on a long life.

The individual anecdotes are well told and often fascinating. Still, in their sheer mass, they tend to become repetitious and cloying. Readers are bound to feel themselves lost among all the stories and, as they read, to wonder just where Cardozo is taking them. For this reason, I have severely edited my translation of the text and present here something less than half the original. (All omissions are marked in the translation with ellipses.) For the reader's convenience, I have divided the translated text into fifteen numbered sections; the original Hebrew has no such divisions.

It is not easy to summarize so rambling a document. The next several paragraphs attempt a bird's-eye view of those portions of the text that are represented in the translation, with the aim of giving the reader some sense of the coherence that underlies its apparent confusion. I give a particularly close paraphrase of the opening section, this being the part of the text that the reader is likely to find the most difficult.

Cardozo begins with his critique of *Abraham's Tamarisk* (section 1). The book's treatment of the Zohar, he says, is elementary and simplistic, a throwback to the days before Isaac Luria. A spirit-guide's revelations are only as good as the living human being through whom they are channeled, says Cardozo, and Mordecai Ashkenazi is—well—limited. The spirit-guide himself seems limited. The fact of being dead, after all, does not necessarily improve one's intelligence, and the spirit-guide might in his lifetime have been one of Moses Cordovero's disciples. (This will explain, for Cardozo, why he seems so oblivious to Luria's epoch-making advances in Kabbalistic learning.)[3] Cardozo's conclusion: Truth must spring *from the earth*, and spirit-guides are not necessarily reliable guides to the Mystery of Divinity.

A remark of the correspondent's leads Cardozo into a discussion of the "Christianizing" heresy of Samuel Primo. He moves from there into a description of the persecution that he had himself endured from this arch-heretic, which culminated in his expulsion from Primo's city of Edirne in the fall of 1697 (section 2).[4]

Cardozo's thoughts now turn, as they often do, to the dramatic and catastrophic years of the early 1680s, which he seems to have looked back on as the pivotal period of his life. At the beginning of the decade, he was master of the spirit world, his lectures attended by angels and biblical prophets as well as by living human beings (section 3). But then came the failed Redemption of 1682 (section 4) and its dreadful sequelae: demonic visitations, the great apostasy at Salonica (section 5).

Cardozo undertakes to define his own, true path and how it differs from the errors of his opponents (section 6). As a supernatural demonstration of the truth of his way, he offers the fact of his dominion over the spirits of the blessed dead, whom he can assign to his disciples as spirit-guides (section 7). To illustrate his point, he tells two stories from the golden days of early 1682: seances at the home of Solomon Galimidi, attended by such departed dignitaries as Moses Maimonides, Nathan of Gaza, and Sabbatai Zevi himself (sections 8–9). (I have slightly abridged the translation of section 8, omitting the technical details of the halakhic discussion.)

These stories lead Cardozo back, once more, to the perennially troubling subject of the failed Redemption. He was deprived, at that time, of his power over the spirits. He and his students were exposed, at the demons' instigation, to "the most indescribable evils," such as the spreading of the rumor that Cardozo had never been circumcised (section 10).

Cardozo returns, more briefly now, to the qualitative distinctions between himself and his opponents, which he compares to the distinction between Moses and the Egyptian wizards (section 11). He speaks once more of the persecutions he suffered at his enemies' hands, and of how these persecutions utterly failed to accomplish their purpose. God's interventions in Cardozo's life, moreover, are evidence that the faith he preaches is the true one. On more than one occasion, when Cardozo was in mortal peril, God provided a miraculous rescue. On other occasions, when Cardozo was tempted to shirk his destined obligation of revealing to the world the Mystery of Divinity, the Lord showed His power and His wrath by sending plagues to kill Cardozo's children (section 12). And, if this were not enough proof of the truth of Cardozo's Deity, we are offered one more example: the horrific death of Cardozo's old patron Solomon Galimidi, who had turned apostate to the faith that Cardozo had taught him (section 13).[5]

3.

As his reminiscences draw to a close, Cardozo reflects upon himself and the meaning of his own life (sections 14–15). He seems to take for granted—surprisingly, perhaps—that he is not a Messiah of any kind. He is, rather, the fulfillment of what he understands to be a prophecy, found in one of the "Faithful Shepherd" portions of the Zohar: "Worthy is he who struggles, in the final exile, to know the Shechinah, to honor Her through all the commandments, and to endure much distress for Her sake."[6]

Cardozo quotes this passage not only at the end of his long and convoluted narrative, but also at its beginning (section 1). Shall we understand it as the framework within which the narrative unfolds, the statement of the essential theme of the narrative? This seems to me likely. It is striking, moreover, that his understanding of the Zoharic passage seems to change in the course of the text. When he begins to write, he understands the passage as applying generally to all zealous investigators of the Mystery of Divinity. When he concludes, he treats it as having been spoken in specific reference to himself.

Cardozo, and no one else, is "the man who struggles to know the Shechinah." He covets this title intensely. He jealously defends his own special right to it against other possible claimants. He defends his claim most passionately against his old hero and rival, the long-dead Sabbatai Zevi (section 14). Cardozo lived, taught, and suffered—he seems to tell us—as the Shechinah's special devotee. He is Her expositor, Her defender, Her lover.[7] We may perhaps allow ourselves to interpret him in the cultural context of the Spain in which he grew up, and call him Her knight-errant.

He wanders, everlastingly, in the service of his Lady. His life takes shape, in this "autobiographical letter," as a long quest to defend Her nobility, proclaim Her glory, and win Her favor.

"Autobiographical Letter"[8]

1.

I am in receipt of your letter, and of the attached volume *Abraham's Tamarisk*.[9] I have already dispatched, via Izmir, a pamphlet criticizing a few of the author's interpretations of passages from the Zohar. Here, too, I can offer only a very few observations, for I have been ill for the past twenty-eight days and was not able to read the greater part of the book.

The author's spirit-guide, it must be acknowledged, derives from the sphere of holiness [and is not a demon]. Yet he communicates in a manner so unsophisticated that we may think the book perfectly suited for novices in Kabbalistic learning. The Zohar may be expounded in many ways, and this spirit-guide seems to limit his wisdom to the capacity of the [human] vessel that receives it. (Or, alternatively, he may himself have been one of Cordovero's students.)[10] I shall endeavor to learn, before the ship [that bears this letter] sets sail, who he is and what rank he occupies [in the world of spirits].

The fine points of Kabbalah are, in any event, no longer relevant. Redemption depends upon the knowledge of its essentials. Who is God? What is His "Name"—that is, His holy Shechinah?[11] The Bible says: "He desired Me, and I rescued him; I will raise him high, because he has known My Name...and I will show him My salvation" [Ps 91:14–16]. Our rabbis say that the Jews cry out in their exile but go unanswered because they do not know the divine Name. By the "Name," the rabbis do not intend the word itself—even the Gentiles know that it is YAHVEH—but rather the One invoked through that Name, whom we have forgotten in our exile....

All intelligent people ought to do their utmost to come to a true understanding of the Mystery of Divinity on the basis of what is written in the Zohar, the Gemara, and the rabbinic *aggadot*. They must not rely, in this matter, on any spirit-guide, for spirit-guides are granted no authority to reveal the identity of the Deity, the existence of His Name, or the divinity of His Shechinah. It is "from the earth" that truth must sprout [Ps 85:12]; and it is our solemn obligation to expend our labors and our energies in zealous quest after that secret.

That is why the Faithful Shepherd tells us (in the Torah portion *Pinhas*, page 239 [of the Mantua edition of the Zohar]):[12] "Worthy is that man who struggles, in the final exile, to know the Shechinah, to honor Her through the Torah's commandments, and to endure much distress for Her sake...."

2.

You say that you have heard from the emissary, who is related to a certain rabbi [Samuel Primo], that he is in possession of certain "extraordinary doctrines concerning the Mystery of Divinity" that have been confided to him.[13] These "extraordinary doctrines" are none other than those of which the angel spoke to [the prophet] Daniel, when he told him about King Constantine the Great, who accepted the belief that Jesus was at once human and divine and held to the doctrine of the Trinity. This king, the angel said, would "speak extraordinary doctrines upon the God of gods" [Dan 11:36]. "The God of gods" is the Blessed Holy One; "upon" Him [that is, above Him] is the First Cause; and the Christians have turned the First Cause into a Trinity.

The man I have mentioned [Primo], who had better remain nameless, believes [a doctrine similar to Christianity]: that the Blessed Holy One has withdrawn into His Root, and the Messiah [Sabbatai Zevi] is thus wholly divine. This infection has spread among the greater number of the most distinguished rabbis of our time: in Salonica, in Istanbul, in Adrianople. These damned souls, like the rabbi who stands at their head, take no account of what the Tannaim and Amoraim have said in the Talmud. The Zohar they repudiate, claiming it to be obscure and difficult. We know all this for a fact: clear, certain, and admitting no doubt.

We made inquiry into the source from which our contemporary rabbis, who had heard Sabbatai Zevi's words, might have derived this extraordinary heresy. And from Rabbi Ezra Halevi— the man called Pietist, who is now in Jerusalem, engaged in assiduous study of our treatises—we received the following answer:

> "If Sabbatai Zevi told us once," said [Rabbi Ezra Halevi], "he told us a hundred times"—"us" meaning *me and all the rabbis who were in his presence*—"if he told us once he told us a hundred times that he was destined to be administrator of the upper and the lower realms, raised higher than Metatron.[14] And from these words they inferred that he would be raised to the rank of Divinity."

(This need occasion no surprise, inasmuch as Rabbi Nathan [of Gaza] has written to this effect in several of his treatises, one of which we now have in hand, and those rabbis, who think of [Nathan] as a "prophet by consensus,"[15] took him at his word.)

> "But I myself," Rabbi Ezra added, "did not understand him to be telling us that he was going to become a Divinity. I took his meaning to be that, when the Jewish people are raised to the rank of angels, he is to be supreme over all creation, in accord with our sages' interpretation of [Isaiah's prophecy that begins], 'Behold My servant shall prosper' [Isa 52:13]."[16]

There is more. I was at Edirne when word arrived that Sabbatai Zevi had died at Alkum [Dulcigno]. I went to the great scholar, the Honorable Rabbi Jacob Ashkenazi, and I said to him: "Sabbatai Zevi is dead. What says Your Worship to that?" And he replied: "If Sabbatai Zevi is dead, you had best find yourself another God."[17]

Rabbi Ezra testifies as well that he always used to hear Sabbatai Zevi declare, on the subject of Divinity, that "the Blessed Holy One, the world's Creator, is the Second Cause embodied within the *sefirah Tif'eret*."[18]

When it came to my attention that a certain rabbi [Samuel Primo] had burned my treatise *Abraham's Morn*, I waged a terrific struggle against him. I told him, in the presence of the entire Jewish community [of Edirne], that he was a deceiver and seducer of the Jewish people. That very night, by consent of the rabbis and officials of thirteen congregations,[19] he ordered it proclaimed throughout the town that no one might come to my house to learn Torah from me.

The officials visited me the next morning, protesting that they had not really wanted to issue that proclamation. "You are the adherents and enthusiasts," I told them, "of a man who denies the Torah! I can promise you to bring, within a fortnight, solid proofs from Istanbul that he [Primo] believes the Messiah to be divine. But me, who believe in God and in Moses His servant, you have repudiated! Therefore: by the Lord of hosts, the God of my faith! all your houses, and the synagogues, shall go up in flames."

For the few days that remained to me before I left Edirne, I publicly proclaimed their doom to them all. While I was loading my seven wagons for the journey to Rodosto, Rabbi Mordecai Geron, one of the town magnates, appeared before me. Speaking in the name of many individuals in the congregations, he begged me not to leave town. They would, he said, compensate me for my damages. But no: "Have I not sworn," I said to him, "that all your houses and your synagogues are to burn? How am I to stay in this town?"[20] ...

3.

You may well wonder: What could have motivated that rabbi to burn my treatises, to seduce the people of Adrianople into misbelief, to issue public proclamations against anyone's coming to my house to learn Torah from me? The answer is that, in his zeal for the divine status of his master [Sabbatai Zevi], he felt himself obliged to destroy any treatise that went against his faith. And *Abraham's Morn* is a treatise held in such high regard in the celestial realms that, at the beginning of the year 5442 [1681–82], a decree was issued on behalf of those souls that had departed this world without knowledge of the Name, granting them permission to visit me and hear what I was revealing concerning the Mystery of Divinity in speech and in writing. The ancient patriarchs, and the greatest authorities in the world of the departed,[21] were correspondingly ordered to communicate God's faith to all souls.

I myself knew nothing of this, although I had been told that sooner or later this decree was to be issued in the [celestial] academies. But, in that year, I summoned four or five of my students [in Constantinople] to come listen to my reading of *Abraham's Morn*: Yom Tov Mevorakh, whose spirit-guide was Rabbi Isaac Luria; Mansur Kiaya of Damascus,[22] whose spirit-guide was Rabbi Abraham Yakhini; Samuel Galimidi, to whom the prophet Samuel had attached himself (though he did not reveal himself completely, but only made his voice audible);[23] my son Ephraim, who had many spirit-guides under the leadership of Roshi, who appeared to him in my likeness; and Isaac Shalom, whose spirit-guide was Rabbi Asher Kohen of Salonica.[24]

These men were in my presence as I began to read *Abraham's Morn* to them and to others who were with them,[25] explaining it as I went, and, as I did so, they saw[26] above us innumerable spirits. Near me, on my right, sat Abraham, Isaac, and Jacob, Moses and Aaron, David and Solomon, all by themselves. On my left was Rav Hamnuna Sava, right beside Samuel the prophet; Rabbi Simeon ben Yohai was the third; and Rabbi Isaac Luria, Rabbi Asher Kohen, and Rabbi David Habillo. The air of the house was filled with an enormous crowd of spirits, quite apart from those who sat on my left, and Messiah ben David [Sabbatai Zevi] and Roshi stood among them. All of them were listening to me read and interpret the treatise, just as though they were among my students. Some of those who had spirit-guides could see them in their entirety and could describe the characteristics of the faces they saw, whereas those who did not have spirit-guides saw them as shadows. After two hours, when I had completed my lecture, my auditors—corporeal and ghostly alike—departed.

This went on for some twenty-one days. Father Abraham came to listen to what I was saying; we could observe the movements and currents made [in the air] by those seven Pillars of the World.[27] I was perfectly stunned at this and prayed to the Lord that I might understand it. "Surely"—said I to Joseph, son of my wife Judith, when he came to visit—"surely Abraham,[28] Moses, and the other five must have incomparably fuller knowledge of God's Divinity than I do. Why on earth should they come here day after day to listen to what I have to say?"

Yet he swore to me most vigorously that such was indeed the case.

"When the departed souls have not known God's Divinity," he told me, "all of their virtues can avail them nothing as far as knowledge of this Mystery is concerned, either in Paradise or anywhere else. The angels know it, of course, but when they try to talk about theology, none of the souls can grasp their meaning. That is why the decree has been issued that anyone who knows God's Divinity must impart the knowledge to all souls worthy of that greatness. But they must do so in accord with what is written in the treatise *Abraham's Morn*, for they have been ordered to use precisely those similes that Your Worship used in that book. That is why they are obliged to come down here and listen to you: so that they will be able to use your methods to communicate to the departed souls the identity of the God of Israel and of His mighty Shechinah."

4.

For it had already been announced throughout the celestial realms that that year [1681–82] had been fixed as the beginning of the Redemption. But, thanks to the horrid blasphemies of the three cities—Istanbul, Izmir, and Edirne, where God's Divinity and the lofty holiness of His mighty Shechinah were blasphemed in public—the intended Redemption was canceled. That is why God has afflicted them with earthquakes, plagues, conflagrations....

I was bitterly disappointed that Redemption failed to arrive. Again and again it had been promised us: by the Messiah [Sabbatai Zevi], by Elijah, by numerous saints in the Academy On High who brought us the message "Thus saith the Lord of Hosts, God of Israel: In the month Nisan of this year shall your Redemption commence." In Tammuz 5441 [June 17–July 15, 1681], I was granted a heavenly sign to that effect, much like the sign that the prophet Samuel gave the Israelites to convince them they had sinned in demanding a king.[29] I prayed that there be a great windstorm, accompanied by hail and rain, that all this should take place, moreover, on the European side [of the Bosporus, at Istanbul] and not the Anatolian side. The black clouds thickened as I prayed, and hardly was my prayer finished than the storm winds began to blow, with pelting rains and considerable hail, just as I had requested, yet neither raindrop nor hailstone fell on the Anatolian side at Uskudar. Many similar signs and portents promised Redemption for the year 5442.

[Yet Redemption did not arrive;] and, using the Torah's own arguments, I protested against this strange, this uncanny deed that the Lord had wrought.[30] And He replied: "Was it in vain, then, that Isaiah wrote his fifty-ninth chapter, inscribing therein, truly, this extraordinary event?"

> If so, justice is far removed from us
> And righteousness does not overtake us.
> We hope for light, but find only darkness...
> We hope for justice, but there is none;
> For salvation, but it is far removed from us.
> For our sins and our iniquities are many...
> Murder; denial of the Lord;

—as happened in Jeremiah's time, when people "denied the Lord, and claimed He is something other than what He is" [Jer 5:12], and the people of the three cities [Istanbul, Edirne, Izmir] have uttered precisely this monstrous blasphemy for all to hear—

> Abandonment of our God; oppressive, apostate speech [...]
> That is why justice is turned backward
> And righteousness stands far off:
> Because truth stumbles in our streets,
> Propriety receives no welcome,

Truth is lacking,
And the one who abjures evil is made to seem demented.
The Lord saw this, and it displeased Him
That there was no justice… [Isa 59:9–15].

5.

My pen cannot make proper sense of this!—how and why the Lord has yet again concealed His face. Not only have holiness and truth become profaned, not only have all portents proven false, in a manner most unlawful and unjust, but in place of Redemption a most horrible punishment has been inflicted upon us. Lying spirits, emerging from the Realm of the Demonic, have managed to seduce many rabbis of our time, in Salonica and elsewhere, away from the Torah and the Faith.

Seven months before the event, I wrote to my disciples in Istanbul and Izmir, telling them what was to transpire and warning them not to be caught in this dreadful trap. When the time was ripe, the lying spirits set out for Salonica. But first they came to me.

This is how it happened:

I lived four years by the Dardanelles.[31] On Tammuz 11, 5443 [July 5, 1683], one hour before nightfall, as I was descending into my garden from my upper chamber, I looked up and saw the moon. "I see what appear to be shapes on the moon," I said to the people of my household. They looked and said, "There are four shapes: Messiah ben David, Rabbi Nathan, Rabbi Isaac Luria, and a fourth shape that looks to be a woman."[32] (Those who saw them were my wife Sarah, my son Ephraim, a serving boy of ours, Rabbi Raphael Morales, and a certain man from Ancona.)

Now I could see them clearly. "After our meal," I told the others, "we shall say the evening prayer. They shall tell us then what their appearance in the moon today may betoken. It has been many years since they visited us, sitting and speaking with us. This is a certain indication that something new has come to be, and after the prayer, we shall know what it is."

About a half-hour past nightfall they began to speak with us from the moon, loudly, in human voices. We could hear them as distinctly as though they were conversing with us in the garden. I told them that the spot was ritually pure and that they might stand upon the trees, which they proceeded to do. They spoke that night for about two hours.[33] They imparted attractive interpretations of the Bible, considered according to its literal meaning. They discussed Kabbalistic subjects with accuracy. And, after bidding us adieu, they departed.

The next day they visited me in my upper chamber, conversing with me as was their wont. I did not recognize them; I believed they really were the Messiah, and Rabbi Isaac Luria, and Rabbi Nathan.

They came to me in that manner for three days. It never ceased to puzzle and distress me that they had appeared within the moon and had behaved so extraordinarily as to speak with us from heaven. It was on the night of the fourth day that I remembered the plague of lying spirits that was destined to befall. So, when I spoke with them the next morning, I chose my words deliberately, hoping thus to unveil their true intention.

In the midst of our discussion, I turned to the man who bore Luria's shape. "Are you really Rabbi Isaac Luria?" I asked him.

He replied: "I am your teacher and your pupil: your teacher in Kabbalah, your pupil in theology."

"Suppose," I then said to him, "that the Tetragrammaton written with *aleph*s,[34] which has the numerical value of forty-five, is vocalized in such-and-such a way. Where [within the World of Emanation] is it to be located?"

"In [the Person of] the Holy Ancient One," he said.

"The Holy Ancient One has three heads," I told him. "Which of them is it in?"

"The second head," he said, "the one called 'Nothingness.'"

"You cannot possibly be the Rabbi Luria!" I declared. "Rabbi Luria has written, in his *Treatise Concerning the Three Heads*, that the Sacred Name of Forty-five is in the head called 'Patient.'"

"Those two heads," he replied, "are located within each other. In view of their union, we may apply to the one the name of the other."

Eventually, before the day was out, they did concede that they were not the Messiah, Rabbi Isaac Luria, and Rabbi Nathan. Out of pure love for me, however, they had taken on the shapes of those persons in order to rescue me from any belief that might be false. For surely, they supposed, I would listen to them.

They took as their starting point the acknowledged principle that "it is the First Cause that decides, of Its own will, who is to be the reigning Deity. Now, sad to say, the sins and disbeliefs of the Jewish people have brought about that the Deity in Whom you believe, and Whom it is your goal to proclaim the world over, has been stripped of His power. That is why you are doomed to a life of harried wandering, deprived of all repose, persecuted and scorned, why you cannot succeed at anything. You have seen that, in YAHVEH's name, you were promised Redemption. Yet that promise turned out to be a fantastic lie. The truth is that it is Samael [Satan] who now holds the power and that is why the Gentiles dominate the world."

They debated with me—to make a long story short—for days on end. At last they said to me: "You maintain, do you not, that we come from the demonic realms? That your God's dominion encompasses everything, and that He therefore rules over us? That this is the God who drowned Pharaoh in the sea? Who sent an angel to wreak slaughter in Sennacherib's camp because he had blasphemed Him, and then killed Sennacherib himself at the hands of his sons? Who worked His will also upon Nebuchadnezzar?[35] Well now, we are heaping worse blasphemies on Him than any of them ever did"—and here they spoke the sacred Tetragrammaton with the most virulent insults and curses, and challenged me to "call upon Him; let Him send fire to burn us up!"

I answered them:

"If there is any God other than the Lord—that Lord whom I recognize and in whom I believe, and for whose sake I suffer all those torments you have mentioned—I curse that God! You believe in some God, other than Him who is rightly called by the name YAHVEH? Then let him be banned! Let him be damned and his name be damned! Now go ahead: ask him to burn me up. I am flesh and blood, after all. If I am burned, the flame will be entirely visible. But you are spirits; and, when [God] destroys you, there will be no way to know it. Off with you now to Salonica! There is nothing for you here."

"How long will you keep on persecuting me?" I asked them another day. They answered: "Until you are dead. For it is our God's pleasure to do to you as the Lord did to Pharaoh."

Not many days afterward, I fell dangerously ill of the disease called *kausos*, that is, *fiebre ardiente* ["burning fever"].[36] One of those spirits came one day and stood at my bedside, all dressed in black. When they finally left me alone, they said to me: "You are a great scholar, possessed of the most immense knowledge. Peace be upon you." To which I replied: "There is no peace, saith the Lord, to the wicked" [Isa 48:22].[37]

I thereupon dispatched an account of the entire episode to Rabbi Elijah Kohen and to the pietist Daniel the Beloved [Bonafoux] in Izmir, bidding them read the letter themselves and then burn it, for I did not want the students to know what had happened. They did as I had asked. When the very same spirits turned up at Izmir in the shapes of the Messiah, Isaac Luria, and Rabbi Nathan, trying to seduce them and the students into misbelief, they got nowhere with them, for they were able easily to recognize them.

They went then to Salonica. There, equipped with their visions and with their ability to pronounce the Sacred Name as written, they induced the people to abandon the Torah of Moses. You have already heard the story from the rabbis who fled to Leghorn.[38]...

6.

I shall explain to you, now, what is distinctive about my knowledge of and faith in God and His Shechinah. I shall tell you how it differs from the faith of all those fellows who so pride themselves that seraphim and angels and celestial saints have appeared to them, done miracles for them, poured wisdom into them, and instructed them in the Mystery of Divinity in ways so different from my own.

To begin with, I have always made my views public property, and I did not keep them secret. I wrote numerous treatises, in accord with Torah and Kabbalah, and I never tried to prevent any interested person from reading or hearing them. Never did I make anyone swear that he would not reveal what I was telling him. All the others have done just the opposite.

Second, whenever those spirit-guided people undertook to write or speak about the Mystery of Divinity, they all fell into misbelief. They betook themselves to wells that had no water in them—only snakes, only scorpions[39]—and they wrote heresies. Thus did Rabbi Nathan [of Gaza]; thus did Joseph ibn Zur,[40] and others of their ilk. Neither I nor any of my students who had spirit-guides ever fell into this trap. It would not have occurred to my students to defend these men or the spirits who supplied them with their ideas, who believed that the Messiah was destined to become a deity.

One further distinction: Whenever our spirit-guides ordered us to perform some Mending-rite *[tiqqun]*, they prescribed for us only such supplicatory prayers as are found in the Torah and the Prophets, in a manner entirely lawful. They all were steadfast in the knowledge of God and in His Faith, worshiping Him truly and righteously and in accord with His precepts.

All those who received revelations from spirits—my students excepted—went on to abandon the divine precepts. Not content with donning the turban [that is, converting to Islam], they violated both Written and Oral Torah. They acted on the principle that, to bring the Redemption, one must violate the Sabbath, eat leaven on Passover, and abandon the teachings about the Deity that our ancient rabbis had set forth in the Gemara, *Mekhilta*, *Sifra*, *Sifrei*, and the other *aggadot*.[41] We, by contrast, held firmly to those teachings. We were prepared to suffer death by every kind of torture, if only we might uphold the truths taught by our rabbis, even in those recondite passages that people are wont to call "tainted texts," but which I, thanks to the wisdom with which God has gifted me, have shown to be the loveliest texts of all.

With good reason, then, did the spirit-guides in Izmir declare (when they first began to manifest themselves) that "Abraham Michael Cardozo is the present-day heir to Solomon's wisdom!"…

7.

God did yet another marvelous wonder in order to demonstrate to the entire world of spirits that there is no God other than Himself, the Deity whom I have recognized and proclaimed. I was granted the power to distribute spirit-guides at my pleasure, to assign whomever I wanted as spirit-guide to whomever I wanted. Rabbi Isaac Luria was assigned to Rabbi Sabbatai Sardina in Izmir, for example; Rabbi David Habillo to Rabbi Daniel Israel [Bonafoux]; Rabbi Asher Kohen to Isaac Shalom;[42] and, along the same lines, in Constantinople. Similarly, if I were to decide that a certain spirit-guide should no longer function as such, he would obey me. I did this several times with Rabbi Isaac Luria.

For the sake of His own honor, moreover,[43] God gave me the power to send at my discretion anyone I pleased to the saints' graves to talk with their spirits. I might dispatch one of my students or many of them; all the spirits would promptly emerge from their graves in perceptible shapes and give lucid replies to whatever questions I had sent them to ask. Yet I did not provide them with any special prayer or prayer-intention or sacred name; I did not order them to bathe beforehand or to avoid greeting anyone.

Rabbi Elijah Kohen was astounded at this. Rabbi Isaac Luria, after all, would not go himself to a saint's tomb, or send any of his students there, without sanctification and immersion, without a prayer-intention or some sacred name or combination of names. Yet sometimes he was answered and sometimes not.

"Suppose," I told [Kohen], "that I were to send men who are holy and wise, and in a state of purity, equipped with a prayer-intention or a sacred name or a special prayer. You might then say that these preparations were what qualified you for this.

"It is obvious that Rabbi Luria and his disciples were your superiors in holiness and purity. But it was I who struggled my way toward knowledge of God, and who made known to the Jewish people His Divinity and the sanctity of His Name. It was through my *Abraham's Morn* that all the celestial spirits came to recognize Him, so that His fame might spread through the heavens and my merit through this world. That is why He, who is God of the spirits of all flesh, has ordained that all spirits must reveal themselves at my slightest command, or to anyone I may choose to send."

—And this did not happen once or twice, but went on for many years!

It once happened that the students expressed some doubt about the power God granted me, in the year 5442, over all spiritual entities, such that no creature from Metatron down—none of the souls in hell, and self-evidently none of those in Paradise— could refuse my summons. Thus they witnessed on Purim night, 5442 [March 24, 1682], when I bade damned souls come from hell. I even summoned Rejeb Bey,[44] and, as I sat at table, he came and spoke with us....

8.

I shall detail one experience of ours, from which you may infer a myriad of others.

At the end of Adar 5442 [ca. March 10, 1682], I went to Ortakoy,[45] to the house of the late Solomon Galimidi, with the intent of lodging in one of his son Samuel's rooms. About twenty people were there at the time. On the Sabbath, Master Solomon and the men who had spirit-guides—all those who were in the house—came to visit me in my room. Master Solomon said to me: "Would Your Worship care to dine with us upstairs today?"

"I shall eat here by myself," I replied. "But do not leave yet.

Passover is approaching, and there is one of its laws that I must open for discussion."

Thereupon I said, in his presence: "Master of the Universe! let the late Rabbi Hayyim Benveniste[46] be present here." And he appeared on my right side, at some considerable distance from me; for Master Solomon Galimidi and the rest were sitting in disarray on my left....

[Cardozo now reminds Benveniste's ghost of an episode that had taken place while he was alive. A young student had asked Benveniste a highly technical question, grounded in a passage from the legal writings of Maimonides, about the preparation of dough during Passover. Benveniste had answered with some harshness; and an argument had ensued.]

"Well now," I said to him [Benveniste's ghost], "who was the young scholar who asked you that question?"

He replied: "It was Sabbatai Zevi."

Then, said I: "Master of the Universe, let Sabbatai Zevi be present here!" And he came and sat down quite close to me.

I asked him if he remembered that dispute.

"Remember it I do," he said.

(Three or four of those seated in the room were able to see them,[47] and they described their features. The late Rabbi Hayyim was wearing a blue cap and a woolen caftan,[48] while Sabbatai Zevi wore a white turban like that of a Turk. He was handsome, his face shining.)

"The dispute," said I, "turned on the question of Maimonides's intent....So let Maimonides be present here, and let us hear it from his own mouth!"

Then came Maimonides and sat down near Rabbi Hayyim.

Master Solomon and the others were wholly astounded. "Do you see them in human form?" he inquired of the company. And Yom Tov Mevorakh, Samuel Galimidi, Isaac Shalom, my son Ephraim, and Shem Tov[49] all answered him: "We can see them and understand what they say, as we see you and hear your voice."

Just at that moment, Mansur Kiaya of Damascus walked into the room. "Sit down by the door," I said to him, "and tell me who they are who sit here."
"I see nothing at all," he answered.
"Look closely into this corner," said I.
He said that he saw nothing.
I said: "I shall now summon Rabbi Abraham Yakhini, opposite you;[50] and he will give you power to see."
Then came Rabbi Abraham Yakhini. As he revealed himself to Mansur, the latter said: "I see my rabbi; and in that corner there is also a man with a *bonete mavi* and a *fereje de suf, su barba blanca como la nieve, y es hermoso de cara*" ["...with a blue cap and a woolen caftan, his beard white as snow, and he has a handsome face"].[51]
"Ask him his name," I said.
"Hayyim Benveniste," he replied.
"And who is beside him?"
"A certain red-faced man," he answered. "He looks like an Arab, *y en su oreja una halqa*" ["...and in his ear is an earring"].[52]
"And what is his name?"
"Rabbam" ["their master"], he said.
I said: "[You mean,] the Rambam" [Maimonides].
"Both ways," he said.[53]
(When Master Samuel [Solomon?] Galimidi[54] heard all this he became silent and immobile as a rock, whether from fear or from astonishment I do not know.)
I proceeded to discuss with Maimonides at some length the dispute between the two scholars [Benveniste and Sabbatai Zevi] and told him to deliver his verdict loud enough that all the men with spirit-guides might hear it. And I said to Yom Tov Mevorakh: "Declare you whatever it is that Maimonides says."
And he said:

"I wrote clearly enough. If he wants to make slippery arguments to the contrary, what do I care?"[55]...

[The ghost of Maimonides having thus waffled, Cardozo himself undertakes to resolve the question in Sabbatai

Zevi's favor. The assembled spirits are apparently convinced—]

And, with that, they departed in great joy.

9.

In view of the utter amazement with which Master Solomon and the rest had responded to this event, I summoned him to me that evening, after the Sabbath was over. "I have already told you," he said to me, "that it was Rabbi Nathan Shapira—who was guest in my house for two and a half years—who made a Jew out of me. It was he who told me all my sins and provided me with a mending for them. Why is it that Your Worship did not summon him?" To which Mansur, Yom Tov, and Samuel responded: "Why, there he is sitting right next to you!"

I told him to come close to me. I laid upon Rabbi Nathan Shapira the task I deemed fitting for him: to be Master Solomon's spirit-guide. "But you must now [Cardozo tells the ghost] provide him some way to prepare and to sanctify himself, for he is wholly occupied with toll collections and has no free time. And now I shall determine if he is properly mended or not. If the Tetragrammaton takes shape on his forehead as it appears in the Torah, I shall know that the mendings he has performed on his soul have taken effect. But if the letters are inverted, such that what ought to be on bottom is on top, it will be clear to me that he has not yet been mended of his prior sins."

[Master Solomon] was exceedingly fearful at this, lest he find himself entirely humiliated. (One man, in whose mending I had invested considerable effort, had indeed experienced the like: the Tetragrammaton had, in our presence, appeared inverted upon his forehead. Yom Tov Mevorakh asked Rabbi Isaac Luria what this meant, whereupon the Tetragrammaton vanished and the words HE IS A DEMON took shape on the man's forehead. When he learned of this, he wept bitterly, yet the rabbi [Luria] declared that that man could not be mended, for he would deny God. He eventually went to Egypt and, having abandoned all belief, renounced Judaism. Later he fled from there; if I am not much mistaken, he currently resides in Leghorn. His name is Elijah Yanni.)[56]

But, as it happened, the Tetragrammaton appeared on his forehead in its proper form, and, underneath it, the name SHADDAI ["the Almighty"].

"Sit you there," I said to him [Galimidi], "and you shall see something akin to what happened earlier today." And I rose and prayed to the Lord that the saints I should summon would be present with us. And I summoned Sabbatai Zevi and Rabbi Nathan Benjamin [of Gaza].

As they arrived, the house filled with spirits. I hardly need say that Rabbi Simeon ben Yohai, Rabbi Isaac Luria, Rabbi Abraham Yakhini, Rabbi Asher Kohen, and Roshi were present. Rabbi Moses Bosnak of Tripoli was, I believe, also there.

This is what I said [to Sabbatai Zevi]:

"Zemah Maimon, our emissary from Tripoli, brought us from Adrianople and Comargene many of the writings of Rabbi Nathan. At one point, in discussing the creation of the world, he [Nathan] poses the question of why it had not been created earlier than it was. And he writes:

"'I heard from AMIRAH [Sabbatai Zevi][57] a most excellent reply, namely, that this question has no end. Had the world been created one thousand or two thousand years earlier than it was, the same question could still be asked, inasmuch as the world has to have had some beginning. But the Creator has it within His power to create it at whatever time is appropriate for its creation.'

"I wrote a long letter and dispatched it by special courier to Edirne, along with my treatise *Abraham's Morn*, to be delivered directly to Your Worship. Your Worship, however, was by that time already in Alkum, in Albania, so Master Elijah Zevi [Sabbatai's brother] and Rabbi Hayyim Abulafia opened the letter and read it along with the treatise. When I arrived in Izmir, he told me that 'we read the letter and the treatise three times over, and were not able to understand a word'; so they sent them on to Your Worship in Alkum.

"Now, what I should like to know is this: Is the reply Your Worship gave, as I saw it in Rabbi Nathan's writings, really yours?"

"It was mine," he said. And Rabbi Nathan put in: "Have I the power to say or write in AMIRAH's name anything that is not truly his?"

"And is that reply correct, do you think?"

The Messiah answered: "It is unsatisfactory."

"Your Worship," said I, "has already read my letter. But I wish now to expound upon it orally, so that those who have not read the letter may understand the issue at stake." And I went on to lecture for an hour or so, explaining—as I had written in my letter—that no fewer than three heresies were contained within [Sabbatai Zevi's] reply.[58]

When I was done, AMIRAH kissed my face and blessed me. He, and Rabbi Simeon ben Yohai, and all the saints who were present hugged me and kissed me. I gave them my blessing as well, and they departed in peace. This was the sort of thing we used continually to experience.

10.

Then came the failed Redemption. Rabbi [Isaac Luria] came with the patriarch Joseph and Rabbi Abraham Yakhini to relate in the strictest confidence that my power would be gone, that I would rule no more over any spirit. They ordered them [Cardozo's disciples?] to write all this down, and the three of them signed their names to it. And so it came to pass.

Yom Tov Mevorakh appeared before me one day, awash in tears. Rabbi Luria had told him that the proclamation had gone forth: the gates of paradise were to be closed; no longer were spirit-guides permitted to appear on earth below. He then bade him farewell and departed. Mansur and Isaac Shalom brought much the same story....

We suffered the most unspeakable, the most indescribable

evils: persecution, humiliation, ridicule. Samael [Satan] began by inciting the slander that I was still uncircumcised, and nearly everyone in Istanbul and Edirne came to believe that this was so.

The wealthy and powerful Joseph Uzziel happened on one occasion to be in Haskoy, where I lived.[59] It was the middle of the night; they had been feasting, drinking, getting themselves drunk, and they told two men—an apostate, one of them—to summon me on pretext of a sick call. Once I got there, they would examine me by force. The men did not want to do this. "We are afraid of his curse," said they. The host, Master Jacob Vilisid,[60] told Uzziel and his sons that "if you examine him and he turns out to be circumcised, he will be perfectly justified in excommunicating you"; that I had, moreover, many friends in Istanbul; and that everyone would find the act repugnant. The next morning they came and told me all that had happened. And [Uzziel's] elder son died; and a thunderbolt—*rayo*, as it is called [in Spanish]—fell upon the younger son's head and burned him up.

Once this ugly rumor had died away, the demons proceeded to an act that practically defies human belief.

What happened was this: We had completed the Mending-rite for [the *sefirah*] *Malkhut*, and I and all of my students—those in Istanbul, and even those in Brusa and Izmir—wanted to perform the Mending-rite [for the *sefirah Yesod*, the divine phallus][61] in Uskudar, in my sister Rica's house. We were seated; all the preparations necessary for that tremendous procedure had been completed; I wanted to begin reciting the lecture—when three women showed up, claiming that they needed to have just one word with me.

I left the room. One of the women asked me if there was any blemish in my circumcision. And, when she saw how shocked I was at her question, she added: "There is very great value in having this information. Indeed, I came here yesterday from Edirne for just this purpose."

Just to be rid of her, I told her I had something there like a bean, like a small *verruga* ["wart"].[62] Whereupon the two other women declared: "This lady told us yesterday about [the blemish] that you just said you had! And there is something else as well."

She then said: "Moses our Master and Aaron the priest appeared to me in Edirne. They sent me to speak with you and to tell you to mend one thing about your circumcision. That done, the salvation of Israel can begin. It depends on you. I shall return tomorrow."
They went off, and I returned to the room. The students wanted to know what had happened. I told them that the woman had asked me if my circumcision were in any way blemished; that she had gone on to tell me about [the blemish] that I had; and that what she had said was quite amazing.[63]
The upshot was that the Mending-rite for *Yesod* was not performed that day. They [?][64] kept up their probing and questioning. The damned woman said that I was uncircumcised, that Moses and Aaron had dispatched her from Edirne to tell me that I needed to get myself circumcised, and that she was obliged to pour all her energies into this project. Given that I had told the students that the woman was speaking the truth, they became confused. Some of them had their doubts whether I was circumcised or not. Some of them, remembering the long-forgotten libel, even believed her.

Let me explain just what that "blemish" was that I had mentioned to her. I was born circumcised. When I arrived in Leghorn from Spain, the circumciser Joseph Gabbai disfigured me by circumcising me, whereas all he ought to have done was draw some blood.[65] Once I had healed, there remained a gathering of flesh about the size of a bean, in a location far from the corona and near the body. I assumed it was that bit of flesh that the woman was asking about. I had told her that the "Moses our Master and Aaron the priest" who had sent her to me were really arch-demons, who had attached themselves to her from the year 5426 [1665–66] onward.[66] Off she went, therefore, to the rabbis of Istanbul, and I became the butt of insult and ridicule. She went around telling everybody that Redemption depended on me, that if only I would have myself circumcised it would be here at once, with the result that they made a joke of her, which did rather sweeten my own humiliation.
Some time afterward I went to Edirne. There she was, spouting the most extraordinary things, screaming at me at the top of her lungs in the middle of one marketplace: "How long are you going

to keep the Jewish nation trapped in exile? Circumcise yourself, and have pity on this nation!" The Jews seized her, forced her into a house, and shut the door on her. But the incident left me utterly abashed, and the rumor that I was uncircumcised spread so widely in Edirne that I was obliged, when I engaged in public disputation with a certain rabbi [Samuel Primo],[67] to challenge three circumcisers who were present in the crowd to examine me in a private room. They flatly refused.

You may see from this how powerful Samael is, and how he managed to prevent us from performing the Mending-rite for *Yesod.* For he knows how vast a virtue the rite possesses....

11.

The power of the Demonic is a matter of common knowledge. Did not the Egyptian wizards perform the same wonders as did Moses and Aaron—the latter to prove that YAHVEH is the true God, the wizards to perform auguries and to confirm Pharaoh in his denial of God? Every one of the signs and the tokens, the miracles and the wonders, that God did through the agency of Moses and Aaron had as its purpose to demonstrate to the Jews that He was the God of their ancestors and the universal creator, YAHVEH His name. This was demonstrated by those signs that Moses and Aaron could perform and the wizards could not. (So they acknowledged when the sons were slain: "This is the finger of God.")[68] And we are obliged to remember all God's deeds; so He has commanded us.

In precisely this way, it is my own solemn obligation to inscribe a true account of all that the Lord has done in this generation, to prove that He alone is God. The proof of His divinity lies in the distinction between me and everyone who rejects me. I clearly and irrefutably prove that the God of my faith is the God of Abraham, Isaac, and Jacob, YAHVEH His name. I prove this from Torah and Mishnah, from Gemara and Kabbalah, always with evidence and arguments that appeal to the intellect. Those who excommunicate me, by contrast, can offer no argument whatever. They publish nothing; they write no treatises. Like bats they flutter about in darkness, chirping to one another about some alleged "mystery," by which their souls are in fact plundered and shattered.[69]

But I am like an eagle. My students, too, see as though by noonday sunlight. [My opponents,] sorcerers that they are, have been able through the power of the spirits manifested to them to bring about that their supporters see lights and figures, letters and signs. But they cannot assign everyone spirit-guides at their will, as I have done for the past twenty-two years. Nor can they dispatch anyone to make inquiries at the graves either of saints or of sinners, as I have done and as I continue to do....

12.

Do I now have the same power I had in 5442 [1681–82]? you ask. The truth is that my power has not diminished in the slightest. But no one in this city is capable of seeing, though they do indeed visit me daily (Turkish grandees among them) to learn from me what the future holds. I must tell you, moreover, that the Constantinople rabbis and their men are fully aware that one rabbi from Constantinople boasts of being Messiah ben David; they know all about his deluded adherents.[70] But they have never reprimanded them, nor persecuted even one of them, nor taken any account of their having held assemblies. For there is no spark of zeal in their hearts for the honor of God or His Torah.

So it is in Edirne as well. [Samuel Primo's] heretic faith is a matter of common knowledge, yet they have done nothing to bring it into disrepute. Their scorn and abuse has always been reserved for me and my students, who study the Torah, keep its commandments, and believe in the God of Israel. It is permitted, they say, to shed my blood, and they persecute with all their power, having tried thirteen times to destroy and expel me. Yet "it is they who have stumbled and fallen, while we stand firm and proud" [Ps 20:9].

Twelve rabbis issued a decree—they voted on it, they recorded it, they signed it—declaring my life to be legitimate prey. They excommunicated me in all the districts of Constantinople, except for Haskoy and Ortakoy. They sent copies of the full text of the decree to Brusa, Edirne, Izmir, Rodosto, Gallipoli and Izmit, with the intent that they excommunicate me, which the people of Rodosto, Gallipoli, and Izmit refused to do. What was their reason? That I had been slandered; I had allegedly told everyone to eat on the Ninth of Av, whereas the truth was exactly the opposite.[71]

That was when I left Constantinople for the first time and went to Rodosto. When the signed decree reached Rodosto, they handed it over to me, for if I wished to bring evil upon them, I could.[72] But, before a year had passed, God killed all [the signatories], apart from Rabbi Joseph Katzavi, who had signed under duress, and Rabbi Chelebi Brodo, who had begged my pardon.

I came back from Rodosto to Constantinople on Tevet 8, 5442 [December 19, 1681]. I departed again in Iyyar of that year [May-June 1682] in the greatest public disgrace and humiliation, the Redemption having failed. I spent something like five years by the Dardanelles and in Gallipoli,[73] after which I returned to Constantinople for a third time and remained there until 5456 [1695–96]. God never abandoned me to my enemies' desires. The bans and excommunications they pronounced accomplished nothing whatever, nor did any of their schemes to prevent me from giving instruction in my house or to injure any one of my students.

Most recently they have joined forces with the captain [of the] Carabusa, with whom they knew I had quarreled.[74] Many people, the *kiaya* Elijah Falcon[75] among them, had gone to testify that I had administered poisoned medicine to that aged Christian, to kill him in accord with the wishes of the Venetian Senate, and that, he having been warned, the medicine was given to a dog, which thereupon died. He went to the kaimakam[76] on the very day that I had been summoned to attend his steward, so that I was there when the Christian came in demanding judgment against me. He and all his supporters went out disappointed, dejected, and grieving[77]—the steward, indeed, would have beaten the Jews who came to testify that I had poisoned him, were it not for their failure to appear before him—and within a few days he had fallen into my power.

A miraculous rescue! much like the episode in Izmir when twenty-three witnesses—the elders and dignitaries—came into the *mahkeme* [Islamic court] to testify, before a judge and fifteen Muslim religious scholars assembled by my enemies, that I had said that within sixteen months Sultan Mehmed would be assassinated by a Gentile from the East, and that the sun would not then shine[78] in its normal manner. Everyone thought I would be taken directly to execution! But they did not touch one hair of my head, for my God rescued me in a most marvelous way. And, when Osman Pasha and Rejeb Bey were killed in Tripoli, not one of those who had agreed to pay the three thousand *leventes* for his [Osman's] assassination was spared, other than myself. For the mufti stood up and loudly proclaimed: "Any believer in Muhammad who lays a hand on the Jew doctor, is no believer in Muhammad!"[79]

All of this demonstrates the truth of my belief in the Deity, and the truth of the Deity in whom I believe. Even the death of my sons and daughters constitutes clear proof that the God of our faith is the true God, a jealous and avenging God. For each time I resolved not to speak of the Mystery of His Divinity, He would cause them to die.

The first time was in Izmir, in the year 5438 [1677–78]. Sorely troubled by the demons, I angrily declared[80] that from 5425 [1664–65] onward I had had enough suffering, that I would no longer reveal the Mystery of Divinity to anyone. God was enraged at me. I heard a voice proclaim: "Because you have thought and spoken this thing, the Lord's anger shall burn against you and against your house till you are destroyed from the face of the earth." Three days afterward, from the first through the fifteenth of Tammuz [June 21–July 5, 1678]—the period, our sages tell us, when Satan dominates the world[81]—the plague began, and I lost thirteen people, besides contracting the plague myself. I reversed my decision and craved God's pardon.

Again in Istanbul, in 5447 [1686–87], I shut the doors to my house to prevent students from reading with me. Within a few days I lost four people, and myself contracted the plague. On this last painful occasion I have just described, I had said to all the students:

"I have tried with every ounce of my strength to make known God's divinity in this city. Yet I am continually persecuted, and you are made objects of scorn. One cannot rely on miracles, yet miracles and marvels are precisely what I need if I am to survive the abuse they constantly heap on me. Blasphemy and insult proliferate, and I am the cause of it. My best course, I find, is to keep silent, and to obey the words of Scripture: 'Hush! one must not mention the Lord's name' [Amos 6:10]. Do not come any more to study with me, therefore; and let God do whatever He pleases."

There were thirty-two students in my house that night, all of them dreadfully grieved. I had had four small sons, and, after midnight, God struck them down with plague. When I got up in the morning, I found there a student named Jacob Ammon. "Hurry!" I said to him. "Go tell the students to come as usual to hear wisdom expounded." All my sons contracted the plague. I had a son named Isaac who was with his nurse in Balat;[82] he too came down with the plague that night. I repented my intention, I cried aloud, but all to no avail. Every one of them died.

God has furthermore taken revenge on everyone who has learned from me His Divinity and then denied it, and from this too it is evident that He is a God of honor who pays His enemies back....

13.

When I left Constantinople, I said to Master Solomon Galimidi:

"Our Redemption is far off. I am going wherever the spirit takes me. You may believe whatever you please about the Messiah and the Redemption. But be very careful indeed about the Deity whom I have made known to you, and make sure that you are not seduced from His faith by Yom Tov Romano or others of that ilk."[83]

303

"God forbid!" he said. "Why would Your Worship suspect me of so awful a thing?"

Five [?] years passed.[84] On the second day of the New Year festival [September 30, 1685], while I was in Gallipoli, five students visited me; one of them was Meir Alcaire, the husband of Master Solomon Galimidi's sister. "What new thing," they asked me, "has transpired in the celestial realms?"[85]

"Master Solomon Galimidi," I told them, "has been condemned to a horrible death. An evil sky shall cover him; a stormy sea shall he travel; and an evil land shall he tread."

They asked me why, and I had no idea.

That evening his sister came wailing. "What can I do?" I asked her. "Go tell him the decree; let him beg mercy for himself."[86] I also wrote to Samuel Galimidi and Yom Tov Mevorakh.

On Tevet 1, 5446 [December 28, 1685] I went from Gallipoli to Constantinople with my mother-in-law and my sister Luna's son Benjamin. Perhaps, I thought, I could save him. I sent a message to his son Samuel: Let him tell his father, I said, that "he must not spend Purim in Constantinople. His friend Suleiman Pasha, the new vizier, has written ordering him to Edirne; and so he must do." But he stubbornly refused.

So I sent to Master Moses de la Garsa, who was gravely ill, in the small hours of Friday morning [March 8, 1686]. "What on earth," he said to me, "can have brought Your Worship to Yeni Khan at a time like this?"[87] I replied that Solomon Galimidi was on the verge of a gruesome death. He was grieved and said to me: "I will go on Saturday evening to tell him, so that he can repent." But snow began to fall that Saturday, and it fell steadily for three days, so that he could not go from Constantinople to Ortakoy.

On Shushan Purim [Monday, March 11], Master Solomon stepped into his small boat, intending to go from Ortakoy to Constantinople. But all of a sudden a north wind blew up into a terrific storm, accompanied by snow, darkness, cloud, and fog. It carried him more than a hundred miles.[88] When he stepped onto land, he died of the cold. The birds and the beasts nibbled a bit of his flesh and his [...];[89] thereby carrying out the sentence against him in every particular.

Rabbi Isaac Luria communicated to us that, when [Galimidi] had cast all his sins into the sea on the first day of the New Year, he had included as one of his "sins" the faith in divinity that he had learned from me.[90] Yom Tov Romano had indeed seduced and deluded him, and so had Rabbi Jacob Alfandary....

14.

I am no Messiah. But I am the man of whom the Faithful Shepherd [Moses] spoke when he addressed Rabbi Simeon ben Yohai and his companions: "Worthy is he who struggles, in the final generation, to know the Shechinah, to honor Her through the Torah's commandments, and to endure much distress for Her sake."[91]

Now, if I were not to speak [publicly] of the unity of the Shechinah's holiness—to tell how She is a divinity in the full sense of the word—how should distress and persecution be my lot? *Tiqqunei Zohar*, similarly, declares that man "worthy" who has the Shechinah's faith in his heart and in his mouth, who fears neither celestial nor earthly beings.[92] It follows that anyone who has come to recognize the unity and exaltation of the Shechinah must publicly express that faith. For, if he did not do so, what reason would he have to fear anyone?

No one in this generation has struggled more than I have to know the mystery of the Shechinah. I have achieved recognition of Her reality and Her root [in the realm above the *sefirot*]; I have consequently come, through Her,[93] to know the Blessed Holy One in truth....And every day they concoct new arguments by which to rationalize their persecution of me and my students....

You may well ask:

You claim in this letter that everything that happened in the generation of Rabbi Simeon ben Yohai and his students has again happened, and continues even now to happen,[94] among you and your students. This you offer as proof that we are living in "the final generation, the end of days"—in the words of Elijah.[95]

If this is so, we need to know: who are you? You admit that Messiah ben David [Sabbatai Zevi] is currently in Paradise, and you have sworn that you are not Messiah ben Ephraim.

I have already written you that our Redemption will soon be made reality, by the two [!] tribes of Reuben, Gad, and Asher. They have been living in Arabia Felix for more than thirty years now, under the leadership of Messiah ben Ephraim, as we find written in the *Zohar Hadash* on the Torah portion *Balaq*.[96] Soon, with God's help, they will come forth from there via Arabia Deserta and [Arabia] Petraea.[97] God will do the most marvelous signs and portents, set forth in Isaiah and Jeremiah, on their behalf.

I, however, am one of those men of whom God spoke through Jeremiah, that at the end of the exile "they shall speak each to his brother and each to his comrade, saying: Know the Lord!" [Jer 31:33]. They "speak," that is to say, to the select few, in secret as it were, for fear of the rabbis and leaders of the generation.

After the Redemption—that is to say, after the war of Gog and Magog—will come the fulfillment of the [other] Scriptures: "I will be magnified and sanctified and known by the Gentiles, and they shall know that I am the Lord" [Ezek 38:23]. "Israel shall know from that day forward that I am the Lord their God" [Ezek 39:22].[98] [When that happens,] "they shall no longer teach, each his brother and each his comrade, saying, Know the Lord," for, when Redemption comes, "they shall all know Me, from the least of them to the greatest" [Jer 31:33]. For "the earth shall be filled with the knowledge of the Lord" [Isa 11:9], through the manifestation of Messiah ben David, who shall come forth from Paradise at the time of the Gog-Magog war, endowed with a superior spirit, for the purpose of this inquiry [in quest of the divine knowledge].[99]

You are yourself witness to that which is known to most of the Diaspora: that I alone am wisely, intelligently, knowledgeably revealing the Divinity of God, drawing upon Torah, Prophets, and Writings, Mishnah, and Gemara. I have never made any of my students take an oath to keep the mystery hidden. Quite the contrary: they are to tell others what I have made known to them. This knowledge comes through the religious tradition and not in accord with what spirit-guides have told me. They have learned from me, indeed, that in matters of theology I do not trust any spirit or any angel, not Elijah, not Metatron....

There is no conceivable way, however one wants to look at it, that Sabbatai Zevi can have been the subject of the Faithful Shepherd's remarks in the Zohar and the *Tiqqunim*. At the end of the exile will appear a man who—fearless of celestial and earthly creatures alike—will struggle to know the Shechinah and to communicate knowledge of Her to the broad public. For Her sake, moreover, that man will take upon himself much suffering, hardship, persecution. Now, Sabbatai Zevi did not reveal the mystery of the Shechinah; he would not even give anyone a complete exposition of the Divinity of God without an accompanying threat of excommunication. He never so much as permitted, much less commanded, anyone who had heard from him the Mystery of Divinity to reveal it to anyone else.

Yet we have it on the authority of our ancient rabbis that Israel cannot leave its exile till the Tetragrammaton becomes complete! We cry out in our exile and get no answer because we do not know the sacred Name [the fourth letter of which is a representation of the Shechinah].[100]...And the reason for this is that the Jewish people is destined to forget the Shechinah's holiness, to forget that She is fully divine, to fall into the abhorrent claim that She is only a created entity, not sacred at all. (Thus do Saadiah Gaon in his *Book of Beliefs*, in the chapter on the divine unity; Maimonides, in many places in the book of the *Perplexed*; and those under their influence.)

In the Torah portion *Pinhas* [Zohar, III, 239a], the Faithful Shepherd is quoted as saying: "Worthy is he who struggles, in the final exile, to know the Shechinah." What is the nature of this knowledge? "Honoring Her through the Torah's commandments," that is to say, performing them for Her sake, for it is She who is called God of Israel. We have made exhaustive inquiries of everyone who, under oath, had been made privy to Sabbatai Zevi's theology.

He never spoke, even to them, of the existence of the Great Name [that is, the Shechinah]. They have no knowledge of it whatsoever. Yet it is by virtue of that knowledge, and only by virtue of that knowledge, that we can have salvation.

Our ancient rabbis have said that King Messiah will tell every Jew who his father is, that is to say, his Father in heaven, God, whom they have forgotten in their exile. Sabbatai Zevi has not done this. He has not openly proclaimed to the Jewish people the divinity of the Shechinah, the existence of the Great Name, the truth of God. Even if he was aware of all this, his awareness was for himself alone, as was Father Abraham's.

But he must fulfill what is written of him. When he emerges from Paradise—as he will, during the war of Gog and Magog—he will reveal it all to the entire Jewish people, and to the Gentiles as well....

15.

I shall state the matter briefly. A solemn oath has been imposed upon me[101] to make my best efforts to know God, and that is precisely what I have done. I have made full public disclosure, to my brethren and comrades, of God's true reality and the mystery of His Great Name and the divinity of His Shechinah. Never did I speak in secret. Never did I tell the Jewish race to seek [God][102] in vain, or in some faith that has no grounding in Torah, but rather with knowledge and sound judgment.

Does anyone care to criticize me? Well, then, let him refute me in writing, for all Jewry to read. Does anyone claim himself my equal? Let him prepare a systematic exposition [of his theology] that is to be preferred to my demonstration of the deity of the eternal God.[103]

For there is no Deity, other than the Lord.

Chapter 13
Epitaph

[We do not know where Cardozo is buried, or what, if anything, is written on his grave. Let this inscription— written on the title page of one manuscript of *Abraham's Morn*,[1] by an otherwise unknown copyist named Solomon ben David—serve as Cardozo's epitaph.]

This (with God's help) is the Book entitled
ABRAHAM'S MORN

When humble Solomon ben David perceived the greatness of this book, he said: "Here is a man of true authority,[2] who sees vision Divine; who reveals depths hidden even from visionary Ezekiel!" And he raised his poetic voice, and he said:[3]

Hear me, dear friends, and grow wise;
Rejoice, and sing out in delight;
For the secrets of God are revealed!
Their splendor doth brilliantly shine

'Pon a heart, perceptive and keen,
That hungrily, all its life long
Shall banish all sorrow and pain,
As yearning fulfilled doth become.

What god is as great as our God,
Who created, who fashioned us all?—
Our Monarch, our Glorious Pride[4]—
With lion's great voice shall He roar.[5]

He, *Father's dear Holy Son*,
In His love did create all that be.
And this is the excellent pearl
That's become revealed—to Abraham.

Notes

Note to the Reader

1. Jacob Sasportas, *Sefer Zizat Novel Zevi*, ed. Isaiah Tishby (Jerusalem: Bialik Institute, 1954), p. 368.
2. Yosef H. Yerushalmi, *From Spanish Court to Italian Ghetto: Isaac Cardoso* (New York and London: Columbia University Press, 1971).
3. There is a further complication, in that the Jewish day begins at sundown. When, therefore, Cardozo speaks of an event that took place on the night of Heshvan 15, 5457, he is referring to the night of November 9 (not November 10), 1696. Heshvan 15 began that year at sundown on November 9 and ended at sundown on November 10.

Part One

1. Yerushalmi, *From Spanish Court*, p. 69.
2. Elijah Kohen, *Sefer Merivat Qodesh (Book of the Holy Quarrel)*, in *Sammelband kleiner Schriften über Sabbatai Zebi und dessen Anhänger* [Hebrew], ed. Aharon Freimann (Berlin: Itzkowski, 1912), p. 5: *yemino 'asuqah be-ishah u-semolo ba-ashishah*.

Chapter 1

1. Cardozo, *Ani ha-mekhunneh (I Am the Man They Call...)*; in ms 1677 of the Jewish Theological Seminary of America, New York (=ms Adler 1653), fol. 1a; cf. the publication by Carlo Bernheimer, "Some New

311

ABRAHAM MIGUEL CARDOZO

Contributions to Abraham Cardoso's Biography," *Jewish Quarterly Review*, New Series, 18 (1927–28), p. 112, and the translation below, chapter 8.

2. Cervantes, *Don Quixote*, trans. Motteux-Ozell (New York: Modern Library, 1930), pp. 137, 492. Cervantes's own feelings about the New Christians can perhaps be inferred from the immense sympathy he shows for the plight of his character Ricote the Morisco, one of the Spanish Muslims-turned-Christian whom Philip II expelled in 1565 (ibid., pp. 805–810).

3. *Ani ha-mekhunneh*, fol. 1a.

4. As among the Marranos' descendants in New Mexico, in the 1990s: Kathleen Teltsch, "Scholars and Descendants Uncover Hidden Legacy of Jews in Southwest," *New York Times*, November 11, 1990, p. 16.

5. Cecil Roth, *History of the Marranos* (New York: Harper & Row, 1932), pp. 195–295.

6. Translations of Da Costa, *Exemplar Humanae Vitae*, are from Leo W. Schwarz, *Memoirs of My People* (New York: Farrar & Rinehart, 1943), pp. 84–94. The dates are from H. P. Salomon and I. S. D. Sasson, "Introduction," in Uriel Da Costa, *Examination of Pharisaic Traditions = Exame das Tradições Phariseas: Facsimile of the unique copy in the Royal Library of Copenhagen* (Leiden: E. J. Brill, 1993).

7. Cardozo, untitled text; in ms 1723 of the Jewish Theological Seminary of America, New York (=ms Adler 2432), fol. 175a; published by Gershom Scholem, "Lidi'at ha-Shabbeta'ut mi-tokh kitvei Qardozo," in *Studies and Texts Concerning the History of Sabbetianism and Its Metamorphoses* (Jerusalem: Bialik Institute, 1982), p. 294.

8. Cf. Colette Sirat, *A History of Jewish Philosophy in the Middle Ages* (Cambridge: Cambridge University Press; Paris: Maison des Sciences de l'Homme, 1985), pp. 2–3.

9. *Ani ha-mekhunneh*, fol. 1a (Bernheimer, "Some New Contributions," p. 113).

10. Cardozo's autobiographical letter, in Isaac R. Molho and Abraham Amarilio, "Autobiographical Letters of Abraham Cardozo" [Hebrew], *Sefunot* 3–4 (1960), pp. 220, 230; translated below, chapter 12.

11. Yerushalmi, *From Spanish Court*, pp. 55, 66–83, 151–54.

12. Sasportas, *Zizat Novel Zevi*, p. 270.

13. Nissim Yosha, "Ha-reqa' ha-filosofi le-te'olog shabbeta'i— qavvim le-havanat torat ha-elohut shel Avraham Mikha'el Qardozo," in Aharon Mirsky, Avraham Grossman, and Yosef Kaplan, eds., *Galut ahar golah: mehqarim be-toledot 'am Yisra'el muggashim le-Professor Hayyim Beinart* (Jerusalem: Ben-Zvi Institute, 1988), p. 555.

NOTES

14. Cardozo, untitled text, ms JTS 1723, fol. 174b (Scholem, "Lidi'at," p. 294). Scholem mistakenly reads *mimmennu* for *mimmenni*. It is true that Cardozo has been speaking in the third person, of Messiah ben Ephraim; but now he reveals, through a "Freudian slip" of the pen, that the Messiah he is thinking about is none other than himself. On Messiah ben Ephraim, and Cardozo's self-identification with this figure, see below, chapters 3.3, 7.2.

15. Ibid., fol. 164b; cf. below, chapter 11, n. 21.

16. Cardozo, *Sefer Boqer Avraham (Abraham's Morning)*, ms Oxford, Bodleian Library 1441, fol. 28b.

17. Cardozo, *This Is My God (Zeh eli ve-anvehu)*, chapters VIII, XVI; published by Gershom Scholem, "Drush zeh eli ve-anvehu le-Avraham Mikha'el Cardozo," in *Studies and Texts Concerning the History of Sabbetianism and Its Metamorphoses* (Jerusalem: Bialik Institute, 1982), pp. 349, 367; translated below, chapter 10. (On the use of Roman and Arabic numerals, see "Note to the Reader.")

18. Cardozo, untitled text, ms JTS 1723, fol. 171a (Scholem, "Lidi'at," p. 291).

19. Ibid., fol. 170a (Scholem, "Lidi'at," p. 289).

20. Yerushalmi, *From Spanish Court*, p. 203.

21. Louis Ginzberg, *The Legends of the Jews* (Philadelphia: Jewish Publication Society of America, 1942–47), 1:186–217; Elena Romero, *Coplas Sefardíes: Primera selección* (Córdoba: Ediciones El Almendro, 1991), pp. 41–48.

22. *"A los vente diyas lo hue a visitar, / lo vido de enfrente mancebo saltar, / mirando en el cielo y bien atentar / para conocer al Dio de la verdad."* Cf. Ginzberg, *Legends of the Jews*, 1:189–91.

23. *Ani ha-mekhunneh*, fol. 1b (Bernheimer, "Some New Contributions," p. 113); translated below, chapter 8.

24. *Tanakh*, a word composed of the Hebrew initials of Torah, Prophets, and Writings, remains a standard Jewish designation for the Hebrew Bible.

25. Da Costa: "I had not been [in Amsterdam] very long before I observed that the customs and ordinances of the modern Jews were quite different from those commanded by Moses. Now if the Law was to be observed according to the letter, as it expressly declares, the Jewish interpreters are not justified in adding to it interpretations quite contrary to the original text. This provoked me to oppose them openly" (Schwarz, *Memoirs of My People*, p. 86).

26. *Ani ha-mekhunneh*, fol. 2a (Bernheimer, "Some New Contributions," p. 114); translated below, chapter 8.

27. *Sefer Boqer Avraham*, fols. 23a–24a.

28. Cardozo, untitled text, ms JTS 1723, fol. 233b (quoted in Yosha, "Ha-reqa' ha-filosofi," p. 566). Cardozo's testimony to the prevalence of Deism among the Venetian aristocracy of the seventeenth century supplements and confirms some of the suggestions of David Wootton, *Paolo Sarpi: Between Renaissance and Enlightenment* (Cambridge: Cambridge University Press, 1983). See, for example, page 40: "…according to…a pseudonymous attack on Venice published in 1607, Sarpi had been reported to Clement VIII for belonging to an 'academy,' an intellectual association, in which nobles and others participated, where it was generally accepted that the immortality of the soul was to be rejected on philosophical grounds.…It is perhaps indicative that a reply defending Venice…contested the doge's membership of [this academy], not its existence."

29. *Sefer Boqer Avraham*, fols. 23a–24a.

30. Untitled text, ms JTS 1723, fol. 233b.

Chapter 2

1. *Ani ha-mekhunneh*, fol. 2a (Bernheimer, "Some New Contributions," p. 114); translated below, chapter 8.

2. For the discussion that follows, see Gershom Scholem, *On the Mystical Shape of the Godhead: Basic Concepts in the Kabbalah* (New York: Schocken, 1991), pp. 140–96.

3. Cf. Matthew 18:20: "Where two or three are gathered together in my name, there am I [Jesus] in the midst of them." The Holy Spirit, in its role as ever-present Comforter (John 14:15–27), is a reasonable analogue to the rabbinic *Shechinah*.

4. Plato's myth (in the *Symposium*) of the primordial human androgyne had made its way into rabbinic Judaism in ancient times (*Midrash Genesis Rabbah* 8:1; cf. Ginzberg, *Legends of the Jews*, 5:88–89), and lay ready at hand for the Kabbalists.

5. But cf. Yehuda Liebes, "*De Natura Dei*: On the Development of the Jewish Myth," in *Studies in Jewish Myth and Jewish Messianism* (Albany, N.Y.: State University of New York Press, 1993), pp. 42–54. Liebes's discussion stresses the continuities between the rabbinic and the Kabbalistic concepts.

6. I am indebted to the translations of Daniel Chanan Matt, *Zohar:*

NOTES

The Book of Enlightenment (Ramsey, N.J.: Paulist Press, 1983), for this way of rendering *ha-qadosh barukh hu.*

7. Raphael Patai, *The Hebrew Goddess,* 3d ed. (Detroit: Wayne State University Press, 1990).

8. Elliot Wolfson, "Crossing Gender Boundaries in Kabbalistic Ritual and Myth," in Mortimer Ostow, *Ultimate Intimacy: The Psychodynamics of Jewish Mysticism* (London: Karnac Books, 1995), pp. 255–337. It must be acknowledged that Wolfson's views are far from universally accepted, and that the reading of the Shechinah given by Scholem (*Mystical Shape,* pp. 140–96) continues to be very influential. Cf. Isaiah Tishby, *The Wisdom of the Zohar: An Anthology of Texts* (London and Washington: Littmann Library of Jewish Civilization, 1989), 1:371–87; and the authors cited by Wolfson, pp. 378–79.

9. Scholem, *Mystical Shape,* p. 192; referring to Elijah de Vidas, *Reshit Hokhmah, Sha'ar ha-Qedushah,* chap. 16, section 31, ed. Hayyim Yosef Waldman (Jerusalem, 1984), p. 455. In some editions of the Passover Haggadah, such as that prepared by Rabbi Nathan Goldberg (New York: Ktav, 1949), one finds each of the ritual acts of the Passover meal prefaced by a Kabbalistic formula, discreetly left untranslated: "Behold, I am prepared and at the ready, to perform the commandment of [e.g.] the first of the four cups: for the purpose of uniting the Blessed Holy One and His Shechinah; through the agency of that Hidden and Concealed One; in the name of all Israel." The "Hidden and Concealed One" is the supreme Kabbalistic *sefirah, Keter.* (See below for a sketch of the sefirotic system.)

10. *Ani ha-mekhunneh,* fol. 2a (Bernheimer, "Some New Contributions," p. 114).

11. Ibid.

12. Elijah Kohen's brutally hostile biography of Cardozo (*Sefer Merivat Qodesh,* written in 1707), which is our major source for the narrative of Cardozo's life, says nothing of any stay in Egypt. But another hostile source, Jacob Sasportas, does mention it (writing in 1668 or 1669): "[Cardozo] had been in Leghorn; then he went to Egypt; and from there he went a-wandering, till he settled himself in Tripoli" (*Zizat Novel Zevi,* p. 270). We know that Cardozo was in Leghorn in 1659, and that he went from there to Tripoli (below, chapter 3.5). His stay in Egypt must belong to an earlier period; his claim that he studied with Hayyim Kohen, if true, would date it before 1655, for Kohen died in that year (Scholem, cited in the following note). Was Cardozo in Leghorn at the beginning of the 1650s, as well as at the end of the decade?

13. Cf. the doubts expressed by Scholem, "Ha-ta'alumah be-'enah 'omedet," in *Researches in Sabbateanism* [Hebrew], ed. and supplemented by Yehudah Liebes (Tel Aviv: Am Oved, 1991), p. 267.

14. *Abraham's Morn (Drush Boqer de-Avraham)*, ms Ginzburg (Moscow) 660, fol. 5a. This text must not be confused with *Sefer Boqer Avraham*, an entirely distinct work whose title I render as *Abraham's Morning*. See below, chapter 4, n. 2.

15. *Ani ha-mekhunneh*, fol. 2b (Bernheimer, "Some New Contributions," p. 115).

16. Ed. Mantua, the basis of most subsequent editions of the Zohar. A one-volume edition, in large format, was printed at Cremona in 1559–60.

17. On Moses de Leon and the Zohar, see the introductory material in Matt, *Zohar*, and Tishby, *Wisdom of the Zohar*. Yehuda Liebes has advanced the suggestion that Moses de Leon did not write the Zohar all by himself but in collaboration with a circle of kindred spirits: "How the Zohar Was Written," in *Studies in the Zohar* (Albany, N.Y.: State University of New York Press, 1993), pp. 85–138.

18. Cardozo, *Epistle to the Judges of Izmir*, in Gershom Scholem, "Iggeret Avraham Mikha'el Qardozo le-dayyanei Izmir," in *Studies and Texts Concerning the History of Sabbetianism and Its Metamorphoses*, p. 310; translated below, chapter 9.

19. The quotations that follow are taken from *This Is My God*, chapters IX and XI (Scholem, "Drush zeh eli," pp. 350–51, 353–54). The first sixteen chapters of this treatise are fully translated below, chapter 10.

20. The origin of the term *sefirot* is unclear. Scholem thinks it was coined by the author of an ancient esoteric text, *Sefer Yezirah (Book of Creation)*, as an unusual word for "number." The ten *sefirot* were thus originally the ten primary numbers. See Scholem, *Origins of the Kabbalah* (Philadelphia: Jewish Publication Society, 1987), pp. 25–29. The strange phrase *sefirot belimah*, used by the author of *Sefer Yezirah*, occurs once in the midrashic literature: *Numbers Rabbah* 14:12.

21. Singular of *sefirot*.

22. The names of the *sefirot* beneath *Binah* are based roughly on 1 Chronicles 29:11: *lekha YHVH ha-gedullah ve-ha-gevurah ve-ha-tif'eret ve-ha-nezah ve-ha-hod*, "Yours, O Lord, is the Greatness and the Power and the Splendor and the Eternity and the Glory." The Kabbalists often refer to the *sefirah* that comes after *Binah* as *Gedullah*, "Greatness," on the basis of this verse. (They normally prefer to speak of it as *Hesed*, reflecting its actual functioning as the divine Grace.) The biblical passage's subsequent

reference to "Kingdom" *(ha-mamlakhah)* underlies the name of the tenth *sefirah: Malkhut*, "Kingship."

23. Because, in the Bible, circumcision is the "sign of the covenant."

24. *Ani ha-mekhunneh*, fol. 21a. See below, chapter 7.3.

25. Joseph Avivi, *Binyan Ariel* (Jerusalem: Misgav Yerushalayim, 1987), pp. 20–32.

26. This is vividly conveyed in the awkward and defensive remarks of Menahem Azariah of Fano in his preface to *Pelah ha-Rimmon* (an abridgement of Cordovero's encyclopedic *Pardes Rimmonim*), written about 1600, under the influence of Israel Sarug's version of Lurianism.

27. Cf. Moshe Idel, "'Ehad me-'ir u-shnayim mi-mishpahah'— 'iyyun mehuddash bi-ve'ayat tefuzatah shel qabbalat ha-Ari ve-ha-shabbe-ta'ut," *Pe'amim* 44 (1990), pp. 5–30.

28. Avivi, *Binyan Ariel*, pp. 46–71.

29. Borrowed, in rabbinic Hebrew, from Greek *prosopon*.

30. E.g., Gershom Scholem, *Major Trends in Jewish Mysticism*, 3d ed. (New York: Schocken, 1954), pp. 269–71.

31. Untitled text, ms JTS 1723, fols. 196b, 246a.

32. On the Hebrew terms used by Jewish writers (normally polemical) for the Trinity, see Daniel J. Lasker, *R. Hasdai Crescas: Sefer Bittul Iqqarei Ha-Nozrim* (Ramat-Gan: Bar-Ilan University Press, 1990), pp. 21, 58–59.

33. Following Scholem's understanding of the names *Ze'ir Anpin* and *Arikh Anpin*; but see the criticism in Elliot R. Wolfson, "Constructions of the Shekhinah in the Messianic Theosophy of Abraham Cardoso, with an Annotated Edition of Derush ha-Shekhinah," *Kabbalah* 3 (1998), p. 46.

34. Lurianic writers speak also of the Persons of "the Holy Ancient One" *('Attiqa Qaddisha)* and "the Ancient of Days" *('Attiq Yomin)*. These figures largely overlap with "the Patient One," though there are subtle distinctions among the three.

35. Song of Songs 4:9–12, 5:1–2.

36. Matt, *Zohar*, pp. 19–20. See also the passage cited in the next note.

37. There is a particularly fine example of this in his unpublished *Abraham's Morning* (ms Oxford 1441, fols. 25a–26). Pharaoh's sages, Cardozo explains, were essentially correct in calling the God of Moses "Son of the Wise, Son of Ancient Kings" *(Midrash Exodus Rabbah* 5:14, drawing upon Isaiah 19:11), for God is the "Holy Son" of *Hokhmah* and *Binah*, and these are called, respectively, "the Wise" and "the Ancient Kings."

38. *This Is My God*, chapter XI (Scholem, "Drush zeh eli," p. 353); translated below, chapter 10.

39. The Zohar finds this hinted at in Genesis 36:31–39, which enumerates the "kings that reigned in the land of Edom, before there reigned any king over the children of Israel." Each of these kings, except the last, is said to have died. Hence the designation, "Death of the Kings." See Scholem, *Major Trends*, pp. 265–68; notes to chapter XI of *This Is My God*, translated below, chapter 10.

40. *Qelippot*, "shells," is one standard Kabbalistic designation for the demonic realm. Another is *sitra ahra*, "the Other Side." From the very beginnings of Kabbalah, its theoreticians cherished elaborate beliefs about demons and the demonic hierarchy, which they assumed to be constructed in a manner mirroring and imitating the divine hierarchy. ("The Other Side," says the Zohar [III, 192a], "imitates the Divine the way an ape imitates a human being.") Thus, there are ten demonic *sefirot*, and, in the Lurianic system, five demonic "Persons." The roots of the demonic, furthermore, lie within the Divine: the strict Justice of the *sefirah Gevurah*, isolated from the rest of the *sefirot* and therefore untempered with Grace, turns evil.

41. *'Ez Hayyim*, VI.iii.2 (*Sha'ar me'ut ha-yareah*, chap. 2, ed. Yehudah Zvi Brandwein [Jerusalem: n.p., 1988], 2:186).

42. Ibid., 2:190.

43. *This Is My God*, chapter VI (Scholem, "Drush zeh eli," p. 345); translated below, chapter 10. Cf. above, p. 20.

44. *Ha-galut ha-mar ve-ha-nimhar ha-zeh*: *'Ez Hayyim*, VI.iii.1 (ed. Brandwein, 2:184); Cardozo, *This Is My God*, chapter IV (Scholem, "Drush zeh eli," p. 341). The language is drawn from Habakkuk 1:6.

45. On the following paragraphs, see Gershom Scholem, *On the Kabbalah and Its Symbolism* (New York: Schocken, 1965), pp. 118–57.

46. See above, n. 9.

47. Scholem, *On the Kabbalah and Its Symbolism*, pp. 149–50.

48. See, in addition to Scholem, David J. Halperin, "The Son of the Messiah: Ishmael Zevi and the Sabbatian Aqedah," *Hebrew Union College Annual* 67 (1996), pp. 153–56; Moshe Idel, *Messianic Mystics* (New Haven and London: Yale University Press, 1998), pp. 308–20.

49. *Sha'ar ha-Kavvanot, Drushei ha-laylah*, 4 (ed. Brandwein, 1:352).

NOTES

Chapter 3

1. Cardozo, *Epistle to the Judges of Izmir*, in Scholem, "Iggeret...le-dayyanei Izmir," p. 320; translated below, chapter 9.

2. Alban Butler, *Lives of the Saints*, ed. Herbert Thurston and Donald Attwater (New York: Kenedy, 1962), 3:184–87; from William Caxton's English translation (printed 1483) of the thirteenth-century *Golden Legend*.

3. Abraham seeks after the true God and reasons his way from one possible candidate to the next, till he finally arrives at the truth. Christopher seeks, in a similar way, after "the greatest prince that was in the world." Like Abraham, Christopher is threatened with death by fire, at the hands of a wicked pagan king; like Abraham, he is miraculously rescued. Arrows shot against Christopher are ineffective, so Abraham (Ginzberg, *Legends of the Jews*, 1:232). Abraham, like Christopher, is a giant (ibid.; and n. 97), and perhaps the *Golden Legend*'s claim that "Christopher was of the lineage of the Canaanites, and...served and dwelled with the king of Canaan" is an echo of Abraham. Abraham is an idol-smasher; so are two of Christopher's female converts. I do not wish to offer any hypothesis to explain these resemblances; my point is only that they are likely to have helped Abraham become conflated with Christopher in Cardozo's mind.

4. Origen, *Contra Celsum*, I, 55 (*Origen: Contra Celsum*, trans. Henry Chadwick [Cambridge: Cambridge University Press, 1965], pp. 50–51). As we shall see in chapter 9, Cardozo prefers to forget that there is any Talmudic or midrashic support for this "collective" interpretation of Isaiah 53.

5. S. R. Driver and Ad. Neubauer, *The Fifty-Third Chapter of Isaiah According to the Jewish Interpreters* (reprinted New York: Ktav, 1969).

6. From Nachmanides's account of the Barcelona disputation of 1263; in Hyam Maccoby, *Judaism on Trial: Jewish-Christian Disputations in the Middle Ages* (Rutherford, N.J.: Fairleigh Dickinson University Press; London: Associated University Presses, 1982), p. 111.

7. E.g., *Midrash Numbers Rabbah* 11:2, *Ecclesiastes Rabbah* 1:28. The former passage was particularly beloved of Sabbatai Zevi's believers (of whom we shall presently have a great deal more to say): "'My beloved is like a gazelle' [*zevi*; Song 2:9]....Just as a gazelle reveals itself, then again hides itself, so the First Redeemer was revealed and then concealed. Rabbi Berechiah said in Rabbi Levi's name: Like the First Redeemer, so the Final Redeemer. The First Redeemer, Moses, was revealed to them and again

concealed from them...so the Final Redeemer will be revealed to them and then concealed from them." Baruch of Arezzo uses this passage as an epigraph for his hagiography of Sabbatai Zevi, *Memorial to the Children of Israel (Zikkaron li-vnei Yisra'el)*, in Freimann, *Sammelband kleiner Schriften über Sabbatai Zebi und dessen Anhänger*, p. 45.

8. *Coryats Crudities* (London, 1611; reprinted London: Scolar Press, 1978), p. 236.

9. From Paul Rycaut's account of Sabbatai Zevi: *The History of the Turkish Empire from the Year 1623 to the Year 1677* (London, 1680); earlier published by John Evelyn, under his own name, in *The History of the Three Late Famous Impostors* (London, 1669); reprinted as *The History of Sabatai Sevi the Suppos'd Messiah of the Jews* (Los Angeles: William Andrews Clark Memorial Library, 1968), p. 86.

10. Ephraim, in the Bible, is a son of the patriarch Joseph. The Bible uses both names as collective designations for the northern Israelite tribes.

11. "Book of Zerubbabel," trans. Martha Himmelfarb, in *Rabbinic Fantasies: Imaginative Narratives from Classical Hebrew Literature*, ed. David Stern and Mark Jay Mirsky (New Haven and London: Yale University Press, 1990), pp. 71–81; "Secrets of Rabbi Simeon ben Yohai," in Yehudah Even-Shmuel, *Midreshei Ge'ullah* (Jerusalem and Tel Aviv: Bialik Institute, 1954), pp. 195–97. (The phrase *bereh de-sitna u-de-avna* occurs in the latter source.) See also David Berger, "Three Typological Themes in Early Jewish Messianism: Messiah Son of Joseph, Rabbinic Calculations, and the Figure of Armilus," *AJSReview* 10 (1985), pp. 141–64.

12. *Ra'ya Mehemna*, printed as part of the Zohar.

13. Zohar, III, 276b. See the fuller discussion of this passage in the special introduction to chapter 9, below; and Abraham Elqayam, "The Absent Messiah: Messiah Son of Joseph in the Thought of Nathan of Gaza, Sabbatai Zevi, and A. M. Cardozo" [Hebrew], *Da'at* 38 (1997), pp. 42–47.

14. Untitled text, ms JTS 1723, fols. 133a-b.

15. On Abulafia, see Idel, *Messianic Mystics*, pp. 58–100; on Molcho, ibid., pp. 144–52, and Salo Wittmayer Baron, *A Social and Religious History of the Jews*, vol. 13 (New York: Columbia University Press; Philadelphia: Jewish Publication Society of America, 1969), pp. 109–15.

16. Zohar, I, 139a–40a; basing itself on the numerical value of the word *ha-zot* in Leviticus 25:13. (On the science of *gematria*, by which one draws inferences about the hidden meaning of biblical passages on the basis of the numerical values that can be assigned to the Hebrew words,

see the introduction to chapter 11, below.) See Abba Hillel Silver, *A History of Messianic Speculation in Israel* (Boston: Beacon Press, 1927), pp. 92, 138–39.

17. Gershom Scholem, *Sabbatai Sevi: The Mystical Messiah* (Princeton, N.J.: Princeton University Press, 1973), pp. 88–93.

18. Ibid., pp. 138–42.

19. Reported by Thomas Coenen, *Ydele verwachtinge der Joden...* (Amsterdam, 1669), p. 9; I am grateful to my colleague Professor Peter Tax for his help with the Dutch. Cf. Scholem, *Sabbatai Sevi*, p. 127.

20. Cardozo, *Epistle to the Judges of Izmir*, in Scholem, "Iggeret...le-dayyanei Izmir," pp. 320–21; translated below, chapter 9.

21. He describes himself as having been "abused, insulted, dreadfully tormented" (Sasportas, *Zizat Novel Zevi*, p. 289, quoting a letter written by Cardozo nine years later, in 1668).

22. Ibid. In Tishby's edition of the letter Cardozo represents himself as having been in Tripoli in 5424 (1663–64). Freimann's edition (p. 87), however, gives 5423 (1662–63) as the date, and this is supported by the parallel narrative in the *Epistle to the Judges of Izmir* (below, chapter 9).

23. Kohen, *Sefer Merivat Qodesh*, p. 9.

24. In the 1668 letter, quoted in Sasportas, *Zizat Novel Zevi*, pp. 290–91, he speaks of "one of my wives" *(ahat mi-nashay)* and "a certain wife of mine" *(ishti pelonit)*.

25. Ibid., p. 368 (Sasportas's narrative, written a year or so after the events it describes).

26. Untitled text, ms JTS 1723, fols. 171b (bottom)–73b (Scholem, "Lidi'at," pp. 291–93, where we find, among other nuggets of misinformation, that Muhammad "was born...a Christian. Once he had believed in Jesus. But when he became a man of importance, he rejected the Pope and became an Arian."

27. Stanford J. Shaw, *The Jews of the Ottoman Empire and the Turkish Republic* (Washington Square, N.Y.: New York University Press, 1991), p. 82.

28. *Epistle to the Judges of Izmir*, in Scholem, "Iggeret...le-dayyanei Izmir," p. 319; translated below, chapter 9.

29. Alfred W. Crosby, *The Measure of Reality: Quantification and Western Society: 1250–1600* (New York: Cambridge University Press, 1997), pp. 106–7. I owe this reference to Joanne Seiff.

30. Patrick Moore, *Watchers of the Stars: The Scientific Revolution* (London: Michael Joseph Ltd., 1973), p. 117.

31. Frances Yates, *The Rosicrucian Enlightenment* (Boulder, Colo.: Shambhala, 1978), pp. 44, 48; index, s.v., "Stars, new." The phrase "wild

excitement" is taken from page 91 (where Yates speaks also of "the Rosicrucian furore").

32. *Epistle to the Judges of Izmir*, in Scholem, "Iggeret...le-dayyanei Izmir," pp. 321–22; translated below, chapter 9.

33. Marvin Lowenthal, trans., *The Memoirs of Glückel of Hameln* (New York: Schocken, 1977), p. 46.

34. R. B. Serjeant and Ronald Lewcock, *San'a': An Arabian Islamic City* (London: World of Islam Festival Trust, 1983), p. 398.

35. Robert Latham and William Matthews, eds., *The Diary of Samuel Pepys* (1666; Berkeley and Los Angeles: University of California Press, 1972), 7:47.

36. The "Epistle to Raphael Joseph." Text in Sasportas, *Zizat Novel Zevi*, pp. 7–12; English translation, by R. J. Zwi Werblowsky, in Scholem, *Sabbatai Sevi*, pp. 270–75. The quotation given below is my own translation.

37. David J. Halperin, "Sabbatai Zevi, Metatron, and Mehmed: Myth and History in Seventeenth-Century Judaism," in *The Seductiveness of Jewish Myth: Challenge or Response?* ed. S. Daniel Breslauer (Albany, N.Y.: State University of New York Press, 1997), pp. 287–89.

38. *Epistle to the Judges of Izmir*, in Scholem, "Iggeret...le-dayyanei Izmir," p. 319; translated below, chapter 9.

39. Ibid., p. 326; not included in the translation of the *Epistle* given below. Nathan, it is true, had anticipated (in the "Epistle to Raphael Joseph") that "the ingathering of the Diaspora communities will not take place at that time [1666 or 1667]. Rather, the Jews will enjoy high status right in their present localities." This expectation has perhaps inspired Cardozo. But, in Nathan, this arrangement is provisional; there will be a general ingathering in the time after Sabbatai Zevi's return from the River Sambatyon. Cardozo seems to envision it as permanent.

40. Franz Landsberger, *Rembrandt, the Jews and the Bible* (Philadelphia: Jewish Publication Society, 1946); cf. the far more cynical portrayal by Gary Schwartz, *Rembrandt: His Life, His Paintings* (New York: Viking, 1985). As to the links between Rembrandt's subjects and Sabbatai Zevi's believers: Ephraim Bueno, whose portrait Rembrandt painted, joined with Abraham Pereira in 1656 to found the Or Torah yeshivah (*Encyclopedia Judaica*, s.v. "Bueno"). Bueno died in 1665, but Pereira survived him, to become an almost fanatical propagandist for Sabbatai Zevi (see the index to Sasportas, *Zizat Novel Zevi*, s.v. "Pereira").

41. I do not know who coined the phrase "Dutch Jerusalem." Salo Baron uses it as the title for his chapter on the Jews in the early modern

NOTES

Netherlands in volume 15 (1973) of his *Social and Religious History of the Jews.*

42. Aaron Sarfatti, to Sasportas; in Sasportas, *Zizat Novel Zevi,* p. 29.

43. Isaac Nahar, to Sasportas; in Sasportas, *Zizat Novel Zevi,* p. 49.

44. The others were the Seventeenth of Tammuz, the Fast of Gedaliah, and the greatest of them all: the summertime Fast of the Ninth of Av, the day the Temple was actually destroyed.

45. Sasportas, to Nahar; ibid., p. 56.

46. *Ha-ma'asim ha-mekhu'arim,* in *Epistle to the Judges of Izmir,* in Scholem, "Iggeret...le-dayyanei Izmir," p. 303; translated below, chapter 9.

47. Scholem, *Sabbatai Sevi,* pp. 396–405.

48. As in the chilling episode (from April 1666) reported, with full approval, by Baruch of Arezzo, *Memorial to the Children of Israel,* pp. 53–55.

49. So Scholem, *Sabbatai Sevi,* p. 459, apparently following Sabbatian sources such as Baruch of Arezzo, *Memorial to the Children of Israel,* pp. 52, 55, 64. But Rycaut's assertion—that Sabbatai was imprisoned at "the Dardanelli, otherwise called the castle of Abydos"—does seem to contradict this and to suggest that Sabbatai's prison was at the narrowest part of the straits of the Dardanelles, some twenty-five miles south of Gallipoli (*contra* Scholem, who quotes the passage from Rycaut). Cf. below, chapter 12, n. 31.

50. The Hebrew word for "the Almighty" could be shown, by an advanced technique of *gematria* (manipulation of the numerical value of Hebrew letters and words; see the introduction to chapter 11, below), to have the same numerical value as *Sabbatai Zevi.*

51. Baruch of Arezzo, *Memorial to the Children of Israel,* pp. 55–56.

52. See the letter from Primo published by Abraham Amarilio, "Te'udot shabbeta'iyyot mi-ginzei Rabbi Sha'ul Amarilio," *Sefunot* 5 (1961), pp. 271–72, which breathes hatred, rage, and lust for persecution. The letter is undated. Its concluding hope that Sabbatai will "come out of prison in order to reign" (the language is from Ecclesiastes 4:14) might suggest the period of imprisonment in 1666, but perhaps Primo is thinking of Sabbatai's attachment to the Turkish court as a sort of gilded imprisonment.

53. Joseph Halevi of Leghorn, quoted in Sasportas, *Zizat Novel Zevi,* p. 172.

54. Cf. Gershom Scholem, "Redemption Through Sin," in *The Messianic Idea in Judaism and Other Essays on Jewish Spirituality* (New York: Schocken, 1971), pp. 94–99.

55. On the rabbi's powers, see Shaw, *The Jews of the Ottoman Empire*, pp. 59–63.

56. Sasportas, *Zizat Novel Zevi*, pp. 289–308, 359–68.

57. Ibid., pp. 289, 297.

58. Meir Rofe, writing in May 1675, in Isaiah Tishby, "R. Meir Rofe's Letters of 1675–80 to R. Abraham Rovigo" [Hebrew], *Sefunot* 3–4 (1960), p. 93.

59. As far as I know, there is no reference to Cardozo in any of Nathan's writings.

60. The references to Nathan in Cardozo's so-called autobiographical letter, written a few years before his death, are extremely chilly and critical. See below, chapter 12.

61. Below, chapter 12; cf. chapter 7.2.

62. *Epistle to the Judges of Izmir*, in Scholem, "Iggeret…le-dayyanei Izmir," p. 324; translated below, chapter 9.

63. Sasportas, *Zizat Novel Zevi*, pp. 289–97. Aharon Freimann published a slightly different text of the letter, from ms Halberstam 40, in *Sammelband kleiner Schriften über Sabbatai Zebi und dessen Anhänger*, pp. 87–92. On the date, see Tishby's note to *Zizat Novel Zevi*, p. 308. It is not clear who the recipient of the letter might have been. Sasportas represents it as having been addressed to Isaac Cardozo and assumes that it constitutes Abraham's answer to the "witty," jocular letter he had received from his brother earlier that spring. The internal evidence of the letter, however, does not support Sasportas's assumptions. The recipient is assumed to be someone who believes in Sabbatai Zevi and who is prepared to treat Cardozo with awed respect. (The letter begins: "Inasmuch as you have believed the truth of what I have written you about our Messiah, I shall satisfy your wishes and your needs, and tell you everything about which you asked me.") Neither of these characteristics would suit Isaac Cardozo any more than does the obvious assumption that the recipient will be able to understand and digest a complex argument in Hebrew. It seems to me likely that it is a circular letter, intended for several of Cardozo's correspondents; this explains how Sasportas can represent it as having arrived in Leghorn while Nathan of Gaza was there in the late spring of 1668, and also as having come into the hands of Abraham de Souza in Amsterdam. Cardozo's brother-in-law, Abraham Baruch Henriquez, lived in Amsterdam (Yerushalmi, *From Spanish Court*, p. 321). Perhaps he was the person, or one of the people, for whom the letter was intended—as Scholem at one point surmised, on the basis of ms Halberstam 40 (Scholem, "Iggeret…le-dayyanei Izmir," p. 300). I must acknowledge,

however, that there is one bit of internal evidence for Isaac Cardozo as the addressee: the letter's allusion to Clara Nunez as someone whom the reader will instantly recognize (Sasportas, *Zizat Novel Zevi*, p. 291). Clara was martyred at an auto-da-fe in Seville in 1632 and would presumably be very well known to someone who was an adult in Spain at that date, as Isaac Cardozo certainly was. Would she have been familiar to others in the Sephardic Diaspora some thirty-six years after her death?

64. Sasportas, *Zizat Novel Zevi*, p. 291. Many scholars have called attention to this passage; see, e.g., Yerushalmi, *From Spanish Court*, pp. 303–6, 313–43.

65. Cf. Halperin, "Sabbatai Zevi, Metatron, and Mehmed," pp. 271–308.

66. Abraham Elqayam makes a similar point in "The Absent Messiah," pp. 54–56.

67. *This Is My God*, chapter III (Scholem, "Drush zeh eli," p. 340); translated below, chapter 10.

68. Yates, *The Rosicrucian Enlightenment*.

69. *Abraham's Morn (Drush Boqer de-Avraham)*, ms Ginzburg 660, fol. 2a.

70. Nathaniel Bradley, "A Narrative of the Revolutions in Tripoli in November and December 1672" (unpublished manuscript: State Papers Foreign, Public Record Office, London, SP71/22[i], 62–67), fol. 63a. See also L. Charles Féraud, *Annales Tripolitaines* (Tunis: Librairie Tournier; Paris: Librairie Vuibert, 1927), pp. 126–29. Féraud, pp. 115–19, describes a previous mufti's involvement in plots against Osman. This evidence of the Muslim clergy's longstanding hostility to Osman may provide a context for Cardozo's claim that the mufti intervened to save Cardozo's life. I am grateful to my research assistant, Ms. Joanne Seiff, for helping me track down these sources, and to Mr. Robert Clements, of the Public Record Office, for providing me with a copy of the Bradley manuscript.

71. Cardozo's autobiographical letter, in Molho and Amarilio, "Autobiographical Letters," pp. 213–14; translated below, chapter 12.

72. Ibid., p. 228; translated below, chapter 12.

73. Bradley, "A Narrative of the Revolutions," fol. 64b.

74. Cardozo's autobiographical letter, in Molho and Amarilio, "Autobiographical Letters," p. 228.

75. Sasportas, *Zizat Novel Zevi*, pp. 361–62.

76. Ibid., pp. 362, 368; Kohen, *Sefer Merivat Qodesh*, p. 10.

77. Yerushalmi, *From Spanish Court*, pp. 313–43. I would modify Yerushalmi's narrative in one respect: I do not accept, as Yerushalmi does,

Sasportas's claim that Cardozo's Hebrew letter of 1668 was addressed to his brother (see above, n. 63).

78. Sasportas, *Zizat Novel Zevi*, p. 368; Kohen, *Sefer Merivat Qodesh*, p. 10. Sasportas seems to claim that Cardozo went to Adrianople from Leghorn and that he arrived there in February 1675, and he seems to have been misinformed on both counts. We have the testimony of the Sabbatian Meir Rofe, which is certainly to be relied on, that Cardozo left Leghorn at the very end of May 1675 and that he was in Izmir (not Adrianople) before September of that year (Tishby, "R. Meir Rofe's Letters," pp. 92–96, 101–3.

79. The original Spanish text of the decree is published in Bernheimer, "Some New Contributions," pp. 127–29. I am very grateful to my former student, Mr. Jonathan I. Tepper, for providing me with an English translation.

Chapter 4

1. *Drush Boqer de-Avraham (Abraham's Morn)*, ms Ginzburg 660, fol. 2a.

2. Not to be confused with another of Cardozo's theological essays, *Sefer Boqer Avraham*, which was written some fifteen years afterward: Yosha, "Ha-reqa' ha-filosofi," p. 554 n. 77. The two titles are nearly identical. To keep the two separate, in English, I make an artificial but consistent distinction between *Abraham's Morn* (=*Drush Boqer de-Avraham*) and *Abraham's Morning* (=*Sefer Boqer Avraham*). The date of *Abraham's Morn* is not quite certain, but it cannot have been composed before 1670 (for the "twenty-two years" mentioned at the beginning surely cannot have begun before Cardozo's move to Venice in 1648) or after November 30, 1672 (the date in the colophon to ms Berlin-Marburg 501; see Scholem, *Sabbatai Sevi*, p. 881 n. 130 [who mistakenly gives the Hebrew date as 2 Kislev 5433; it is actually 11 Kislev]; Yehuda Liebes, "Mikha'el Qardozo—mehabbero shel sefer 'Raza de-Mehemanuta' ha-meyuhas le-Shabbetai Zevi ve-ha-ta'ut be-yihusah shel 'iggeret magen Avraham' le-Qardozo," in *On Sabbateaism and Its Kabbalah: Collected Essays* [Hebrew] [Jerusalem: Bialik Institute, 1995], p. 38, and p. 298 nn. 33–35; Yosha, "Ha-reqa' ha-filosofi," p. 568). Yosha thinks it "practically certain" that the date in the Berlin manuscript is the date of the copying and not of the original composition of the text. He is probably right: it is hard to imagine that Cardozo could have completed a work like *Abraham's Morn* during the tumultuous days of the

revolution in Tripoli. But Yosha is too precise when he dates it to 1670. The "twenty-two years" surely did not begin *before* 1648, but they may have begun afterward, and we need not assume that Cardozo began writing the book immediately after their completion.

3. Cf. Zohar, III, 238b *(Ra'ya Mehemna)*: Moses will emerge from his present concealment, in the "nighttime" of exile, when the "morning" of Redemption arrives; "as it is said, 'The morning brightened' [Gen 44:3]—this is Abraham's morn *[boqer de-avraham]*." It seems likely that Cardozo thought of himself as the "Abraham" indicated in this passage, for shortly afterward, in this same context, comes the passage that Cardozo applies to himself in his so-called autobiographical letter: "Worthy is he who struggles, in the final exile, to know the Shechinah, to honor Her through all the commandments, and to endure much distress for Her sake!" (III, 239a; see the introduction to chapter 12, below).

4. *Drush Boqer de-Avraham (Abraham's Morn)*, fol. 2a.

5. Ibid., fols. 11b–12a.

6. *This Is My God*, chapter I (Scholem, "Drush zeh eli," pp. 336–37), drawing upon rabbinic midrash; translated below, chapter 10.

7. From Proverbs 30:31. On Sabbatai's banishment, see Scholem, *Sabbatai Sevi*, pp. 872–84.

8. Elijah Zevi, Sabbatai's brother, was later to tell Cardozo that the packet had come into his hands (in Adrianople, presumably), that he and a second man had read the letter and treatise "and were not able to understand a word," and that they had forwarded the materials to Sabbatai Zevi (Molho and Amarilio, "Autobiographical Letters," pp. 216–17; translated below, chapter 12). After Sabbatai's death Elijah Zevi allegedly retrieved the treatise from among his brother's effects and sent it to Cardozo in Rodosto (ibid., pp. 200–201, reading *bihyoti* for *bihyoto*. We have only Elijah Zevi's word for it that the treatise was ever out of his possession, and Elijah Zevi was obviously hostile to Cardozo, as we see from his smug and totally unjustified dig at the clarity of *Abraham's Morn*). This is all the more or less reliable evidence we have concerning the fate of Cardozo's packet. Cardozo claims to have heard a story in the late spring of 1682, from one Ali Chelebi (ibid., pp. 200, 217–18; the name is to be supplied in the second passage, from the first), of how Sabbatai Zevi had expressed, just before his death, the greatest admiration for Cardozo and his writings. But the story seems to me a creation of Cardozo's own desperate wishes, just like the high praise and approval that Cardozo had received, not long before, from Sabbatai Zevi's ghost (ibid., pp. 216–17; translated below, chapter 12).

9. The assumption I express in this paragraph, that Cardozo wrote *Abraham's Morn* with Sabbatai Zevi in mind, is not contradicted by the fact that he also gave copies of it to other people—in later years, he would use it as a primer for his theology—and that it seems to have been read and copied at least once before he sent it to Sabbatai Zevi in Adrianople (see above, n. 2).

10. Untitled text, ms JTS 1723, fol. 185a.

11. Gershom Scholem, "Hadashot lidi'at Avraham Qardoso," in *Researches in Sabbateanism* [Hebrew], ed. and supplemented by Yehuda Liebes (Tel Aviv: Am Oved, 1991), pp. 394–98.

12. *Drush Boqer de-Avraham (Abraham's Morn)*, fols. 2a–3a.

13. These entities are not limited to the First Cause. Cardozo, who tends to identify the "body" of God (see below) with the Lurianic "Person" of the Irascible One, understands the "soil," "water," and "air" on which the tree depends as symbolizing the three higher "Persons" of Mother, Father, and Patient One, respectively.

14. *Drush Boqer de-Avraham (Abraham's Morn)*, fol. 35b. Cardozo bolsters his argument with an extraordinary interpretation of the traditional Jewish prayer *'alenu le-shabbeah*. The prayer begins, as Cardozo understands it: "It is our duty *to improve* the Lord of all"—understanding *le-shabbeah* as though it were *le-hashbiah* (against the ordinary translation of the verb, "to praise"). It continues: "…and to give greatness to the Fashioner of Creation." People normally understand "to give greatness" as meaning "to ascribe greatness," but Cardozo takes it literally. By our worship, we *give* Him something He did not previously have.

15. Cardozo makes this charge, that contemporary Judaism is an imitation of Islam, in ms JTS 1723, fols. 181a, 183a-b.

16. It is not clear whether Cardozo has been influenced, directly or indirectly, by the Gnostic thinkers of late antiquity. (Gershom Scholem thought he was; Nissim Yosha has argued that he was not; see Yosha, "Ha-reqa' ha-filosofi," pp. 541–71.) There is a contemporary analogue to the distinction made by Cardozo in a famous passage of Pascal (part of a passionate hymn of reconciliation to the God whom he had just experienced, in a close brush with death, in November 1654): "God of Abraham, God of Isaac, God of Jacob, not of the philosophers and the scholars…Just Father, the world has never known you, but I have known you" (quoted in Will and Ariel Durant, *The Age of Louis XIV* [New York: Simon & Schuster, 1963], p. 58). But it seems highly unlikely that Pascal would have claimed, as did Cardozo, that his distinction between the two deities was the sober and literal truth.

17. *This Is My God*, chapters VII, XIII (Scholem, "Drush zeh eli," pp. 347, 359); translated below, chapter 10.

18. Untitled text, ms JTS 1723, fols. 233a-b. Cf. ibid., fols. 170b–71a (Scholem, "Lidi'at," pp. 290–91): "Is it any wonder, then, that many of the intelligent folk among our people nowadays—philosophically trained, most of them—repudiate the words of our sages? That some of them question the truth of the Torah, and some deny it outright? They have strong reasons; their arguments are philosophically well grounded. But it is all because they believe that God—the God of Israel who gave [the Torah]—is the First Cause….Once these people come to realize the identity of the God who has hidden His face from us, they change their opinion. They confess the truth of the Torah, and of our sages' teachings." We need not assume that Cardozo is referring specifically to Spinoza (who published his *Theological-Political Treatise* in 1670, about the time that Cardozo was putting the finishing touches on his "Mystery of Divinity"). But he was certainly familiar with the current of thought to which Spinoza belonged and was concerned to provide an intellectually satisfying alternative.

19. Genesis 1:27; the Song of Songs. See *Sefer Boqer Avraham* (*Abraham's Morning*), fols. 23a–24a.

20. Cardozo's autobiographical letter, in Molho and Amarilio, "Autobiographical Letters," p. 212. I can think of no way to reproduce Cardozo's wordplay in English.

21. *Sefer Boqer Avraham* (*Abraham's Morning*), fols. 23a–24a. Cf. *This Is My God*, chapter XVI (Scholem, "Drush zeh eli," pp. 365–67); translated below, chapter 10.

22. E.g., Philip Birnbaum, *Daily Prayer Book* (New York: Hebrew Publishing Company, 1949), pp. 71–72. Cardozo makes frequent use of this argument: e.g., *Ani ha-mekhunneh*, ms JTS 1677, fol. 7b; and the fragmentary chapter XVIII of *This Is My God* (ms JTS 1677, fols. 20a-b; not published by Scholem or translated below).

23. *This Is My God*, chapter XVII (Scholem, "Drush zeh eli," pp. 368–69); translated below, chapter 10.

24. In Cardozo's developed thought, as represented by the untitled treatise of ms JTS 1723, there are three cardinal entities in the "World of *Ein Sof*." The first is the nameless, bodiless, genderless First Cause. The second is the Cause-Above-All-Causes (*'illat 'al kol ha-'illot*), which is emanated from the First Cause and, like the First Cause, is absolutely simple (as opposed to being composite). The third is the Cause-of-Causes (*'illat ha-'illot*), which is emanated from both the First Cause and the

329

Cause-Above-All-Causes and which is the "soul" that fuses itself with the Irascible One to become God. The roots of this theosophy are complex. Cardozo draws upon the doctrine of three supernal "lights," which appears in the speculations of certain thirteenth-century Kabbalists (Scholem, *Origins of the Kabbalah*, pp. 349–54; Mark Verman, *The Books of Contemplation: Medieval Jewish Mystical Sources* [Albany, N.Y.: State University of New York Press, 1992]), and attaches to these "lights" a terminology drawn from the later strata of the Zohar. His triad, moreover, is very suggestive of the "three primal hypostases" of Plotinus: Elmer O'Brien, *The Essential Plotinus* (Indianapolis, Ind.: Hackett Publishing, 1964; I am grateful to my colleague Lance Lazar for calling my attention to this book), pp. 90–105, from *Enneads* V, 1; cf. Bertrand Russell, *A History of Western Philosophy* (New York: Simon & Schuster, 1945), pp. 284–97. It does not seem that Cardozo had formulated the doctrine of the triad when he wrote *Abraham's Morn*, for throughout that work he consistently uses "Cause-of-All-Causes" *('illat kol ha-'illot)* as a synonym for the First Cause and does not show the slightest inkling that there exists a lower entity with almost the same title.

25. Cardozo distinguishes between the "rational soul" *(nefesh ha-sikhlit)* and the "speaking soul" *(nefesh ha-medabberet)*, thus giving a new twist to the technical terminology of the medieval philosophers, who had used the term "speaking soul" to designate the rational soul (e.g., Ibn Tibbon's translation of Maimonides, *Guide to the Perplexed*, I, 41, II, 10). You can have a "speaking soul" without having the godlike "rational soul," as we see from the snake in the Garden of Eden, who obviously has a "speaking soul"—he is quite eloquent—but not a rational one. Similarly, in the World of Emanation, the Irascible One has been endowed by the higher entities with the equivalent of a "rational soul," while his evil twin, Samael (=Satan), has only a "speaking soul." The Irascible One has received his "body," his "speaking soul," and everything else that is his from his divine "parents," the "Persons" of Father and Mother. The same is presumably true of Samael. But only the Irascible One has been gifted, in addition, with the loftier rational soul that makes Him God. See ms JTS 1723, fols. 118a, 149b–50a, 153b–54a.

26. The character of the "Great Name" and the intermediary role that it seems to play in the process of divine incarnation are among the most obscure elements of Cardozo's theology. I cannot claim to understand them.

27. Untitled text, ms JTS 1723, fols. 165a-b.

28. Ibid., fols. 134a-b; cf. 154b–55a.

29. From the brief text entitled *Tiqqun*, which follows after *Ani ha-mekhunneh* in ms JTS 1677; fol. 1a.

Chapter 5

1. Cardozo's autobiographical letter, in Molho and Amarilio, "Autobiographical Letters," pp. 203–4; translated below, chapter 12.2.

2. Letter from Meir Rofe to Abraham Rovigo (October 25, 1677) (Tishby, "R. Meir Rofe's Letters of 1675–80 to R. Abraham Rovigo," pp. 113–14). Elijah Zevi also brought back with him some of the Messiah's personal effects—including, if we are to take his word for it, the copy of *Abraham's Morn* that Cardozo had sent Sabbatai Zevi a few years earlier (above, chapter 4, n. 8).

3. Scholem, *Sabbatai Sevi*, pp. 886–87.

4. Baruch of Arezzo, *Memorial to the Children of Israel*, p. 67.

5. Meir Benayahu, *The Shabbatean Movement in Greece* [Hebrew] (Jerusalem: Ben-Zvi Institute, 1971–77 [=*Sefunot* 14]), pp. 27–32.

6. We know her name from a poem her father wrote in honor of the marriage (ibid., pp. 365–66) and from an allusion in a half-insane letter that Sabbatai Zevi sent off to Filosoff the following year (Baruch of Arezzo, *Memorial to the Children of Israel*, pp. 67–68). In a letter written shortly after the year 1700 (Molho and Amarilio, "Autobiographical Letters," p. 201), Cardozo calls her *ester ha-zevuyah*, "swollen-bellied Esther"—a bitter pun on her name, Esther Zevi, by which Cardozo alludes to Numbers 5:21–22, 27 and hints pretty broadly that Esther had been up to no good during the three days she spent sequestered with her younger brother Jacob (below, chapter 6, n. 20). (Cardozo surely plays also on the similar-sounding word *zevu'ah*, "hypocrite.") Needless to say, Cardozo's feelings about Esther Zevi had soured very drastically by the time he wrote this letter.

7. Halperin, "The Son of the Messiah," pp. 143–219.

8. Kohen, *Sefer Merivat Qodesh*, p. 13.

9. Ibid., pp. 11–12. Kohen quotes a letter, apparently written in transit, in which Cardozo promises the Redemption for the Jewish year 5440, which ended on September 23, 1680. Cardozo therefore cannot have left Izmir after this date. This seems to be contradicted by Cardozo's remark, made more than twenty years afterward, that he left Izmir for Brusa on Iyyar 18, 5441 (May 6, 1681; Molho and Amarilio, "Autobiographical

Letters," p. 222). I am disposed to attribute the latter to some confusion in Cardozo's memory. (Cf. below, chapter 12, n. 5. Scholem seems to have wavered on this point: contrast the date given in Scholem, "Rabbi Eliyahu ha-kohen ha-itamari ve-ha-shabbeta'ut," in Yehuda Liebes, ed., *Researches in Sabbateanism* [Hebrew] [Tel Aviv: Am Oved, 1991], pp. 454, 456, with Scholem, *Kabbalah* [New York and Scarborough, Ontario: New American Library, 1974], p. 397.)

10. Bonafoux's vision, quoted in *Sefer Merivat Qodesh*, pp. 10–11, is signed by twenty-two witnesses, including Elijah Kohen of Izmir.

11. Molho and Amarilio, "Autobiographical Letters," p. 210 (translated below, chapter 12) and p. 222.

12. Israel Zinberg, *A History of Jewish Literature: The German-Polish Cultural Center* (New York: Ktav, 1975), pp. 165–69. Scholem has convincingly demonstrated the identity of Cardozo's disciple with the author of *Midrash Talpiyyot* and *Shevet Musar*: "Rabbi Eliyahu ha-kohen," pp. 453–77.

13. My account of the episode combines two sources: "Autobiographical Letters," p. 229 (translated below, chapter 12); and *Ani ha-mekhunneh*, fol. 29a. In the latter passage Cardozo speaks of his having had two wives at the time. We might guess that two of the four wives who had traveled to Leghorn with Cardozo had been divorced or had died, or, perhaps, that Cardozo was embarrassed by the number of his wives and preferred to reduce it. The extraordinary statement in *Ani ha-mekhunneh*, fol. 36b (Bernheimer, "Some New Contributions," p. 127), that Cardozo lost fifty-three of his children, surely rests upon a scribal error of *nun-gimel* ("fifty-three") for *yod-gimel* ("thirteen").

14. Baruch of Arezzo, *Memorial to the Children of Israel*, pp. 54–55.

15. Kohen, *Sefer Merivat Qodesh*, p. 10; cf. Elqayam, "The Absent Messiah," pp. 57–59.

16. Above, chapter 2.5.

17. Cf. Molho and Amarilio, "Autobiographical Letters," p. 227 (not translated here), where Cardozo is instructed by the ghost of one Rabbi Isaac Crescas that he must not perform *tiqqunim* in Izmir.

18. Kohen, *Sefer Merivat Qodesh*, p. 25. I assume that *y-b yayin* is to be read *u-b' yayin*.

19. Ibid., pp. 17–18.

20. *Epistle to the Judges of Izmir*, in Scholem, "Iggeret...le-dayyanei Izmir," pp. 319–20; translated below, chapter 9.

21. He swears "by the existence of the Cause of all causes and the Occasion of all occasions, whose name is the Lord" *(bimezi'ut 'illat kol ha-*

'illot ve-sibbat kol ha-sibbot adonay shemo). During this period, if we may judge from *Abraham's Morn*, *'illat kol ha-'illot* was Cardozo's term for the First Cause, which was *not* the being whose name was the Lord. The entity, by whose "existence" Cardozo swore, therefore had no existence. If, as I suspect, Cardozo swore an oath that was misleading though not technically false, he was far from the only person of his time to do so (see, e.g., Perez Zagorin, *Ways of Lying: Dissimulation, Persecution, and Conformity in Early Modern Europe* [Cambridge, Mass.: Harvard University Press, 1990], pp. 193–220; I am grateful to my colleague John Headley for referring me to this book).

22. Molho and Amarilio, "Autobiographical Letters," p. 213; translated below, chapter 12.

23. Ibid.

24. Ibid., pp. 207–8; translated below, chapter 12.

25. Ibid., pp. 214–16; translated below, chapter 12.

26. The Hebrew word *maggid* literally means "one who tells."

27. R. J. Zwi Werblowsky, *Joseph Karo: Lawyer and Mystic* (Philadelphia: Jewish Publication Society, 1977). On the views of Cordovero and Vital, see ibid., pp. 74–83; cf. pp. 265–66.

28. Vital, by contrast, sharply distinguished revelation by *maggidim* from revelation by souls of departed saints (see the preceding note).

29. On the date of Yakhini's death, see Scholem, "Avraham Mikha'el Qardozo: Drush qodesh yisra'el la-adonay," in Liebes, *Researches in Sabbateanism*, p. 429.

30. Also David Habillo, a Palestinian Kabbalist (d. 1661) who was an associate of Sabbatai Zevi in the latter's younger days and who was reputed to have had a *maggid* of his own. See Scholem, *Sabbatai Sevi*, pp. 172–74; Avraham Yaari, in *Encyclopedia Judaica*, s.v. "Habillo"; Werblowsky, *Joseph Karo*, p. 13 (citing Azulay, *Shem ha-Gedolim*).

31. Sasportas, *Zizat Novel Zevi*, p. 291; Freimann, *Sammelband kleiner Schriften über Sabbatai Zebi und dessen Anhänger*, p. 88. The story reappears in the *Epistle to the Judges of Izmir* (Scholem, "Iggeret...le-dayyanei Izmir," p. 323), but with the really interesting details omitted. See below, chapter 9.

32. Following the reading of ms Halberstam, and supposing (with Freimann) that the meaningless *hmh* is to be read *ba'ah*. We need a verb in this spot, and the parallel in the *Epistle* suggests that this, and not Tishby's proposed *qamah*, is the correct one.

33. *Ha-ish she-hu 'al roshekha*. (I assume, of course, that little Rachel did not actually say this in Hebrew.)

34. Molho and Amarilio, "Autobiographical Letters," p. 217 (not translated here). The passage implies that Roshi was banned from visiting Cardozo after the failed Redemption. (Understand *ve-attah tukhal la-vo* as a question, directed by Cardozo to Roshi, and read the following word as *ve-heshiv*. Cardozo, or the scribe who copied this letter, often interchanges the letters *aleph* and *hei*.)

35. Scholem, "Drush qodesh yisra'el," p. 437; see below, chapter 11. This text implies fairly strongly, although it does not say explicitly, that the significance of the name Roshi is that it is composed of the four letters *(resh-aleph-shin-yod)* that the first word of the Torah (*bereshit*, "in the beginning") shares with the last word (*yisra'el*, "Israel").

36. *'Al rosham*; a play on his name? (Cf. *ha-ish she-hu 'al roshekha*; above, n. 33.)

37. Molho and Amarilio, "Autobiographical Letters," p. 207.

38. The fuller account is in "letter 2" (Molho and Amarilio, "Autobiographical Letters," pp. 190–92, supplemented by "letter 3" (ibid., p. 200). On the dating of the events, see below, chapter 6, n. 33.

39. Ibid., p. 192; on p. 200, the hat is called *gappello*. Cf. Ruth Matilda Anderson, *Hispanic Costume 1480–1530* (New York: Hispanic Society of America, 1979), pp. 41, 177, and accompanying illustrations, from which it would appear that the sombrero, worn by men and women alike, was a distinctly Spanish article of headgear. There was, of course, nothing comic about the sombrero. The humorous association the word often has nowadays is a product of certain modern North American stereotypes.

40. Molho and Amarilio, "Autobiographical Letters," p. 219 (not translated here).

41. Ibid., p. 228 (translated below, chapter 12); Kohen, *Sefer Merivat Qodesh*, pp. 12–13.

Chapter 6

1. Cardozo's "letter 3" (Molho and Amarilio, "Autobiographical Letters," p. 201).

2. Kohen, *Sefer Merivat Qodesh*, pp. 13–14.

3. Cardozo's "letter 3" (Molho and Amarilio, "Autobiographical Letters," p. 201.

4. Kohen, *Sefer Merivat Qodesh*, p. 20.

5. See chapter 12, nn. 31, 73.

6. Molho and Amarilio, "Autobiographical Letters," p. 229 (translated below, chapter 12).

7. Kohen, *Sefer Merivat Qodesh*, p. 22.

8. Ibid., p. 21.

9. Cardozo gives us two versions of the story that follows: in his so-called autobiographical letter (Molho and Amarilio, "Autobiographical Letters," pp. 208–10; translated below, chapter 12); and in the untitled text, ms JTS 1723, fols. 109a–10b (Scholem, "Lidi'at," pp. 281–83).

10. Velazquez's *Immaculate Conception* is now in the National Gallery, London. For a reproduction, see Antonio Dominguez Ortiz, Alfonso E. Perez Sanchez, and Julian Gallego, *Velazquez* (New York: Metropolitan Museum of Art, 1989), p. 30. The upper part of the moon is illuminated in this painting by the light that shines from the Virgin herself (for she is the "woman clothed with the sun, with the moon under her feet" of Revelation 12:1, which inspired this mode of depiction). Assuming that the painting Cardozo saw was similar in this respect, it is easy to see how the appearance of the gibbous moon on the evening of Tammuz 11 (July 5, 1683) might have triggered his unconscious memory of it. On the Immaculate Conception in Christian art—especially, that of seventeenth-century Spain—see Peter Murray, *The Oxford Companion to Christian Art and Architecture* (Oxford: Oxford University Press, 1996), pp. 239–40. I am grateful to Professor Lazar and to my wife, Rose Halperin, for helping me locate these references.

11. Untitled text, ms JTS 1723, fol. 171b (Scholem, "Lidi'at," p. 291).

12. Untitled text, ms JTS 1723, fols. 167a-b.

13. So the version in ms JTS 1723. The version in the so-called autobiographical letter (translated below, chapter 12) attributes the blasphemies to all three of the demons, not just the one who has taken on Sabbatai Zevi's form.

14. Ms JTS 1723, fol. 110b. (The parallel in the so-called autobiographical letter does not give the Spanish.) *Hakham* is Hebrew for "sage." My former student Jonathan I. Tepper informs me that *muncho* is a familiar Judeo-Spanish variant for *mucho*.

15. On the entire episode, see Benayahu, *The Shabbatean Movement in Greece*, pp. 79–108; also Gershom Scholem, "The Crypto-Jewish Sect of the Dönmeh (Sabbatians) in Turkey," in *The Messianic Idea in Judaism and Other Essays on Jewish Spirituality*, pp. 147–54.

16. Shall we see, in this foursome, the model for Cardozo's four moon spirits? If so, we must suppose that he created at least part of his vision after the fact, after he had learned what had happened in Salonica.

17. Our source for the following details is a deposition delivered in Jerusalem, probably around the year 1702, by one Moses ben Jacob ibn Habib—a scholar, born probably around 1660, who hailed from Salonica and had known Solomon Florentin personally. The text of the deposition is preserved in Jacob Emden, *Torat ha-Qena'ot* (Amsterdam, 1752), pp. 25a–26a; discussed by Meir Benayahu, "Mafteah le-havanat ha-te'udot 'al ha-tenu'ah ha-shabbeta'it birushalayim," in *Studies in Mysticism and Religion Presented to Gershom G. Scholem* (Jerusalem: Magnes Press, 1967), pp. 35–40.

18. Molho and Amarilio, "Autobiographical Letters," p. 211.

19. Benayahu, *The Shabbatean Movement in Greece*, pp. 96–99; cf. below, chapter 12, n. 38.

20. Cardozo therefore calls her *ester ha-zevuyah*, "swollen-bellied Esther," implying that she is like the guilty wife of Numbers 5:27, who sequesters herself with her lover, whose "belly shall swell," therefore, in the course of the Ordeal of Bitter Waters. (See Numbers 5 and the rabbinic interpretation of that chapter in Mishnah *Sotah*; above, chapter 5, n. 6.)

21. Kohen, *Sefer Merivat Qodesh*, p. 22.

22. Ibid., p. 26.

23. Molho and Amarilio, "Autobiographical Letters," pp. 229–30; translated below, chapter 12.

24. See below, chapter 12, n. 65.

25. Molho and Amarilio, "Autobiographical Letters," pp. 220–21; translated below, chapter 12.

26. Ibid., p. 229; translated below, chapter 12.

27. Kohen, *Sefer Merivat Qodesh*, p. 26: *sarei ha-qarabusah ha-nozri*. I regret that I have been unable to discover anything whatsoever about this group, or about the etymology (or even the correct spelling) of its name. Robert Mantran, *Istanbul dans la seconde Moitié du XVIIe Siècle* (Paris: A. Maisonneuve, 1962), gives no information that might shed light on the question; and the suggestions of Heinrich Graetz and David Kaufmann, cited by Freimann in his footnote to *Sefer Merivat Qodesh*, seem to me little more than guesswork. (Scholem's statement that Cardozo was "under the protection of some eminent Christian diplomats" [*Kabbalah*, p. 398] seems to rest upon Graetz's conjecture.) Kohen (p. 27) gives the name of the brother of the head of the Carabusa (*ah sar ha-qarabusah*, following the reading of ms Ginzburg [Moscow] 681, fol. 80a) as Don Francisco, which would suggest that the group's leadership, at least, was Spanish. When Cardozo speaks of *ha-qapitan qarbusah* (see next

note), I assume that he means, "the captain *of* the Carabusa," and that his phrase is equivalent to Kohen's *sar ha-qarabusah*. There is no way, otherwise, to reconcile Cardozo's usage with Kohen's clear testimony that "Carabusa" is the name of a group, not of an individual.

28. Molho and Amarilio, "Autobiographical Letters," p. 228; translated below, chapter 12.12.

29. Kohen, who is much obsessed with what he imagines to have been the goatish virility of Cardozo's old age, claims that he was banished by the Jewish community on a morals charge: he had gotten his servant's daughter pregnant and then tried to marry her (*Sefer Merivat Qodesh*, p. 29).

30. Ibid., p. 30. Cardozo gives his own account of this episode (Molho and Amarilio, "Autobiographical Letters," p. 205); however, he gives the misleading impression that it took place after his expulsion from Edirne in 1697. In fact, it happened during his earlier stay in Rodosto, in 1696: "Thursday, the first of Iyyar," when Cardozo inscribed his proclamations of doom against "the three blaspheming cities of Istanbul, Edirne, and Izmir," was May 3, 1696. (Iyyar 1 fell on Thursday in 1696, 1699, and 1706.)

31. Kohen, *Sefer Merivat Qodesh*, p. 31: Cardozo's patients come clamoring to his door, purses in hand, but he is too busy making love with his wife to attend to them. Cardozo mentions in a letter, apparently written in 1701, that he has prescribed massage therapy for an Englishman in Candia, much to the patient's satisfaction (Molho and Amarilio, "Autobiographical Letters," p. 190. The reference to David Franco shows that he is writing from Candia [see Kohen, *Sefer Merivat Qodesh*, pp. 35–36]. The letter is dated "Sunday, Tammuz 4." Tammuz 4 fell on Sunday in 1697, 1701, and 1704; the letter's allusions to Judah Hasid point strongly to 1701 as the date).

32. Kohen, *Sefer Merivat Qodesh*, p. 31.

33. The date may be inferred from the following considerations: We know from Elijah Kohen that, after Cardozo was driven out of Edirne, he went to Rodosto (*Sefer Merivat Qodesh*, p. 31). Cardozo speaks in two of his letters (Molho and Amarilio, "Autobiographical Letters," pp. 191, 200) of his having been in Rodosto on Heshvan 15 (year unstated), when the Turkish sultan returned from a humiliating military defeat by the Christians, and of having lived two months earlier in Edirne, from which he had departed "in a fury." The defeat of which Cardozo speaks is certainly the catastrophic Battle of Zenta on September 11, 1697, when Mustafa II's troops were crushed by Eugene of Savoy, and thirty thousand Ottoman soldiers may have lost their lives (Alan Palmer, *The Decline and*

Fall of the Ottoman Empire [New York: M. Evans, 1992], pp. 24–25). Heshvan 15 of that year fell on October 30; the devastated Turkish army, it would seem, took seven weeks to march back to home territory. It follows that Cardozo left Edirne some time in September or October 1697. From his statements (Molho and Amarilio, "Autobiographical Letters," p. 191), it would appear that Cardozo was already in Edirne when he received news of an event that had taken place in Izmir on the night of Heshvan 15 of the *preceding* year (November 9, 1696); it follows that he was in Edirne before the end of 1696. Kohen therefore seems to have been wrong in claiming that Cardozo was in Edirne only three months (*Sefer Merivat Qodesh*, p. 30). (The dates given in Cardozo's "letter 2" will best cohere if we read "5456" in the last line of "Autobiographical Letters," p. 190, in place of "5457"; the reference is to the earlier part of 1696, when Cardozo was still in Rodosto.)

34. Kohen, *Sefer Merivat Qodesh*, p. 30. I translate *hin 'erko be-khetem lo yesulleh* in accord with Rashi's understanding of Job 28:16, 41:4.

35. Above, chapter 3.7.

36. Cardozo, "letter 3" (Molho and Amarilio, "Autobiographical Letters," p. 195).

37. For Kohen as a young man in 1707, see Scholem, "Rabbi Eliyahu ha-kohen," p. 456.

38. The data is presented in Meir Benayahu, "Te'udah 'al polmos 'im kat shabbeta'it be-'inyan perush ha-elohut," *Sefunot* 1 (1956), pp. 118–27; many of the interpretations I give here, however, are my own. We may see an indirect admission of Romano's old relationship to Cardozo in the touchy defensiveness with which Romano denies, in his preface to *Sefer Merivat Qodesh* (pp. 1–2; see below), that any such relationship existed. He admits that "I dwelt for many days cheek by jowl with the snake [Cardozo]," but insists that—thanks be to God!—he never once budged from his faith. Clearly he had been questioned and criticized on this point.

39. Romano's story is thus parallel to that of Hayyim Alfandary; see below, chapter 12, n. 70.

40. Benayahu, "Te'udah," p. 124. Benayahu understands the passage to mean that Romano had previously accused Cardozo of being a "Christianizer." But it seems clear that Cardozo is pointing the finger at Romano and not the other way around.

41. See above, section 2.

42. Benayahu, "Te'udah." The text published by Benayahu is obviously a letter from Cardozo to his disciples in Constantinople. Samuel

Galimidi is still alive at the time of writing and a leader in the Constantinople circle. Cardozo himself is somewhere other than in Constantinople. All this would point to the letter's having been written during the latter part of Cardozo's Dardanelles period, say 1685 or 1686.

43. Kohen, *Sefer Merivat Qodesh*, p. 7, referring to the "treasury" (*mikhman*, from Dan 11:43) of the deceased "Isaac Roman," whom we know from the signature to the preface to have been Yom Tov's father. Keep in mind that Kohen's information on the Messianic enthusiasm of 1665–66 was essentially what Romano had fed him, and it will no longer seem surprising that he knew nothing of Samuel Primo's role in the movement.

44. Kohen, *Sefer Merivat Qodesh*, pp. 1–2.

45. On the *yeshiva* in the Ottoman cities of early modern times, see Shaw, *The Jews of the Ottoman Empire*, pp. 98–99.

46. Cardozo, "letter 3" (Molho and Amarilio, "Autobiographical Letters," p. 197); "letter 4" (ibid., pp. 204, 205, 207). The passages on pp. 204 and 207 are translated below, chapter 12.

47. Kohen, *Sefer Merivat Qodesh*, pp. 30–31; Molho and Amarilio, "Autobiographical Letters," pp. 195, 204, cf. pp. 197, 200. (The passage on page 204 is translated below, chapter 12.) I draw upon all these sources for the following account, discounting the parts that obviously derive from Kohen's malice or Cardozo's wishful thinking. Cf. also *Ani ha-mekhunneh*, fols. 28b–29a (Bernheimer, "Some New Contributions," pp. 123–24). Benayahu's note to "Autobiographical Letters," p. 204—that Cardozo claims in *Ani ha-mekhunneh* to have gone from Edirne to Izmir after the confrontation with Primo—is based on a misreading of the text. What Cardozo says is that after having begun to publicize God's Divinity in North Africa (in the 1670s), he went to Izmir.

48. Following Psalm 122:5.

49. Kohen uses the language of Job 18:2, as understood by Rashi.

50. Molho and Amarilio, "Autobiographical Letters," p. 204 (translated below, chapter 12). Cardozo represents himself as having delivered this speech to the community officials, in private, the morning after his confrontation with Primo. But in "letter 3" he presents a very similar speech as part of the confrontation itself. I assume that he said much the same thing on both occasions.

51. So Cardozo (Molho and Amarilio, "Autobiographical Letters," p. 204). Kohen gives the number of wagons as six, but he is copying from Numbers 7:3.

Chapter 7

1. Cardozo's autobiographical letter, in Molho and Amarilio, "Autobiographical Letters," p. 231; translated below, chapter 12.

2. Kohen, *Sefer Merivat Qodesh*, p. 37.

3. Ibid., p. 36. Cardozo perhaps alludes to his fortunetelling activities in Molho and Amarilio, "Autobiographical Letters," p. 227; translated below, chapter 12.12: "...they do indeed visit me daily (Turkish grandees among them) to learn from me what the future holds."

4. A pun on Cardozo's name and the Italian word *cardo*, "thistle."

5. This and the following paragraphs are from Kohen, *Sefer Merivat Qodesh*, p. 37.

6. I am not sure of the disciple's real name. Kohen first introduces him (at the top of p. 27) as "Weepingwillow Ashkenazi Halevi" (*kippah ha-ashkenazi ha-levi;* the *kippah* is taken from Isaiah 9:13, 19:15). He is paired with Moses Bulla, here and again on page 33, where Bulla is equated with the *agmon* of the Isaiah passages. The story of Halevi's marriage to Cardozo's daughter Zilpah is on page 29. As usual, Kohen loads the story with lurid details: Zilpah is wildly promiscuous, sleeps with Cardozo's students, is already pregnant when Halevi takes her to bed; he divorces his wife in order to marry her or else takes her as a second wife (Kohen cannot quite make up his mind which will sound more scandalous), etc. etc.

7. Cardozo, *Epistle to the Judges of Izmir*, in Scholem, "Iggeret...le-dayyanei Izmir," p. 324; translated below, chapter 9.

8. Molho and Amarilio, "Autobiographical Letters," p. 211: *she-afillu hu be-safeq mashiah*.

9. Ibid., p. 200.

10. *Ani ha-mekhunneh*, fol. 8a (Bernheimer, "Some New Contributions," p. 116); translated below, chapter 8.

11. See below, chapter 11.

12. *Ani ha-mekhunneh*, fol. 1a (Bernheimer, "Some New Contributions," p. 112); translated below, chapter 8. Cardozo regularly signed himself *aleph-mem-koph mem-bet-aleph*, which can be reasonably understood only as "Abraham Michael Cardozo, Messiah ben Ephraim." See, for example, Kohen, *Sefer Merivat Qodesh*, pp. 6, 13, and the remarks of Romano and Kohen on pp. 1, 4 (of which the former is obviously a parody of *Ani ha-mekhunneh*). For Cardozo to call himself "Abraham Michael Cardozo, Michael ben Abraham" would be quite meaningless.

13. Above, chapter 3.3.

14. *She-yiddaqer*: untitled text, ms JTS 1723, fols. 133a-b.

NOTES

15. Zohar, III, 239a *(Ra'ya Mehemna)*; quoted by Cardozo, with minor variations, in his autobiographical letter, in Molho and Amarilio, "Autobiographical Letters," pp. 203, 231–34. See the translations of these passages, and my notes on them, in chapter 12, below.

16. Ibid., p. 233; translated below, chapter 12.

17. *Ani ha-mekhunneh*, fol. 34b: *davar zeh satum ve-hatum 'ad sof ha-galut* ("this matter is hidden and sealed up, until the end of the exile").

18. Ibid., fols. 2a-b (Bernheimer, "Some New Contributions," pp. 114–15); translated below, chapter 8.

19. Ibid., fol. 21a. Cardozo here states explicitly that this was the issue concerning which the Kabbalists of Egypt disappointed him. On fol. 27a, he acknowledges that the term *Shechinah* can at times be employed for the *sefirah Malkhut*. He denies, however, that this exhausts its meaning.

20. This is a brief and much oversimplified presentation of Cardozo's difficult doctrine of the Shechinah. Cf. the magisterial treatment by Wolfson, "Constructions of the Shekhinah," pp. 11–143.

21. Above, chapter 2.5. Cf. the passages from *Drush ha-Shekhinah* published by Wolfson, pp. 99–100, 133–35.

22. *Tiqqun* (in ms JTS 1677), fol. 1a; quoted above, chapter 4.5. Cf. Wolfson, "Constructions of the Shekhinah," p. 134.

23. Cervantes, *Don Quixote*, p. 6.

24. Cardozo may be compared, in this respect, with St. Ignatius of Loyola (1491–1556), and I am grateful to my colleague, Professor Lance Lazar, for suggesting to me the possibility of making this comparison. At the age of about thirty, Ignatius turned away from a libertine life as courtier and soldier. His mind, like Don Quixote's, was "all full of tales like Amadis de Gaul and such books"; he therefore conceived the "knightly" idea (in 1522) of "keep[ing] a vigil of arms one whole night…before the altar of Our Lady of Montserrat, where he had resolved to lay aside his garments and to don the armor of Christ" (*Autobiography*, 17, in George E. Ganss, ed., *Ignatius of Loyola: The Spiritual Exercises and Selected Works* [Mahwah, N.J.: Paulist Press, 1991], p. 75). Shortly before conceiving this plan, Ignatius had pondered the idea of killing a Moor who had impugned the perpetual virginity of Mary, "for it seemed that he had done wrong in allowing the Moor to say such things about Our Lady, and that he ought to sally forth in defense of her honor" (*Autobiography*, 15). The collocation of these two events might suggest that Ignatius had transferred to the Virgin his chivalric fantasies of service to the "Lady." Cf. W. W. Meissner, *Ignatius of Loyola: The Psychology of a Saint* (New Haven, Conn., and London: Yale University Press, 1992), pp. 60–65; and,

for an analogous shift in the medieval troubadour literature, Marina Warner, *Alone of All Her Sex: The Myth and Cult of the Virgin Mary* (London: Pan Books, 1976), pp. 134–59. Might we imagine a similar process in Cardozo? Cardozo's youth, like Ignatius's, was fairly wild; Cardozo had once "played guitars, sang *villancicos*, and composed comedies" (Yerushalmi, *From Spanish Court*, p. 322, quoting Cardozo's Spanish letter to his brother), but later turned his poetic talents—and, presumably, much of his libido—toward "composing an original hymn about the Shechinah's having gone back up to Her proper place" (*Epistle to the Judges of Izmir*, in Scholem, "Iggeret...le-dayyanei Izmir," p. 322; translated below, chapter 9). Did Cardozo, like Ignatius and Don Quixote, read books of knight-errantry? They surely must have been accessible to him: Ariosto's *Orlando Furioso* was the single most popular non-Jewish book on any subject among Mantuan Jewish readers at the end of the sixteenth century, and a few Jews were reading *Amadis di Gaula* as well (Shifra Baruchson, *Books and Readers: The Reading Interests of Italian Jews at the Close of the Renaissance* [Hebrew] [Ramat-Gan: Bar-Ilan University Press, 1993], pp. 176, 180). A library of six thousand books, such as Cardozo claims his brother Isaac had in Venice (and evidently put at Cardozo's disposal; below, chapter 8), can hardly have been without a few specimens of the genre.

25. *Ani ha-mekhunneh*, fol. 34b, quoting, in immediate succession, Zohar III, 239a (the passage quoted at the beginning of this section) and *Tiqqunei Zohar* 21 (62a).

26. Moses Hadas, ed., *Solomon Maimon: An Autobiography* (New York: Schocken Books, 1947), pp. 39–40.

27. Elisheva Carlebach, *The Pursuit of Heresy: Rabbi Moses Hagiz and the Sabbatian Controversies* (New York: Columbia University Press, 1990), p. 84.

28. Yehuda Liebes, "Mikha'el Qardozo—mehabbero shel sefer 'Raza de-Mehemanuta,'" pp. 35–48. Aside from this, the earliest publication of a Cardozo text that I am aware of was in 1865, by Nahum Brüll: "Mikhtav be-'inyan sod ha-elohut neged kat sh-z," in *Bet ha-Midrash*, ed. Weiss (1865), 1:63–71, 100–103, 139–42.

29. Carlebach, *The Pursuit of Heresy*, pp. 75–159.

30. Yehuda Liebes, "Ha-yesod ha-ideologi she-be-folmos Hayon," in *On Sabbateaism and Its Kabbalah*, pp. 49–52.

31. Carlebach, *The Pursuit of Heresy*, p. 98.

32. See above, chapter 3.6.

33. Scholem, "The Crypto-Jewish Sect of the Dönmeh," pp.

142–66; Dan Ross, *Acts of Faith: A Journey to the Fringes of Jewish Identity* (New York: Schocken Books, 1982), pp. 83–98; Moshe Temkin, "Shabbtai Tzvi Would Be Proud," *The Jerusalem Report* (May 24, 1999), pp. 34–36.

34. In the Dönmeh commentary on the Torah portion *Lekh Lekha*, written in the eighteenth century by Judah Levi Tovah (in Judeo-Spanish) and published in Hebrew translation by Isaac R. Molho and Rivka Shatz, "A Sabbatian Commentary on *Lekh-Lekha* (Gen. 12–17)" [Hebrew], *Sefunot* 3–4 (1960): pp. 452, 453, 458 (veneration of Cardozo); pp. 438–39, 444, 451, 493 (polemic against the worship of the First Cause); even Roshi appears, on page 515! Tovah's formulation on page 493 is particularly striking: Abraham and Lot quarrel, because "Lot wanted to return to the idolatry practiced by the inhabitants [of Canaan]…none of whom recognized or worshiped the Creator of All, but rather they—except for Abraham—directed all their worship toward the First Cause. [Recall that, according to Cardozo, the Muslims call the First Cause by the name Allah!]….And Lot wanted to worship the First Cause and not the Blessed Holy One…and he believed that the Creator was the First Cause." Cardozo, to paraphrase a source cited in the preceding endnote, would have been proud. Cf. Rivka Shatz-Uffenheimer, "Portrait of a Sabbatian Sect" [Hebrew], ibid., pp. 398–400; Moshe Attias, *Sefer shirot ve-tushbahot shel ha-shabbeta'im* (Tel Aviv: Dvir, 1948), pp. 55–56, 131.

35. It is entirely typical of Cardozo that he believed all his life in the authenticity of the Greek texts that had been passed off in antiquity as the writings of "Hermes Trismegistus," a marvelous sage of ancient Egypt. (Cardozo assumed that Hermes was the teacher of the biblical Pharaoh and used the Hermetic writings in a most ingenious manner to reconstruct the issues at stake in the confrontation between Pharaoh and Moses.) If Cardozo had lived in the sixteenth century, he would have been in the best of company, for leading European intellectuals, like Giordano Bruno, took the authenticity of the Hermetic books for granted and allowed their own ideas to be deeply influenced by them. Yet these texts were shown in 1614—thirteen years before Cardozo was born—to be forgeries, composed in the early centuries of the Christian Era. By the middle of the seventeenth century, nearly all informed people had abandoned them. (See Frances A. Yates, *Giordano Bruno and the Hermetic Tradition* [Chicago and London: University of Chicago Press, 1964].) Yet Cardozo would continue, for another fifty years, not only to believe in the Hermetic writings, but to show himself unaware that anybody had ever raised a question about them.

36. Wayne Shumaker, *Renaissance Curiosa* (Binghamton, N.Y.: Center for Medieval and Early Renaissance Studies, 1982), pp. 15–52.

37. *Tiqqun*, in ms JTS 1677, fol. 1b; cf. above, chapter 4.5.

Chapter 8

1. I translate extracts from the treatise *Ani ha-mekhunneh* from ms 1677 of the Jewish Theological Seminary of America, New York (=ms Adler 1653), fols. 1a–3b, 7b–8a. Most of the material here translated was published by Carlo Bernheimer, "Some New Contributions to Abraham Cardoso's Biography," *Jewish Quarterly Review*, New Series, 18 (1927–28), pp. 112–16. But Bernheimer's text is filled with strange errors, which often make it difficult or impossible to understand; e.g., the meaningless *hippani da'at u-zefirah rabbah* (in the second paragraph of my translation), for the manuscript's straightforward *hanani da'at u-zekhirah rabbah*. I therefore translate directly from the manuscript, without reference to Bernheimer, by courtesy of the Library of the Jewish Theological Seminary of America.

2. On this elusive passage, see above, chapters 3.3, 7.2.

3. Hermes Trismegistus ("thrice-great Hermes") was a fabled sage of ancient Egypt, whom Cardozo supposed to have been the teacher of the biblical Pharaoh. (See *This Is My God*, chapter VII; translated below, chapter 10. Cardozo normally calls him by the Spanish form of his name, based on the Latin: Mercurio, or Mercurio Termegisto.) On the so-called Hermetic writings, to which Cardozo here alludes, see chapter 7, n. 35. I do not know what Cardozo means by "the books of Cadmus." In Greek mythology, Cadmus was a Phoenician prince who founded Thebes; in the Middle Ages, he was sometimes seen as a "type" of Christ (H. David Brumble, *Classical Myths and Legends in the Middle Ages and Renaissance: A Dictionary of Allegorical Meanings* [Westport, Conn.: Greenwood Press, 1998], pp. 59–60; I am grateful to my colleague Professor Lance Lazar for directing me toward this resource). I am not aware of any tradition that he was a philosopher or an author. But he was said to have "brought letters [that is, the alphabet] from Phoenicia to Greece," and perhaps that was enough to suggest to Cardozo—who was a great deal less conversant with the thought and literature of the Gentile world than he liked to believe—that Cadmus had written books.

4. The Hebrew verb *mehavveh*, "to bring into existence," is from the same root as *YAHVEH*. Cardozo's father supposes that Moses used the

word YAHVEH to indicate the First Cause, by pointing to a particularly significant action of the First Cause. The biblical quotations in this paragraph are from Exodus 6:3 and 3:15.

5. This is precisely the position that Spinoza assails in the seventh chapter of the *Theologico-Political Treatise*, trans. Samuel Shirley, *Baruch Spinoza: Theological-Political Treatise* (Indianapolis, Ind., and Cambridge: Hackett Publishing Company, 1991), pp. 103–6.

6. "Leghorn" must be Cardozo's mistake for "Venice." The rabbis he names lived and taught in Venice, and this is in fact the place where the Cardozo brothers settled when they left Spain in 1648. It is *perhaps* possible to understand Cardozo as meaning that he came to Leghorn and afterward studied in Venice, but this seems very strained.

7. An abridged quotation from *Midrash Exodus Rabbah* 3:6. Cf. *This Is My God*, chapter XV; translated below, chapter 10.

8. BT Berakhot 6a, 7a, translated among the Background Texts to chapter 10; see also chapter 10, n. 174.

9. For references to the sources of this discussion, see the notes to *This Is My God*, chapter VI (below, chapter 10). On the issue of the Shechinah, see above, chapter 2; on Saadiah and Maimonides, chapter 1.4; on Ibn Migash, chapter 10, n. 52.

10. The Five Books of Moses are traditionally divided into 54 "portions," each one being read in the synagogue on a given Sabbath, so that the entire Pentateuch is publicly read aloud in the course of a year. Each portion is designated by its opening word, or sometimes, its first significant word. (See Table II at the end of the "Note to the Reader" for a list of these portions.) Cardozo normally uses the name of the Torah portion to cite any text (like the Zohar) that is structured as a commentary on the Pentateuch.

11. See *This Is My God*, chapter VI; translated below, chapter 10. The *'Amidah* is an extended series of benedictions—most of which are in fact petitions—that forms the core of each and every prescribed Jewish worship service, whether public or private.

12. On Kohen and the Vitals (father and son), see above, chapter 2.4. On Benjamin Halevi (d. 1672), and Cardozo's claim to have met him in Egypt, see Scholem, "Ha-ta'alumah be-'enah 'omedet," pp. 252, 265–69; idem, *Sabbatai Sevi*, index, s.v. "Benjamin ha-Levi, R." "Rabbi Iskandrani" (*'skndrny;* not *'skndry,* as Bernheimer transcribes the name) is perhaps Abraham Skandari, master of a distinguished Cairo *yeshiva* in the mid-seventeenth century. See S. Shtober's introduction to Yosef Sambary,

Sefer Divrei Yoseph (Jerusalem: The Zalman Shazar Center and the Dinur Center, 1981), p. 6.

13. Titles of ancient midrashic texts; cf. above, chapter 1.4.

14. Zechariah 14:9, which the Kabbalists understood as describing the internal unification of the Deity. For Cardozo, God's Name is a designation for the Shechinah. What the verse speaks of, therefore, is the unity of the male and female aspects of the Deity.

15. BT Berakhot 7a, translated among the Background Texts for chapter 10: God requests of Rabbi Ishmael ben Elisha, "My son, bless Me," that is, bring down upon Me "blessing" from the First Cause. Cf. above, chapter 4.3.

16. The consequence of Maimonides's error is this: If God is the First Cause, which trancends all gender, the female Shechinah cannot be divine. But now suppose, in accord with the true teaching of the Bible and the ancient rabbis, that God is a gendered, androgynous being distinct from and subordinate to the First Cause (above, chapter 4.3). The question of the Shechinah's divinity will begin to look different. Cf. above, chapter 7.3.

17. The Tannaim (singular, *Tanna*) were those ancient rabbis who lived in the period from the destruction of the Temple in 70 C.E., to the compilation of the Mishnah in the early third century (see above, chapter 1.4). Their immediate successors, who developed and elaborated upon their work—roughly, during the third through the fifth centuries C.E.— were the Amoraim. Still later were the Geonim, the legal scholars of the early Middle Ages (see above, chapter 1.4).

18. *Midrash Numbers Rabbah* 14:2. See Background Texts to chapter 10, below; and *This Is My God*, chapters II, III, XIV.

19. On Messiah ben David and Messiah ben Joseph (or ben Ephraim), see above, chapter 3.2–3.

Chapter 9

1. From Cardozo's preface to the *Epistle to the Judges of Izmir*; below.

2. On the date, see Scholem, "Iggeret...le-dayyanei Izmir," pp. 298–303.

3. Sasportas, *Zizat Novel Zevi*, pp. 289–97 (on Sasportas, see above, chapter 3.6); cf. Freimann, *Sammelband kleiner Schriften über Sabbatai Zebi und dessen Anhäuger*, pp. 87–92.

NOTES

4. Tishby's note to Sasportas, *Zizat Novel Zevi*, p. 308.

5. Ibid., p. 270.

6. See above, chapter 3, n. 63.

7. Yerushalmi, *From Spanish Court*, pp. 313–43.

8. Ibid., p. 322.

9. There is an extended discussion of prophecy, and the requirements for accepting a prophet as such, in Maimonides's *Code of Jewish Law, Laws of the Fundamentals of the Torah*, chapters 7–10. Cardozo and his contemporaries would have acknowledged the authoritative status of this discussion. Cf. the treatment of the same problem in Sasportas's letter to Joseph Halevi, of the third week of November 1666 (Sasportas, *Zizat Novel Zevi*, pp. 142–49).

10. Hebrew *navi muhzaq*. Cardozo believes that one can become a "prophet by consensus" by repeatedly working evidentiary miracles (below, p. 158); as against Sasportas (previous note), who insists that you are not a "prophet by consensus" until you have a substantial prophetic career to point back to.

11. Origen, *Contra Celsum*, I, 55 (above, chapter 3, n. 4).

12. Cardozo has a point when he claims this to be the rabbinic consensus, though he overstates it. The classical rabbinic sources normally do not deal with Isaiah 53 at all. But one midrash (*Tanhuma, Toledot* #14, and parallels) explicitly applies 52:13 to the Messiah, and this would seem to carry the rest of the passage with it. BT Sanhedrin 98b, moreover, quotes 53:4 in reference to the Messiah. *Midrash Ruth Rabbah*, 5:6, applies to the Messiah the key text for Cardozo's argument: *ve-hu meholal mi-pesha'enu* (53:5), which Cardozo takes to mean: "he was profaned on account of our sins."

13. We may wonder why Cardozo begins his list of "markers" with the assertion that the Messiah must be an ordinary human being. The point seems of small importance to his argument, especially since few Jews would be inclined to contest him. His real aim, surely, is to advertise his opposition to Christianity.

14. Scholem, *Sabbatai Sevi*, pp. 741–47, where the text is partly translated. The original may be found in Sasportas, *Zizat Novel Zevi*, pp. 260–62; Baruch of Arezzo, *Memorial to the Children of Israel*, pp. 59–61. The date is given as Shevat 25, 5428 (February 7, 1668).

15. Gershom Scholem, *Major Trends in Jewish Mysticism*, pp. 156–204; Pinchas Giller, *The Enlightened Will Shine: Symbolization and Theurgy in the Later Strata of the Zohar* (Albany, N.Y.: State University of New York Press, 1993).

16. Hebrew *ve-hu meholal mi-pesha'enu*. See below.

17. See above, chapter 3.2, 7.1; and below, pp. 152–53. For Moses as a full-blown Messianic figure in Cardozo's thinking, see below, chapter 11.

18. Cf. Richard G. Marks, *The Image of Bar Kokhba in Traditional Jewish Literature* (University Park, Pa.: Pennsylvania State University Press, 1994).

19. *Midrash Lamentations Rabbah* 2:4. On the term *Tannaim*, see above, chapter 8, n. 17.

20. For a discussion of this figure, see above, chapter 3.3.

21. Cf. the remarks of Elqayam, "The Absent Messiah," p. 60.

22. *'Erev rav*; an expression drawn from Exodus 12:38, where the Israelites leaving Egypt are joined by a "rabble" (or, as most translations give it, "mixed multitude"). It is this rabble, and not the true children of Israel, who are responsible for the Israelites' sins and rebellions in the desert (Num 11:4). It is their descendants, according to the author of *The Faithful Shepherd*, who drag the Jews in each generation into sin, and into disloyalty to their true leaders. Unfortunately—still according to *The Faithful Shepherd*—it is the rabble who tend to become the rabbis and leaders of the Jewish community.

23. The Hebrew roots for *being wounded* and *being joined* are identical.

24. I translate the text published by Gershom Scholem, "Iggeret Avraham Mikha'el Qardozo le-dayyanei Izmir," in *Studies and Texts Concerning the History of Sabbetianism and Its Metamorphoses* (Jerusalem: Bialik Institute, 1982), pp. 298–331, from ms Hamburg 312 (with comparison of ms Halberstam 40). I have not myself consulted the manuscripts. The Bialik Institute, Jerusalem, which published Scholem's text, kindly granted me permission to publish this translation.

25. Numbers 15:2. The Torah portion *Shelah*, which contains this verse, was read in the synagogue in 1669 during the week 10–16 Sivan (9–15 June). (The year 1669 is not found in the *Epistle* itself, but Scholem has made a reasonably strong case for it: "Iggeret...le-dayyanei Izmir," pp. 298–303.) Cardozo dates his writing, in accord with the common practice of his time, by quoting some passage from the Torah reading for the week. Numbers 15:2 is particularly significant for him, not only because of its Messianic overtones—Sabbatai Zevi was to restore the Jewish people to the Holy Land—but because of a peculiarity in the word *moshavotekhem* ("in which you are to dwell"). The central four letters, extracted from the word and re-vocalized, spell the name *Sabbatai*.

26. These episodes took place in 1667 and 1668: Scholem, *Sabbatai Sevi*, pp. 718–49, 764–81.

27. The language *ha-ish ha-mehullal* is taken from Isaiah 53:5. We shall presently see how Cardozo expounds this passage.

28. The "four fasts" (as Cardozo calls them, at the end of the *Epistle*) were the Tenth of Tevet, the Seventeenth of Tammuz, the Ninth of Av, and the Fast of Gedaliah (the day after Rosh Hashanah). The Talmud (Rosh Hashanah 18b, cf. Ta'anit 28b) understands these to be the fasts mentioned in Zechariah 8:19, and understands all of them to commemorate sad events connected with the destruction of the Temple. The passage from Zechariah promises that in Messianic times they will cease to be fasts and become days of rejoicing, and those who believed that the Messiah had come in the person of Sabbatai Zevi acted accordingly. (See above, chapter 3.6.) Cardozo assures his readers that, although he had stopped observing the fasts during the Messianic excitement of 1666, he has now returned obediently to the orthodox practice.

29. That is, the congregations; taking *qehillot* as the antecedent for *'immam*, despite the inconsistency in gender. It is also thinkable that the antecedent is the more remote *m'k-t*, in which case "them" should be replaced by "you."

30. *Midrash Lamentations Rabbah* 1:51.

31. The language of "consuming" the Messiah is drawn from BT Sanhedrin 98b, 99a. The former passage speaks of people eating *shnei mashiah*, which, in context, certainly means "the years of the Messiah," but which lends itself to Cardozo's distortion into *shnei meshihim*, "the two Messiahs." On the dual Messiah (Messiah ben David, Messiah ben Ephraim), see above, chapter 3.2–3.

32. This "rabbinic" teaching seems in fact to be of medieval origin. It was fairly widespread, in one version or another, among the Safed Kabbalists: Scholem, *Sabbatai Sevi*, pp. 56–57; Yehuda Liebes, "Meshihiyyuto shel Rabbi Ya'aqov 'Emden ve-yahaso la-shabbeta'ut," in *On Sabbateaism and its Kabbalah*, pp. 405–7, nn. 155, 180.

33. Paraphrasing BT Sanhedrin 98b.

34. *Pirqei de-Rabbi Eliezer*, chap. 30. I assume Cardozo is reading *u-vimehem ya'amod zemah ben david*, "and in their [the Muslims'] days the Sprout, son of David, will arise," as though it were *u-venehem ya'amod zemah ben david*, "and among them the Sprout...will arise."

35. *Midrash Tanhuma, Toledot* #14 (in Buber's edition, #20).

36. A rough quotation of *Midrash Shemuel* 19:1, which invokes Isaiah 53:5. Cardozo probably took it from Moses Alsheich's commentary on Isaiah 53, where it is attributed vaguely to "our rabbis" (Driver and Neubauer, *The Fifty-Third Chapter of Isaiah*, 2:259).

37. A free quotation of BT Sanhedrin 93b.

38. Paraphrased from BT Sanhedrin 98b.

39. *Midrash Pesiqta Rabbati*, ch. 37 (ed. Friedmann, p. 163a).

40. Paraphrased from *Midrash on Psalms*, 18:5 (ed. Buber, p. 69a).

41. *Ra'ya Mehemna* (Zohar, III, 125b), commenting on Isaiah 53:9. See the Background Texts. The same Zoharic passage was used by Nathan of Gaza, at the beginning of 1668, in defense of Sabbatai Zevi's apostasy: Scholem, *Sabbatai Sevi*, p. 741.

42. This is a reasonably accurate summary of Jewish exegesis of Isaiah 53. Cf. E. B. Pusey's introduction to Driver and Neubauer, *The Fifty-Third Chapter of Isaiah*, pp. lx–lxiii; Rav Asher Soloff, *The Fifty Third Chapter of Isaiah According to the Jewish Commentators, to the Sixteenth Century* (Madison, N.J.: Drew University, 1967), p. 8.

43. See above, n. 38.

44. Paraphrased from Isaiah 28:21.

45. See above, p. 134.

46. Cardozo perhaps refers to BT Sanhedrin 50b, which, however, hardly makes the etymological point very explicitly.

47. BT Sanhedrin 76a envisions the possibility that "profaning one's daughter" *(tehallel et bittekha)*, taken by itself, might refer to a priest's marrying his daughter to a non-priest and thus depriving her of her sacral status. Cardozo presumably refers to this passage (hardly "many passages"!).

48. A free quotation of Ezekiel 36:23.

49. Deuteronomy 34:6. The exegesis to which Cardozo refers is found in the Zohar, III, 280a *(Ra'ya Mehemna)*; cf. III, 125b. (See the Background Texts.)

50. The verse is applied to the Messiah in two midrashic passages— *Ruth R.* 5:6, *Midrash Samuel* 19:1—and also in Zohar II, 212a. The Sabbatians liked to see in Moses a "type" of the Messiah ben David (Sabbatai Zevi, that is), and Cardozo accordingly reads these passages in the light of *Ra'ya Mehemna*'s application of Isaiah 53 to Moses.

51. Zohar, III, 276b *(Ra'ya Mehemna)*; see the Background Texts. The Zoharic passage seems to represent Messiah ben Ephraim as being saved from this fate by the atoning sacrifice of Moses—a fact that Cardozo prefers to gloss over.

52. Cardozo normally uses "uncircumcised" *('arelim)* to mean Christians.

53. Whom Cardozo claims to have once been among his teachers of Kabbalah; above, chapter 2.2, 2.4. Kohen quotes the Zoharic phrase *'atid le-*

ithallela bein ummin de-'alma (III, 277a) as though it applied to the Messiah (*Torat Hakham* [Venice, 1654], p. 18b). Cf. Scholem, *Sabbatai Sevi*, pp. 53–55.

54. The noun "Messiahs" is plural, yet the accompanying verb and the antecedent pronouns are singular and suggest that Cardozo has a single "Messiah" in mind. The context would favor the plural reading.

55. Cardozo explains the peculiar shift from second to third person as pointing to a change in subject. The second person is the Jewish people, the third person is the Messiah, and the prophet makes a comparison between the two.

56. Reading *she-hu* for *she-lo*, which is necessary to make sense of the passage and which accords with the parallel in Cardozo's letter of 1668 (in Sasportas, *Zizat Novel Zevi*, p. 294). In the earlier version of his argument, Cardozo had quoted a "biblical" passage, "Edom transgressed from beneath Israel" *(va-yifsha' edom tahat yisra'el)*, that in fact does not exist. (The error may be significant: "Edom," in medieval and early modern Jewish usage, is a standard designation for Christendom.) Here he corrects himself.

57. BT Sanhedrin 98b, which quotes Isaiah 53:4 and thus supports Cardozo's contention that the terms "afflicted" and "smitten"—associated with leprosy in rabbinic Hebrew—indeed refer to the Messiah's being a leper. (It does *not*, of course, suggest that his "leprosy" consists of his "dwelling outside the camp of Israel"; that is Cardozo's contribution.) But Cardozo seems to be quoting the Talmudic passage from memory, for his attribution of the statement to Rabbi Judah the Patriarch is a garbling of what the Talmud actually says.

58. I do not know Cardozo's source for this statement. The association of "life" with Torah, however, follows easily from such passages as Proverbs 3:18.

59. The Hebrew for "Glory to the righteous" is *zevi la-zaddiq*. This obviously could be read as a reference, by name, to Sabbatai Zevi, and Sabbatai's followers did not pass up the chance so to read it. Cardozo tactfully refrains from explicitly making the point.

60. This is plainly how Cardozo construes the difficult Hebrew text of the verse. The American Jewish version (1917) translates: "I waste away, I waste away, woe is me! The treacherous deal treacherously; yea, the treacherous deal very treacherously."

61. Using the language of Isaiah 53:6.

62. Reading *u-varur*.

63. Following the reading of ms Halberstam; cited by Scholem, "Iggeret…le-dayyanei Izmir," p. 310n.

64. The clue to Cardozo's "mystery" is provided in a parallel passage from Cardozo's Hebrew letter of 1668 (Sasportas, *Zizat Novel Zevi*, p. 297). It is reasonably clear from the parallel that Cardozo understands Isaiah 52:13—53:12 as applying, on the deepest level, to the Shechinah, understood here as the *sefirah Malkhut*, which is manifested on the historical plane by Messiah ben David. (See below, p. 153, and chapter 11.) Cardozo writes, in the 1668 letter, that the Shechinah is "disfigured" (Isa 52:14), in that "the nine *sefirot* possessed by *Malkhut*, which She has received in addition [to the single *sefirah* that essentially and properly belongs to Her], have become enclothed in the Demonic...enclothed in the Profane, and the Divine effluence is thus channeled toward the enemies of Israel [for their benefit]. This is why it was absolutely inevitable that the holy Messiah become enclothed in profane garb—this being the meaning of 'profaned on account of our sins' [Isa 53:5]—in order to extract the effluence, for the benefit [?] of Holiness, and to extract Holiness itself from the profane, which is the Demonic, the clothing, the Turk." In the Kabbalistic tradition, the Jerusalem Temple is a representation of the *sefirah Malkhut*. This is why, for Cardozo, the disfiguring "enclothement" of *Malkhut* within the Demonic is mirrored by the "enclothement" of the Temple within the "profane garb" of a Muslim shrine—as well as by Sabbatai Zevi's "enclothement" in the "profane garb" of a Turkish courtier. (On the Lurianic conception of the Shechinah's loss of Her nine *sefirot* to the Demonic, see above, chapter 2.5.) Cf. the beginning of the translation of *Israel, Holiness to the Lord* (below, chapter 11), where the "disfigurement" of Isaiah 52:14 is understood of both *Malkhut* and *Tif'eret*. The background for Cardozo's thinking may be found in the writings of Hayyim Vital, who, unlike Cardozo, seems to apply the "disfigurement" specifically to *Tif'eret*: "...when the nine *sefirot* of *Malkhut* are enclothed in the demonic Lilith, it is the Irascible One who is essentially affected by the loss, for it is from Him that [these *sefirot*] derive...and this is the hidden meaning of the biblical passage, 'In the same way his appearance is disfigured from that of a man' [Isa 52:14]" (Brandwein, *'Ez Hayyim*, VI.iii.2–3: *Sha'ar me'ut ha-yareah*, chaps. 2–3, 2:191–92). It is inconvenient for Cardozo, of course, that a biblical prophecy referring to a *male* figure must be applied to the specifically *female* aspect of Divinity, but cf. the introduction to chapter 11, below.

65. Presumably referring to Zohar, I, 237b.

66. *Ve-lo amar limeta'ev mi-goy o limetu'av mi-goy.* Cardozo alludes in passing to an exegetical difficulty in the Hebrew text: that it seems to

require a passive verb *(metu'av)* but provides an active verb instead *(meta'ev)*.

67. A free quotation from Maimonides's *Mishneh Torah, Hilkhot Melakhim*, 11:4. (See Background Texts.)

68. Where, in antiquity, the Great Sanhedrin used to convene.

69. BT Sanhedrin 93b. Cardozo erroneously splits one Talmudic passage into two.

70. Earlier, as we have seen, Cardozo has understood this verse differently, to mean that the Messiah will hide his own face from *us*, the Jewish people. (Hebrew *mimmennu* can mean either "from him" or "from us.")

71. Maimonides, *Epistle to Yemen*, part 4; in Abraham Halkin and David Hartman, *Crisis and Leadership: Epistles of Maimonides* (Philadelphia: Jewish Publication Society, 1985), pp. 122–23.

72. Scholem ("Iggeret...le-dayyanei Izmir," p. 313n) claims that the reference is to Nachmanides's commentary on Isaiah 53, but I have been unable to find any relevant passage in that source. More likely, Cardozo alludes to Nachmanides's comment on Deuteronomy 34:11, where the biblical text is interpreted to mean that the distinction between Moses and the other prophets lies not in any one specific miracle—for Joshua, Elijah, and Elisha also did dramatic miracles comparable to those of Moses—but in the uniqueness of the ensemble (ed. Chavel, 2:504–5).

73. The biblical passage refers to the Messiah.

74. Reading *hagur* for *hoger*. Or, perhaps, the word should be deleted.

75. For explanation of the Kabbalistic concepts involved, see above, chapter 2.

76. See Cordovero, *Pardes Rimmonim, Sha'ar 'Erkhei ha-Kinnuyim*, s.v. *mal'akh*; and Zohar, I, 205b, where *Malkhut* is identified with both *go'el* ("redeemer") in general and *ha-mal'akh ha-go'el* (Gen 48:16) specifically. The Messiah is thus to be identified with the *sefirah Malkhut* both in that he is "Redeemer," and that he has already been identified with the "kingship" (the literal meaning of *malkhut*) of David.

77. Apparently referring to Zohar, II, 123a, which, however, speaks of *malkhut david* instead of *malkhut bet david*.

78. Both "shining mirror" and "Torah" are appellations for the *sefirah Tif'eret*. (So also is the "sun," mentioned in the following sentence.)

79. Psalm 118:20, commonly applied to the *sefirah Malkhut* (e.g., Zohar, I, 7b). Cardozo's point is that if one wants to rise to knowledge (=*Tif'eret*), one must first have faith (=*Malkhut*)—which is impossible, if one already has knowledge.

80. The second imprisonment would thus correspond to Sabbatai Zevi's imprisonment at the fortress of Gallipoli in the summer of 1666. It is not clear what Cardozo means by the first imprisonment. Scholem ("Iggeret...le-dayyanei Izmir," p. 302) denies that he is talking about the first phase of the imprisonment of 1666 in Constantinople, before Sabbatai Zevi was transferred to Gallipoli. Scholem's argument is that the Sabbatians never made a distinction between the two. Yet it is difficult to read Paul Rycaut's account of Sabbatai's successive imprisonments, in Constantinople and in Gallipoli—the first in "the most loathsom and darkest Dungeon in the Town," the second marking a "removal...from a worse Prison to one of a better air"—without thinking how natural and plausible such a distinction would be. (John Evelyn, *The History of the Three Late Famous Impostors*, pp. 68–72; see above, chapter 3.7, and chapter 3, n. 9.) Cardozo, like many of the Sabbatians, cannot resist bragging about the honor that Sabbatai Zevi received in Gallipoli. He apparently does not notice that it undercuts his argument.

81. Following Scholem's emendation of *ba-galut* to *be-galuy*.

82. Matthew 5:17–20.

83. Presumably, by practicing Judaism even after his formal conversion to Islam.

84. The rationale for which rested squarely upon his Messianic claims. See above, n. 28 and chapter 3.6.

85. I see no alternative to beginning the sentence with *ve-'od ha-hitnazzelut she-hitnazzel* and placing the period before rather than after these words (as Scholem does). Cardozo's point is apparently that Sabbatai Zevi could not have defended himself before the sultan as effectively as he did, unless he were in full possession of his faculties.

86. Reading, with Scholem, *biqqesh* for *qibbel*.

87. Alluding to Isaiah 53:7. Cardozo's point is that Sabbatai Zevi was entirely passive during his transition from Judaism into Islam.

88. Cardozo fulfills these promises in the third part of the *Epistle*, which I have not included in this translation (see the introduction to this chapter): Scholem, "Iggeret...le-dayyanei Izmir," pp. 324, 330.

89. Alluding to Isaiah 59:15. I am not sure what "dreadful events" (*me'ora'im ra'im*) Cardozo is referring to.

90. April-June 1668, following his appearance in April before the rabbis of Venice (Scholem, *Sabbatai Sevi*, pp. 764–75).

91. That is, in addition to His having granted a full prophetic revelation to Nathan of Gaza, as Cardozo has earlier explained.

92. *Liftoah piv el ha-satan.* It is not clear what "adversary" Cardozo

has in mind. Perhaps it is literally Satan, but then what will become of his arguments that demons cannot act without God's permission?

93. See above, chapter 6.4.

94. This would be remarkable. Jews in Muslim countries were normally prohibited, at least in theory, from riding horses (Shaw, *The Jews of the Ottoman Empire*, p. 82; Scholem, *Sabbatai Sevi*, p. 241).

95. *Be-vadday she-lo…ba'avur galuti ki en li galut*—an extraordinary statement, which suggests that "exile" is for Cardozo less a matter of locality than of mode of life. Cf. above, chapter 3.6, and chapter 3, n. 39.

96. Referring to BT Shabbat 31a.

97. *'Illat kol ha-'illot ve-sibbat kol ha-sibbot.* "Cause of all causes" was Cardozo's regular designation, in the early 1670s, for the First Cause. (The phrase occurs regularly in this sense throughout *Abraham's Morn.*) We might infer from this oath that, as of 1669, Cardozo had not yet evolved his fundamental distinction between the First Cause and the God "whose name is the Lord." Or, alternatively, we might suppose that he is deliberately misleading his readers, with an oath that he knows to be self-contradictory and therefore meaningless. The latter seems to me the more likely option. See above, chapter 5.4.

98. That is, about the end of 1660, assuming Scholem is right in dating the *Epistle* to June 1669. But Scholem has provided good reason for emending the number "eight" to "five," and dating Cardozo's dream to the end of 1663 ("Iggeret…le-dayyanei Izmir," p. 320n).

99. Scholem supposes that these were two *successive* nights. This is plausible and will make good sense of the story. But Cardozo does not say it in so many words.

100. *U-mahshevotay 'al roshi be-mishkavi.* Cardozo is obviously drawing on Daniel 7:1, and probably 7:28 as well. (His use of the Daniel verses is even clearer in the parallel passage from his 1668 letter: Sasportas, *Zizat Novel Zevi*, p. 289.) But it is not wholly clear what he is trying to say.

101. In his 1668 letter, Cardozo says the woman was "the sister of my wife Judith" (Sasportas, *Zizat Novel Zevi*, p. 290).

102. "Lunatic," *meshugga'*, is a common Jewish polemic term for the Prophet Muhammad. I am not aware of its being used elsewhere for a muezzin.

103. We know from Cardozo's 1668 letter that this "premonition," as well as the star's actual appearance, took place in 1666. There were two months of Adar in 1666—a second Adar is inserted into the Jewish lunar calendar every few years, in order to keep it in step with the sun—and it

is not clear which of the two Cardozo has in mind. A few paragraphs further on, he speaks explicitly of "First Adar" (February 6–March 7, 1666), so I assume that "Adar" here is Second Adar. This is particularly plausible, in that the Purim festival and other special days of Adar fall in Second Adar, whenever the calendar includes two months of that name, so Cardozo might well have thought of Second Adar as *the* month of Adar.

104. That is, the Sabbath before Passover.

105. This Abraham Nunez is presumably identical with Abram Nunes Provençal, who appears at the head of the signatories to the decree of the Community Council of Leghorn (October 26, 1676), excommunicating Cardozo and anyone who might communicate with him (Bernheimer, "Some New Contributions," pp. 127–29; cf. above, chapter 3.9). The bad blood between the two men apparently went back some years, as we learn from an odd story in Cardozo's Hebrew letter of 1668: "Eight months ago, I received word that a certain profanation [*hillul*] lay in store for me. Three months ago, they [supernatural beings, presumably] came to let me know that the trouble was imminent. And lo and behold! a certain vicious lunatic of an unbeliever, Abraham Nunez by name (Clara's uncle), went completely out of his mind and began screaming the most unheard-of accusations against me and the people of my household, right out in public, to Turks and Jews and Christians alike. I was in no small danger! But they came to tell me that it would all end with his going off in tears, and so it did. The Bey actually wanted to kill him, but I would not permit him to be harmed. I, meanwhile, continued to be honored ever more highly. For the truth did come out" (Sasportas, *Zizat Novel Zevi*, p. 291). It is not easy to make sense of this curious tale, or to square Cardozo's apparent hatred of Nunez (in 1668) with his invoking him as witness to the extraordinary star (in 1669). We must assume, I think, that Nunez was known to the "judges of Izmir" as a man to be taken seriously, who had, moreover, no tolerance for Sabbatian belief. His having seen the star, therefore, was likely to impress them all the more. (It is striking, by the way, that in his 1668 letter Cardozo speaks of the episode with Nunez as a "profanation" [*hillul*]—the word he normally applies to the "profaned" Messiah, Sabbatai Zevi. Surely he is developing the parallelism between Sabbatai Zevi and himself.) On Abraham Nunez's niece Clara, see above, chapter 3, n. 63.

106. The text says "four times," but this does not seem well to fit the context.

107. The Kabbalists had developed an elaborate myth, which Cardozo shared, of the exile and degradation of the Shechinah from "Her

proper place" (Scholem, *On the Kabbalah and Its Symbolism*, pp. 146–53; above, chapter 2.5). We here see Cardozo making pious use of his youthful talent for poetry.

108. Cardozo gives a very important variant of this story in his Hebrew letter of 1668 (above, chapter 5.5).

109. According to Jewish law, a woman who has completed her period of menstruation must immerse herself in a ritual bath *(miqveh,* often spelled *mikvah)* before she is again permitted to make love.

110. Cf. the version of this story in Cardozo's 1668 letter, which gives the date of the event: "In the month of Adar 5427 [February 25–March 25, 1667], I was sick, emaciated, and weak. I told one of my wives to immerse herself [so we could make love]. They did not want to, on account of my illness, till I revealed the secret. I am about to beget a male child, I told them. His name will be Ephraim, and he will not die, as the first one did. Such and such would happen on the day he was to be born. I also said that he would be born on a Sabbath. They waited, and all the predictions came true. Not one of them failed" (Sasportas, *Zizat Novel Zevi*, p. 291).

111. Cardozo does not mention this episode in his letter of 1668. It is at least thinkable that Asher's impending birth was "announced" to him after that letter was written, that it was still impending as of June 1669, and that Cardozo expected major Messianic developments to take place during the intervening months. (The name Asher and the biblical phrase "Happy are you," are both derived from the same Hebrew root.)

Chapter 10

1. *This Is My God*, chapter III; see below, n. 38. The quotation is also from chapter III.

2. For the details, see above, chapter 6.1–4.

3. As indicated in the "Note to the Reader," I use "chapter(s)" with a *Roman* numeral to refer to one or more of the chapters into which Cardozo divided *This Is My God*. "Chapter(s)" with an Arabic numeral, by contrast, refers to a chapter or chapters in this volume.

4. Chapter XII: *mi hu ha-elohim.*

5. "Blessed be He and blessed be His Name for all eternity! Amen, amen, selah! Forever!" We would expect to find a doxology of this sort at the very end of a treatise, not in the middle.

6. The manuscript evidence is, on this point, more confusing than helpful. Two manuscripts survive: ms 1677, in the library of the Jewish Theological Seminary of America, New York (=ms Adler 1653; henceforth, ms JTS); and ms Jerusalem 8° 491, in the National and University Library, Jerusalem (henceforth, ms Jerusalem). A third manuscript, according to Scholem ("Drush zeh eli," pp. 332–35), was once in the possession of the religious academy of the Jewish community of Leghorn, Italy, but vanished during World War II. Ms JTS contains, as indicated above, seventeen full chapters and a portion of an eighteenth. It breaks off in the middle of chapter XVIII, without any explanation. Ms Jerusalem also ends in the middle of a chapter: chapter XIV. The Leghorn manuscript was evidently divided into two parts, of which part one contained fourteen chapters, while part two contained twelve chapters and a portion of a thirteenth. It is very difficult to explain why three different manuscripts all break off in the middle of a chapter—but not the same chapter. It is difficult to explain why the Leghorn manuscript seems to have been so much longer than mss JTS and Jerusalem, or what we are to do with its "part one" and "part two." (The end of chapter XIV does not seem to mark a major division of the text.) Shall we assume that the chapter divisions in the Leghorn manuscript were different from those in the other two? Or that Cardozo kept on adding postscripts to the original sixteen chapters of *This Is My God* until it had swollen to the dimensions of the Leghorn manuscript, and that ms JTS marks an earlier stage of this process? But then why does ms Jerusalem have *fewer* than these sixteen chapters? And why do all three mss end in the middle of a chapter? For the present, at least, these questions seem unanswerable.

7. See above, chapter 4.3.

8. From chapters III, X, XV; the missing passages are supplied (but with only minimal explication) in nn. 32, 94, 173.

9. Above, chapters 3.8, 4.1.

10. As was brought home to Cardozo, many years earlier, by a learned monk of Venice. See above, chapter 2.1, and chapter 8.

11. See above, chapter 2.3.

12. Above, chapter 1.4, and chapter 8.

13. The text was published by Gershom Scholem: "Two New Theological Texts by Abraham Cardozo" [Hebrew], in *Sefunot* 3–4 (1960), pp. 271–300; reprinted as "Drush zeh eli ve-anvehu le-Avraham Mikha'el Cardozo," pp. 332–69. On the two manuscripts used by Scholem, see above, n. 6. I translate Scholem's edition but have occasionally corrected his readings on the basis of ms JTS. (I have not consulted ms Jerusalem.)

These corrections are indicated in my notes. The Ben-Zvi Institute, Jerusalem, which originally published Scholem's text in *Sefunot* 3–4, kindly granted permission to publish this translation.

14. The designation of the wilderness generation as *dor de'ah*, "the generation of knowledge," is drawn from midrashic passages such as *Midrash Numbers Rabbah* 19:3.

15. For the full context of this passage—which is vital for understanding Cardozo's thinking—see the Background Texts for this chapter. Cardozo was not the only Sabbatian writer to make use of it (see Scholem, *Sabbatai Sevi*, p. 226, quoting Nathan of Gaza).

16. Scholem's readings here are misprints. Read, with ms JTS, *male'…lanu*.

17. On this method of citing the Zohar, see the "Note to the Reader."

18. Paraphrased from Zohar, I, 128a-b *(Midrash ha-Ne'elam)*. Cardozo's final sentence does not seem to have any warrant in the source.

19. I read *li-zekhut* in ms JTS for Scholem's *lizkor*.

20. *Sifrei* to Deuteronomy, para. 346.

21. Alluding to *Midrash Numbers Rabbah* 14:2 (see the Background Texts), significantly omitting the fourth of these independent inquirers: the Messiah. See below.

22. So ms JTS, referring to Zohar, I, 69b, which, however, is part of the Zohar to *Noah* and not *Bereshit*. Scholem incorrectly gives the page number as 49. (Cardozo often, though not uniformly, cites the Zohar by the page number of the Mantua edition, which was in his time, as it remains today, the standard edition of the Zohar.)

23. A slightly free Hebrew translation of Zohar, I, 73a.

24. Zohar, I, 128a *(Midrash ha-Ne'elam)*.

25. Zohar, I, 130b. Cardozo abridges the passage (which he translates from Aramaic into Hebrew) and misunderstands its opening words: *let atar penima'ah be-khol innon* does not mean "there is no place that is concealed from them," but "there is no place [i.e, heavenly chamber] that is so interior, among all these [heavenly chambers]," as the chamber that is reserved for those who know the Mystery of God.

26. The language is very suggestive of John 1:49: "Rabbi, you are the Son of God, you are the King of Israel" *(Rabbi, tu es Filius Dei, tu es Rex Israel)*. Surely here, as often, we have an imprint of the young Cardozo's Catholic upbringing, which the adult Cardozo could not erase.

27. Cardozo uses the language of 2 Kings 17:9. I am assuming he understood the verse as Kimhi interpreted it, and I translate accordingly.

(In his comment on Hosea 7:13, Kimhi links that verse to 2 Kings 17:9, while in his comment on 2 Kings 17:9, he quotes Ezekiel 8:12. The fact that Cardozo juxtaposes the same three verses leads me to think that his understanding of them has been influenced by Kimhi.)

28. *Midrash Numbers Rabbah* 14:2; see Background Texts.

29. As understood by Kimhi.

30. The first part of this sentence is a close paraphrase of Zohar, II, 175b. The second part does not occur in the Zohar but is perhaps inspired by *Midrash Samuel* 13:4.

31. I do not know any rabbinic source for this assertion. Scholem cites *Midrash Leviticus Rabbah* 19:5, but the first part of this passage only vaguely supports Cardozo, and the second part seems to contradict him (in that it speaks of the "many days" as if they were in the past). Cardozo's claim, however, seems a reasonable extrapolation from Kimhi's comment on 2 Chronicles 15:3.

32. Cardozo inserts here a parenthetical note: "We have already seen [from 2 Chronicles] that they would have no knowledge of the Divinity those 'many days' they were to worship idols, for they would remain without a true God. That is why the prophet says, 'without *teraphim*': *teraphim*, of the sort that Rachel stole [Gen 31]. He means by this that they will have no false gods that can respond to their inquiries, as they had in ancient times." The point of this note is not wholly clear, but seems to be as follows: Cardozo is troubled by Hosea's reference to *teraphim*, which he understands as idols that can be used for divination. (He normally takes for granted that idols have supernatural power of a somewhat limited kind, derived from demonic sources. See, for example, his discussion in the untitled text, ms JTS 1723, fols. 159a–62b.) If the Jews are without God (the "king" of Hosea 3:4), why should they be at the same time without idols? And Cardozo seems to answer that the Jews indeed worship idols for at least part of their exile, but, unlike the old days when they committed idolatry in the Holy Land, the idols are no longer capable of responding to their inquiries.

33. *Midrash Leviticus Rabbah* 19:5. The Sanhedrin was the supreme religious and civil court of the Jewish people in ancient times. It ceased to function after the Second Temple was destroyed.

34. On the Gemara, see above, chapter 1.4. I translate this sentence in accord with the parallel in *Abraham's Morn* (ms Ginzburg 660, fol. 34a), which reads in part: *ve-khen tir'eh she-kol ha-dinim ahar ha-talmud ba-goyim 'al sevarah zeh omer kakhah ve-zeh omer kakhah va-amittut ha-'inyan lo noda' lanu*. Should we correspondingly emend, in our text, *kelalei ha-gemara* to

kelalei ha-sevara, and translate, "deduced...on the basis of logical princi-ples"? This is plausible, but the text as we have it will also yield a coher-ent meaning.

35. Quoted, in BT Shabbat 138b, in opposition to the view (which Cardozo has just cited) that "the Jews are destined to forget the Torah."

36. Cardozo is perhaps drawing on Zohar, III, 13b. The notion that the Torah is the mystical Name of God is widespread among the Kabbalists: Scholem, *Kabbalah*, pp. 168–74.

37. Cardozo has presumably confused this verse with the very sim-ilar Proverbs 9:10.

38. This might suggest that Cardozo knew that the Temple had been destroyed in the year 70 C.E., not, as was more conventionally believed, in 68 (Sasportas, *Zizat Novel Zevi*, pp. 80, 100). The reading of the Jerusalem manuscript, "5445" (for "5446"), suits the chronology of Abraham Ibn Daud. (Gerson D. Cohen, *The Book of Tradition by Abraham Ibn Daud* [Philadelphia: Jewish Publication Society, 1967], p. 24: "The Temple was destroyed in the year 3829 [68–69 C.E.].")

39. The context in Isaiah suggests the possibility that these words are spoken by Gentiles (so Rashi and Kimhi).

40. *Midrash Genesis Rabbah* 45:21.

41. The language is drawn from Daniel 9:24, with some alterations. (The biblical text has: "to bring the eternal righteousness...to anoint the Holy of Holies.") What does Cardozo intend by "the Holy of Holies"? Rashi explains the phrase in Daniel as referring to the Ark and the rest of the sacred furniture to be brought by the Messiah; Saadiah refers it to the Second Temple (so Ibn Ezra, if I understand him correctly). The Vulgate translates *Sanctus sanctorum*, and Jerome's commentary seems to assume this is Christ. Might Cardozo have followed the Christian interpretation, transferring it from Christ to the Jewish Messiah?

42. See above, chapters 2.5, 5.3; and below, chapter 11.

43. The *sefirah Gevurah*, the divine attribute of severe judgment.

44. *Midrash on Psalms*, chapter 150, thus interprets Ezekiel 39:7–8.

45. This is actually quoted from Zephaniah 3:9, which Kimhi understands to apply to "the nations who have survived the war of Gog."

46. Zohar, III, 23a (following Scholem's emendation of *Vayyera'* to *Vayyiqra'*).

47. Zohar, III, 130b. The term *Idra* refers to either of two sections of the Zohar (the *Idra Rabba*, III, 127b–45a, or the *Idra Zuta*, III, 287b–96b), devoted to particularly esoteric speculations on the nature of the Deity.

48. The language is drawn from Jeremiah 31:33.

49. *Mi-pahad ha-yehudim.* The phrase is strikingly reminiscent of John 20:19. A parallel passage in *Ani ha-mekhunneh* (ms JTS 1677, fol. 13a) uses the language of Psalm 64:2: *mi-pahad oyev.*

50. "The redemption" is certainly, as Scholem says, a mistake for "the divine unity." Cardozo refers to Saadiah's *Book of Beliefs and Opinions*, II, 10. Cf. chapter 8, above, where Cardozo describes how a sermon by a learned monk of Venice awakened him to the problem described in this chapter.

51. Cf. *Guide*, I, 25, 64, where Maimonides speaks of the biblical "glory" as God's "created light."

52. Cardozo regularly refers to the great Spanish Talmudist Joseph ibn Migash (1077–1141), along with Saadiah and Maimonides, as one of those who consider the Shechinah a created entity. I do not know what specific passage of Ibn Migash's writings he is referring to. Cf. Scholem's note on this passage, "Drush zeh eli," p. 345n.

53. Interpreted as in BT Megillah 29a, *Midrash Leviticus Rabbah* 32:11, *Numbers Rabbah* 7:10, with the Bible's active verb ("I have sent away") read as though it were a passive.

54. Both passages occur in Isaiah 50:1, but in reverse order. The Zohar (I, 27b; III, 75a) interprets "your Mother" as the Shechinah.

55. Scholem cites as a possible source Zohar I, 203a, which represents the Shechinah as Jeremiah's "Rachel weeping over her children" (31:14).

56. *Ha-rabbanim.* Cardozo cannot here intend the ancient rabbis of the Talmud, midrash, and Zohar, but rather the medieval authorities he has earlier cited. Cf. the use of *ha-rabbanim* in the untitled text, ms JTS 1723, fol. 233b.

57. Nachmanides, *Commentary* on Genesis 46:1 (ed. Chavel, 1:244–52, especially 250–51), on which Cardozo bases much of his argument.

58. On the '*Amidah*, see above, chapter 8, n. 11. Cardozo gives a very free paraphrase of BT Yoma 53b, which does not in fact mention the Shechinah. Rashi, commenting on the passage, says that the worshiper "envisions the Shechinah as being before him," and perhaps this is the basis of Cardozo's reading of the passage as prescribing prostration to the Shechinah.

59. Cardozo gives a very free quotation, not from anywhere in BT 'Avodah Zarah, but from BT Hagigah 14a.

60. Cardozo gives an inexact quotation from BT Ketubbot 111b, which attaches the midrash to Deuteronomy 4:4, not 10:20.

NOTES

61. *Midrash Song of Songs Rabbah* 5:1.

62. *Fathers According to Rabbi Nathan*, Version A, chapter 34.

63. Jonathan ben Uzziel and Onkelos are traditionally regarded as the translators (respectively) of the Targums on the Prophets and the Pentateuch. These Targums (ancient Aramaic translations of the Bible) loom very large in Nachmanides's arguments, to which Cardozo has earlier alluded.

64. Abraham ben David (ca. 1125–98) was a prominent halakhic authority of southern France, whom later generations regarded—whether rightly or wrongly—as a pioneer Kabbalist. On Nachmanides (1194–1270), see chapter 1.4, above. Bahya ben Asher was a Kabbalist of the fourteenth century, author of a popular Kabbalistic commentary on the Pentateuch.

65. On Rashi (1040–1105), see above, chapter 1.4. *Tosafot* is the name given to a series of supplements to Rashi's commentary on the Talmud, written by halakhic authorities in northern France and Germany in the twelfth and thirteenth centuries, and printed opposite Rashi on the Talmud page. Cardozo extends the word to refer to the authors of the Tosafot.

66. The biblical reference is to an angel whom the Lord sends before the Israelites. The rabbinic and Kabbalistic tradition, starting from BT Sanhedrin 38b, applies the verse to a divinized super-angel, Metatron. See Halperin, "Sabbatai Zevi, Metatron, and Mehmed," pp. 271–308.

67. This parenthetical remark has an extremely complex background. The midrash tells us, and the Zohar repeats, that wherever the Bible attaches the conjunction "and" before the Tetragrammaton ("and the Lord..."), it is referring to God acting in conjunction with His celestial court (e.g., *Midrash Exodus Rabbah* 12:13; Zohar, I, 64b; see below, chapter X). In the symbolic code of the Zohar, this "court" represents the Shechinah (e.g., Zohar, III, 117a *[Ra'ya Mehemna]*; *Tiqqunei Zohar*, 21 [p. 45a]; cf. Cordovero, *Pardes Rimmonim, Sha'ar 'Erkhei ha-Kinnuyim*, s.v. *bet din*). When the rabbis speak of "Him and His Court," therefore, they are hinting at the pair of the Blessed Holy One and His Shechinah—fused, inseparably, into the single Hebrew word that corresponds to the phrase "and the Lord."

68. *Moreh zedeq*. Cardozo perhaps draws the phrase from *Midrash on Psalms* 102:3.

69. Cardozo shared this notion, that Aristotle had converted to Judaism, with his brother Isaac and with many of their Jewish contemporaries. See Yerushalmi, *From Spanish Court*, pp. 449–50; and the legend

cited and rejected by Leone Modena (Israel Zinberg, *A History of Jewish Literature: Italian Jewry in the Renaissance Era* [New York: Ktav, 1974], p. 154), which, like Cardozo, makes Aristotle a pupil of Simeon the Righteous. (Simeon was a semi-legendary high priest of ancient Jerusalem, famed for his saintliness, wisdom, and prophetic powers. The Talmud, Yoma 69a, represents him as having met and received the homage of Alexander the Great.)

70. Cardozo refers to the Hermetic literature, which sixteenth-century intellectuals falsely believed to be the work of the ancient Egyptian sage Hermes Trismegistus. See above, chapter 7, n. 35.

71. Nachmanides, on Exodus 5:2 (ed. Chavel, 1:300).

72. Cardozo uses the Spanish word.

73. Paraphrased from *Midrash Genesis Rabbah* 68:4.

74. Paraphrased from *Midrash Exodus Rabbah* 3:12.

75. See above, chapter 1.4.

76. Hebrew *parzufim*, the same word that Cardozo and the Kabbalists use for the anthropomorphized entities in the World of Emanation, and which Cardozo glosses as *personas*. See above, chapter 2.4.

77. *Ve-ha-sod mi mi-mi be-mi bara elleh.* This brief sentence is very cryptic, and I am not at all sure what Cardozo is hinting at. In the code language of Kabbalah, the word "who" in Isaiah 40:26 stands for the *sefirah Binah*, the "Supernal Mother." Isaiah's "these" are the lower *sefirot* that emerge from this "Mother's" womb (Tishby, *Wisdom of the Zohar*, 1:328–31). "Who created These" therefore means, in the Kabbalistic interpretation: *Binah* created the lower *sefirot*. Now, the central figure among the lower *sefirot* is *Tif'eret*, the essential and central part of the "body" of the divine being whom Cardozo calls the "Holy Son" or the "Delightful Son" *(bera qaddisha, ha-ben ha-nehmad)*. Cardozo, moreover, tends to equate the supernumerary *sefirah Da'at*—which ordinary Kabbalists made the third member of the *Hokhmah-Binah-Da'at* triad—with the "mind" of the "Holy Son." So he is perhaps saying here that the Christians got hold of the authentic Kabbalistic teaching that the "Holy Son" emerges from *Binah*'s womb, and corrupted it into the "begetting" of the Second Person of the Trinity. ("Jesus's disciples," Cardozo says elsewhere, "were not expert in the depths of theology, and therefore got themselves muddled on many issues" [Scholem, "Hadashot," p. 407; cf. *Sefer Boqer Avraham*, ms Oxford 1441, fols. 26b–27a]). Cf. below, n. 79. Cardozo's language, "the 'Who' from the 'Who'" *(mi mi-mi)*, remains peculiar. Is it possible that he originally wrote, "the 'What' from the 'Who'" *(mah mi-mi)*, combining the ideas of Zohar, I, 3b–4a, and II, 79a-b, III,

191b, and that this was corrupted by a scribe who (understandably) missed his point? It must be noted that Cardozo quotes *mi bara elleh* in *Sefer Boqer Avraham*, fol. 35a, apparently applying the biblical phrase to his Hidden God: *'ad she-ba-dor ha-aharon...yassigu min ha-katuv ba-sefarim mi bara elleh.*

78. The four "sciences" Cardozo enumerates in this sentence are, in Hebrew, *hokhmat ha-higgayon, h. ha-teva', h. ha-nefesh,* and *h. ha-mezi'ut.* For the meaning of the first three terms, see the entry on *hokhmah* in Jacob Klatzkin, *Thesaurus Philosophicus* [Hebrew] (Berlin: Eschkol, 1928), 1:290–99. Klatzkin does not list *hokhmat ha-mezi'ut* (literally, "the science of existence"), and I am speculating as to its meaning. The parallel passage in *Abraham's Morn*, fols. 2b–3a (quoted in Yosha, "Ha-reqa' ha-filosofi," p. 556), lists *h. ha-higgayon, h. ha-teva', h. ha-mezi'ut, h. ha-nefesh,* and *h. ha-ruhaniyut.* Yosha glosses the last of these terms as "metaphysics," and *h. ha-mezi'ut* as "meteorology." But I do not know his basis for this, and remain uncertain how meteorology would be a useful propaedeutic for the study of the Trinity. I translate the ambiguous text of *This Is My God* in accord with the parallel in *Abraham's Morn*, which makes entirely clear that it is the Christians—not Cardozo himself—who prohibit discussion of "this mystery" to anyone without the proper educational background.

79. Cardozo takes for granted that the Christian Trinity is a distortion of some genuine Kabbalistic triad. But which triad does Cardozo have in mind? In his so-called autobiographical letter, Cardozo contrasts the "false" Christian Trinity with the "true" Kabbalistic triad of "*Hokhmah, Binah,* and *Da'at,* otherwise called Father, Mother, and Holy Son...whereas the Gentile Trinity refers not to the *sefirot* but to the First Cause, which they believe to consist of a Father, Son, and Spirit" (Molho and Amarilio, "Autobiographical Letters," p. 223; the passage is *not* included in the translation of this text in chapter 12, below). Does Cardozo believe that the Christian Father-Son-Spirit is a distortion of the Kabbalistic Father-Mother-Son? This would suit his oblique hint in the preceding paragraph, that the "mystery" of the Trinity is somehow connected with the *sefirah Binah* (above, n. 77). But Cardozo's writings suggest other possibilities as well. He hints in one passage that the Christian Trinity is a distortion of the Kabbalistic doctrine of the three primordial lights (Scholem, "Hadashot," p. 406; a similar claim had been made nearly three hundred years earlier, in Profiat Duran's polemic against Christianity: Scholem, *Origins of the Kabbalah,* p. 354). Elsewhere, Cardozo seems to imply that the Christians have distorted the triad of First Cause (=Father), the Creator-God of the Bible (=Son), and the

Shechinah (=Holy Spirit), and this last triad is the most central to Cardozo's own thinking (see Scholem, "Hadashot," pp. 408–9, 414–15; *Sefer Boqer Avraham*, fols. 26b–27a). Cf. also Cardozo's triad of super-sefirotic entities: above, chapter 4, n. 24.

80. Cardozo uses the language of Kabbalah—"sparks of holiness…the demonic" *(nizozot ha-qedushah…ha-qelippah)*—to explain Christian doctrine.

81. Jonah 1:6, following the exposition in *Pirqei de-Rabbi Eliezer*, chap. 10.

82. *Midrash Exodus Rabbah* 8:2, Tanhuma *Va'era* #9; following Ezekiel 28:2, 29:3.

83. This passage does not exist in the Bible. It is evidently a misquotation of 1 Samuel 17:8, perhaps influenced by Joshua 17:18, Daniel 2:45.

84. See above, chapter III.

85. Cardozo uses the language of Psalm 25:14.

86. *Sefirot belimah* is the cryptic phrase used in the *Sefer Yezirah* to refer to the numbers from one to ten (see Scholem, *Major Trends*, p. 77). It occurs in *Midrash Numbers Rabbah* 14:12, which speaks of "the ten divine utterances by which the world was created, the ten *sefirot belimah*." Kabbalistic writers naturally understood the phrase to refer to the ten Kabbalistic *sefirot*. (The meaning of the word *belimah* remains a mystery.)

87. *Midrash Genesis Rabbah* 12:15.

88. E.g., BT Shabbat 55a.

89. E.g., *Midrash Exodus Rabbah* 1:36.

90. E.g., *Midrash Genesis Rabbah* 33:3.

91. Cardozo mixes in evidence from the Zohar (III, 231b, for example) with his Talmudic and midrashic citations.

92. Cf. PT Ta'anit 2:1 end (9a).

93. An inexact quotation of *Midrash Leviticus Rabbah* 29:9–10, according to the traditional printed editions.

94. For the meaning of this sentence, see above, n. 67. I have omitted the sentence that follows, which is so complicated, and requires so much background to understand, that retaining it in the text would have had no effect but to bewilder the reader. "And they [the rabbis] read the word *be-hibbare'am* [in Gen 2:4] as though it were *be-hei bera'am*: God created [heaven and earth] 'using the letter *Hei*' [e.g., *Midrash Genesis Rabbah* 12:2], using, that is to say, the attribute that is designated 'the Lesser Letter *Hei*' [e.g., Zohar, I, 93a]." The "Lesser Letter *Hei*" is Kabbalistic

code for the *sefirah Malkhut*, through which, according to the Kabbalists, God created heaven and earth.

95. Cf. Israel Davidson, *Thesaurus of Mediaeval Hebrew Poetry* (reprinted New York: Ktav Publishing House, 1970), 2:324, no. 1432.

96. This quotation is not in fact taken from the *Sifrei* or from any other rabbinic source. It is from the Pentateuch commentary of a fourteenth-century Kabbalist named Bahya ben Asher and, as such, is useless for Cardozo's argument. Cardozo seems to have had no awareness of the true source of the passage, for he frequently uses it in his various writings to demonstrate that God is neither any one of the *sefirot* nor the totality of them all, but something distinct from and superior to them.

97. Cf. Martin Hengel, *Judaism and Hellenism* (Philadelphia: Fortress Press, 1974), pp. 153–57.

98. I translate the biblical passage in accord with the commentaries of Rashi and Ibn Ezra.

99. Above, chapter VI.

100. From Exodus 3:14.

101. As in the word *hallelu-yah*, "praise the Lord."

102. As in Genesis 15:2, and frequently in the Bible. In rendering these passages into English, many translations print "GOD" in small capitals. They indicate thereby that the Hebrew has the Tetragrammaton (*YHVH*, normally assumed to have been pronounced *YAHVEH*, and normally translated into English as "the LORD"), but that these four consonants are marked with the vowels normally used for *Elohim*, "God."

103. Both *El* and *Elohim* are normally rendered "God" in English translations of the Bible.

104. See above, chapter X. The quotation does not quite suit Cardozo's purpose here.

105. On the Tannaim and Amoraim, see above, chapter 8, n. 17. *Sefer Yezirah (Book of Creation)* is a brief but extraordinarily baffling text, written in late antiquity and traditionally attributed to the patriarch Abraham. Its central subject seems to be the role of letters and numbers within the process of creation. *Bahir* is an early Kabbalistic text, perhaps written in the twelfth century, traditionally attributed to the late first-century (C.E.) Rabbi Nehunyah ben ha-Kanah. The *Tiqqunim*, or *Tiqqunei Zohar*, is a collection of seventy exegetical essays (of varying length), supplementary to the Zohar. It seems to have been written about the year 1300, shortly after the Zohar itself, but, like the Zohar itself, it claims to go back to the rabbis of the second century C.E. Cardozo takes for granted the antiquity of all these

texts, as well as of the Zohar. Hence, he imagines that Luria "revealed anew to the world the doctrine of the ancients."

106. See above, chapter 2.4. Cardozo attaches the qualifier *di-veri'ah* ("of Creation") to the title *Adam Qadmon*, on the ground that Primordial Adam was the source of the ten original *sefirot*, whose "Shattering" eventually made Creation possible. (See his explanation in *Israel, Holiness to the Lord*: Scholem, "Drush qodesh yisra'el," pp. 440–41.) I do not know whether this usage is original with Cardozo, or whether it goes back to Luria and his disciples.

107. *Midrash Genesis Rabbah* 9:2: "God created worlds and destroyed them, until He created the present worlds. He said, These please Me; the others did not please Me." Kabbalists, as far back as the Zohar, understood these "worlds" to be *sefirot*, and the midrash to allude to an earlier sefirotic system that had somehow been destroyed. In this light, they gave a symbolic interpretation to the biblical list of the "kings that reigned in the land of Edom, before there reigned any king over the children of Israel" (Gen 36:31–39): the "Edomite kings" were a system of *sefirot*, which had perished—the Bible speaks over and over of the *deaths* of the kings—before the rise of the current, "Israelite" system. On the basis of these Zoharic passages, Luria constructed his myth of the "Shattering of the Vessels," to which Cardozo here alludes. (See Scholem, *Major Trends*, pp. 265–68, for the background; and above, chapter 2.5.)

108. See above, chapter 2.4, where I explain why I translate *parzufim* as "Persons."

109. Cf. above, chapter 2.3–4. One may think of the "Irascible One" as being the single *sefirah Tif'eret*; or the six *sefirot* of which *Tif'eret* is the nucleus; or all ten *sefirot* (since each *sefirah* has ten *sefirot* of its own); or, as here, the nine *sefirot* that remain once *Malkhut* has been subtracted. (There is a further complication in this passage, in that *Keter* has been detached from the sefirotic system, as too lofty to be joined with the other *sefirot*; and an additional *sefirah* called *Da'at*, conceived as offspring and synthesis of *Hokhmah* and *Binah*, inserted in its stead.)

110. See above, n. 86.

111. Following ms Jerusalem: *megalleh sham ha-s-r ahduto u-qedushato*.

112. Menahem Recanati was an Italian Kabbalist of the late thirteenth and early fourteenth centuries. On Nachmanides and Abraham ben David, see above, n. 64. To judge from Cardozo's letter to Samuel de Paz (below, n. 114), the citation of Abraham ben David refers to the commentary to *Sefer Yezirah* printed in Abraham ben David's name. (By the time Cardozo wrote this letter, he had become aware that the commen-

tary had been misattributed; so the text of ms JTS 1677, *perush le-sefer yezirah ha-mekhunneh ha-ra'avad gam ki enennu.*)

113. The quotations from Nachmanides are not very exact, and I am entirely unable to locate the source of the second of them. Nor would I swear by the accuracy with which Cardozo depicts the views of the people he cites here.

114. As Scholem observes ("Drush zeh eli," p. 354n). The identification is guaranteed by parallels to these remarks in a letter Cardozo wrote to one Samuel de Paz: Brüll, "Mikhtav," pp. 63–71, 100–3, 139–42; *Iggeret*, in ms JTS 1677 (from which the last portion of the text, printed on pp. 101–3 of Brüll's edition, is omitted).

115. Ibid., p. 67 (in Brüll's edition); fol. 3b (in ms JTS 1677).

116. Cardozo draws on Talmudic legends concerning the translation of the Septuagint (BT Megillah 9a, PT Megillah 1:9), which enumerate a number of changes the translators made "for King Ptolemy"—including switching the sequence of the first three words of the Book of Genesis.

117. Paraphrasing *Pirqei de-Rabbi Eliezer*, chap. 3.

118. Translated in accord with Kimhi, the context in Cardozo, and Cardozo's gloss of *yiqra'* as *yakhriz be-qol gadol.*

119. The Neoplatonists, presumably.

120. Cardozo's argument becomes intelligible against the background of Bahya ben Asher's commentary on Exodus 20:2. Why, Bahya asks, does God introduce Himself as the one "who brought you out of the land of Egypt," and not the one "who created heaven and earth"? He answers that the Israelites were not eyewitnesses of the Creation, as they were of the Exodus; the miracles that accompanied the Exodus, moreover, incorporated the Creation, inasmuch as they demonstrated God's ability to alter the order of nature.

121. This is an echo of Cardozo's argument that God is "blessed"— as the Jewish liturgy attests—and therefore in need of blessing ("additional benefit") conferred upon Him by some superior Being (see above, chapter 4.3). The First Cause is entirely self-sufficient and has no superior; "blessing" the First Cause, therefore, is an exercise in pointlessness.

122. A hot topic of medieval Jewish philosophy; see Julius Guttmann, *Philosophies of Judaism* (Garden City, N.Y.: Doubleday, 1964), index, s.v. "world." Nachmanides, in his comment on Exodus 13:16, gives belief in the eternity of the world as a prime example of irreligion.

123. Referring to the Zohar's accusation (I, 56a-b) that the people before Noah's flood used their supernatural knowledge to practice black magic and, in the words of Job 21:15, to defy God.

124. Drawing upon a widespread midrashic explanation of the divine name *Shaddai* (normally translated "Almighty"): *she-dai*, the One who (*she-*) said "Enough!" (*dai*) to the world. See BT Hagigah 12a, *Midrash Genesis Rabbah* 46:3, Zohar, III, 254b.

125. *Midrash Genesis Rabbah* 8:10.

126. Cardozo presumably refers to Zohar, I, 221b, III, 107b, where, however, Adam speaks these words to the animals, not the angels.

127. *Qedem* can mean both "the east" and "antiquity." Modern translators assume the former meaning in Genesis 11:1; the rabbis of the midrash, the latter.

128. Following *Midrash Genesis Rabbah* 38:6–7 (in accord with which I read *lanu* for the second *lo*); cf. Zohar, I, 74b. In the midrash, the words are attributed to the builders of the Tower of Babel, who propose to construct at the top of their tower an idol that will brandish its sword against God.

129. Referring perhaps to passages like the bottom of I, 73b, where Nimrod's name is explained as meaning that "he rebelled *[merad]* against the Exalted King."

130. Scholem observes that the text is difficult and seems corrupt. With Scholem, I read *ella* before *ba'avur*, and I assume that the plurals *herefu ve-giddefu* should be taken as singular. Ginzberg (*Legends of the Jews*, 1:216–17) summarizes the midrashic story of Abraham's near-martyrdom in a fiery furnace.

131. *Genesis Rabbah* 41:7, following Genesis 13:12.

132. Deleting *ha-s-r* after *hayah*; the word presumably originated from a dittograph of *hayah*. Otherwise the passage will make no sense.

133. The midrash is taken from *Midrash Genesis Rabbah* 74:16. Cardozo employs the phrase "Other God" (Exod 34:14), in accord with Zoharic usage (e.g., Zohar, I, 29a; III, 179a, 277b [*Ra'ya Mehemna*]), to refer to the "other side," the demonic counterpart to the divine spheres.

134. *Midrash Exodus Rabbah* 5:14, following Isaiah 19:11. Cardozo expands his discussion of the midrash in *Abraham's Morning (Sefer Boqer Avraham)*, ms Oxford 1441, fols. 25a–26b, where he credits Pharaoh's sages with keen insight into the nature of the Jewish God.

135. Cardozo leaves the thought unfinished. He develops his point at the beginning of chapter XIV, and, more fully, in the untitled text, ms JTS 1723, fols. 168a-b: The Jews of Elijah's time were uncertain "whether it was the Honored Name [YAHVEH] who was God, or whether it was Baal; 'Baal' being Samael [Satan]…whose power had grown so formidable at the time that the Jews found themselves plunged into doubt. Was Baal

the Branch that grew from the Supernal Root [that is, the First Cause]...? Or was our blessed God...the Branch...? This is why Elijah said to the people, 'How long will you hesitate between two Branches? If the Lord is God, follow Him; but, if Baal, follow him'" [1 Kgs 18:21]. Those whom Elijah addressed, in other words, never wavered in their belief that the First Cause was the Root of Divinity. Their perplexity concerned the Branch.

136. The Aramaic phrase quoted by Cardozo occurs in Daniel 5:3 and several times in the Book of Ezra (4:24, 5:2, 16, 6:18, cf. 6:12). But the passage he has in mind is surely Ezra 1:3 (in Hebrew).

137. *Ke-fi ha-zemanim ve-ha-otot*; literally, "according to the times and the signs." I do not know an exact parallel to Cardozo's expression and admit that my translation is conjectural. Cf. *Ani ha-mekhunneh*, ms JTS 1677, fol. 5a: the Gentiles did not believe that the Jewish God was the Creator, but they did concede His greatness, "each one according to his time" *(kol ehad ve-ehad le-fi zemano)*. Has Matthew 16:3—*signa autem temporum non potestis scire?*—perhaps influenced Cardozo's usage?

138. Scholem perceives here an allusion to Acts 17:23. Cardozo perhaps subtly attacks the view, attributed in this passage to Paul, that the "unknown God" of the Athenians is identical with the biblical Creator.

139. *To'avotav*, in ms Jerusalem, is presumably a polemic allusion to the specifically pagan cultic ordinances. The better ms (JTS) omits the word.

140. See above, n. 135.

141. Paraphrased from *Midrash Deuteronomy Rabbah* 2:20.

142. Cf. 2 Chronicles 33:14. The relevance of this sentence to Cardozo's argument is unclear. Perhaps he means, as the Bible seems to indicate, that Manasseh *came to realize* that Yahveh was God, after He had saved him from his torments at the hands of the Assyrians.

143. Cardozo's argument requires the insertion of *lo'* in this sentence.

144. Exodus 15:11. The midrash *Pirqei de-Rabbi Eliezer*, chap. 42, puts the second part of this verse ("Who is like You, exalted in holiness?") into Pharaoh's mouth.

145. *'Al ha-ye'or ve-'al nilus*. I am not sure what distinction Cardozo makes between the "river" (normally equated with the Nile) and the "Nile." Cf. the Vulgate, and the traditional Jewish commentators *(Miqra'ot Gedolot)*, on Genesis 41:1, Joshua 13:3, Isaiah 23:3, Jeremiah 2:18.

146. Referring to the third plague, in which the blow of Aaron's rod turned the dust of Egypt into gnats. Cardozo seems to assume that, in speaking of "God," the wizards are referring to the First Cause.

147. Numbers 14:15–16, conflated with Deuteronomy 9:28.

148. Free quotation from Palestinian Talmud, Hagigah 2:1 (9b). Cardozo perhaps inserts this episode to indicate that not only the biblical heroes, but the Talmudic rabbis as well, were fully aware that the biblical Creator and the First Cause are two distinct beings. Very little is known of the historical Elisha ben Abuyah, beyond that he was a Palestinian rabbi of the early second century C.E. But, for reasons that are unclear, an extraordinarily powerful and moving cycle of legends grew up around him, which represented him as an almost Faust-like figure, a profoundly learned and sensitive man who became a tragic rebel against God (PT Hagigah 2:1, BT Hagigah 14b–15a). Cardozo refers here, very tangentially, to one of these legends.

149. This is not a quotation from any rabbinic text that I am aware of but seems to be Cardozo's inference from *Midrash Numbers Rabbah* 14:2. How could Hezekiah have come to know God on his own, unless his contemporaries had previously lost this knowledge?

150. *Midrash Numbers Rabbah* 14:2. See the Background Texts to this chapter.

151. The following account of the Mosaic "catechism" is based, very loosely, upon Zohar, II, 25a *(Ra'ya Mehemna)* and 161a. The distinction between the God of Israel and the First Cause, so dear to Cardozo, is entirely missing from these sources.

152. Rabbinic midrash explains that the "Solomon" of the Song of Songs is God, the "Blessed Holy One," and that His "bride" is the people of Israel. Kabbalistic interpreters, building upon the midrash, identified "Solomon" with the male aspect of divinity (the Blessed Holy One, the *sefirah Tif'eret*), and His "bride" with the female aspect of divinity, the *sefirah Malkhut*. On Solomon's "mother," see Tishby, *Wisdom of the Zohar*, I, 356; III, 1256.

153. *Sefer Boqer Avraham*, ms Oxford 1441, fols. 23b–24a, 26a-b. Cf. above, chapters 2.4, 4.4.

154. Shared, that is, by Gentile pagans and by all Jews, idolatrous and faithful alike. Cardozo prefers to forget that the spread of Christianity took place well before the completion of the Gemara.

155. The numeral is missing from the manuscripts, which leave at this point a blank space. Scholem supplies "nine." But, given that this chapter is oriented toward the Kabbalistic theories of Deity set forth at the end of chapter XI, "eleven" seems more likely. Conceivably, Cardozo was himself uncertain which chapter he was referring back to.

156. *Midrash Exodus Rabbah* 29:5. The midrash attaches "I have no

brother" to the second clause in Isaiah, "I have no son" to the third. Cardozo's version makes better sense; he has altered the text, consciously or unconsciously, in the way that was later to be proposed by the midrash commentator Zev Wolf Einhorn.

157. Ms JTS reads *ne'ezalot*, not *ka'azilut* (Scholem).

158. There follows a very free quotation from *Exodus Rabbah* 3:6, adapted in accord with Kabbalistic beliefs—detailed in Cardozo's explanatory remarks—about the significance of the divine names. Cf. above, chapter 8, the text to which n. 7 is attached, where Cardozo tells us how he first became acquainted with this midrashic passage.

159. We must insert (or understand) *zot* after *be-middah*, if the sentence is to make sense.

160. Again, a free quotation of *Midrash Exodus Rabbah* 3:6.

161. The *Zohar Hadash* is "a collection of pieces and complete works from the Zoharic literature that were missing from the printed editions [of the Zohar] and assembled from manuscripts by the Kabbalists of Safed" (Tishby, *Wisdom of the Zohar*, 1:105, n. 3). Scholem was unable to find the source of this quotation, in *Zohar Hadash* or anywhere else, and I can do no better. I do not know what the antecedent of "their" is supposed to be. The *sefirot* themselves? Or Abraham's contemporaries?

162. See above, chapter X.

163. *Sefer Yezirah* 1:2, considerably abbreviated.

164. Free quotation of Zohar, III, 70a, omitting the passage's conclusion, which is not altogether congenial to the argument Cardozo is making here: "He is they and they are He, like the flame that clings to the coal, without any distinction."

165. *Zohar Hadash*, ed. Reuven Margaliot (Jerusalem: Mossad Harav Kook, 1994), p. 111b.

166. Probably summarizing *Tiqqunei Zohar*, pp. 122b–23b. Scholem gives *Tiqqunei Zohar* 131a-b as the source of Cardozo's citation, but I cannot find there anything corresponding to this passage.

167. Cf. Margaliot, *Zohar Hadash*, pp. 109a, 111a.

168. I am not quite sure what Cardozo intends by the plural *'olamot*. I assume he means the three lower "worlds" of the Kabbalists (Creation, Fashioning, and Making) that are below the World of Emanation. On the very difficult Kabbalistic conception of the four "worlds" (which I have not discussed at all in chapter 2), see Scholem, *Kabbalah*, pp. 118–19; and, from a very different perspective, Aryeh Kaplan, *Innerspace: Introduction to Kabbalah, Meditation, and Prophecy* (Jerusalem: Moznaim, 1990), pp. 21–36. Cf. below, chapter 11, the text to which n. 50 is attached.

169. The reading *'w-'* (*abba ve-imma*, "Father and Mother") makes no sense. I see no alternative but to emend it to *t-t* ("*Tif'eret*"); which, at least in the script of ms JTS 1677, is very close graphically to *'w-'*. Read: *she-ha-sefirah tif'eret hu ha-bore' ve-hu elohei yisra'el.*

170. Using the language Cardozo has earlier attributed to *Tiqqunei Zohar.*

171. This is the standard Kabbalistic interpretation of the midrashic statement that "the patriarchs are themselves the *merkavah*," that is, the divine Chariot described by the prophet Ezekiel (*Midrash Genesis Rabbah* 47:6, 82:6).

172. *Eno*, and not Scholem's *enan*, is the correct reading of ms JTS.

173. I omit here a few very difficult sentences in the text: "It was precisely to eliminate the possibility of this error that Rav Hamnuna Sava spoke as he does in the Zohar on the Torah portion *Ha'azinu*: 'It is to the Possessor of the Nose that I pray. It is of the Possessor of the Nose that I ask mercy.' [Zohar, III, 130b. Cardozo's attribution of the quote to the Zohar on *Ha'azinu* is mistaken. As Scholem points out, he has confused the *Idra Rabba* (which he is actually quoting) with the *Idra Zuta*.] The 'nose' is used throughout [the Zohar] as a representation of *Tif'eret*. Rav Hamnuna Sava is therefore saying that he does not pray to the *Tif'eret* of the 'Holy Ancient One,' but only to its spirit. Surely, then, he would not have prayed to the *Tif'eret* of the 'Irascible One.'" The difficulties of making the Kabbalistic allusions in this passage intelligible to the modern reader are out of all proportion to its value in strengthening Cardozo's argument.

174. BT Berakhot 6a refers to God's phylacteries, 7a to His prayers. (See the Background Texts to this chapter.) God's studying Torah is mentioned in BT 'Avodah Zarah 3b, His fringed garment in *Midrash Pesiqta Rabbati* 15:17. On these "tainted texts," and their importance for Cardozo, cf. above, chapters 1.4 and 4.3.

175. *Midrash Genesis Rabbah* 19:4: "The serpent began to slander his Creator [to Eve]. God, he said, ate from this Tree [of Knowledge] and created the world. He now tells you not to eat from it, in order that you should not create other worlds. Any craftsman, you see, hates his competitors." Cardozo apparently thinks that the "Tree" in question is the sefirotic structure (often envisioned as a tree) and that the midrash hints at the doctrine that Cardozo will presently state explicitly: "Making use of the *sefirot*, and drawing upon the power of the Infinite [First Cause], [God] created and administers everything that exists" (*'immahen bara kol ha-nimza'im mi-koah ha-en-sof u-manhig otam*).

374

176. BT Hullin 60b; cf. *Midrash Genesis Rabbah* 6:3. According to the Talmud, God "diminished the moon" in punishment for her having tried to aggrandize herself at the sun's expense, and afterward regretted it. The Kabbalists, whom Cardozo follows, understood the "moon" to be symbolic of the Shechinah and the moon's "diminution" to refer to the Shechinah's exile (Scholem, *On the Kabbalah and Its Symbolism*, pp. 151–53), or, in the Lurianic system, the loss of the nine *sefirot* that She had received from the Irascible One, in order to build Her up as a complete Female Person. (Vital, in Brandwein, *'Ez Hayyim*, VI.iii.2, *Sha'ar Me'ut ha-Yareah*, chap. 2; 2:186–91. On this very difficult notion, see above, chapter 2.5.) To "atone" for this loss—that is, to "mend" it—God requires human assistance.

177. *Be-haskamah a[hat]* (ms JTS). The reading Scholem gives, *bahem kemah a[meru]*, is unintelligible.

178. *U-mi shalah yado bo bi-devarim elu yinnaqeh has ve-shalom.* This is to be understood as a rhetorical question, modeled after 1 Samuel 26:9. Cardozo is referring to Deistic critics of the Jewish God (see above, chapter 1.4, and chapter 4, n. 18), as well as Christian opponents of the Talmud. Cf. the text published in Scholem, "Hadashot," pp. 419–20: "…the believers in Jesus have declared them all [Talmudic statements of the sort Cardozo cites here] to be shocking heresies. The Pope of Rome, indeed, has on their account prohibited the reading of the Talmud even to the Jews in his domains."

179. *Midrash Genesis Rabbah* 8:9; quoted in *Yalqut* to Genesis, #14. (The *Yalqut* is a medieval compilation of midrashim, quoted from rabbinic sources.) Cardozo has added the words "but rather like Us" to the text and has suppressed its original conclusion ("nor the two of them without the Shechinah") in order to make it support his argument more convincingly. I am not aware of any commentator on the passage who says precisely what Cardozo says "the commentators" say, but it is perhaps a legitimate extension of the *Mattenot Kehunnah*'s interpretation. Cf. the fuller discussion of this midrash in *Sefer Boqer Avraham*, ms Oxford 1441, fols. 12b–13a.

180. Zohar, I, 103a-b (cf. Tishby, *Wisdom of the Zohar*, 1:400): the Shechinah's "husband" (=the Blessed Holy One) is unknown, except insofar as he can be perceived via the *sefirot*, which Proverbs 31:23 refers to as "gates." Scholem identifies Cardozo's second allusion as I, 233a, but the passage does not seem to me to fit.

181. II, 138b; translated in Tishby, *Wisdom*, 3:1029.

182. Scholem misreads the letter *nun* ("50") as *gimel* ("3").

183. I am unable to locate Cardozo's reference.

184. Quoted, rather freely, from Zohar III, 109b *(Ra'ya Mehemna)*. Moses, as the "Faithful Shepherd," is the speaker throughout the passage.

185. Scholem was unable to find a source for this.

186. On *Yezirah* and *Bahir*, see above, n. 105. *Berit Menuhah* is a fourteenth-century Kabbalistic text, attributed (falsely, according to Scholem) to one Abraham of Granada.

187. The language is taken from Isaiah 44:6, as expounded in *Midrash Exodus Rabbah* 29:5. See chapter XV, above.

188. Cardozo fulfills this promise, not in the surviving chapters of *This Is My God*, but in other writings, e.g., *Drush ha-kinnuyim*, published in Scholem, "Hadashot," pp. 410–11. It is clear from this fuller passage that his observation here has an anti-Christian thrust: the Blessed Holy One cannot be said to be "son" of the First Cause, in the way that the Christians falsely claim their Second Person to be the "son" of the First.

189. And now we understand why, according to the Talmud, He begins His prayer with the words, "May it be the will from within Me" (BT Berakhot 7a; see the Background Texts, above).

190. Cardozo does not keep this promise, at least within the extant chapters of *This Is My God*. In other writings, however (*Sefer Boqer Avraham*, ms Oxford 1441, fol. 26b; untitled text, ms JTS 1723, fols. 76b, 262b), he explains God's phylacteries as the "Father" and the "Mother" (=the *sefirot Hokhmah* and *Binah*), following *Tiqqunei Zohar* 30 (p. 74b), Zohar, I, 147a-b; III, 262b.

191. Cardozo here alludes, in very vague and general terms, to his difficult and complex doctrine of the Shechinah. See Wolfson, "Constructions of the Shekhinah," pp. 11–143; above, chapter 7.3.

192. Following Kabbalistic tradition, Cardozo understands the female aspect of Deity as the "Name," containing and encasing the male aspect.

Chapter 11

1. For background on the concept of *tiqqun*, and Cardozo's *tiqqunim*, see above, chapters 2.5 and 5.3.

2. See above, chapters 5.6—6.2.

3. Scholem tries to fix a *terminus ante quem* for the text, on the ground that Cardozo speaks about the activities of the "spirit-guides" *(maggidim)* with what seems unqualified approval. He could not have

maintained this attitude, Scholem argues, after hearing of the apostasy at Salonica in 1683, which he blamed on the seductions of evil spirits (Scholem, "Drush qodesh yisra'el," p. 428; cf. below, chapter 12.5). The argument does not seem to me entirely compelling.

4. *Midrash Leviticus Rabbah* 36:4. "Rabbi Berechiah said: 'Heaven and earth were created only through the merit of Jacob, whose name is Israel. How do we know this? [Genesis 1:1 says:] "In the beginning God created the heavens and the earth." And "the beginning" specifically designates Israel; as it is written, "Israel is holiness to the Lord, the beginning of His yield."'"

5. On the two Messiahs, see above, chapter 3.2–3. On Cardozo's Messianic self-perception in this text, cf. Elqayam, "The Absent Messiah," pp. 63–68, which approaches the issue from a Jungian perspective.

6. For a full discussion of Roshi, see above, chapter 5.5. The first word of the Torah, *bereshit*, contains the four Hebrew letters of the name *Sabbatai* (BR'ŠYT, בראשית). They are, however, out of order, and their disarrangement hints at how confused and ineffective a Messiah Sabbatai Zevi was. Cardozo's Messianic name *Roshi*, by contrast, "shines directly within the word *bereshit*," in the proper order of its letters (BR'ŠYT, בראשית). The name *Sabbatai* may be discovered within the Torah's last word, *yisra'el*, provided one is persuaded by the Kabbalistic maneuvers through which Cardozo equates the letter *lamed* with both *tav* and *bet*. The four letters of *Roshi* are obviously present within *yisra'el* (YSR'L, ישראל); they are, indeed, the four letters that *bereshit* and *yisra'el* have in common. But now they, like *Sabbatai* in *bereshit*, are out of order. This is because Cardozo, like Sabbatai Zevi, appears now in "Israel"—that is, among the Jewish people—in a mode that is confused, distorted, bewildering. (*Gam hu nihyah be-yisra'el be-vilbul*; text in Scholem, "Drush qodesh yisra'el," p. 437.)

7. See the preceding note.

8. Scholem, "Drush qodesh yisra'el," p. 432.

9. Ibid.

10. Ibid., p. 440.

11. See above, chapter 2.3.

12. Joanne Seiff pointed out to me this implication of Cardozo's "maleness," over against Sabbatai's "femaleness."

13. Quotations in this paragraph are from Scholem, "Drush qodesh yisra'el," p. 437. The designation of *Malkhut* as *aspeqlariyah she-enah me'irah*, "the mirror that does not shine," is familiar from Kabbalistic sources.

Cardozo had associated the phrase with Sabbatai Zevi as early as 1669, in his *Epistle to the Judges of Izmir*; above, p. 153.

14. Scholem, "Drush qodesh yisra'el," p. 440.

15. See above, chapter 2.3.

16. See, for example, Tishby, *The Wisdom of the Zohar*, 1:335 (quoting Zohar, III, 289b–90a): "*Hokhmah*…produced a river [=*Binah*], which welled up and emerged in order to water the garden [=the World of Emanation], and it entered the head of *Ze'ir Anpin* ["the Irascible One"], and became a brain, and from there it proceeded and surged through the whole body [of *Tif'eret*] and watered all the plants [=the *sefirot*]." Cf. Tishby, 3:1304 (quoting Zohar, III, 69a-b), where the "river" (Hebrew *nahar*) is equated with "light" (Aramaic *nehora*).

17. Tishby, *Wisdom*, 1:266 (Zohar, II, 42b–43a), 442 (Zohar, II, 166b–67a).

18. See above, chapter 4.4.

19. Cf. the somewhat different Kabbalistic understanding of Isaiah 52:13—53:12, reflected in the *Epistle to the Judges of Izmir*: above, chapter 9, n. 64.

20. Zohar, III, 189a, 192a. Cf. the very powerful passage translated in Matt, *Zohar*, p. 77: "Just as it is on the side of holiness, so it is on the other side: male and female embracing one another. The female of Sama'el is called Serpent….Two evil spirits joined together…" (from Zohar, I, 148a, *Sitrei Torah*).

21. See the preceding note. Cardozo discusses the anatomy of the demonic at some length in the untitled text, ms JTS 1723, fols. 164a–76a (partly published in Scholem, "Lidi'at," pp. 286–95). In this important passage, he explains that Samael was once, like the Irascible One, a sefirotic "body" within the World of Emanation. The two, indeed, were twins; they had emerged, fused together, from the womb of the "Supernal Mother" (= the *sefirah Binah*), as Esau and Jacob emerged from Rebecca's womb. One of the super-sefirotic beings "chose" the Irascible One (as God would later choose Jacob) and fused with the Irascible One to become His soul. Thus it was that the Irascible One *became* God. But Samael, like Esau, was rejected. He responded by rebelling against the Irascible One, with the result that he was cast down permanently from the World of Emanation. (The Christians borrowed this story from the Jews, Cardozo says, and they called Samael by the name Lucifer.) Samael's "female," the Snake, apparently fell with him; the two are now the nucleus of the demonic hierarchy, as the Blessed Holy One and His Shechinah are the nucleus of the Divine. It would seem (though Cardozo is not wholly explicit on this point) that

the Snake manifests herself as the Virgin Mary, whom the Christians worship as "queen over all the seraphim of heaven and the apex of all creation," and whom Cardozo designates as the demonic counterpart to the Shechinah. Further, just as there are two divine Messiahs, so there are two demonic Messiahs: Jesus, corresponding to Messiah ben Ephraim; and Muhammad, corresponding to Messiah ben David.

22. Elijah Kohen (the biographer, not the disciple) lists a "mending of the rods" *(tiqqun ha-maqelot)* among Cardozo's "ridiculous" *tiqqunim*, alongside "the *tiqqun* of the lamps," "the *tiqqun* of the *paras*" (פאראש; I do not know what this word means), and "the *tiqqun* of the stone that they placed at the crossroads" *(Sefer Merivat Qodesh*, p. 5). Shortly before this passage, Kohen quotes the text of a letter supposedly sent to Cardozo by various heavenly dignitaries through the mediation of the "prophet" Yom Tov Mevorakh. Here we read of Cardozo's practicing something called *tiqqun ha-mattot. Mattot*, not *maqelot*, is the word Cardozo uses for "rods" in *Israel, Holiness to the Lord*. I assume that *tiqqun ha-maqelot* and *tiqqun ha-mattot* refer to the same ritual, and it is essentially the same as the one set forth in our text.

23. The displacement from Judah to Messiah ben David is entirely appropriate: the ancient kingdom of Judah was ruled by David's dynasty.

24. We learn the location of "Messiah ben David's fountain" (which the Sabbatian believers normally called "the fountain of our Lord," *fonteyn van onse Heer*) from Coenen, *Ydele verwachtinge der Joden*, pp. 55–56, 137; cf. Scholem, *Sabbatai Sevi*, pp. 109–10. According to Coenan, Sabbatai Zevi used to pray at that spot during his teen years, and later made it into a place of pilgrimage for his faithful; they were first to visit the nearby grave of Sabbatai's mother and afterward to drink water from the spring. (I am grateful to my colleague Professor Lance Lazar for his help with Coenen's Dutch.)

25. Scholem, "Drush qodesh yisra'el," p. 432. The image of Moses as the "body," whose two "arms" are the two Messiahs, is drawn from several passages in *Ra'ya Mehemna*: Zohar III, 153b, 243a-b, 246b, 278b.

26. Cardozo's wavering on the gender of the "bringer of good news" is perhaps, in part, exegetically grounded. Isaiah 40:9 speaks of a *mevasseret ziyyon* (feminine), while 41:27 and 52:7 have a masculine *mevasser*.

27. Benayahu, *The Shabbatean Movement in Greece*, p. 81.

28. Above, chapter 5, n. 6; chapter 6, n. 20.

29. Carl G. Jung, *A Psychological Approach to the Dogma of the Trinity*, chap. 5, in *The Collected Works of C. G. Jung, Psychology and Religion: West*

and East, 2d ed. (Princeton, N.J.: Princeton University Press, 1969), 11:164–92; cf. Halperin, *The Faces of the Chariot: Early Jewish Responses to Ezekiel's Vision* (Tübingen: J.C.B. Mohr, 1988), pp. 190–93. Elqayam, "The Absent Messiah," pp. 80–82, also applies the Jungian quaternity to the understanding of Cardozo's thought, but he comes to conclusions that are substantially different from mine. (He does not discuss the four Messianic figures in this passage or the four people on the moon.)

30. See above, chapter 6.3; below, chapter 12.5.

31. We may perhaps detect one more "quaternity" of this sort in a doctrine that Cardozo attributes to Sabbatian "heretics" like Samuel Primo and Hayyim Alfandary (Scholem, "Hadashot," p. 419). These people claim, says Cardozo, that there are four primordial existents: the Supreme Infinite, the First Cause, the Primordial Will, and "His Mighty Shechinah." Cardozo accuses his opponents of having deliberately fixed on the number four in order to avoid sounding trinitarian. (The strategem is futile, Cardozo says. Once one has posited the absurd notion of a multiplicity of primordial entities, it hardly matters whether they are three or four.) The essential point is that there does seem to be a quaternity here, and its fourth member is female.

32. For example: You can count the total number of *letters* in a word or phrase, and add that number to the *gematria* value of the word or phrase. If there is more than one word in the phrase, you can add the number of *words* to the *gematria* value. You can add an extra "one" to the *gematria* value, for the *totality* of the word or the phrase. You can supplement the *gematria* value in all the ways noted here, or some of them, or none of them. (For an example of how this might work, see below, n. 64.) And this is only the beginning. See Scholem, *Kabbalah*, pp. 337–43.

33. Scholem, *Major Trends in Jewish Mysticism*, pp. 297–98; cf. idem, *Sabbatai Sevi*, pp. 235–36; Halperin, "Sabbatai Zevi, Metatron, and Mehmed," p. 292. Scholem points out that the ancient Gnostic sect of the Ophites (or "Naassenes," from Hebrew *nahash*) similarly venerated the serpent. "Were it not for the fact that the raw material of this [Sabbatian] Kabbalistic doctrine is actually to be found in the Zohar and in the Lurianic writings, one would be tempted to postulate an intrinsic, though to us obscure, connection between the first Sabbatian myth and that of the ancient Gnostical school…who placed the mystical symbolism of the serpent in the center of their Gnosis" (*Major Trends*, p. 298).

34. Beginning of chapter 8, above.

35. I translate the text published by Scholem, "Two New Theological Texts by Abraham Cardozo" [Hebrew], *Sefunot* 3–4 (1960),

pp. 245–300; reprinted in "Avraham Mikha'el Cardozo: Drush qodesh yisra'el la-adonay," in Liebes, *Researches in Sabbateanism*, pp. 425–52. (The material actually translated is contained in pp. 441–52.) I am grateful to the Ben-Zvi Institute, which published *Sefunot* 3–4, for granting permission to publish this translation. Scholem used two manuscripts for his edition: ms Jerusalem 8° 1495, in the National and University Library, Jerusalem, and ms Gaster 1430, in the British Museum, London. I have not consulted the manuscripts.

36. See above, chapter 4.4. In the immediately preceding passage ("Drush qodesh yisra'el," pp. 440–41), Cardozo gives a detailed and very complex analysis of the various "Adams" of the super-sefirotic worlds, and how they may be identified with the supreme "Causes" spoken of in the later strata of the Zohar. Cardozo's theory of the super-sefirotic entities is the most abstruse aspect of his theological system, and the only one concerning which his views seem to have shifted significantly over the years. I see no point in discussing it here in any but the most general terms.

37. The *sefirah Hokhmah* ("Wisdom") is often equated in the Zohar with the "Eden" of Genesis 2:10, which is the source of the "river" of divine effluence. See above, n. 16. Cf. also below, the text preceding n. 65; where *Hokhmah* is Sabbatai Zevi's sefirotic source of inspiration, which withdrew itself from him when he appeared on earth.

38. The Hebrew *benei adam*, "humanity," used in Isaiah 52:14, can be understood literally as "the children of Adam." As we have seen (above, n. 36), Cardozo takes "Adam" to refer to one or another of the super-sefirotic entities. Adam's "children" will then be the sefirotic (and therefore inferior) beings whom the Kabbalists designate as "Irascible One and His Female" or, alternatively, *Tif'eret* and *Malkhut*. See above, chapter 2.3–4.

39. That is, God's "soul" abandoned His "body," leaving the body comatose. For an explanation of this strange conception, see above, chapter 4.4.

40. On "the original 'Mending,'" see above, chapter 2.5.

41. Comprising the six *sefirot* from *Hesed* through *Yesod*.

42. The "Holy King" (*malka qaddisha*) is God, conceived in both His aspects of "body" and "soul." Cf. Scholem, "Drush qodesh yisra'el," p. 434, line 7, where the nine *sefirot* from *Hokhmah* through *Yesod* (including *Da'at*, an extra *sefirah* that appears in some lists) are called *gufa de-malka qaddisha*, "the body of the Holy King." Cardozo, using the language of Genesis 2:10–14, speaks of this divinity as "watering" the "Five Persons."

43. On the disciples Elijah Kohen and Daniel Bonafoux, see above, chapter 5.2. Of the spirit-guides, Nathan of Gaza, Isaac Luria, and the prophet Samuel require no further introduction. (Samuel is presumably included as a spirit-guide because of the biblical story of how a medium raised his ghost to reveal the future to King Saul [1 Sam 28].) On Yakhini and Habillo, see above, chapter 5, nn. 29–30. Asher Kohen seems to have been a Salonican scholar (see below, chapter 12, nn. 24, 42). In his note on this passage (*Researches in Sabbateanism*, p. 442n), Scholem gives the date of Kohen's death as 1645; cf. Benayahu, *The Shabbatean Movement in Greece*, p. 50.

44. *Even* is suggestive of *binyan*, "building," and the verb *banah*, "to build." Earlier, in a passage omitted from the translation, Cardozo had spoken of the Primordial Adam "building worlds and destroying them," in reference to the imperfect *sefirot* that existed before the Shattering. In this passage, which I abridge drastically, Cardozo sketches out a series of Kabbalistic associations of the word *even*.

45. The phrase "smooth stones," *avanim mefullamot* (following Scholem's very plausible emendation), is taken from BT Hagigah 12a, read in the light of Zohar, I, 16a. (Cf. Cordovero, *Pardes Rimmonim, Sha'ar 'Erkhei ha-Kinnuyim*, s.v. *avanim mefullamot*.)

46. Cardozo does not quote the entire passage, but he indicates clearly that it is all to be recited.

47. Cardozo mixes in the language of Genesis 2:8, *'eden mi-qedem*.

48. In a passage that I omit from the translation, Cardozo's "menders" go on to recite a series of biblical passages, linked with one another by the theme of "stones": Job 28:5–6, Isaiah 28:16, 54:11–13, 62:10–12. They must concentrate, as they recite the texts, on the Kabbalistic "intentions" concealed within the biblical words and letters. Through these words and these intentions, they will build up the "stones" of the Realm of Holiness (that is, the *sefirot*), as in Isaiah 54:11, and clear away the corresponding "stones" that are the demonic powers (Isa 62:10).

49. Psalm 51:17, which functions in the Jewish liturgy as the introduction to the *'Amidah* prayer.

50. The four Hebrew letters of the Tetragrammaton (*yod-hei-vav-hei*) here represent the four Kabbalistic "worlds" of Emanation, Creation, Fashioning, and Making, each of which has its own *sefirot*. (This notion of the four "worlds" is a complication of the Kabbalistic system that I chose to leave out of my discussion of Kabbalah in chapter 2. Cf. above, chapter 10, n. 168.)

51. The language of this sentence, *be-or ha-panim ha-nir'im panekha*, is strange, and I am not certain of the meaning. Cardozo's point seems to

be that the hidden "soul" of Deity, which he here addresses, may be perceived within its more evident manifestations.

52. These names are various combinations, with different vowellings, of the Tetragrammaton *(YHVH)*, *Ehyeh* ("I Am"; Exod 3:14), and *Adonai* ("the Lord").

53. The "will" is a manifestation of the First Cause, which lies "within" the God whom Cardozo worships and to which God Himself offers prayer. One invokes the "will" through the God that encases It. See *This Is My God*, chapter XVI; above, chapter 10, n. 189.

54. A normal Kabbalistic designation for *Yesod*.

55. An uncommon equation. Normally the sun is understood as a symbol for *Tif'eret*.

56. The ancestor of King David (Ruth 4:18–22).

57. I am not sure what Cardozo means by *le-mattah*, "below." "Land" is regularly used in the Kabbalah to designate the *sefirah Malkhut*, and it seems possible that Cardozo means that the "voice" of *Tif'eret* is being heard within *Malkhut*, and in these lower realms (below the "land") as well.

58. Literally, *tif'eret yisra'el*, "the glory of Israel."

59. Compare Cardozo's discussion of the prophetic status of Nathan of Gaza, in the *Epistle to the Judges of Izmir* (above, chapter 9).

60. Why does Cardozo speak as though Moses has already made his appearance? And why does he omit to mention the appearance of Messiah ben Ephraim—that is, himself? I do not know.

61. I assume that the word *qol*, after *be-arzenu*, is a scribal error, and I do not translate it.

62. The network of allusions in this passage is unusually dense, even for Cardozo. A *qav* is a rabbinic dry measure, approximately equivalent to two quarts. The Talmud (Ta'anit 24b) says that the pious Hanina ben Dosa "is satisfied with one *qav* of carobs from one Sabbath eve to the next." *Qav harovim* is, literally, "*qav* of carobs." But the word *harovim* has overtones of "ruin," and thus seems to Cardozo to hint at the Kabbalistic myth of the primordial "Shattering"—the "Death of the Kings"—in the sefirotic realms. And *qav* has the numerical value of 102—it is, indeed, the way one would normally write the numeral in Hebrew—and thus corresponds to *Zevi*. There are two *Zevis*, Cardozo is saying. One represents death and destruction; that is Sabbatai Zevi. The other represents life and mending, and this, of course, is Cardozo. Cf. Scholem's remarks on the Sabbatian legend of the *ba'alei qavin*: "Barukhyah rosh ha-shabbeta'im be-Saloniki," in Liebes, *Researches in Sabbateanism*, pp. 380–83.

63. Zohar, II, 14a.

64. This is one of Cardozo's most complex and arbitrary numerical calculations. It works as follows: "The name of the first is Pishon" = 804. The phrase has eleven letters, which brings us up to 815. "Sabbatai Zevi" = 814. Add an extra "one" for the totality of the name—and, voila! 815. (On this procedure, see above, n. 32.)

65. *Rehovot ha-nahar*, a place-name mentioned in Genesis 36:37 and 1 Chronicles 1:48. Even before Cardozo, the Lurianic tradition had identified "the broad places of the river" with *yesod de-imma*, the genital organ of the Lurianic "Person" of the Mother (Vital, in Brandwein, *'Ez Hayyim*, II.i.4: *Sha'ar Drushei Nequdot*, chap. 4, 1:114; cf. Zohar, III, 142a, and above, n. 16). Cardozo now builds upon this identification, and locates the metaphysical source of his own existence in "the Mother's genital."

66. So he tells us in his autobiographical sketch (above, chapter 8). Cardozo plainly regarded the name of his birthplace as significant, for he makes very sure that his reader knows the meaning of the Spanish name. The river imagery of *Israel, Holiness to the Lord* now provides the clue to what Cardozo perceived that significance as having been.

67. Deriving *perat*, "Euphrates," from *perot*, "produce," and referring to *Malkhut*'s pivotal role in the process of creation.

68. For a discussion of who the *Mevasseret Ziyyon* might be, see the introduction to this chapter.

69. Alluding to BT Hagigah 12a; see above, n. 45.

70. The word *'šr* does not make sense in context. Perhaps read *ahar*, "afterward"?

71. The word *kittot*, used here and in the next paragraph, might well be translated "sects." Does it refer to the religious divisions of the Gentile world? To "sects" of Sabbatian believers whom Cardozo regarded as heretics (like the apostates at Salonica)? Or, perhaps, to "bands" of demons?

72. Cardozo's point is that, when the demonic "stones" are worn away, the hopes of their all-too-human Gentile adherents will perish as well. I have translated the difficult Job passage in accord with the commentary of Ibn Ezra.

73. The reading *b'bym*, in the 1991 edition of Scholem, "Drush qodesh yisra'el," p. 450, is a misprint. Scholem's original publication of the text (*Sefunot* 3–4 [1960], p. 269; see above, n. 35) has the correct reading *ba'avanim*.

74. I translate the verse as Cardozo evidently understood it.

75. The sentence is difficult. We may assume that Cardozo has

identified the biblical "stones of the field" with the stones of the Shechinah, for "field" is a familiar Kabbalistic symbol for the *sefirah Malkhut*. "Covenant" symbolizes *Yesod*; hence the divine penis, *Yesod* (= Cardozo) is already "with" the Shechinah's stones.

76. I do not know what Cardozo means by "the field and the garden" *(ba-sadeh u-va-gan)*. No "garden" seems to have been mentioned so far, and it is possible that something is missing from the text. On "Messiah ben David's fountain," see above, n. 24.

77. This verse, called the *Shemaʿ*, has become Judaism's central statement of belief. Cf. the end of *This Is My God*, chapter I (translated above, chapter 10).

78. Which I assume to have extended from I, 206a (the beginning of the comment on *va-yiggash elav yehudah*) to the bottom of 206b. The citation of "page 207" (instead of 206) is an error, either Cardozo's or Scholem's.

Chapter 12

1. Scholem, *Kabbalah*, p. 275; *Halomotav shel ha-shabbetaʾi R. Mordekhai Ashkenazi* (Jerusalem: Schocken, 1938), pp. 5, 9, 18–19; Tishby, "R. Meir Rofe's Letters," pp. 82–84.

2. Molho and Amarilio, "Autobiographical Letters," pp. 183–241; the quotation is from the introduction, p. 185. The name of the family of the second author, which preserved the manuscript (with other important Sabbatian manuscripts) and brought it from Greece to Israel after World War II, is normally spelled "Amarillo." I follow the author's preference, as indicated in the English summaries in *Sefunot*. (For the story of the Amarillo manuscripts, see Scholem, *Sabbatai Sevi*, p. xiii.)

3. Yehuda Liebes remarks on the absence of any trace of the Lurianic system in the Kabbalistic teaching of *Abraham's Tamarisk*: "Perush sifra di-zeniʿuta," in *On Sabbateaism and Its Kabbalah*, pp. 153–54. On Cordovero and Luria, see above, chapter 2.4.

4. See above, chapter 6.6–7.

5. Cardozo repeats at this point a few of the stories, familiar to us from the *Epistle to the Judges of Izmir*, of the portents that he had experienced just before Sabbatai Zevi's appearance (Molho and Amarilio, "Autobiographical Letters," pp. 230–31; omitted from the translation). The stories are not quite the same as they had been thirty years earlier—

in place of a paralytic sister-in-law (above, chapter 9, n. 101), we are introduced to a blind sister—and I suspect that Cardozo's memory was beginning to fail.

6. Zohar, III, 239a *(Ra'ya Mehemna)*. Cardozo's quotations of the passage are a bit free, and they do not agree exactly with one another. He seems also to have read (or misremembered) *amar ra'ya mehemna*, in place of our text's *ameru ra'ya mehemna*, for he plainly understands Moses to have been the speaker of these words and not the person addressed (by the assembled rabbis).

7. This last point is implied in the continuation of the passage from the *Faithful Shepherd*: "...as it is said, 'The Bride's reward is [for?] the suffering' [BT Berakhot 6b, very much reinterpreted]. 'And he lay down in that place' [Gen 28:11]: if he [the devotee] possesses the twenty-two letters of the Torah, She lies with him." (The expositor understands *va-yishkav* in the biblical verse as though it were *yesh k-b*, "there are twenty-two.")

8. I translate the text published by Isaac R. Molho and Abraham Amarilio, from one of the Dönmeh manuscripts brought from Salonica by Amarilio's family (details given above, n. 2). I am grateful to the Ben-Zvi Institute, Jerusalem, which published the text in *Sefunot* 3–4, for granting permission to publish the translation. I have not consulted the manuscript.

9. Published in Fuerth, 1701. See the introduction to this chapter.

10. See above, n. 3.

11. When the Bible and the rabbis speak of God's "Name," Cardozo believes, they are not speaking simply of the word "Yahveh," but of the female aspect of the Divinity (the Shechinah) in which the male aspect encases and manifests Himself. See above, chapter 2.

12. See below, n. 91.

13. I do not know who this "emissary" *(shaliah)* might have been. Nor is it clear whether the third-person pronouns in this sentence refer back to the emissary or (as I think more likely) to Primo.

14. In Jewish literature of late antiquity, Metatron appears as the name of a super-angel, a human being (the biblical Enoch) who has been raised to angelic and indeed near-divine status. (One of his titles is *Lesser Yahveh*.) He continues to play a prominent role in the Zohar and other Kabbalistic texts. Sabbatai Zevi's own self-perceptions, as well as the perceptions of Sabbatai by many of his followers, seem to have been heavily influenced by the mythology that surrounded the figure of Metatron, hence the comparison Sabbatai makes in this passage. (See Halperin,

"Sabbatai Zevi, Metatron, and Mehmed," pp. 271–308.) Cardozo himself, as far as I can tell, had no particular interest in Metatron.

15. *Navi muhzaq*; see above, chapter 9, n. 10.

16. That is, the prophecy of the "Suffering Servant," which Cardozo—and, obviously, Ezra Halevi—understood to refer to the Messiah. See Cardozo's *Epistle to the Judges of Izmir* (above, chapter 9; especially n. 12).

17. We know practically nothing about Jacob Ashkenazi, other than that he died not long before 1680. The obscurity that surrounds the man is itself something of a mystery, since he seems to have been widely regarded in the 1670s as one of the leading intellectuals of the Sabbatian movement, perhaps second only to Nathan himself (Cardozo, in Molho and Amarilio, "Autobiographical Letters," pp. 217–18; cf. Halperin, "The Son of the Messiah," p. 162). I do not know precisely what Ashkenazi meant by the remark Cardozo here attributes to him—surely, one of the most memorable epigrams in the Sabbatian literature—and I very much wish that Cardozo had not decided at this point to change the subject.

18. On the special significance of the *sefirah Tif'eret* as the embodiment of God, see above, chapter 2.3.

19. *Qehillot*. The Jewish community, in a large Ottoman city like Edirne, might be divided into many autonomous *qehillot* "according to national, provincial and even city origins…each with its own Rabbi, synagogue, hospital, cemetery, schools and slaughterhouse, and each providing members with secular and religious leadership" (Shaw, *The Jews of the Ottoman Empire*, p. 48). In the paragraphs that follow, Cardozo seems to use the word *qehillot* in the unusual sense of synagogue buildings.

20. On this episode, which took place in the fall of 1697, see above, chapter 6.6–7.

21. *Be-erez ha-hayyim*, literally, "in the land of the living." Given the context, I think "the living" must be a euphemism for the blessed dead. Cf. BT Berakhot 18a-b, and the use of *bet hayyim* ("house of life") as a euphemism for a cemetery.

22. *Manzur qiyaya shel sha'm*; we shall hear more of him below. His surname is apparently a dialectal variant of Turkish *kethuda*, "steward" (see below, n. 75). The biographer Elijah Kohen refers to him as "Eliezer of Damascus," after the biblical character who is Abraham's steward (*Sefer Merivat Qodesh*, p. 15, following Gen 15:2).

23. Reading *ella* in place of *ve-lo*.

24. On these spirit-guides *(maggidim)*, see above, chapter 11, n. 43 (where they are attached to members of the Izmir circle). On the concept

of the spirit-guide, and the identity of Roshi, see above, chapter 5.5; on Yom Tov Mevorakh and Samuel Galimidi, see chapter 5.3.

25. The text has *ve-lo aherim 'immahem*, but the context shows this must be wrong; others besides Cardozo and his five disciples were present. I presume the original reading must be *ve-la-aherim 'immahem*. See also the next note.

26. *Ve-lo ra'u*, "they did not see," seems impossible. I think we must emend to *ve-elleh ra'u*.

27. The seven biblical saints, from Abraham to Solomon, mentioned in the preceding paragraph.

28. The use of *aleph-hei* as an abbreviation for "Abraham" is very unusual, but the context does not seem to allow for any alternative. (*Adam ha-rishon* [Adam], *eliyahu ha-navi* [Elijah], and *adonenu ha-mashiah* [the Messiah] will not suit the context. *Aharon ha-kohen* [Aaron] is possible, but Aaron ought to come after Moses, not before.) Perhaps we should emend to *aleph-aleph, avraham avinu*.

29. 1 Samuel 12:16–18.

30. In canceling the promised Redemption. The language is taken from Isaiah 28:21.

31. *Ba-migd[al]ot*, literally, "in The Towers." I am not sure whether the reference is to Gallipoli (as Molho and Amarilio say, in their footnote on this passage) or to Canakkale (Kale-i Sultaniye, "the Sultan's castle," near ancient Abydos), twenty-five miles to the south, at the narrowest and most heavily fortified part of the straits of the Dardanelles. The designation, "The Towers," would seem to me to favor the latter option, as would Cardozo's subsequent reference to having lived "in The Towers and in Gallipoli" (below, n. 73).

32. That is, Sabbatai Zevi, Nathan of Gaza, Luria, and a mysterious woman. On this episode, and the identity of the woman, see above, chapter 6.3, and the introduction to chapter 11.

33. It seems that *kol oto ha-laylah* must go with what follows rather than with what precedes. (*Va-ya'asu ken kol oto ha-laylah* would imply that they stood in the spot all night long, whereas the sequel suggests that they left after two hours.) The use of *kol*, however, is awkward. Is it perhaps a dittograph for *ken*?

34. The reference is to a refined technique of *gematria*, in which the Tetragrammaton can be given different numerical values according to how one spells the names of the four letters that comprise it. (For the details, see Scholem, *Kabbalah*, pp. 341–42.) Each of these different values is then linked to one or another divine manifestation within the sefirotic

world. (Cf. Cardozo's remarks on *havayah de-alafin*, from *Tiqqunei Zohar Hadash*, in the untitled text, ms JTS 1723, fol. 222a.) The Lurianic "Person" of the Holy Ancient One overlaps with the Patient One but is not quite identical to it. See Scholem, *Kabbalah*, p. 141; and idem, *Major Trends in Jewish Mysticism*, p. 270.

35. Cardozo refers to 2 Kings 19, Daniel 4.

36. *Kausos* (literally, "burning") is the Greek technical term for the disease, which Cardozo had learned from his medical books. *Fiebre ardiente* is how one would call the disease in lay language. See the Loeb Classical Library *Hippocrates*, vols. V–VI, trans. Paul Potter (Cambridge, Mass.: Harvard University Press and London: William Heinemann, 1988), "Index of Symptoms and Diseases," s.v. "Ardent fever"; and the Loeb *Celsus: De Medicina*, trans. W. G. Spencer (Cambridge, Mass.: Harvard University Press and London: William Heinemann, 1935), 1:140 (II.8.19): *febrem autem ardentem, quam Graeci causoden vocant....*

37. Cardozo tells the same story, with some variations, in the untitled text, ms JTS 1723, fols. 109a–10b. His variant of the conclusion is particularly interesting: "One of those black-clad beings stood for fourteen days by the head of my bed. Afterward they departed, and bade me 'Peace.' I said to them, 'There is no peace, saith the Lord, to the wicked.' They answered, 'Gran hakham eres, muncho sabes.' I said to them, 'Off with you to Salonica! There is no food for you here.'" (The Spanish means, "You are a great scholar, you know much." My student Jonathan I. Tepper informs me that *muncho* is a common Judeo-Spanish variant for *mucho*.) On Cardozo's "fourteen days," see Hippocrates, *Affections*, 11: "Ardent fever *[kausos]*...has its crisis, when it is shortest, on the ninth day, when it is longest, on the fourteenth day" (5:20–23; see preceding note).

38. That is, the Sabbatian scholars who remained faithful to Judaism and who were forced out of Salonica by Jacob Querido's persecution. See Benayahu, *The Shabbatean Movement in Greece*, pp. 96–99; and chapter 6.4, above.

39. Like the pit into which Joseph was thrown, according to the rabbinic midrash (BT Shabbat 22a, Hagigah 3a, *Midrash Genesis Rabbah* 84:16, on Genesis 37:24).

40. A Sabbatian prophet who appeared in Morocco toward the end of 1673, claiming to be Messiah ben Joseph and prophesying the Redemption for Passover 1675. He caused a very considerable stir among the Jews of North Africa and seems to have died in 1676 or shortly thereafter. There is a brief notice about him in Sasportas, *Zizat Novel Zevi*, pp. 368–69, and a fuller account in Baruch of Arezzo, *Zikkaron li-vnei Yisra'el*,

pp. 73–76; cf. Elie Moyal, *The Shabbetaian Movement in Marroco* [sic]—*Its History and Sources* [Hebrew] (Tel Aviv: Am Oved, 1984), pp. 116–34.

41. *Mekhilta, Sifra,* and *Sifrei* are the names of three ancient midrashic texts. On the terms *aggadot* and *Gemara,* see above, chapter 1.4.

42. Cf. chapter 11, n. 43. It would appear that Habillo remained Bonafoux's spirit-guide over the long term, while Isaac Luria and Asher Kohen were reassigned at least once to other disciples.

43. Reading *shel* for *'al.*

44. See above, chapter 3.5, 3.9.

45. A village on the western shore of the Bosporus, just outside Istanbul, about three miles north of the mouth of the Golden Horn. Murray's *Handbook for Travellers in Constantinople, Brusa, and the Troad* (London: John Murray, 1900), p. 95, describes it as "a large and not very clean village inhabited principally by Armenians and Jews, and celebrated for its gardens." Jews had settled there in the seventeenth century (Mantran, *Istanbul,* p. 59).

46. A distinguished halakhic scholar, chief rabbi of Izmir from 1662 until his death in 1673. He was the first and foremost of the "judges of Izmir" whom Cardozo had addressed in 1669. Cardozo apparently had ties with his family, for Elijah Kohen (the biographer) claims that Cardozo got possession of Benveniste's personal library after his death, and, desperate for cash, sold it for a pittance. (It would appear that the books were a gift of Benveniste's widow. But it is also possible that the suffix of *ishto* refers to Cardozo, not Benveniste, in which case Cardozo will have married a close relative of Benveniste's and gotten the books from her.) See Kohen, *Sefer Merivat Qodesh,* p. 31.

47. Understanding *otam* for *oto.*

48. *Fereje.* On the use of this word for the caftan, see Robert Mantran, *La Vie Quotidienne à Constantinople au Temps de Soliman le Magnifique* (n.p: Hachette, 1965), p. 258.

49. Molho and Amarilio suggest this is Shem Tov Shemaiah, who appears a few years later as part of the Izmir circle (above, p. 256). Cf. Kohen, *Sefer Merivat Qodesh,* p. 5.

50. I am not sure whether Cardozo means that he will summon Yakhini *from* a position opposite Kiaya's or *to* a position opposite Kiaya's. We have already seen that Cardozo had assigned Yakhini—who had died only a few months before the time this story is supposed to have taken place—to be Kiaya's spirit-guide.

51. *Mavi, fereje,* and *suf* are all Turkish words, the last a loan-word from Arabic. (I am grateful to my former student, Jonathan I. Tepper, for

his help with the language of this passage.) On *fereje*, see above, n. 48. On *bonete*, "cap," as a distinctively Jewish form of headgear (as opposed to the Muslim turban), see Scholem, "Perush mizmorei tehillim me-hugo shel Shabbetai Zevi be-Adrinopol," in Liebes, *Researches in Sabbateanism*, p. 111, and n. 73; and cf. Samuel Romanelli, *Travail in an Arab Land*, trans. Yedida K. Stillman and Norman A. Stillman (Tuscaloosa, Ala., and London: University of Alabama Press, 1989), p. 66.

52. The last word is Arabic (cf. below, n. 55). Kiaya's Syrian origin will explain why his Spanish is peppered with Arabic words.

53. *Rambam* is the standard Hebrew designation for Maimonides (from the initials of his name, **R**abbi **M**oses **b**en **M**aimon). *Rabbam* would mean "their master." Kiaya is apparently doing his best to come up with the answer Cardozo wants to hear, but is not altogether sure what that answer is. He therefore says something that sounds more or less like *Rambam* but can be construed as the neutral "their master," in the event that the invisible person sitting next to Benveniste is not supposed to be Maimonides after all.

54. "Samuel" is surely an error for "Solomon."

55. This answer is of course no answer at all. Yom Tov Mevorakh obviously has no idea what answer Cardozo expects Maimonides to give, and he invents, in his desperation, a brilliantly meaningless piece of equivocation. Mevorakh's imagination seems to have been stimulated by the "earring" that Maimonides's ghost (according to Kiaya's description) was wearing for the seance. The Arabic word that Kiaya had used for "earring," *halqa*, sounds very much like the Hebrew root *hlq*, which turns up twice in "Maimonides'" second sentence (*im hefzo lahloq bi-sevarot halaqot…*; reading *hlqwt* for *hlwqwt*), and presumably it was Kiaya's use of this word that inspired Mevorakh's creativity.

56. This story aside, we know practically nothing about Elijah Yanni. He seems still to have been a member in good standing of the Constantinople circle as of Heshvan 25, 5442 (November 6, 1681), for Elijah Kohen represents him as participating on that date in Cardozo's "*tiqqun* of the seven shepherds and eight princes of mankind," along with the Galimidis, Yom Tov Mevorakh, Mansur Kiaya, and ten other men (*Sefer Merivat Qodesh*, p. 16 bottom). The story Kohen tells on page 19, which seems to take place shortly before the failed Redemption of 1682, points to considerable tension between Yanni and the Galimidis.

57. AMIRAH is a standard Sabbatian designation for Sabbatai Zevi. It is comprised of the initials of the phrase *adonenu malkenu yarum hodo*,

"our Lord and King, may his majesty be exalted." See Scholem, *Sabbatai Sevi*, p. 263.

58. It is hard to imagine, at first sight, how the banal remark attributed to Sabbatai Zevi could have been perceived to contain anything remotely "heretical," much less the "three heresies" detected by Cardozo. For informed speculation on what the "heresies" might have been, see Nissim Yosha, "Ha-beri'ah ve-ha-zeman: 'vikkuah' te'ologi-filosofi shel Qardozo 'im Natan he-'azati," in *Mehqerei Yerushalayim be-mahshevet Yisra'el* 12 (1996), pp. 275–84.

59. Haskoy was, in the seventeenth century, one of the principal Jewish neighborhoods of Istanbul (Mantran, *Istanbul*, p. 69). It remains so today.

60. Cf. Scholem, "Te'udah le-toledot Nehemyah Hayyun ve-ha-shabbeta'ut," in Liebes, *Researches in Sabbateanism*, p. 484. Scholem assumes that Vilisid was Cardozo's landlord. It seems to me more likely that he was the host of the party where Uzziel's scheme was hatched, and I have translated *ha-ba'al ha-bayit* accordingly. Baruch of Arezzo's list of the forty-one Constantinople householders (including Solomon Galimidi) who pledged in 1666 to devote their resources to persecuting people who did not believe in Sabbatai Zevi (*Zikkaron*, p. 55; cf. above, chapter 5.3), includes a name that can be read "Joseph Vilisid." I assume that Joseph Vilisid was a relative of Jacob Vilisid, probably his father.

61. It is evident from the sequel that the *tiqqun* was directed toward the "Mending" of *Yesod*, and it is surely no coincidence that the ritual was interrupted by the unwelcome announcement that Cardozo's own phallus was substantially in need of "mending."

62. Latin *verruca* is still the standard medical term for "wart." See below, n. 65.

63. This, the reader will observe, is not precisely what happened. There is no reason to think that the woman had any idea of the existence of Cardozo's genital wart until he made the mistake of telling her about it.

64. The students? The three women? People in general?

65. Cardozo refers to the Jewish practice of *hattafat dam berit*, the drawing of a drop of blood from the remains of the foreskin of an adult convert who has already been circumcised. According to rabbinic legend, several biblical heroes—notably, Moses—were born already circumcised (Ginzberg, *Legends of the Jews*, 5:273–74, 399; cf. Halperin, "The Son of the Messiah," p. 149). I suppose it is possible that Cardozo, like them, was born without a foreskin. But, even assuming this, his story is incoherent. Why would Joseph Gabbai have tried to circumcise a man who was

already without a foreskin? And what exactly would he have cut away? One is tempted to suppose that the accusations were in fact true, and that Cardozo was never circumcised (cf. Yerushalmi, *From Spanish Court*, p. 202). But then why does Cardozo seem to have been so eager to get himself examined? His genital wart, moreover—"far from the corona and near the body"—can hardly be related to anything that Gabbai may have done; it seems virtually certain that it was venereal in origin. (I am indebted to my wife, Rose Halperin, M.D., for pointing this out to me.) I am inclined to conjecture that Cardozo had acquired a case of venereal warts while he was a young man in Spain, presumably from one of the ladies of Madrid whom he spent his nights serenading (above, chapter 1.3). The condition persisted for much of his life. He was on some level aware of how he had come by it, and it caused him intense shame. (There is a ferocious Kabbalistic taboo against "desecrating" the sacred organ of the covenant by inserting it into an "unclean" woman like a Gentile or a prostitute [Tishby, *The Wisdom of the Zohar*, 3:1364–72].) The tension between his contradictory impulses—to confess the fact of how he had "blemished" the precious organ and to conceal it from others and from himself—is what underlies the confusion and incoherence of his narrative.

66. The year of the Sabbatian Messianic enthusiasm.

67. See above, chapter 6.7.

68. Exodus 8:15. Cardozo has the context wrong. The reference is to the third plague (gnats), not the tenth (the slaying of the firstborn). The error presumably springs from Cardozo's wish to see the Divine and the Demonic as nearly equal in power; it is only in the final testing that the Divine shows itself stronger. It is also striking that Cardozo speaks of the killing of the "sons" *(banim)*, not of the "firstborn," and that, in a few more paragraphs, he will speak of God's killing his own sons. (Cardozo certainly knew better. See *This Is My God*, chapter XIV [translated above, chapter 10]; and his unpublished treatise *The Lord Is Good to All*, ms JTS 1677, fol. 5a. The error recurs, however, in the untitled text, ms JTS 1723, fol. 78a.)

69. Cardozo refers to Sabbatian "heretics," like Samuel Primo. He puns on the Hebrew words *sod* ("mystery") and *shod* ("plundering, devastation"). The phrase *shod va-shever* is taken from Isaiah 59:7, 60:18, Jeremiah 48:3.

70. Cardozo refers to Hayyim Alfandary, whose story he has told at length in a passage omitted from the translation. Alfandary, Cardozo claims, had once been a student of his, who would travel to Constantinople to hear Cardozo's lectures, and who was even willing to incur Samuel Primo's wrath by defending Cardozo in his presence. But

eventually he fell into the grip of the demons. He betrayed Cardozo and joined forces with Primo. He taught that Sabbatai Zevi was now divine and that he himself (Alfandary) had taken Sabbatai's place as Messiah ben David. If Cardozo is to be believed, Alfandary even encouraged people to convert to Islam and to desecrate the Torah. See Molho and Amarilio, "Autobiographical Letters," pp. 222–26; Scholem, "Hadashot," pp. 418–19.

71. This episode took place in the late summer of 1681. See Kohen, *Sefer Merivat Qodesh*, p. 12–13 (where the "slander" of which Cardozo complains is of course repeated); above, chapter 5.6.

72. It is not clear just what Cardozo means by this remark. By "evil," does he mean the reprisals that the Rodosto authorities might bring upon themselves by refusing to comply with the decree from Constantinople? Or does the clause explain why they handed the document over to Cardozo: they were intimidated by the supernatural "evil" that Cardozo might inflict upon them? Or does "them" refer to the signatories on the decree, whom the Rodosto authorities have exposed to Cardozo's supernatural revenge by revealing to him who signed the document? All three options are thinkable, and the sequel perhaps points to the last.

73. *Ba-migdalot u-ve-gallipoli*. See above, n. 31.

74. On this strange, obscure, and disturbing episode, see above, chapter 6.5 and chapter 6, n. 27.

75. *Kiaya* is one of a very large number of variants of the Turkish word *kethuda*, which means "steward" or "lieutenant" (Albert Howe Lybyer, *The Government of the Ottoman Empire in the Time of Suleiman the Magnificent* [Cambridge: Harvard University Press, 1913], pp. 96, 125; cf. the entry in the modern *Oxford Turkish Dictionary*, which glosses *kethuda* as "steward"). Cardozo uses the word three times in this paragraph. The second and third times, it certainly refers to the personal steward of the kaimakam (see the next note), and I have translated it accordingly. (Recall that one of Cardozo's disciples, Mansur of Damascus, bore the surname *Kiaya*, "steward.") But the chief rabbi of Istanbul also had a *kiaya* ("lieutenant"), to whom he delegated the task of representing the Jewish community before the Ottoman government (Mantran, *Istanbul*, pp. 59–60; Shaw, *The Jews of the Ottoman Empire*, pp. 42–43; Mantran and Shaw use the form *kahya*). I have no doubt that Elijah Falcon was *kiaya* in this official sense of the word—which, obviously, made him as formidable an enemy within the Jewish community as Cardozo could ever dread to have.

NOTES

76. The Grand Vizier's deputy, who, in the seventeenth century, functioned effectively as the governor of the city of Constantinople: Mantran, *Istanbul*, pp. 126–28.

77. Reading *mappahei nefesh* [based on Job 11:20] *kefuyei rosh ve-avelim* [based on Esther 6:12, with *kefuyei* substituted for *hafuy*].

78. Reading *ta'ir* for *he'ir*.

79. On this episode, see above, chapter 3.9. I am not aware of any evidence, outside this passage, that foul play was involved in Osman's death, and it is possible to understand Cardozo to mean that the assassination was plotted but never actually carried out. By *leventes*, Cardozo means the *Leeuwendaalder* ("lion-dollars"), an originally Dutch currency that enjoyed great popularity in the Ottoman Empire (Mantran, *Istanbul*, pp. 240–42; Konrad Schneider, in Michael North, *Von Aktie bis Zoll: Ein historisches Lexikon des Geldes* [Munich: C. H. Beck, 1995], pp. 224–25). He elsewhere refers to these coins as *arayot*, "lions" (Molho and Amarilio, "Autobiographical Letters," p. 231).

80. Reading *u-ve-kha'as* (not, as do Molho and Amarilio, *u-ve-nes*).

81. Perhaps an inaccurate reference to the midrashic tradition that the demons are at large from Tammuz 17 through Av 9 (Ginzberg, *Legends of the Jews*, 3:186).

82. A district of Istanbul, on the other side of the Golden Horn from Haskoy, with a very large Jewish population (Mantran, *Istanbul*, p. 59).

83. On Cardozo's old enemy Yom Tov Romano, and his role in the composition of Elijah Kohen's biography, see above, chapter 6.6.

84. This is clearly a mistake. Cardozo left Istanbul in the spring of 1682; the next episode takes place in the fall of 1685. Perhaps we are to read *sheloshah* ("three") in place of *hamishah* ("five").

85. An appropriate question for the Jewish New Year, when God decides upon the fate of persons and nations for the coming year.

86. Cardozo seems to address these words to both Alcaire and his wife (Galimidi's sister). On Meir Alcaire, and his Sabbatian background, see Scholem, *Sabbatai Sevi*, p. 429.

87. I do not know where Yeni Khan (New Inn) was located. There is a structure of this name in modern Istanbul, but it was not built until 1764, well after Cardozo's time (Hilary Sumner-Boyd and John Freely, *Strolling Through Istanbul: A Guide to the City* [Istanbul: Redhouse Press, 1972], p. 183).

88. That is, Galimidi intended to travel the three miles or so down the Bosporus, from Ortakoy to Istanbul. But the storm carried his boat into the Sea of Marmara.

89. *Wšyʻw*. I do not know what this word means.

90. Cardozo refers to the traditional Jewish rite of *tashlikh*, performed on the first day of the New Year festival, in which one goes to a body of water and symbolically throws one's sins into it. Galimidi's act—for which, of course, Cardozo has no evidence whatever beyond the testimony of Isaac Luria's ghost—neatly explains for Cardozo why, on the second day of the festival, Galimidi was condemned to death.

91. Zohar, *Raʻya Mehemna*, III, 239a. The text of the Mantua edition is slightly different from Cardozo's quotation; in particular, it speaks of "the final exile" instead of "the final generation." Cardozo presumably has allowed himself a small liberty. (He again quotes the passage, somewhat more accurately, in the sequel.)

92. A close paraphrase of *Tiqqunei Zohar* 21 (ed. Zhitomir, p. 62a).

93. Reading *bah* for *lah*.

94. Omitting the word *li* before *ve-yesh*, which is meaningless in context and best explained as a scribal error: the copyist began to write *wyš* as *lyš*, perhaps initially assuming that it was an abbreviation for *le-yisra'el*. He wrote only the first two letters, then stopped and corrected his error.

95. *Tiqqunei Zohar* 6 (ed. Zhitomir, p. 24a), where the prophet Elijah, descended from heaven, is addressing Rabbi Simeon ben Yohai and his students.

96. *Zohar Hadash*, ed. Margaliot, p. 56b: "On that day the Ten Tribes will be aroused to wage war against the four corners of the earth, along with the Messiah who is anointed over them...that Messiah being of the tribe of Ephraim, a descendant of Jeroboam son of Nebat...." The geographical details, and the singling out of the tribes of Reuben, Gad, and Asher, seem to be Cardozo's own contribution to the eschatological prophecy.

97. "Arabia Felix (Latin: 'Happy, or Flourishing, Arabia'), in ancient geography, the comparatively fertile region in southwestern and southern Arabia (in present-day Asir and Yemen), a region that contrasted with Arabia Deserta in barren central and northern Arabia and with Arabia Petraea ('Stony Arabia') in northwestern Arabia..." (*Encyclopaedia Brittanica*).

98. Neither of these two quotations is exact. Cardozo changes the word order of the second and makes a small but significant change in the first, replacing *le-ʻenei goyim rabbim* ("by many nations") with *le-ʻenei ha-goyim* ("by the Gentiles").

99. *Mukhtar bihidah ba-haqirah ha-zot*. I interpret these difficult words in accord with a similar passage in the *Epistle to the Judges of Izmir*

(above, p. 133), and understand *yehidah* in its Kabbalistic sense of the supreme level of soul. Cardozo's views have changed substantially since 1669, now that Sabbatai Zevi is dead and the "wonderful and terrible [Messianic] acts that are needed to bring us out of exile" have been redefined as the discovery of the secret of God's identity. But Cardozo will not let go the belief that the task of unearthing the long-forgotten knowledge of God, though indeed pursued by the esoteric college of which Jeremiah prophesied, most properly belongs to the Davidic Messiah.

100. Cardozo draws upon Kabbalistic tradition: the last letter, *hei*, of the four-letter Name of God *(YHVH)* is a representation of the Shechinah. As long as the Shechinah is degraded and misunderstood, therefore, the Name remains incomplete.

101. Reading *mushba'* for *mashbia'*. The reference is to Zohar, II, 161b, which describes the oath administered to the soul about to be born. See *This Is My God*, chapter I; translated above, chapter 10.

102. Literally, "seek me" *(baqqeshuni)*, as in Isaiah 45:19, which Cardozo draws upon here.

103. Following Isaiah 44:7, more or less as understood by Rashi, but, for Cardozo's use of the passage to make sense, we must take the preposition in *mi-sumi* as comparative rather than temporal.

Chapter 13

1. Ms Ginzburg 660 (Moscow); translation published by courtesy of the Russian State Library, Moscow.

2. *Mi-zeh u-mi-zeh yazzeh*, literally, "from this and from this shall he sprinkle," which is fairly meaningless. I assume Solomon ben David has inadvertently conflated two Talmudic expressions—BT Berakhot 28a, *mazzeh ben mazzeh yazzeh*, and Ketubbot 17a, *kol min den ve-khol min den semokhu lana*—both of which make essentially the point conveyed in the translation (with implied disparagement of those who are currently in positions of authority).

3. *Vayyissa meshalo vayyomar*, from Numbers 23:7, 18, 24:3, etc. I translate in accord both with the biblical and the present context. But surely Solomon ben David also intends an allusion to his biblical namesake, the author of the Book of *Mishlei* (Proverbs)—who, the wisest of the ancients, now humbly pays tribute to one whose wisdom outshines his own. In the translation that follows, I have tried to convey the poetic

quality of the original. But I do not attempt to replicate its intricate rhymes or its acrostic structure. (The opening letters of the four stanzas, read together, spell out in Hebrew the name *Solomon.*)

4. *Tif'artenu*, an allusion to the *sefirah Tif'eret.*

5. Alluding to Hosea 11:10, and thereby to the Redemption. Solomon ben David replaces Hosea's *yish'ag* with *yinham* for the sake of the rhyme.

Selected Bibliography

Baruch of Arezzo. *Zikkaron li-vnei Yisra'el (Memorial to the Children of Israel)*. In Freimann, *Sammelband kleiner Schriften über Sabbatai Zebi und dessen Anhänger*.

Benayahu, Meir. *The Shabbatean Movement in Greece* (=*Sefunot* 14; Hebrew). Jerusalem: Ben-Zvi Institute, 1971–77.

———. "Te'udah 'al polmos 'im kat shabbeta'it be-'inyan perush ha-elohut." *Sefunot* 1 (1956), 118–27.

Bernheimer, Carlo. "Some New Contributions to Abraham Cardoso's Biography." *Jewish Quarterly Review*, New Series, 18 (1927–28), 97–129.

Brüll, Nahum. "Mikhtav be-'inyan sod ha-elohut neged kat sh-z." In *Bet ha-Midrash*, ed. Weiss, 1 (1865), 63–71, 100–103, 139–42.

Cardozo, Abraham. *Ani ha-mekhunneh (I Am the Man They Call ...)*. New York, Jewish Theological Seminary of America, Ms 1677 (=ms Adler 1653). Cf. Bernheimer.

———. "Autobiographical Letter." See Molho and Amarilio.

———. *Drush boqer de-Avraham (Abraham's Morn)*. Ms Ginzburg 660, Moscow.

———. *Drush qodesh Yisra'el la-Adonay (Israel, Holiness to the Lord)*. See Scholem, "Avraham."

————. *Iggeret le-dayyanei Izmir (Epistle to the Judges of Izmir)*. See Scholem, "Iggeret."

————. *Sefer Boqer Avraham (Abraham's Morning)*. Ms Oxford, Bodleian Library, 1441.

————. Untitled text. New York, Jewish Theological Seminary of America, Ms 1723 (=ms Adler 2432). Cf. Scholem, "Lidi'at."

————. *Zeh eli ve-anvehu (This Is My God)*. See Scholem, "Drush zeh eli."

Carlebach, Elisheva. *The Pursuit of Heresy: Rabbi Moses Hagiz and the Sabbatian Controversies*. New York: Columbia University Press, 1990.

Elqayam, Abraham. "The Absent Messiah: Messiah Son of Joseph in the Thought of Nathan of Gaza, Sabbatai Zevi, and A. M. Cardozo" (Hebrew). *Da'at* 38 (1997), 33–82.

Freimann, Aharon, ed. *Sammelband kleiner Schriften über Sabbatai Zebi und dessen Anhänger* (Hebrew). Berlin: Itzkowski, 1912.

Ginzberg, Louis. *The Legends of the Jews*. Seven volumes. Philadelphia: Jewish Publication Society of America, 1942–47.

Halperin, David J. "Sabbatai Zevi, Metatron, and Mehmed: Myth and History in Seventeenth-Century Judaism." In *The Seductiveness of Jewish Myth: Challenge or Response?* ed. S. Daniel Breslauer, pp. 271–308. Albany, N.Y.: State University of New York Press, 1997.

————. "The Son of the Messiah: Ishmael Zevi and the Sabbatian Aqedah." *Hebrew Union College Annual* 67 (1996), 143–219.

Idel, Moshe. *Messianic Mystics*. New Haven, Conn., and London: Yale University Press, 1998.

Kohen, Elijah. *Sefer Merivat Qodesh (Book of the Holy Quarrel)*. In Freimann, *Sammelband kleiner Schriften über Sabbatai Zebi und dessen Anhänger*.

Liebes, Yehuda. "Ha-yesod ha-ideologi she-be-folmos Hayon." In *On Sabbateaism and Its Kabbalah: Collected Essays*. Jerusalem: Bialik Institute, 1995.

SELECTED BIBLIOGRAPHY

————. "Mikha'el Qardozo—mehabbero shel sefer 'Raza de-Mehemanuta' ha-meyuhas le-Shabbetai Zevi ve-ha-ta'ut be-yihusah shel 'iggeret magen Avraham' le-Qardozo." In *On Sabbateaism and Its Kabbalah: Collected Essays*. Jerusalem: Bialik Institute, 1995.

Liebes, Yehuda, ed. *Researches in Sabbateanism* (Hebrew). Tel Aviv: Am Oved, 1991. [A collection of articles by Gershom Scholem, compiled and annotated by Liebes.]

Mantran, Robert. *Istanbul dans la seconde Moitié du XVIIe Siècle*. Paris: A. Maisonneuve, 1962.

Matt, Daniel Chanan, trans. *Zohar: The Book of Enlightenment*. Ramsey, N.J.: Paulist Press, 1983.

Molho, Isaac R., and Abraham Amarilio. "Autobiographical Letters of Abraham Cardozo" (Hebrew). *Sefunot* 3–4 (1960), 183–241.

Rosenstock, Bruce. "Abraham Miguel Cardoso's Messianism: A Reappraisal." *AJS Review* 23 (1998), 63–104.

Sasportas, Jacob. *Sefer Zizat Novel Zevi*, ed. Isaiah Tishby. Jerusalem: Bialik Institute, 1954.

Scholem, Gershom. "Avraham Mikha'el Qardozo: Drush qodesh yisra'el la-adonay." In Liebes, *Researches in Sabbateanism*.

————. "The Crypto-Jewish Sect of the Dönmeh (Sabbatians) in Turkey." In *The Messianic Idea in Judaism and Other Essays on Jewish Spirituality*. New York: Schocken, 1971.

————. "Drush zeh eli ve-anvehu le-Avraham Mikha'el Qardozo." In *Studies and Texts Concerning the History of Sabbetianism and Its Metamorphoses*. Jerusalem: Bialik, 1982.

————. "Hadashot lidi'at Avraham Qardoso." In Liebes, *Researches in Sabbateanism*.

————. "Ha-ta'alumah be-'enah 'omedet." In Liebes, *Researches in Sabbateanism*.

————. "Iggeret Avraham Mikha'el Qardozo le-dayyanei Izmir." In *Studies and Texts Concerning the History of Sabbetianism and Its Metamorphoses*. Jerusalem: Bialik Institute, 1982.

————. *Kabbalah*. New York and Scarborough, Ontario: New American Library, 1974. (Reprint of Scholem's articles in *Encyclopaedia Judaica*.)

————. "Lidi'at ha-shabbeta'ut mi-tokh kitvei Qardozo." In *Studies and Texts Concerning the History of Sabbetianism and Its Metamorphoses*. Jerusalem: Bialik Institute, 1982.

————. *Major Trends in Jewish Mysticism*. Third edition. New York: Schocken, 1954.

————. *On the Kabbalah and Its Symbolism*. New York: Schocken, 1965.

————. *On the Mystical Shape of the Godhead: Basic Concepts in the Kabbalah*. New York: Schocken, 1991.

————. *Origins of the Kabbalah*. Philadelphia: Jewish Publication Society, 1987.

————. "Rabbi Eliyahu ha-kohen ha-itamari ve-ha-shabbeta'ut." In Liebes, *Researches in Sabbateanism*.

————. "Redemption Through Sin." In *The Messianic Idea in Judaism and Other Essays on Jewish Spirituality*. New York: Schocken, 1971.

————. *Sabbatai Sevi: The Mystical Messiah*. Princeton, N.J.: Princeton University Press, 1973.

Shaw, Stanford J. *The Jews of the Ottoman Empire and the Turkish Republic*. Washington Square, N.Y.: New York University Press, 1991.

Tishby, Isaiah. *The Wisdom of the Zohar: An Anthology of Texts*. Three volumes. London and Washington: The Littmann Library of Jewish Civilization, 1989.

Wolfson, Elliot R. "Constructions of the Shekhinah in the Messianic Theosophy of Abraham Cardoso with an Annotated Edition of Derush ha-Shekhinah." *Kabbalah* 3 (1998), 11–143.

Yerushalmi, Yosef Hayim. *From Spanish Court to Italian Ghetto: Isaac Cardoso*. New York and London: Columbia University Press, 1971.

Yosha, Nissim. "Ha-beri'ah ve-ha-zeman: 'vikkuah' te'ologi-filosofi shel Qardozo 'im Natan he-'azati." In *Mehqerei Yerushalayim be-mahshevet Yisra'el* 12 (1996), 259–84.

———. "Ha-reqa' ha-filosofi le-te'olog shabbeta'i—qavvim le-havanat torat ha-elohut shel Avraham Mikha'el Qardozo." In *Galut ahar golah: mehqarim be-toledot 'am Yisra'el muggashim le-Professor Hayyim Beinart*, ed. Aharon Mirsky, Avraham Grossman, Yosef Kaplan. Jerusalem: Ben-Zvi Institute, 1988.

Index

Note: **Bold type** marks the page or pages where a term is defined or an individual described.

INDEX

INDEX

Other Volumes in This Series

Other Volumes in This Series

Other Volumes in This Series